Guide to

Microsoft® Windows® Server 2003 Command Line Administration

Deborah Haralson

THOMSON

COURSE TECHNOLOGY

Australia • Canada • Mexico • Singapore • Spain • United Kingdom • United States

THOMSON

COURSE TECHNOLOGY

Guide to Microsoft® Windows® Server 2003 Command Line Administration

By Deborah Haralson

Senior Editor:
William Pitkin III

Development Editor:
Amanda Brodkin

Editorial Assistant:
Amanda Piantedosi

Senior Product Manager:
Laura Hildebrand

Quality Assurance Manager:
John Bosco

Marketing Manager:
Jason Sakos

Senior Production Editor:
Elena Montillo

MQA Project Leader:
Nicole Ashton

Text Designer:
GEX Publishing Services

Technical Reviewers:
Ron Houle, Nathan Ullger,
Randy Weaver, Tom Trevethan,
Carolyn E. McLellan

Associate Product Manager:
Nick Lombardi

Product Manager:
Tim Gleeson

Compositor:
GEX Publishing Services

Cover Design:
Steve Deschene

Contents

TABLE OF

Contents

Preface

Welcome to *Guide to Microsoft Windows Server 2003 Command Line Administration*. This book shows you how to administer Windows Server 2003 in a variety of environments from the command line.

DOS may be dead, but the DOS command language isn't. In its place is the environment known as the command line or command prompt. The command line supports a new DOS-like 32-bit language irrevocably linked to Windows Server 2003 that boasts a vast range of functions, commands, and applications. Microsoft provides intermediate and advanced tools specifically for administrative use on the command line within Windows 2000, XP, and Server 2003. Many of these tools have been created because they contain more advanced — and therefore more dangerous — functions than you will find within applications that are traditionally found on the Windows Start menu. These commands range from tools for viewing and administering local and network resources to tools for managing Active Directory configuration, users, groups, and other complex functions. You will learn about the command prompt in such a manner as to dispel any fears or discomfort that usually occurs in the black screen. Once you are thoroughly familiar with how the current Windows command prompt behaves and how to navigate within it, you will learn about the relevance and application of each command. Each command is covered thoroughly with practical usage scenarios, syntax, code examples, and hands-on projects.

This book features the following special information:

- Explanation of commands and functions that make your job easier, faster, and more efficient
- Coverage of commands and functions that you will not find in other GUI-based administrative utilities
- Usage and syntax for each command
- Introduction to remote Active Directory administration

The Intended Audience

This book is intended as a command primer for administrators in charge of Windows Server 2003 systems. The command line topic is usually considered an advanced topic. While this is truly the case, this book seeks to both train novice administrators in the topic and update veteran administrators with the new commands associated with Active Directory.

Unit 1, "Introduction," consisting of Chapters 1 through 3, covers the introductory aspects of the command environment, much of which hasn't changed in years.

Chapter 1, "Introduction to the Command Line," introduces the command environment and explains how to get there and how to configure it.

Chapter 2, "Managing Files," introduces the basic commands that have not changed since DOS. File manipulation and management is at the heart of this entire book, and is absolutely necessary for all aspects of command administration.

Chapter 3, "Batch and Automation," walks you through the programming language that consists entirely of commands and allows you to run commands on demand. Batch programming is particularly important because every command covered in this book can be automated, or placed in a batch program, for ease of use.

Unit 2, "Computer Administration," comprising Chapters 4 through 6, covers commands associated with computer and system information. Many of the commands in this unit function appropriately with both Windows Server 2003 and Windows XP.

Chapter 4, "System Administration," outlines commands that are used for local system configuration and administration.

Chapter 5, "Disk and Data Management," covers those commands that can be used to administer disk drives and the data that lives on those drives. This chapter covers dynamic disks and RAID.

Chapter 6, "User Administration and Data Security," discusses how to create, delete, and administer user accounts and user groups.

Unit 3, "Networking," which includes Chapters 7 through 9, introduces commands associated with networking, including hardware and protocol management.

Chapter 7, "Introduction to Networking," introduces networking, how it works in the Microsoft environment, and which commands can be used to configure networking.

Chapter 8, "Networking a Server," covers **NET**, which is the major command used to configure networking. This chapter also introduces services.

Chapter 9, "Manipulating Network Resources" covers remote network administration.

Unit 4, "Domain Administration," covering Chapters 10 through 12, introduces the Windows Server 2003 domain, its components, and the commands that are essential for domain administration.

Chapter 10, "Active Directory: The Windows Server 2003 Domain" discusses the commands that are used for administering Active Directory.

Chapter 11, "Securing Active Directory" details security options for Active Directory and covers the **DCDIAG** command.

Chapter 12, "Name Resolution Using DNS, WINS, and DHCP" describes commands that are used for DNS, WINS, and DHCP administration and addresses structure naming.

Additional information is also contained in the appendices at the end of the book. **Appendix A** is a command dictionary containing every command covered in this book. **Appendix B** discusses several advanced networking commands, including certificates and DFS.

Features

To ensure a successful learning experience, this book includes the following pedagogical features:

- **Chapter Objectives:** Each chapter in this book begins with a detailed list of the concepts to be mastered within that chapter. This list provides you with a quick reference to the contents of that chapter and is a useful study aid.

- **Screenshots, Illustrations, Tables:** Wherever applicable, screenshots and illustrations are used to aid you in the visualization and execution of common installation, administration and management steps, theories, and concepts.

- **Syntax:** Syntax tables list and explain command options that may be used in combination with the specific command being discussed. Syntax examples use both actual and representative (user-specified) command words. Actual commands should be copied exactly as they appear in the syntax. Representative words appear within angle brackets (< >) and are italicized. For example, the syntax representation of the **ATTRIB *<FILENAME>*** command indicates that you should type the ATTRIB command followed by a filename of your choice. You do not need to type the angle brackets; they are used strictly to indicate the user-specified aspect of the keyword. Syntax shown in italics and separated by a bar character (|) indicates an either/or option for the command. For example, the syntax representation of the **NET USER *<USERNAME>* /PASSWORDREQ: *YES|NO*** command indicates that you should type either YES or NO at the end of the command to require or not require a user password.

- **Hands-on Projects:** These projects contain specific step-by-step instructions that enable you to apply the knowledge gained in the chapter. Hands-on Projects are preceded by the Hands-on icon and a description of the exercise that follows.

- **End-of-Chapter Material:** The end of each chapter includes the following features to reinforce the material covered in the chapter:

  - Chapter Summary: A brief but complete summary of the topics covered in the chapter.

  - Command Summary: A table listing command names and their functions.

  - Key Terms List: A list of key terminology with definitions.

  - Review Questions: Multiple-choice, fill-in, and true/false questions to test the reader's mastery of the most important concepts covered in the chapter.

  - Discovery Exercises: Include theoretical, research, or scenario-based projects that expand on the information contained within the chapter.

- **On the CD-ROM:** On the CD-ROM included with this text you will find a copy of Microsoft Windows Server 2003 180-day Trial Edition software.

Text and Graphic Conventions

Wherever appropriate, additional information and exercises have been added to this book to help you better understand what is being discussed in the chapter. Icons throughout the text alert you to additional materials. The icons used in this textbook are as follows:

Tips are advice or guidelines based on the authors' experiences that provide additional real-world insights into the topic being discussed. Tips also provide solutions to potential problems you may encounter while completing the Hands-on Projects.

Notes are used to present additional helpful material related to the subject being described.

Instructor's Resources

The following supplemental materials are available when this book is used in a classroom setting. All of the supplements available with this book are provided to the instructor on a single CD-ROM.

- Electronic Instructor's Manual: The Instructor's Manual that accompanies this textbook includes additional instructional material to assist in class preparation, including suggestions for classroom activities, discussion topics, and additional projects.

- Solutions: Answers to Review Questions are provided.

- ExamView®: This textbook is accompanied by ExamView, a powerful testing software package that allows instructors to create and administer printed, computer (LAN-based), and Internet exams. ExamView includes hundreds of questions that correspond to the topics covered in this text, enabling students to generate detailed study guides that include page references for further review. The computer-based and Internet testing components allow students to take exams at their computers, and also save the instructor time by grading each exam automatically.

- PowerPoint presentations: This book comes with Microsoft PowerPoint slides for each chapter. These are included as a teaching aid for classroom presentation, to make available to students on the network for chapter review, or to be printed for classroom distribution. Instructors, please feel at liberty to add your own slides for additional topics you introduce to the class.

- Figure files: All of the figures in the book are reproduced on the Instructor's Resource CD, in bit-mapped format. Similar to the PowerPoint presentations, these are included as a teaching aid for classroom presentation, to make available to students for review, or to be printed for classroom distribution.

ACKNOWLEDGMENTS

Firstly, I wish to thank the staff at Course Technology and especially senior product manager Laura Hildebrand and development editor Amanda Brodkin. In addition, I wish to thank reviewers Tom Trevethan, ECPI College of Technology, Nate Ullger, Wake Technical Community College, Carolyn McLellan, Tidewater Community College, Randy Weaver, Rhodes College, and Ron Houle, Central Lakes College, for their input. It takes a leap of faith to write a book whose specific topic is in great demand for those who generally don't know that they need it, as does writing a book that has no topical peers; nevertheless, the command prompt has often been a career-maker for those who master it well. I am especially grateful to acquisitions editor Will Pitkin for understanding the marketability of this topic.

I must also specifically thank Chris Ward for embarking on this project with me, inadvertently becoming the unsung co-author, guiding this book in its embryonic state all the way through to the final touches that only he was qualified and able to provide. Thank you for your sacrifice, panic, blood, sweat, and tears. Thank you also to Robert Barr, for helping Chris (and thus myself) through some hefty deadlines.

Thank you to my husband, Jeff for all of your support.

Read This Before You Begin

The command environment in any operating system is often regarded as a taboo topic for end users and a frightening topic for administrators. To ensure that you gain a solid understanding of core command line concepts, you should read the entire book in order, as most of the chapters build on the knowledge of prior chapters. Students who are already familiar with the basics of command administration may find it more useful to begin with Unit 2. No matter what your level of expertise, you should at least skim all of the chapters in this book, as there are many commands introduced here that are new with Windows Server 2003.

This course assumes a basic level of understanding and experience with regards to Windows Servers and the necessary administrative tasks that are associated with server and network administration.

LAB REQUIREMENTS

The following hardware is required for the Hands-on Projects in each chapter. You should complete the Hands-on Projects in order. The projects assume that you are logged on to your system as Administrator. Your lab should have at least one system capable of running Windows Server 2003, meeting the hardware requirements listed for this operating system on the *www.Microsoft.com* Web site. Windows Server 2003 should be installed prior to beginning this course, preferably as a member server belonging to no domain. To perform some of the projects in Chapter 5 for disk and data management, three hard disks are required on this server. Rest assured that while this is an ideal configuration, it is not required as long as these projects are thoroughly studied.

In this book, you will have the opportunity to install Active Directory. You should have at least two computers running Windows Server 2003 to complete all of the Hands-on Projects. Both your server and network must meet certain requirements before you can install Microsoft Active Directory. To install Microsoft Active Directory you will need a computer running either Microsoft Windows Server 2003, or Microsoft Windows Enterprise Server 2003. You will need at least a 1 GB, NTFS-formatted partition to store Active Directory. Your network must be running TCP/IP and have a DNS server that supports the SRV (service) resource record type. If you are running a BIND (Berkeley Internet Naming Domain) DNS server of 4.3.7 or higher you will be able to handle basic functionality. However, it is recommended that you also have a DNS server that supports dynamic updates as well. For BIND, that would be version 8.2.1 or higher. When installing Microsoft's Active Directory, you will also be given the opportunity to install the DNS service locally if you do not have a DNS server running in your environment. The Hands-on Project that installs Active Directory appears in Chapter 10.

To take advantage of all of the functionality provided by some of the command line utilities written in this book, you will need to install the Windows Support Tools. To perform this procedure, you must be a member of the Administrators group on the local computer. The step-by-step instructions are as follows:

1. Insert the Windows CD into your CD-ROM drive.

2. Click **No** if you are prompted to reinstall Windows.

3. When the Welcome screen appears, click **Perform additional tasks**, and then click **Browse this CD**.

4. Go to the \Support\Tools folder.

5. Double-click the **suptools.msi** file.

6. Follow the instructions that appear on your screen.

The server machine should have the capability of being networked with at least one other computer, preferably running Windows XP. Similarly, Windows Server 2003 installation disk is necessary to install the operating system, support tools, and additional drivers as necessary.

The Hands-on Projects in this book were tested on a variety of operating systems, including Windows Server 2003, Windows 2000, and Windows XP. In many cases, the configuration of your system may cause discrepancies between what you see depicted in the figures in the book and the actual results on your computer screen. These discrepancies are minor and do not affect the outcome of the overall projects.

UNIT
1

THE COMMAND
ENVIRONMENT

1

INTRODUCTION TO THE COMMAND LINE

After reading this chapter and completing the exercises, you will be able to:

♦ Discuss the origins of the command line and its current evolution

♦ Describe the use of the command line for various operating systems

♦ Access the command prompt

♦ Set characteristics for the command window, including font size, color, and presentation

♦ Use variables on the command line to customize program execution

♦ Redirect program output to a file

♦ Use function keys in conjunction with the command line to perform various file management and administration tasks

This book teaches Windows system engineering and administration through the command window environment. In this chapter, you review a short history of Microsoft Windows and DOS, and you learn about the current status of Windows operating systems. Then you learn about some basic tenets of DOS and the command line environments found in Microsoft Windows NT, Windows 2000, Windows XP, and Windows Server 2003. For consistency with industry usage, this text refers to these Microsoft products as NT, 2000, XP, and Server 2003.

OPERATING SYSTEM ORIGINS

An **operating system (OS)** is a program that provides an interface between a user and the hardware on a computer system. It also acts as a foundation for other programs and processes to build upon. Operating systems provide these features to complement and enhance the functionality of the hardware. Operating systems come in different versions and types, based on the platform hardware and necessary features.

The first personal computers were invented by IBM, which contracted Microsoft to create the operating system. The first PC operating system was known as MS-DOS (Microsoft Disk Operating System), or, more commonly, **DOS**. The interface for these early operating systems was simple: It consisted of a keyboard and a monitor. The mouse hadn't yet been invented, and the monitor only displayed white text characters on a black background, because of the limitations of video hardware at the time. DOS required users to interact with the computer using a limited set of commands, options, and syntax.

As you might guess, operating systems have evolved over the years along with hardware technology. Milestones in hardware development occurred with advances in video hardware and the invention of the mouse. These hardware changes led the way for OSs to become more user friendly and visually appealing, and thus the **graphical user interface (GUI)** OS was born. GUI (pronounced "gooey") is a generic term that describes how information is displayed on the screen. A GUI program, or OS, displays a user environment that, along with a mouse, allows objects, files, programs, and environmental settings to be displayed as high-resolution, colored graphical objects, instead of being limited to black-and-white characters.

Today's Windows Server 2003 and XP operating systems are direct descendants of the MS-DOS that ran the first IBM personal computers (PCs) and started the computer industry that we know today. Despite their graphical sophistication, these modern OSs also provide a text interface through which a user can enter text commands. This interface, known as the **command line**, acts like the old DOS in many ways, but offers functionality appropriate to today's hardware and software.

Regardless of how "old fashioned" the command line might seem in comparison to the slick graphics-intensive interfaces of Windows, the command line has an important role in system administration. Many administration features and functions simply aren't available within the GUI environment—the command line is the only means of accessing these tools. Mastery of the command line environment is critical to the success of any system administration effort, regardless of the platform.

While the command line is available in all PC platforms, certain commands may only run in certain environments. Throughout this book, you learn about commands that are exclusive to particular platforms such as Windows Server 2003 but are not available with others.

The command environment that emulates DOS goes by many names. For the most part, the terms *command line*, *command environment*, *command window*, and *command prompt* all refer to the command window that is available from within Windows Server 2003.

The Continuing Importance of the Command Line

Now that you understand how Windows' treatment of the command line has evolved, it is helpful to realize why the command line is still around and why it is important for the information technology (IT) professional to master this environment. Reasons for the command line's ongoing popularity and necessity include its ability to automate tasks, its enhanced control over how a system works, and its advanced administration capabilities that lack GUI utility equivalents.

Over time, Microsoft began to build applications that were strictly for use within the command environment. Most of these programs were created as advanced and expert-level applications for use only by the most fearless system or network administrator. All commands within the current command line environment can be divided into three types:

1. Commands that are holdovers from DOS

2. Commands that mirror GUI tasks

3. Advanced commands that can cause trouble for casual users. Such commands can be accessed exclusively through the command window.

DOS Holdovers

Most of the old DOS commands have at least one GUI equivalent. Several of the more annoyingly unnecessary commands have been eliminated because advances in technology have rendered them obsolete. The remaining DOS commands include general navigation and execution commands such as **DIR** (for listing drive contents), **COPY** (for copying files), **DEL** (for deleting files), and **CD** (for creating directories). For the most part, these commands behave in the same manner as they always have, but Microsoft has enhanced many of these commands with additional features, making them easier to use and understand.

GUI Mirror Commands

Microsoft has created some command line commands that at first might appear to be useless, text-based replicas of GUI applications. After all, why would anyone want to run a command application that is more difficult to use and has fewer features than a similar GUI program? Actually, there are several situations in which you might want to run a command rather than a GUI equivalent. The first such situation is when you want to automate a task by using commands within batch files, and then scheduling the task to occur automatically at any time. Other reasons for running commands include speed, accessibility, and security. Generally, a command runs faster and more reliably than a GUI equivalent utility, program, or tool, and it is more accessible.

Since most command programs are built for specific tasks and don't require graphics, they run faster than most GUI equivalents. Also, many GUI applications require specific installation. In comparison, it is possible to use a few commands from the command line to perform many of the same procedures without running through an installation routine. This means a busy administrator can usually use the command line to access a command from a remote computer without wasting time installing the GUI application or running across the building to his or her own computer.

Additionally, using commands instead of a GUI application makes it more difficult for observers to understand and track what someone is doing, thus increasing security. What's more, there are times when you may be unable to access the GUI of an OS altogether, but you can enter commands from a boot disk, CD, or emergency repair software. Mastery of commands is vital during these times.

Advanced Commands

Advanced commands created specifically for the brave-hearted administrator do not have GUI equivalents or default icons to represent them. These commands include **SC**, which can create a service, and **RSH**, which allows commands to be run on a remote system. Commands such as these are often under-documented. This lack of documentation typically is intended to prevent stray end users from accidentally running the command and causing problems. Sometimes these commands are created simply to provide necessary tools and utilities that don't demand the extra Microsoft developmental efforts associated with creating a GUI application.

Environmental Considerations

Any OS serves several purposes, one of which is to establish an environment, or interface, appropriate for user interaction with programs and program execution. Many operating systems add features and programs to enhance usability and profitability, but the basic interface between the user and the computer is the primary function of the operating system.

All versions of Microsoft Windows establish the operating system environment during system startup—better known as **boot**—by following a complex checklist of steps that load system components, establish memory stacks, and provide interface functionality to the user.

Windows NT, 2000, XP, and Server 2003 all provide command line environments similar to DOS. These versions of Windows establish the proper command environment by loading user and system variables listed in the system properties and within the autoexec.bat file (a standard file associated with the boot process). Similarly, Windows supports older, 16-bit applications by creating command environments for them to launch from.

Automation Scripts and Batch Files

The command line is frequently used for **automation**. Automation involves running one or more commands or tasks without user intervention. Automating a simple yet redundant task can save time and money. For example, assume you need to add 50 new users to a system. On average, the basic user configuration can usually take five minutes to perform. For 50 users, this means more than four hours of your time. However, this level of simplicity is rarely found in the real world. Even small businesses require around 15 minutes of administrator time to generate a new user account, along with all other account and setup information.

If you could automate and tailor the user generation process to your company's needs, you could save a lot of time. Automation occurs in one of two ways: through **scripts** or **batches**. Technically, a batch program is a type of script. Scripts are essentially applications that are written with a specific scripting language in mind, such as Microsoft Visual Basic (VB), and are written within a simple text file rather than a programming application, as would be necessary with any other program or language. A batch program is a type of script whose programming language consists of any command that can be executed at the command prompt. After the commands are entered, the file is saved with a .bat extension and can be executed simply by typing the filename at the command prompt. Batch programs were used with DOS and continue to be used today because of their simplicity and efficiency.

The difference between scripts and batch files lies primarily with the types of commands that are executed within the script, and also with the file extension. **File extensions** consist of the last three letters of the filename and are used as indicators of the purpose and functionality of the file. Batch files end with .bat. VB script files end with .vbs. The batch programming language is easy to understand and is much more rudimentary than the VB programming language. VB is more powerful and complex than batch, with the ability to perform more advanced logic and interface functions. Once a file script is saved, it can be executed from the command line by typing the filename.

Batch scripts can run on any Windows system. Nonbatch scripts are restricted to the 32-bit operating systems (Windows NT, 2000, XP, and Server 2003).

Nonbatch scripts rely on the Windows Scripting Host (WSH) service to run. WSH has caused security problems on some servers, so some administrators manually disable it. If you find that this service is not running on a system you are administrating, ensure that all appropriate security and virus patches have been updated prior to restarting the service.

In addition to automating user and computer accounts, batch and VB script files can be used to perform complex maintenance tasks, such as running data backup, or communications, such as establishing File Transfer Protocol connections. Scripts and batch files are covered in more depth in Chapter 3.

Data and File Manipulation

Another common use of the command line is to copy, edit, move, and otherwise manipulate files and folders (called directories in the DOS environment). While it is often easier to copy and move files and folders within the Windows Explorer application, sometimes it is better for the support professional to do the same tasks using the command line. The command line approach is preferable because it is usually easier to see what changes you have made to a system by quickly looking at the file sizes, number of files, and the directory statistics at the bottom of a directory listing. As you can see in Figure 1-1, the command line yields more information about the system and its contents than does Windows Explorer.

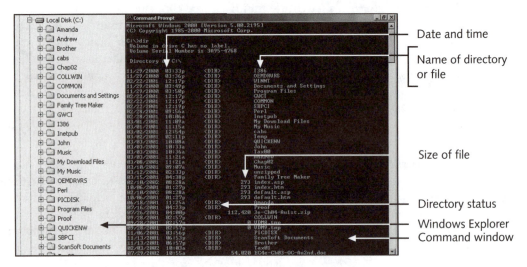

Figure 1-1   The command window and Windows Explorer views of a C drive

Computer Administration

In this book, the term **computer administration** is used as an equivalent to local administration. The tasks that fall under the computer administration umbrella can range from changing hardware settings using the Windows Control Panel tool to changing user characteristics and passwords. Again, two major reasons for command line administration of any sort are automation and scripting. Keep in mind that computer administration applies to the local computer, even when that computer is a server.

Network Administration

Commands available for **network administration**, which is the maintenance of networked computers and software, deal primarily with troubleshooting protocols but can also help determine connectivity status and perform network connection analysis. Many network administration commands have no GUI counterparts. The functionality of network administration commands makes them essential for the troubleshooting administrator and IT professional. Many IT professionals become familiar with the command line just to use these networking commands. You will learn about command line network administration in Unit 3 of this text.

Domain Administration

With Windows NT came the introduction of **domains**, which are logical security boundaries for networks as defined by a network administrator. These logical security boundaries are defined by a centralized database that contains entries for all users, computers, and network resources within domains. This database is called the Active Directory database, and it serves as a sentinel that allows appropriate network resource access to occur and denies inappropriate access based on the entries it contains. To provide redundancy and fault tolerance, this database can exist on more than one server computer, as shown in Figure 1-2. A server that houses such a database is known as a **domain controller (DC)**. **Domain administration**, which is the administration of the Active Directory database, usually occurs using GUI applications. Domain administrators can perform many maintenance and administration functions on a domain from the command line. Many of the more complex domain administration functions are available only from a command line application. You will learn more about domain administration in Unit 4.

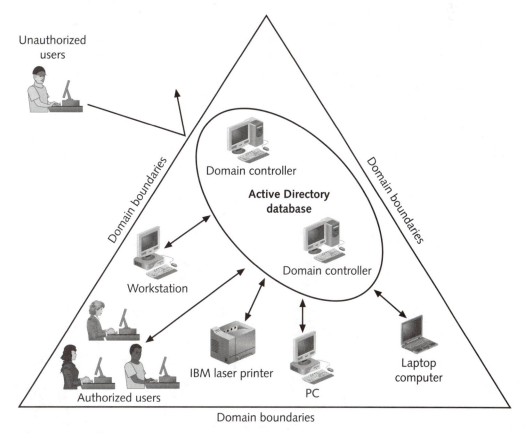

Figure 1-2 A domain

Domain administration always occurs on a domain controller. The DC, like any computer, is subject to standard computer administration commands.

INTRODUCTION TO THE COMMAND PROMPT

Earlier in this chapter, you learned the important role that the command environment plays in today's graphics-based operating systems. With that background, you can now begin learning where the command prompt exists and how to use it.

A **prompt** is the location on the screen where the computer accepts your typed input. A blinking cursor indicates a prompt. The items preceding the blinking cursor (C:\> in the case of the C drive) are also considered part of the **command prompt**, as they always precede the default prompt within a command window.

Using the command prompt begins with accessing it from whatever Windows environment you are using. There are several ways to open the command window and access the command prompt in Windows Server 2003. The first is to navigate to the Start menu, then open All Programs, then open Accessories, and finally open Command Prompt. This process is time consuming, so most users and administrators learn to open a command window by clicking the Start button ▮Start▮, selecting Run, and typing the letters "cmd". Hands-on Project 1-1 walks you through these two methods of opening a command window.

Hands-on Project 1-1

To open a command window using menus:

1. Click the **Start** button ▮Start▮.

2. Point to **All Programs** or **Programs**.

3. Point to **Accessories**.

4. Click **Command Prompt**, as shown in Figure 1-3.

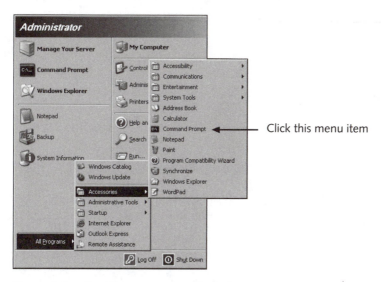

Figure 1-3 Opening a command window

The command window opens and a prompt appears. Your screen should look like Figure 1-4.

Figure 1-4 The command prompt in Windows NT

5. Click the **Close** button ⊠ to close the window.

Now open a command window using the Run line in the Start menu.

6. Click ▓Start.
7. Click the **Run** item.
8. Type **cmd** and press **Enter**.
9. Click ⊠ to close the command window.

People who are accustomed to Windows 98 and Me will notice that the command window looks the same as it does in Windows Server 2003 but that it has a different icon.

Notice that even though the window looks like the prompt shown in Figure 1-4, and in many respects behaves the same, the Windows Server 2003 version of the prompt is called a command prompt. Also, the Server 2003 and XP command prompt is located in Accessories, rather than in the Start menu/Programs option, as it is in other versions of Windows, such as Windows 98 and Windows Me.

Creating a Shortcut

To make the command prompt more accessible and convenient, you can create a **shortcut**. You will learn how to do this in Hands-on Project 1-2. A shortcut is an icon on the Windows desktop that you double-click to launch a program. You can also use this method to create a shortcut on the taskbar next to the Start menu. Users who are familiar with the command environment frequently just select Start, then select Run, and then type cmd to launch a command window.

Hands-on Project 1-2

To create a shortcut to the command prompt:

1. Minimize any applications you have open on the desktop by clicking their **Minimize** buttons .

2. Click the **Start** button , point to **All Programs**, and then point to **Accessories**. Locate the Command Prompt icon on the pop-up menu.

3. Right-click the **Command Prompt** icon and hold down the mouse button.

4. With the right mouse button pressed, drag the icon to the location on the desktop where you want to place the shortcut and release the right mouse button. See Figure 1-5.

Drag icon from menu bar to desktop

Figure 1-5   Creating a desktop shortcut for the command prompt

5. When you release the mouse button, a pop-up menu appears. Click the **Copy Here** option.

Opening and Closing Command Windows Without a Mouse

You can open or close a command window without using a mouse. This feature can be handy if you have lost your mouse functionality. You can launch a window from the Start menu using either the All Programs menu or the Run option. Hands-on Projects 1-3 and 1-4 will teach you these methods.

Hands-on Project 1-3

To open a command window using the All Programs menu:

1. While holding down the **Ctrl** key, press the **Esc** key. The Start menu opens.
2. Press **p** to highlight All Programs. Press the **right arrow** key to display the contents of All Programs. Press **a** to point to Accessories. Press the **right arrow** key to display the contents of Accessories.
3. Press **c** three times to point to the command prompt.
4. Press **Enter** to open the command window.
5. Type **exit** and press **Enter** to close the command window.

> If your Start menu contains more than one menu item that begins with p, a, or c, you can use the up and down arrow keys to navigate to the appropriate menu item, then press the Enter key to select the item.

Now learn another way to open the command window without a mouse.

6. While holding down the **Ctrl** key, press the **Esc** key. The Start menu opens.
7. Press the **up arrow** key until All Programs is highlighted. Press **Enter**.
8. Press the **down arrow** key to highlight Accessories. Press **Enter**.
9. Use the arrow keys to highlight the **Command Prompt** icon. Press **Enter**. The command window opens.
10. Click **X** to close the window.

A third method of opening a command window uses the Start menu's Run option.

Hands-on Project 1-4

To open a command window using the Run option:

1. While holding down **Ctrl**, press **Esc**. The Start menu opens.
2. Press **r** to open the Run dialog box.
3. Type **cmd** in the text box, and then press **Enter**. The command window opens.
4. Type **exit**, and then press **Enter** to close the command window.

You can use this method to access any item within the Start menu hierarchy. Any application can be executed from the Run option, as you did in Hands-on Project 1-4; as long as you know the filename of the program, you can type it on the Run line.

If you don't know what to type on the Run line, click the browse (Alt+B) button to find the program you want to run. Once you click it, you can look at what the Run line has listed so you can type it in manually the next time you want to run it. Ultimately, this can be faster than browsing through Windows Explorer or the Start menu.

The entire command environment exists within a window, which can be closed in the same ways that other windows are closed. While it is possible to close a command window by double-clicking its Minimize button ![minimize] or clicking its Close button ![close], this isn't recommended. Like any other application, the command environment can run processes even when the window isn't active on the desktop. If the command line is running a process when you attempt to close the window using the Minimize or Close buttons, you will receive an error/confirmation message. It is far better to avoid potential problems, and just close the window by typing "exit" at the command prompt, as you learned in Hands-on Project 1-4. If you are running multiple command environments, you will need to close each window individually.

EXIT   Closes the command window.

ANATOMY OF A COMMAND

A command is a program that is specifically run within a command window or environment. A command is run within the command window by typing the name of the command and pressing the Enter key. Most commands are run with **options**. Options are pieces of text that are entered after the command name when running the command. Options serve the purpose of enhancing the command to perform its task in a specific manner as indicated by the option text. An example of an option is the **HELP** command. The **HELP** command, executed by itself, displays a list of the default commands that are available on the system. Options are called arguments and parameters.

HELP   Displays a list of basic commands.

HELP <COMMAND>   Displays help and syntax information for the specified command.

When the **HELP** command is used with an option for the command name itself, it displays details for that command. For example, to obtain information about the **ATTRIB** command, the syntax would be **HELP ATTRIB**.

Hundreds of commands are available for use in the command window, and the options for each of them differ. Most of these commands are not listed using the **HELP** command. No matter what the command is, you can type the command followed by the **/?** option to obtain detailed help and information about the command. Hands-on Project 1-5 shows you how to get help for the **HELP** command.

Hands-on Project 1-5

To get help for the **HELP** command:

1. Click the **Start** button ![Start], and then click **Run**.

2. Type **cmd** and press **Enter**.

3. Type **help /?** and press **Enter**.

The results show the options that are available for the **HELP** command and what they accomplish. You can replace **HELP** with any command to see a list of the options and syntax for that command.

/?   A command option that displays help and syntax for the command.

Figure 1-6 shows the options for the **CMD** command.

![Command Prompt - cmd /?]

```
C:\>cmd /?
Starts a new instance of the Windows XP command interpreter

CMD [/A | /U] [/Q] [/D] [/E:ON | /E:OFF] [/F:ON | /F:OFF] [/U:ON | /U:OFF]
    [[/S] [/C | /K] string]

/C        Carries out the command specified by string and then terminates
/K        Carries out the command specified by string but remains
/S        Modifies the treatment of string after /C or /K (see below)
/Q        Turns echo off
/D        Disable execution of AutoRun commands from registry (see below)
/A        Causes the output of internal commands to a pipe or file to be ANSI
/U        Causes the output of internal commands to a pipe or file to be
          Unicode
/T:fg     Sets the foreground/background colors (see COLOR /? for more info)
/E:ON     Enable command extensions (see below)
/E:OFF    Disable command extensions (see below)
/F:ON     Enable file and directory name completion characters (see below)
/F:OFF    Disable file and directory name completion characters (see below)
/U:ON     Enable delayed environment variable expansion using ! as the
          delimiter. For example, /U:ON would allow !var! to expand the
          variable var at execution time.  The var syntax expands variables
          at input time, which is quite a different thing when inside of a FOR
          loop.
Press any key to continue . . .
```

Options available for **CMD**

Figure 1-6   Help for the **CMD** command

Figure 1-6 shows a variety of options, or switches, that are available for **CMD**. An option is an addition to a command that affects the way the command performs its function. For example, the **/C** option shown in Figure 1-6 modifies the command by terminating the command window after the command executes.

Running Commands from the Run Line

You can use the **CMD** command to launch commands and applications other than the command window from the Run line of the Start menu. In other words, you can run commands without manually opening a command window. For example, using **CMD** on the Run line to open a command window opens the window with the **CMD** command already having been run. The command environment is set up this way to reduce typing and speed up processing.

The following code example, when typed on the Start menu's Run line, opens a command window, runs the **PING** command as shown, and then closes the command window.

```
cmd /c ping 127.0.0.1
```

Figure 1-7 displays the same command as the code example; however, in the figure example, the command window remains open.

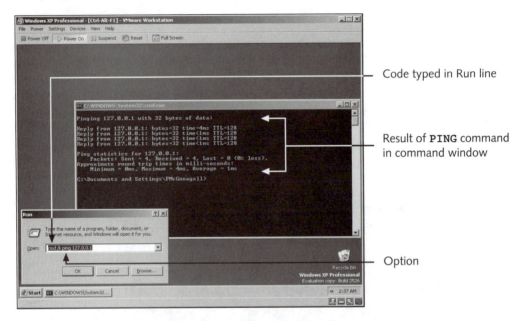

Figure 1-7   Running the PING command from the Run line

CMD   Opens a command window. When run within a command window, it opens another command environment.

Notice that using the **/K** option in Figure 1-7, rather than the **/C** option used in the code example, keeps the command window open. Recall that Figure 1-6 provides information about option functions. If you are running a command that contains a long filename or space, you must add the **/S** option and surround the entire command with quotation marks, for example:

```
cmd /s "c:\program files\newline.bat"
```

Turning Echo Off

If you want to eliminate noncritical messages from appearing on the screen as you are running programs, you can turn echo off. **Echo** is a command line feature that displays noncritical messages on the screen. Running the **ECHO** command with the **/Q** option turns echo off.

C:_
Syntax

ECHO ON	Displays the specified command before executing it.
ECHO <TEXT>	Displays the specified *TEXT* on the screen.

The **ECHO** command is useful in a number of different situations, mostly involving batch programs. Outside of batch, on the command line, **ECHO** can be used to display a message on the screen.

Displaying File and Directory Names

Another particularly nifty option for **CMD** is **/F:ON**, which enables you to display the available file and **directory** names during navigation. Directories (often called folders) are organizational structures for files and other directories. The purpose of creating a directory is to group together files and folders of a particular type and nature. Directories are similar to physical folders that hold documents of a specific type or topic within the same file drawer. They can contain subdirectories or subfolders.

C:_
Syntax

CMD /F:ON Enables display of directory names and filenames (directory and file-name completion).

The **CMD** **/F:ON** command lets you reduce the typing required to locate a file. From within the command window, pressing Ctrl+D multiple times displays the directories available from the root of the C drive. Pressing Ctrl+F multiple times displays the files available from the root of the C drive. This feature, called **directory and filename completion**, is particularly valuable when navigating a lengthy directory of filename entries. Additionally, you can enter on the command line the first letter of the name of the directory or file you are seeking and Ctrl+D or Ctrl+F fills in the rest of the directory name or filename for you. Hands-on Project 1-6 lets you practice with directory and filename completion.

Hands-on Project 1-6

To navigate within a directory using **CMD** **/F:ON**:

1. Click the **Start** button ![Start], and then click **Run**.
2. Type **cmd /f:on** and press **Enter**. The command window opens, with a prompt at C:\\. If the prompt in the command window displays a directory other than

C:\> (such as C:\Documents and Settings\Administrator), type **cd** and then press **Enter**.

3. Type **cd** and then press the **spacebar** once. Hold down **Ctrl** and press **d**. A directory name appears, similar to the one shown in Figure 1-8.

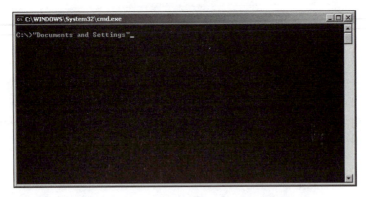

Figure 1-8 Using directory and filename completion

 Directory entries that contain spaces appear with quotation marks surrounding their names. Likewise, any time you type a directory name or filename that contains spaces, you need to surround the pathname or filename with quotation marks.

4. Continuing to hold down the **Ctrl** key, press **d** repeatedly until "Program Files" appears on the screen.

5. Press **Enter**. Your prompt should now read "C:\> Program Files." You have successfully navigated to the Program Files directory.

6. Press the **Close** button ☒ to close the command window.

CUSTOMIZING COMMAND WINDOW SETTINGS

The command window offers several ways to customize its appearance. You can change the size of the window either temporarily or permanently, change the size of the cursor, change the display font, and vary the screen colors. To make any of these changes, right-click the command window's title bar, as shown in Figure 1-9, and select either the Default or Properties option from the pop-up menu. While both the Default and Properties options display the same dialog box, the results of changing one versus the other are drastically different. Changes to the Properties section apply to the active window only and disappear with the next command window that is opened. Any appearance changes you make using the Default option apply to all command windows, including windows that are opened in the future.

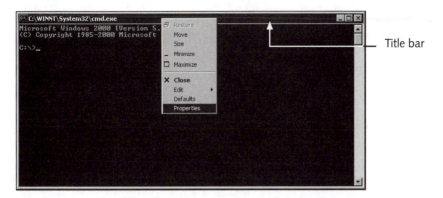

Figure 1-9   The command window settings menu

You can change the command window's size on the fly by resizing the window using the mouse or by clicking the Minimize or Maximize buttons. Most likely, the only time you really want to use the pop-up menu options to change the window size is when you want the command window to always appear at a certain size. In this situation, you would change the default setting of the window size. You also have the option of making the command window full screen; however, beware that if the command window becomes full-screen size, you no longer have easy access to the Default and Properties options for the window itself. Access to these options is available by right-clicking the minimized window instance on the Start menu taskbar.

Hands-on Project 1-7 teaches you how to change the command window's size. You will learn how to change other command window settings in later projects.

Hands-on Project 1-7

To change the command window to be full-screen size:

1. Click the **Start** button , and then click **Run**.

2. Type **cmd** and press **Enter**.

3. Right-click the **command window title bar**, as shown in Figure 1-9. A pop-up menu opens. Click **Defaults**. The Console Windows Properties window opens. Ensure that the Options tab of the Console Windows Properties window is selected.

4. Within the Display Options section, click the **Full Screen** radio button, as shown in Figure 1-10, and then click **OK**.

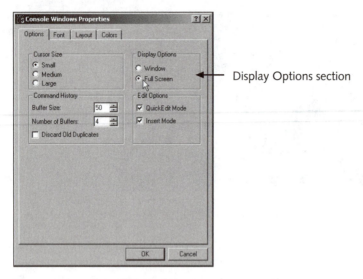

Display Options section

Figure 1-10   Console Windows Properties window

 If your Edit Option section has a checkbox called AutoComplete, make sure that the checkbox is selected.

 An Apply Changes dialog box may appear the first time this function is performed. If necessary, click OK. Notice that the screen immediately flickers and the command environment fills the entire screen. Notice also that the window title bar and control buttons are no longer visible.

5. Type **exit**, and then press **Enter** to close the command window.

6. Click ![cmd], and then click **Run**. Type **cmd** and press **Enter**. Notice that the command window now fills the screen.

 You could also return to Windows by pressing Alt+Tab, by pressing the Windows button (if the keyboard has one, it's labeled with an icon of a flying window), or by pressing Ctrl+Esc. Each of these methods minimizes the command window.

7. Repeat Steps 1 through 4, but change the Display Options setting to Window instead of full screen.

8. Repeat Step 6. This time, the window should appear in Window size.

9. Type **exit** and press **Enter** to close the command window and complete the project.

Copying and Pasting Within the Command Window

As long as the command window is not full-screen size, you can copy and paste text between the window and other applications using the mouse and the title bar. Unfortunately, if you change window properties to full screen, the mouse becomes unavailable to highlight text, and editing capabilities are restricted to what is available from the minimized window located on the Start menu taskbar, as shown in Figure 1-11. Hands-on Project 1-8 teaches you how to copy and paste in the command window.

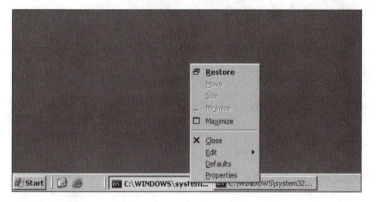

Figure 1-11   Changing full-screen command properties

Hands-on Project 1-8

To copy data from the command window into a text editor:

1. Click the **Start** button ![Start], and then click **Run**.

2. Type **notepad** and press **Enter**. The Notepad text editor application launches in a new window.

3. Click ![Start], and then click **Run**.

4. Type **cmd** and press **Enter**. The command window opens.

5. Type **cd** and press **Enter**.

6. You will need to turn on QuickEdit mode to highlight data within the window. Right-click the **window title bar**, and then click **Defaults**.

7. Within the Edit Options section, ensure that QuickEdit mode is selected. Click **OK** to close the Console Windows Properties dialog box. Type **exit** and press **Enter** to close the command window. Then open a new command window by pressing ![cmd], clicking **Run**, and typing **cmd**. This enables QuickEdit mode.

 If an Apply Properties dialog box appears, click the checkbox next to Save Properties for future windows with the same title and click OK.

8. Type **dir *** and then press **Enter**. The command window lists all of the directories located in the root of the drive.

9. Click the left-most part of the line that contains the Windows directory entry.

10. Press and hold **Shift** while clicking the right-most part of the line that contains the Windows directory entry. The entire line should be highlighted. See Figure 1-12.

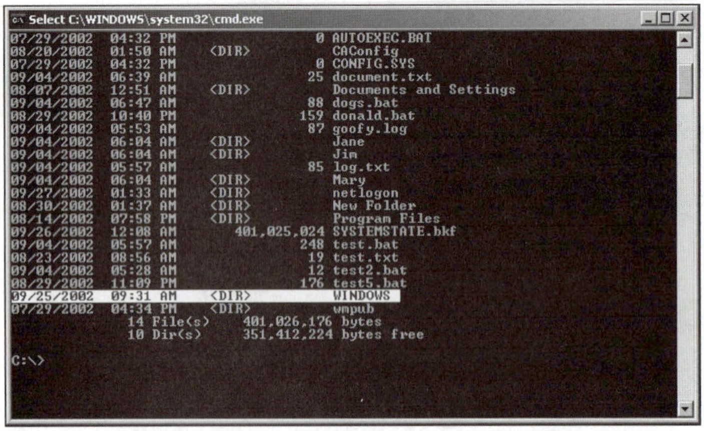

Figure 1-12   Highlighting data in the command window

11. Right-click the title bar of the command window. Point to **Edit** on the pop-up menu.

12. Select **Copy** from the fly-out menu, as shown in Figure 1-13.

Figure 1-13   Copying data within the command window

13. Press and hold **Alt** while pressing **Tab** to make the Notepad window active. Make sure that the Notepad window is the active window. (The Notepad window title bar should be blue and the cursor should be blinking in the main area of the window.) Release **Alt**.

14. To paste the copied text into Notepad, press and hold **Ctrl**. Press **v**. Release the keys.

15. Press and hold **Alt**. Press **f** to activate the File menu. Release **Alt**. Press **x** to exit the File menu.

16. The system prompts you to save the document. Press the **right arrow** key to point to No, then press **Enter**.

17. Type **Exit** then press **Enter** to close the command window.

To paste the text, you could also click Edit on the menu bar, and then click Paste from the drop-down menu.

The text from the command window has now been copied into Notepad. If the text has not been successfully copied, repeat the steps starting with Step 10.

Changing the Appearance of the Command Window

There are several ways of using the **CMD** command with options to change the colors, fonts, and text size of the command window's contents. You may wish to do this to enhance visibility or to display output in different colors to attract the eye. You can change the text and background colors when you launch the command window by adding the **/T:bt** option to **CMD** from the Run line. You will try this method in Hands-on Project 1-9.

C:_
Syntax

CMD /T:<BT>   Opens a command window with the color scheme appropriate to the color codes listed in Table 1-1. **B** is background color. **T** is text color.

COLOR <BT>   Changes the current command window to the color scheme appropriate to the color codes listed in Table 1-1 (on the next page). **B** is background color. **T** is text color.

The easiest method is to change the window properties using the "Command Prompt" Properties window, which is shown in Figure 1-14. You will use this method in Hands-on Project 1-10.

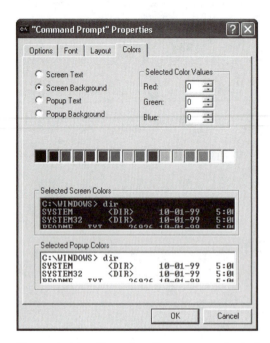

Figure 1-14   Changing the command window background color

Another option is to use the **COLOR bt** command in an open command window, where **bt** is replaced by the codes for background and text numbers or letters. Codes for colors are shown in Table 1-1.

Table 1-1   Command window color codes

Code	Color	Code	Color
0	Black	8	Gray
1	Blue	9	Light Blue
2	Green	A	Light Green
3	Aqua	B	Light Aqua
4	Red	C	Light Red
5	Purple	D	Light Purple
6	Yellow	E	Light Yellow
7	White	F	Bright White

Hands-on Project 1-9

To open a command window with specific colors using **CMD**:

1. Click the **Start** button , and then click **Run**.
2. Type **cmd /t:56** and press **Enter**. The command window appears with a purple background and yellow text.
3. Type **exit** and press **Enter** to close the command window.
4. Click , and then click **Run**.
5. Type **cmd /t:5e** and press **Enter**. Notice that the yellow text is much brighter this time. Any time you change color settings, be sure to carefully plan what you are going to do: It is easy to inadvertently change the text to be so close in color to the background that you cannot see it.
6. Type **exit** and press **Enter** to close the command window.

Hands-on Project 1-10

To change command window colors:

1. Click the **Start** button , and then click **Run**.
2. Type **cmd** and press **Enter**.
3. Right-click the **command window** title bar, and click **Defaults** on the pop-up menu. The Console Windows Properties menu opens.
4. Select the **Colors** tab, and, if necessary, click the **Screen Text** radio button. Make a note of the current colors.
5. If necessary, click the **light gray square** in the middle of the line of squares in the middle of the window to select it, as shown in Figure 1-15.
6. Click the **Screen Background** radio button. Make a note of the current colors.
7. Click the **dark blue square** (second from the left).
8. Click **OK** to close the Console Windows Properties window.

> An Apply Changes dialog box may appear the first time this function is performed. If it does, click OK.

9. Type **exit** and press **Enter** to close the command window.
10. Click , and then click **Run**.
11. Type **cmd** and press **Enter**. Notice that the color changes are now displayed.
12. Repeat Steps 3 through 11, returning the colors to their original settings (noted in Steps 4 and 6).
13. Type **exit** and press **Enter** to close the command window.

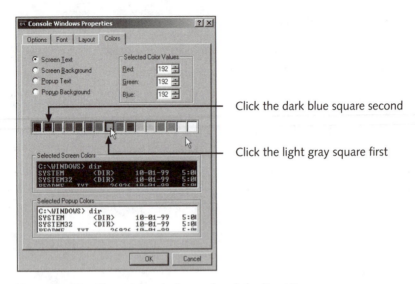

Figure 1-15   Changing window color default settings

Changing the Command Prompt Text

As you learned earlier, a prompt is the text that appears to the left of the cursor when the command window opens. By default, the prompt indicates the current drive and directory, which in Windows Server 2003 is C:\Documents and Settings\Administrator. You might need to change the appearance of this prompt to emulate different environments, shield a user from certain information, or present other information such as the time of day or a username. The command for changing these prompts is **PROMPT**. Recall that a full list of options for **PROMPT** can be displayed within the command window by typing **PROMPT /?**.

PROMPT <OPTION>   Changes the prompt according to the *OPTION* as outlined in Table 1-2.

PROMPT <TEXT>   Changes the prompt according to the *TEXT* entered as the option.

In addition to the options available for **PROMPT**, you can incorporate any word or system variable into the prompt. This is most often done to display frequently referenced information, such as the date, time, or username. Examples of customized prompts are shown in Table 1-2. Unfortunately, there is no quick way to make the results of the **PROMPT** command apply permanently to all command window sessions. One way to permanently apply prompt modifications is to always open the command window using the syntax **CMD PROMPT <OPTIONS> /K**. This syntax opens the command window, changes the prompt, and leaves the window open for further commands.

Table 1-2   Customized prompts and their on-screen appearances

Command Syntax	Display
PROMPT PG	C:\>
PROMPT $D TG	Thu 03/25/2004 15:43:01.15>
PROMPT Time is: $%time%$_Date is: $%date%	Time is: 15:46:04.02 Date is: Thu 03/25/2004
PROMPT Good Morning!$G	Good Morning!>
PROMPT %USERNAME%$G	Johnsmith>

Hands-on Project 1-11 teaches you how to customize the prompt.

Hands-on Project 1-11

To change the prompt to James > :

1. Click the **Start** button [Start], and then click **Run**.

2. Type **cmd** and press **Enter**.

3. Type **prompt James $g** and press **Enter**. Your prompt should look like the one shown in Figure 1-16.

Figure 1-16   Prompt with customized text

4. Type **exit** and press **Enter** to close the command window.

USING VARIABLES IN THE COMMAND ENVIRONMENT

Variables are memory locations that can be used within the command environment to represent data that can change over time. Variables can represent numbers, and they can also represent any combination of words or numbers.

Some variables are automatically created by the system for both internal and user usage. The most commonly used variables are DATE and TIME, which represent the system date and time, and USERNAME, which represents the currently logged-on user. These **environment variables** represent data relevant to the particular system on which they exist, and they can eliminate time and effort in batch programs and on the command line.

Think of variables as placeholders: An example of this idea is a variable that contains the contents of the preamble to the U.S. Constitution. After creating the variable, you could then refer to the variable name (**PREAMBLE**) rather than typing out the full text of the preamble every time you wanted to refer to it.

Variables are created in one of four ways. The first way is to use the **SET** command within an existing command environment. The second way is to use the autoexec.bat file in the root of the boot drive (usually C). You can also create variables within the Windows Control Panel's System/Advanced/Environment Variables option. As you will learn in Hands-on Project 1-12, you can also create variables using My Computer.

You can create variables for use by the user who is currently logged in or for use by the system. System variables can be used by anyone who logs in to the computer, while user variables can be accessed only by the current user. Variables have names, such as **PATH**, and values.

SET   Displays a list of the current environment variables.

SET <*VARNAME*>   Displays information on the specified variable (*VARNAME*).

SET <*VARNAME*>=<*TEXT*>   Defines the specified variable (*VARNAME*) as the specified *TEXT*. The *TEXT* can be any combination of numbers, characters, paths, and so on.

Once a variable has been created, it can be invoked within another command or script by surrounding the variable name with percent signs. Refer back to Table 1-2 and notice how the variable **USERNAME** is invoked as **%USERNAME%**. While the specific variable called **USERNAME** is generated automatically by the system, the same invocation rules apply for all variables.

The syntax for creating a variable within autoexec.bat or on the command line is **SET <*VARNAME*>=<*VALUE*>** where *VARNAME* is the variable name and *VALUE* is the assigned value. Current variables can be viewed in a command window by typing **SET** at the command prompt, then pressing Enter. You could also type **SET <*VARNAME*>** and then press Enter. Hands-on Project 1-12 takes you through these methods.

Hands-on Project 1-12

To view variables:

1. Click the **Start** button [Start], and then click **Run**.

2. Type **cmd** and press **Enter**.

3. Type **set** and press **Enter**. This step displays the environment variables available on your computer. Your screen should look similar to Figure 1-17.

1

```
C:\WINDOWS\system32\cmd.exe                                              _ □ ×
Microsoft Windows [Version 5.2.3663]
(C) Copyright 1985-2001 Microsoft Corp.

C:\Documents and Settings\Administrator.MACHINE>set
ALLUSERSPROFILE=C:\Documents and Settings\All Users
APPDATA=C:\Documents and Settings\Administrator.MACHINE\Application Data
ClusterLog=C:\WINDOWS\Cluster\cluster.log
CommonProgramFiles=C:\Program Files\Common Files
COMPUTERNAME=MACHINE
ComSpec=C:\WINDOWS\system32\cmd.exe
HOMEDRIVE=C:
HOMEPATH=\Documents and Settings\Administrator.MACHINE
LOGONSERVER=\\MACHINE
NUMBER_OF_PROCESSORS=1
OS=Windows_NT
Path=C:\WINDOWS\system32;C:\WINDOWS;C:\WINDOWS\System32\Wbem
PATHEXT=.COM;.EXE;.BAT;.CMD;.VBS;.VBE;.JS;.JSE;.WSF;.WSH
PROCESSOR_ARCHITECTURE=x86
PROCESSOR_IDENTIFIER=x86 Family 6 Model 4 Stepping 2, AuthenticAMD
PROCESSOR_LEVEL=6
PROCESSOR_REVISION=0402
ProgramFiles=C:\Program Files
PROMPT=$P$G
SESSIONNAME=Console
SystemDrive=C:
SystemRoot=C:\WINDOWS
TEMP=C:\DOCUME~1\ADMINI~1.MAC\LOCALS~1\Temp
TMP=C:\DOCUME~1\ADMINI~1.MAC\LOCALS~1\Temp
USERDOMAIN=MACHINE
USERNAME=Administrator
```

Figure 1-17   Environment variables

4. Type **set path** and press **Enter**. The results display the data represented by the variable named **PATH**.

5. Type **exit** and press **Enter** to close the command window.

Hands-on Project 1-13 shows you how to create a new environment variable using My Computer.

Hands-on Project 1-13

To create a variable called `firstname` with the value of `James`:

1. Navigate to My Computer, which will vary in location depending on your system configuration. Right-click **My Computer**, and then click **Properties**. The System Properties window opens.

2. Click the **Advanced** tab, and then click the **Environment Variables** button. An Environment Variables window opens. Notice that the top section contains user variables for the user who is currently logged in. The bottom section contains variables for the entire system.

3. Click the **New** button in the top section for the current user. The New User Variable dialog box opens, as shown in Figure 1-18.

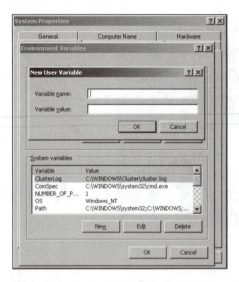

Figure 1-18   New User Variable dialog box

4. Type **firstname** in the Variable name text box. Press **Tab**.

5. Type **James** in the Variable value text box, and then click **OK**. The new variable appears in the list of current user variables.

6. Click **OK** to close the Environment Variables window. Click **OK** to close the System Properties window. Now test that the variable was created successfully.

7. Click , and then click **Run**.

8. Type **cmd** and press **Enter**.

9. Type **set firstname** and press **Enter**. Your command window should look like Figure 1-19.

Figure 1-19   Setting the prompt to the firstname variable

10. Type **exit** and press **Enter** to close the command window.

> **Note**
> Variables created or changed using Advanced System Properties apply to subsequent command windows that you open. Variables created using the SET command apply immediately, but only exist for the duration of the current command window. You can also create variables using scripts, but again, they apply immediately *after* the script is executed and only for the duration of the window from which the script was executed. Variables created or changed within autoexec.bat only apply after the computer has been rebooted.

The PATH Variable

1

The PATH variable is an environment variable used to save time and effort in executing programs from the command line. When the system executes a command or program, it assumes that the program in question resides in the directory (or folder) that the prompt is currently sitting in, which is by default the C:\Documents and Settings\Administrator>, the root of the C drive. If the program is not located in that spot, an error message appears, stating that the program is not recognized. Most programs aren't stored in the root, because they're filed in an appropriate directory for organizational purposes. To execute a program, you must navi-gate to the appropriate directory, and then type the program filename at the command prompt. This can be time consuming, since it's hard to remember the location of every program that you might ever want to run. The PATH variable makes this extra navigation unnecessary. The PATH variable contains a list of directories (separated by semicolons) showing the locations of executable programs (you used this variable in Hands-on Project 1-12). When you enter the name of a program on the command line, the system searches the current directory and also searches every directory listed in the PATH variable for that program. If the program is found, it is automatically executed.

The PATH variable is used not only within the command environment, but also throughout the Windows operating system. To make the PATH variable more readable, and also to enable applications and users to append data to the PATH without completely re-entering the existing PATH contents, you can use the PATH variable even as it is being updated with new data.

For example, assume that you open a command window and type SET PATH at the prompt. You might see something similar to this:

```
Path=C:\WINNT\system32;C:\WINNT;C:\WINNT\System32\Wbem;C:
\Program Files\Network Associates\PGPNT;E:\GRS;
```

Notice that each directory entry path is separated with a semicolon. If you need to add C:\Program Files to the PATH variable to be able to run it from any directory in the command window, one method is to type the entire path over again in a new SET PATH command and add the new data, like this:

```
SET PATH=C:\WINNT\system32;C:\WINNT;C:\WINNT\System32
\Wbem;C:\Program Files\Network Associates\PGPNT;E:\GRS;C:
\Program Files;
```

However, an easier method is to use the PATH variable in a new SET statement, like this:

```
SET PATH=%PATH%; C:\Program Files
```

FUNCTION KEYS

Function keys are at the top of most keyboards and provide shortcut access to frequently used commands. Within Windows, F1 always accesses help, F5 usually represents the refresh function, and F8 and F10 are used to pause the boot process. Other than F1, function key assignments and functionality can vary depending on the application. Table 1-3 shows the actions of the most commonly used function keys within the command environment.

Table 1-3 Function keys and their purpose

Function Key	Action
F1	Displays each letter of the last executed command each time the key is pressed.
F2	Prompts the user to enter the last valid letter from the last command, and the command is displayed up to that letter.
F3	Displays the last executed command.
F5	Displays the last command executed. Pressing F5 again displays the prior command. Performs the same function as the up arrow key. Stops at the oldest command entered since the window was opened.
F6	Performs the same function as Ctrl+Z. No practical usage.
F7	Displays a numbered list of recently executed commands. Highlighting a numbered command executes it at the command prompt.
F8	The same as F5, but it does not stop with the oldest command. Instead, it begins with the most recent command.
F9	Prompts the user to enter a command number in order to avoid typing the command at the prompt. This assumes that the user remembers which command was executed first, which one was executed second, and so on.

OUTPUT REDIRECTION AND LOGGING

Quite often, you may need to log the successes and failures of actions performed within the command environment. Such documentation also comes in handy in recording program results, or output, that you might see within the command window. The process of creating logs in this manner is called **output redirection** or logging. This section provides a brief introduction to output redirection or logging, while Chapter 3 goes into the topic in more depth.

System administrators frequently perform output redirection or logging within batch programs; however, you can redirect the output from any command to a file. To do this, you tag a ><FILENAME> to the end of the command where FILENAME is the name of the file that you want to create. Note that the brackets (>< and <) surrounding FILENAME are required. The file is then created and the output from commands is inserted into the specified file. If you need to add entries to an existing file, add >><FILENAME> (using two >>s) to the end of the command.

><FILENAME> A command option that directs output from a command into the *FILENAME*. If the *FILENAME* does not exist, it will be created. If the *FILENAME* already exists, it will be deleted and re-created.

>><FILENAME> A command option that directs output from a command and adds it to the specified *FILENAME*. If the *FILENAME* does not exist, an error will occur.

Figure 1-20 shows a step-by-step process that uses logging in conjunction with a program called **FC** (file compare) to determine what files are added or modified when a program is installed. This process would be used to determine what files and folders were installed when an application was installed by comparing the directory entries before and after the installation.

FC <FILE1> <FILE2> Compares the contents of both entered files. Displays the differences on the screen.

---

1. Enter this code at the command prompt:
```
TYPE C:\BOOT.INI>C:\BEFORE.TXT
DIR/S C:\>>C:\BEFORE.TXT
```

2. Install the new application (for example, download from the Internet Adobe Acrobat Reader, WinZip, or another application that you do not have currently installed).

3. Type this code at the command prompt:
```
TYPE C:\BOOT.INI>C:\AFTER.TXT
DIR/S C:\>>C:\AFTER.TXT
```

4. Type this code at the command prompt:
```
FC C:\BEFORE.TXT C:\AFTER.TXT>C:\COMPARE.TXT
```

5. At the command prompt, you can type TYPE COMPARE.TXT or EDIT COMPARE.TXT to view the files that were added or modified when the application was created.

Figure 1-20 Process for comparing files to determine modifications

If the primary drive letter is not C, as shown in Figure 1-20, be sure to replace C with your primary drive letter.

Redirection doesn't always have to occur to a file. You can also redirect information to ports, which are data entry/exit points within a computer. One example of a port is a modem. A handy modem troubleshooting method is illustrated in Figure 1-21.

1. Open a command window.
2. At the command prompt, type cd\ and then press Enter.
3. Type edit open.txt and then press Enter.
4. Type AT&F S1 ATDT 123456.
5. Hold down the Alt key, and press F. Release the Alt key, and press X.
6. When the prompt appears to save the file, press Enter.
7. Type edit close.txt and then press Enter.
8. Type ATH.
9. Hold down the Alt key, and press F. Release the Alt key, and press X.
10. Once again, when the prompt appears to save the file, press Enter.
11. At the command prompt, type type open.txt>com1 and press Enter. Replace the COM1 with whichever COM port your modem is connected to. If the modem is working, you should hear a dial tone and the modem attempting to dial.
12. At the command prompt, type type close.txt>com1 and then press Enter.

Figure 1-21   Process for redirecting output to a modem

CHAPTER SUMMARY

❐ The command line is a text-based interface that is available to run commands in the various Windows operating system environments. Commands are available to execute basic and complex tasks, and they include options for administering and manipulating data, files, directories, entire computers, computer networks, and domains. One of the primary uses for commands is the execution of automated tasks through the use of batch files.

❐ Commands allow the user to interact with the computer without using a mouse. In this chapter, you learned how to display help for commands and turn the echo feature on and off to eliminate or display noncritical messages. You learned how to display filenames and directory names, cut and paste between the command window and other environments, and customize the appearance of the command prompt and the command window.

❐ Like placeholders, variables are memory locations that are used in the command environment to make system administration more efficient. Environment variables are system-generated variables that contain information specific to the system, such as system date, time, or user. The **PATH** variable contains a list of directories that shows the locations of executable programs.

❐ Function keys let you take shortcuts in executing commands. Output redirection lets you create documentation of program results using *><FILENAME>* and *>><FILENAME>* syntax, where *FILENAME* is the name of a file that will contain program output.

COMMAND SUMMARY

Command	Function
CMD <COMMAND> /C	From the Start menu's Run line, runs the command and closes the command window.
CMD /F:ON	Turns on directory and filename completion.
CMD /K	From the Start menu's Run line, runs the command and leaves the window open.
CMD /Q	Turns echo off.
CMD /T:BT	Changes the background and text colors: 0=black; 1=blue; 2=green; 3=aqua; 4=red; 5=purple; 6=yellow; 7=white; 8=gray; 9=light blue; A=light green; B=light aqua; C= light red; D=light purple; E=light yellow; F=bright white.
EXIT	Closes the current instance of CMD.
PROMPT	Displays the current prompt configuration.
PROMPT PG	Displays the C:\> prompt.
PROMPT $D	Displays the date as the prompt.
PROMPT $T	Displays the time as the prompt.
PROMPT $G	Displays > as the prompt.
SET	Displays all current environment variables.
SET <VARNAME>=<VALUE>	Creates a new variable called VARNAME and sets the value at VALUE.
SET PATH	Displays the current path.
SET PATH=<PATHDATA>	Sets the path to equal the PATHDATA variable.
SET <VARNAME>	Displays the contents of the VARNAME variable.
SET <VARNAME>=%<VAR1>% %<VAR2>%	Sets the variable VARNAME with the values of the predefined variables VAR1 and VAR2.
><FILENAME>	At the end of the command; creates FILENAME; redirects output to FILENAME; FILENAME can be a file or port.
>><FILENAME>	At the end of the command; redirects output to FILENAME; appends to existing FILENAME; FILENAME can be a file or port.
/?	Displays help.

KEY TERMS

automation — The process of executing a series of tasks using a script, batch file, or other executable program without user intervention.

batch — A type of automation script that uses commands that are written in a plain text file with a .bat extension.

boot — The process in which a computer turns on and loads the operating system.

command line — A text-based interface for running commands.

command prompt — The environment, interface, and location for running commands.

computer administration — The process of administering and maintaining local computer hardware, software, and services.

directory — A logical container on a hard disk that may contain other directories and files.

directory and filename completion — A feature that allows the system to display directory names and filenames based on one or two characters of entered text.

domain — A logical security boundary covering a group of networked computers, user accounts, and other network resources.

domain administration — The process of administering and maintaining the security of objects belonging to a domain.

domain controller (DC) — A Windows NT, 2000, or Server 2003 server that contains the directory service database.

DOS — Disk operating system. The first operating system used on PCs.

echo — A command line feature that displays noncritical messages on the screen.

environment variable — A variable that resides on a computer system and contains data relevant to the system, such as date, time, or username.

file extension — The last three characters of a filename following a period. Directories do not have extensions, and not all files have extensions. The file extension often indicates what application created the file. Examples of extensions are .exe (an executable file), .bat (a batch file), .doc (a Microsoft Word document), .xls (a Microsoft Excel spreadsheet), .gif (a bitmapped color graphics file), and .jpg (a compressed graphics file).

functions keys — The F-numbered keys that provide shortcut access to frequently used commands.

graphical user interface (GUI) — An interface that uses graphics and color to enhance a computer's ease of use and the input/output of commands and data.

network administration — The process of maintaining and administering connectivity between computers on a network. This type of maintenance can involve cables, hardware, and computer administration components such as network card drivers and protocols.

operating system (OS) — A software interface that runs the computer and aids the user in executing programs and utilizing hardware.

option — Text that modifies a command to perform the command in a specific way.

output redirection — The process of directing the output from a given command that would normally appear on the screen elsewhere. Redirection of this sort is usually used for logging but can be used to test data communications.

prompt — The location on the screen where the computer accepts typed input from the user. A blinking cursor indicates a prompt.

script — A specific file that is used to perform multiple tasks and logic. Scripts are generally platform-specific, language-specific, and simpler in nature than a full-blown programming language. Unlike standard programs, scripts do not have to be compiled, but they usually require an agent or service to run them. One exception is batch scripts, whose processing agent is embedded within the command environment.

shortcut — A link to a program or file that is represented by an icon.

variable — A memory location that represents data that can change over time.

REVIEW QUESTIONS

1. Script files can be used to create large numbers of _____ and _____ accounts.

2. A _____ is a logical security boundary covering network resources.

3. Three 32-bit operating systems are _____, _____, and _____.

4. In what situation might it be better to run a command from the command line rather than a GUI application?

5. To find the available options for a command, you use the command plus _____ on the command line.

   a. /$

   b. /@

   c. /switch

   d. /?

   e. /{

6. Describe the difference between a user variable and a system variable.

7. You can change the colors of the background and text of a command window.

   a. True

   b. False

8. It is possible to start multiple instances of CMD within a command window.

   a. True

   b. False

9. Which command changes the prompt to > in a command line environment?

   a. `set prompt`

   b. `change prompt`

   c. `hostname`

   d. `prompt $g`

10. What are the three ways to change an environment variable?

11. What command allows you to navigate between files and directories?

   a. `/F:ON`

   b. `/D:ON`

   c. `/F:Set Directory`

   d. `/D:Set Files`

12. Closing the command window using the Close button ⊠ or Minimize button ▬ while a process is running in the window generates an error message.

   a. True

   b. False

13. Which of the following commands opens a new command environment to operate a new subroutine?

   a. `new`

   b. `open`

   c. `cmd`

   d. `cmd/new`

DISCOVERY EXERCISES

1. Create a variable for `%firstname%=Chris`. Then change the prompt to read `Chris>` using the `%firstname%` variable.

2. Create a variable for `%lastname%=Columbus`. Then create another variable for `%fullname%` using both the `%firstname%` and `%lastname%` variables. Use the **ECHO** command to ensure that the `%fullname%` variable is correct.

3. Append `C:\testpath` to the end of the **PATH** statement with as few keystrokes as possible.

2

MANAGING FILES

After reading this chapter and completing the exercises, you will be able to:

♦ Print output from the command line
♦ Navigate without a mouse
♦ Find and view data in files and directories
♦ Manipulate data
♦ Create new data files and directories

As you learned in Chapter 1, available commands can be displayed on the screen by simply typing "help" at the command line. The purpose of this chapter is to help you become more familiar with basic navigation within the command window by looking at what administrators do on the job: They change and create data and system settings to perform various administrative tasks. To be able to change data, you must first be able to locate it, which you learn about in the first part of this chapter. Once data has been located, you can change it. You will learn about altering data in the second part of this chapter. Creating data, files, and directories is the final step toward the basic knowledge that you must have in order to accomplish nearly every administrative task covered in this book. You will learn about these tasks toward the end of the chapter. This chapter discusses many of the commands listed in Figure 2-1. For a complete listing of commands, you can open a command window and type "help" (without the quotation marks).

```
C:\WINNT\System32\cmd.exe                                              _ □ ×
Microsoft Windows XP [Version 5.1.2600]
(C) Copyright 1985-2001 Microsoft Corp.

C:\Documents and Settings\Administrator>help
For more information on a specific command, type HELP command-name
ASSOC      Displays or modifies file extension associations.
AT         Schedules commands and programs to run on a computer.
ATTRIB     Displays or changes file attributes.
BREAK      Sets or clears extended CTRL+C checking.
CACLS      Displays or modifies access control lists (ACLs) of files.
CALL       Calls one batch program from another.
CD         Displays the name of or changes the current directory.
CHCP       Displays or sets the active code page number.
CHDIR      Displays the name of or changes the current directory.
CHKDSK     Checks a disk and displays a status report.
CHKNTFS    Displays or modifies the checking of disk at boot time.
CLS        Clears the screen.
CMD        Starts a new instance of the Windows command interpreter.
COLOR      Sets the default console foreground and background colors.
COMP       Compares the contents of two files or sets of files.
COMPACT    Displays or alters the compression of files on NTFS partitions.
CONVERT    Converts FAT volumes to NTFS.  You cannot convert the
           current drive.
COPY       Copies one or more files to another location.
DATE       Displays or sets the date.
```

Figure 2-1   Standard command line commands

PRINTING FROM THE COMMAND LINE

As you prepare to learn how to perform various file management tasks, begin by viewing the available commands and printing them out for reference. Hands-on Project 2-1 teaches you how to do this.

Hands-on Project 2-1

To view and print the commands available in the command line environment:

1. Open a command window.

2. At the command prompt, type **help** and press **Enter**. A list of commands appears in the window.

3. At the command prompt, type **help>help.txt** and press **Enter**. Now no commands appear, because the output (what normally appears on the screen) has been sent to the help.txt file, which is created as a result of redirection (>), instead of to the screen.

4. To view the help.txt file, type **type help.txt** and press **Enter**. What you see should be similar to Figure 2-2. Use the mouse to scroll up and down to view the contents of the file.

5. To view the file page by page, type **type help.txt | more** and press **Enter**. Press the **spacebar** to view the next page of the file. You might need to press the spacebar more than once to view the next page.

6. Type **edit help.txt** and press **Enter** to view the file using the Edit program, as you learned in Chapter 1.

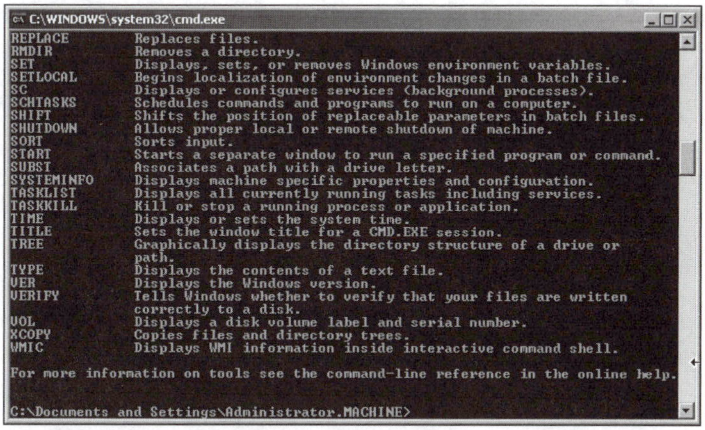

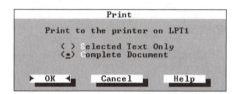

Figure 2-2   Results of the `type help.txt` command

7. Hold down **Alt** and press **f.** A drop-down menu appears from the File menu on the menu bar.

8. To print the command list, press **p** (for printing). A Print dialog box opens, as shown in Figure 2-3. Press **Enter** to print the file.

9. Press and hold **Alt**. Press **f.** Press **x** to exit the Edit program.

Figure 2-3   The Print dialog box within the Edit program

10. Close the command window by typing **exit** and pressing **Enter**.

You now have a hard copy of the commands available for use in the command environment. Keep this list handy for reference throughout this chapter.

Before you learn about more commands, you need to know how the command environment displays data and how to retrieve and view the information you need within the confines of the command window. You will learn about these features in the following sections.

NAVIGATING WITHOUT A MOUSE

The ability to use a mouse is limited within the command environment for several reasons, primarily because mouse technology did not exist when DOS was invented and there has been little need to add mouse functionality over the years. Why so little need? Since

Windows came along, the command window has been considered a basic, no-frills environment. From a technical perspective, mouse functionality increases processing requirements and decreases performance. While the regular Windows interface has additional programs and systems in place to specifically reduce the overhead associated with mouse functionality, those systems also require a certain amount of processing capacity. Put simply, mouse functionality is not really needed within a command window because every task that a mouse would normally perform can be done in other, less processor-intensive ways. Thus, you need to learn how to function without a mouse for the every-day tasks that you will be performing on the command line.

Learning to work mouse-free is a big advantage in the information technology (IT) world. Most of the mouseless techniques described here also apply to the GUI environment. Get into the habit of using the keyboard as much as possible. Here are just a few of the reasons why learning these skills is valuable in the workplace:

- You can perform tasks faster and more reliably than with a GUI.
- A broken mouse, bad mouse driver, or dirty mouse ball can prevent you from working.
- If you can visualize the environment clearly enough, you don't need a functioning monitor to safely restart or modify the system.
- Customized color settings can mask certain menus, commands, and buttons; with keyboard input, these settings don't cause a problem.

Highlighting Data

Often, you need to highlight data within a command application before you can copy, delete, or paste that data. To highlight content within any Windows application, you place the cursor at the beginning of the area, hold down the left mouse button, and drag the cursor to the end of the area you want highlighted. Then you release the mouse button. You can also highlight text without a mouse, using the Shift key, arrow keys, the Home key, and End. To highlight, you navigate to the beginning of the text that you want to highlight, press and hold the Shift key, and then navigate to the end of the text with the arrow keys.

Holding down the Ctrl key and pressing the C key copies the highlighted data, holding down the Ctrl key and pressing the V key pastes the highlighted data, and pressing the Delete key deletes the highlighted data. Pressing the spacebar or typing anything else while data is highlighted replaces the highlighted text with the typed text.

Using the Insert, Home, and End Keys to Highlight Text

Using the Insert, Home, and End keys saves time and effort when navigating within Windows, applications, or in the command environment.

The Home and End keys are used to move the cursor to the beginning or end of a line of text. Holding down Ctrl while pressing Home or End places the cursor at the beginning or end of the entire document. In the command environment, the cursor is a small blinking horizontal line that appears after the command prompt and is exactly the size of one character. Its presence indicates the location where data can be entered. The Insert, Home, and End keys function in the same manner anywhere a cursor exists—either in the command environment or in Windows. The Home and End keys are used most frequently in conjunction with the Shift key while highlighting data, instead of using the arrow keys.

In Hands-on Project 2-2, you will practice using these key combinations to highlight data. The Edit program is discussed in detail later in this chapter. You will use the Edit program here to learn how to highlight, copy, paste, and replace data.

Hands-on Project 2-2

To highlight and manipulate text within the Edit program:

1. Open a command window.

2. Type **edit** and press **Enter**. A window opens, as shown in Figure 2-4.

Figure 2-4 The Edit program

3. Type **Hello There**. Do not press Enter.

4. Press **Home** and hold down **Shift**. Press **End**.

5. The text should be highlighted. Hold down **Ctrl** and press **c**. Release **Ctrl**.

6. Press **End** and then press the **spacebar**. The text should no longer be highlighted.

7. Hold down **Ctrl** and press **v**. Release **Ctrl**. Notice that the previously highlighted text has been pasted onto the line.

8. Use the arrow keys to place the cursor under the "T" of the second "There". Hold down **Shift** and press the **right arrow** key five times to highlight the entire word. Release **Shift**.

9. Type **Yourself**. Notice that "There" has been replaced by "Yourself."

10. Hold down **Alt** and press **f**, and then press **x**. Release **Alt**.

11. The program prompts you to save the file. Press **n** for no.

12. Type **exit** and press **Enter** to close the command window.

Now you know how to navigate the cursor using the arrow keys and the Home and End keys. You also learned how to highlight and replace data without using a mouse. These are valuable (and speedy) skills to have within the command window.

You can also use the Insert key as an alternative to highlighting and replacing data. When the Insert key is on, the cursor changes from a small blinking line to a blinking block. When Insert is on, typing new text is no different than typing when Insert is off. However, if Insert is on and you enter data in the middle of a line, all existing data is written over with the new typed data, character for character. It might seem that the Insert key can be more annoying than useful, because it is easy to accidentally replace an entire line of data, rather than insert it. When used correctly, however, Insert saves effort, which is a good reason to understand exactly what Insert does. You will practice using Insert in Hands-on Project 2-3.

Hands-on Project 2-3

To use the Insert key to replace text:

1. Open a command window.

2. Type **Here is a test of the insert key**. Do not press **Enter**.

3. Press the **left arrow** key 10 times. The blinking cursor should be under the "i" in the word "insert".

4. Press **Insert**. Notice that the cursor changes from a line to a block.

5. Type **mistake**. The line now reads "Here is a test of the mistakekey."

6. Press **Insert** to turn off Insert and press **Esc** to clear the entry.

7. Type **exit** and press **Enter** to close the command window.

Using Alt and Tab to Highlight Text

The Alt key, like Insert, saves time and effort when navigating within command and Windows applications. The Alt key serves to activate menus and hot keys within these applications. Within both Windows applications and command window programs, Alt activates or displays an underscore beneath single letters within individual menu items, buttons, and other features of the window. These letters are used to activate the menu items or buttons represented by the highlighted letter.

The Alt key can activate a menu within an application such as Notepad or Wordpad. The File menu within both of these applications can be accessed using Alt. Holding down Alt displays a line under the first letter of "File" on the menu bar. Pressing the F key then displays the drop-down menu associated with the File menu. Sometimes other letters are underscored in this manner within the drop-down menu. The functions associated with those letters can be activated by pressing the key of the appropriate letter. Additionally, you can use arrow keys to navigate a menu once it has been activated in this manner. Sometimes this is a faster method of navigating menus than using a mouse to navigate and click, since most applications begin with a File menu in the upper-left corner.

Command applications often use the same underscored characters that you are accustomed to seeing in Windows programs; however, several of them highlight or change the color of the character instead of underscoring. Within a menu, a highlighted or underscored character activates the menu when you press the Alt key in combination with the highlighted character. You will learn the specifics of using the Alt key on the command line later in this chapter when you learn how to edit text.

Sometimes applications have different sections or areas on the interface, and you will need to get from one section to another without a mouse to manipulate output or data. The most common example of this is Windows Explorer, where drives and directories are displayed in the left window **pane**, or section, and files and subdirectories are located in the right window pane. Using Tab moves the cursor, or **focus**, from pane to pane so that you can then use the arrow keys to move the focus up and down. The focus is the active section of the screen that is currently highlighted or contains a small dotted rectangle around it. Hands-on Project 2-4 lets you practice moving the focus.

Hands on Project 2-4

To view a file located on the C drive in Windows Explorer without using the mouse:

1. Click the **Start** button ![Start], and then click **Run**. Type **explorer** and press **Enter**.

2. First, you need to change the default settings to display hidden files. Hold down **Alt** and press **t** to activate the Tools menu. Release **Alt**.

3. Press **o**, which displays the Folder Options dialog box.

4. Press and hold **Shift** and press **Tab** to shift the focus to the General tab. Release **Shift**.

5. Press the **right arrow** key once to activate the contents of the View tab.

6. Press **Tab** three times to set the focus inside the Advanced settings window.

7. Press the **down arrow** key 10 times until the Show hidden files and folders option is highlighted. If necessary, press the **spacebar** to select the radio button as shown in Figure 2-5. This enables you to view the boot.ini file within

Windows Explorer. Boot.ini is used to change the default boot settings and options that appear when the system has had more than one operating system installed.

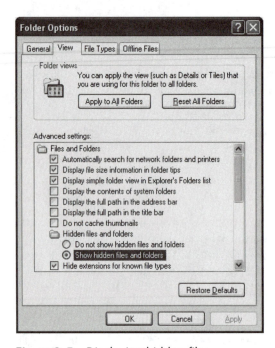

Figure 2-5   Displaying hidden files

8. Press the **down arrow** key twice to highlight the Hide protected operating systems (Recommended) option. Enable this option by pressing the **spacebar**. Press **y** to override the warning that appears.

9. Press **Tab** twice to move the focus to the OK button, and then press the **spacebar**.

Figure 2-6 shows Windows Explorer. The pane on the left is the Folders pane. The pane on the right is the Files pane. The pane that runs horizontally above the Folders and Files panes is the Address pane. Starting from this point, there are two different ways to view the contents of the boot.ini file.

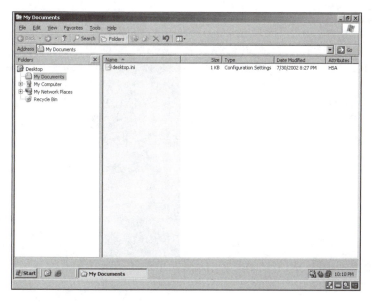

Figure 2-6 Windows Explorer

10. Press **Tab** two times. The Address pane should now have the focus.

11. Press **Tab** two times (the first time the focus shifts to the Close button of the Folders pane, the second time it shifts to the Folders pane itself).

12. Press the **down arrow** key until My Computer is highlighted.

13. Use the right arrow key to point to **My Computer**. Use the arrow keys to point to the **C drive** option. Press the **right arrow** key to select the C drive.

14. Press **Tab** to shift the focus to the Files pane.

15. Press the **down arrow** key until the boot.ini file is highlighted. Press **Enter**. The contents of boot.ini should appear.

16. Close Windows Explorer.

The DOSKEY Command

A command called **DOSKEY** automatically runs when you launch **CMD** from the Run line. **DOSKEY** is a command that causes the system to remember the last 20 commands that were entered at the command prompt, and makes them available again through the up and down arrow keys. Once you select a command, it can be modified using the arrow keys, or cleared with the Esc key.

DOSKEY   Allows the system to maintain a list of previously executed commands, which are available for recall using the up and down arrow keys.

Within the command window, you can press F7 to display a list of all of the commands currently in the **DOSKEY** buffer. You can use the arrow keys to scroll the list and choose a command to display at the command prompt. The Alt+F7 key combination clears the **DOSKEY** buffer. You can also set **DOSKEY** to record a group of commands and assign them a name. This type of recording is called a **macro**. Macros are not used often in the command window because batch files can be used instead, and are far more modifiable.

DOSKEY is valuable when performing redundant tasks, or when trying to change options or arguments for a command to get it to work. Hands-on Project 2-5 lets you practice with **DOSKEY**.

Hands-on Project 2-5

To use **DOSKEY**:

1. Open a command window.

    DOSKEY is loaded with Windows Server 2003. To use **DOSKEY**, you need to have at least one command already entered.

2. Type **cd** and press **Enter**.

3. Press the **up arrow** once. Notice that the previous command appears. Press the **Esc** key to clear it.

4. Type **dir** and press **Enter** to display a list of files.

5. Type **cls** and press **Enter** to clear the screen.

6. Now, view only directories. Press the **up arrow**.

7. Notice that the **CLS** command appears. Press the **up arrow** again. The **DIR** command appears.

8. Type ***.** at the end of the **DIR** command so that it reads "dir ***.**" Press **Enter**.

9. The resulting output should be similar to Figure 2-7. Type **exit** and press **Enter** to close the command window.

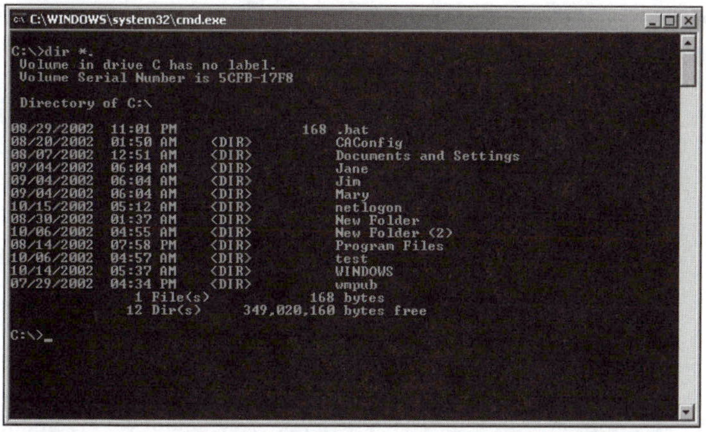

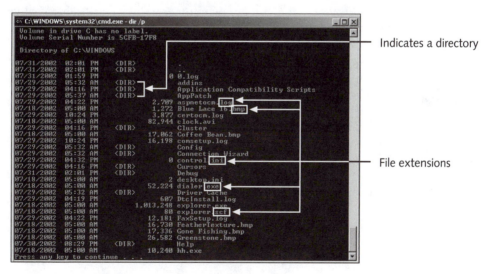

Figure 2-7 Using DOSKEY

Directories, Files, and Extensions

Everything in a computer's hard drive is organized within a strict hierarchy of files and directories (known as folders within Windows Explorer). Each directory can contain files or other directories. Each file and directory has a name that indicates its nature or purpose. Additionally, most files contain an appended three-character **extension**, which is a further indicator of the type of file and its role within the entire system. Examples of file extensions are shown in Figure 2-8.

Figure 2-8 The file and directory structure

In Figure 2-8, the first two columns show the date and time that the files and directories were created or modified. The third column indicates whether the item is a directory. Since only two types of items can exist within a directory—files and directories—the lack of a <DIR> within this column indicates that the item is a file. The fourth column indicates the size of the file in **bytes**. Bytes are the basic units of data size within a computer. One byte equals eight bits, 1,024 bytes are equivalent to a **kilobyte (K)**, and 1,024 kilobytes are equivalent to a **megabyte (M)**. 1,000 M are equivalent to a **gigabyte (G)**.

Keep in mind that Windows Explorer in detailed display (Alt+V, D) shows kilobytes instead of bytes when displaying these file sizes.

The fact that a megabyte is 1,024 K can lead to some annoying arithmetic when estimating the size of a file or the contents of a directory. In general, it is safe to estimate that 1,000,000 bytes = 1 M, and 1,000 M = 1 GB.

Directory entries have no size because they are merely containers. The last column displays the directory name or filename, including any applicable extensions.

Notice in Figure 2-8 that all files have an extension ending with a period and three characters. Files with names that end in .log are generally **text files** that are documents viewable within any text editor (such as Edit, Notepad, and Wordpad). Files with .bmp extensions are **bitmap** graphics files that are viewable with the Microsoft Paintbrush program. They are commonly used for icons, buttons, and other graphics that you see within Windows. Further, .avi files are movies that can be viewed using Windows Media Player; .ini files are used to hold settings for a particular application; and .exe files are program files that are executable.

You might wonder why it is important to know these extensions. Troubleshooting is a big part of any IT professional's life. You might be able to track down a problem by looking at .log or .ini files. Knowing the characteristics of files is a huge factor in figuring out how a program works, and also in solving problems with its execution.

These and other standardized file extensions that you might encounter frequently are displayed in Table 2-1.

Table 2-1 Common file extensions

Extension	Title	Description	Viewable within
.log	log	tracks activity	Edit, Notepad, Microsoft Word, Wordpad
.bmp	bitmap	graphics	Paintbrush
.avi	audio visual interface	movies	Windows Media Player
.ini	initialization	stores default behavior and startup information for applications	Edit, Notepad, Microsoft Word, Wordpad
.exe	executable	program or application	not viewable
.doc	document	word processor	Microsoft Word, Wordpad
.xls	Excel	spreadsheet	Microsoft Excel
.txt	text	straight text (with or without formatting)	Edit, Notepad, Microsoft Word, Wordpad, Excel, and others
.csv	comma-delimited	Data is sorted into columns separated by commas.	any editor (see .txt), Microsoft Excel, most database applications
.tsv	tab-delimited	Data is sorted into columns separated by tabs.	any editor (see .txt), Microsoft Excel, most database applications
.dll	dynamic link library	handles program and system mechanics	not viewable by standard methods
.com	command files	similar to .exe files	not viewable by standard methods
.bat	batch	noncompiled application containing commands	any editor (see .txt)
.msi	Microsoft installer package	installable program package	not viewable by standard methods
.htm	Web page	HTML Web page	any editor (see .txt)
.sys	system files	file-specific	file-specific

Wildcards

Many commands can be executed using what are known as **wildcards**. Wildcards, like the joker in a deck of cards, can be used to represent any character(s) and are used to search for and select multiple files. For example, you can use a wildcard to search for certain types of files, files that begin with particular letters, or files that meet other specific criteria. Wildcards in the command environment are represented by an asterisk (*). An asterisk followed by a period (*.) indicates any or all directories, while an asterisk followed by a period and another asterisk (*.*) indicates any or all files. Wildcards can also be used at the character and extension level by inserting them in place of specific letters or extensions. For example, to search for any file beginning with the character "c", use the wildcard **C*.***. To search for all log files, use the wildcard ***.log**. You can also combine wildcards. For example, to search for any .com file starting with the letters "sym," you would use the wildcard **sym*.com**. To search for any file that ends in "phon," use the wildcard ***phon.***.

Viewing Off-Screen Data

When the command window is maximized, data sometimes extends beyond the visible portion of the monitor (for example, file output). To view the entire contents of output, you can display data one screen at a time by appending the option **|MORE** to the end of a command and pressing the spacebar to display the next page. You used the **|MORE** option when you completed Hands-on Project 2-1 earlier in this chapter.

Clearing the Screen

Sometimes you need to clear the command window of all activity that is being displayed. This is often the case when several commands have been executed whose output remains on the screen, or in between command procedures being run in batch. **CLS** is a command that clears the entire screen of everything except for the command prompt itself.

CLS   Clears the screen.

Stopping a Program

As you learned earlier, you can close the command window by running the **EXIT** command. Sometimes, when a command program hangs or locks up, you may be tempted to just close the window and eliminate the problem. This can cause trouble, however, by abnormally terminating programs or processes currently running within the window. Instead of closing the window, hold down Ctrl and press the C key. This should stop any current process and return to the standard prompt. This halting procedure is commonly known as "break." Ctrl+C also comes in handy when viewing the first few pages of multiscreen output (such as you see when using the **|MORE** command) or in any situation where you don't want to page through the remainder of the screens.

Remember that Ctrl+C within an application copies highlighted data and selected files and folders. Ctrl+C on the command line terminates a running process or procedure.

Occasionally, Ctrl+C can cancel a command that you made by mistake. For example, say you executed a DEL ***.*** command from the C directory, which would delete everything on the C drive. Running Ctrl+C might prevent damage if you run it quickly enough.

FINDING AND VIEWING FILES AND DIRECTORIES

One of the key tasks you will perform as an IT administrator is to locate and view files and directories. Using commands, it is possible to find a file based on its location, specific filename or part of its filename, or contents.

Tree File and Directory Structure

As you learned earlier, files are grouped and placed within directories to make it easier to identify and locate files of a specific type, function, or purpose. The structure of a directory is called a **directory tree**, which describes the outline-like hierarchy of directories that contain subdirectories that contain files. Directory trees may contain multiple levels of subdirectories. The quickest way to envision this file and directory structure on a hard drive is to run the **TREE** command, which you will do in Hands-on Project 2-6. The **TREE** command displays all of the directories and subdirectories that exist on a hard drive in a layout that is similar to an outline.

TREE   Displays the directory structure of a drive.

TREE /F   Displays the directory and file structure of a drive.

Hands-on Project 2-6

To run the **TREE** command:

1. Open a command window.

2. Type **tree c:\ | more** and press **Enter**. The first page of the C drive directory structure is displayed. See Figure 2-9. The first entry on the screen is the directory that is located at the root of the C drive. Subsequent entries that are indented under the first entry are subdirectories. Other entries that are beneath subdirectories and are indented further are sub-subdirectories, and so on.

3. To break the current process, press and hold **Ctrl**. Press **c**. Release **Ctrl**.

4. Type **tree c:\ /f |more** and press **Enter**. Notice in Figure 2-10 that several entries are not connected by lines. These entries are files that reside within the directory listed above them and are visible because you included the **/F** option in the **TREE** command. Directories are always displayed with lines.

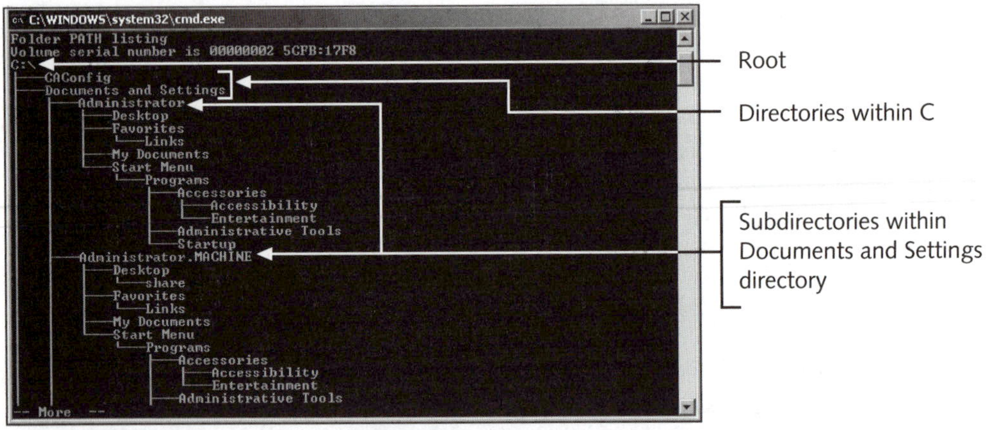

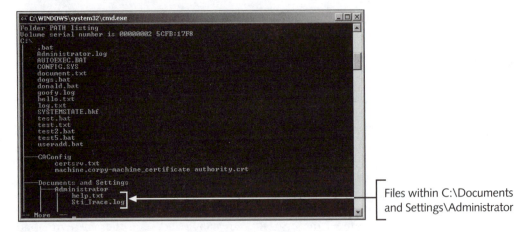

Figure 2-9 Result of running the TREE command

Figure 2-10 Running TREE with the /F option

5. Press and hold **Ctrl**. Press **c**. Release **Ctrl**. Type **exit** and press **Enter** to close the command window.

Navigating Using CD

Now that you know how to view the directories and files that exist on a system, you need a way to move around within the structure. The **CD** command provides this mobility. Recall that the first line in a new command window is the operating system version number. The first line also indicates any service packs that have been applied. In Figure 2-11, Windows Version 5.2.3663 is the OS, which indicates Windows Server 2003. After the copyright information, the prompt appears. By default, the prompt is located in the **profile** directory for the user who is currently logged on (in this case, the Administrator). The user profile directory contains information about settings, icons, and the registry for a user's desktop and system. By navigating within the user profile, you can determine what programs are installed, what the user's desktop contains, where the user has been on the Internet, and lots of other user-specific information.

DIR command

Drive letter and volume

Volume number

Figure 2-11   The profile directory

The directory that is shown in the prompt is the current or active directory. To move to other directories (such as the ones listed by the **TREE** command), use the **CD** command.

C:_
Syntax

CD <DRIVE>:\<DIRECTORY>   Changes the current directory to the new drive and directory.

CD <DRIVE>:   Changes to the root of the new drive.

CD <DRIVE>:   Changes to the last-used directory located on the new drive.

**CD **   Changes to the root of the current drive.

CD ..   Changes to the parent directory of the current directory.

CD ..\<SUBDIRECTORY>   Changes to a subdirectory of the current directory. Also known as a sister directory to the current directory.

The options available with the **CD** command can be subtle in their differences. The best way to become an expert is to learn each one. It is important that you be able to navigate through the directory structure on the system because many programs will not run unless the cursor is located in the directory that contains the program. In Hands-on Project 2-7, you will learn how to navigate through the directory structure.

Hands-on Project 2-7

To navigate to the parent directory and back:

    1. Open a command window. If you are logged on to the system as Administrator, the current prompt should read C:\Documents and Settings\Administrator>.

2. Type **cd c:\documents and settings** and press **Enter**.

3. Type **cd c:\documents and settings\administrator** and press **Enter**.

 Another way of changing directories is to type cd .. and press Enter, and then type cd administrator and press Enter.

4. To move back and forth to the root of the drive, type **cd ** and press **Enter**.

5. Type **cd documents and settings** and press **Enter**.

6. Type **cd administrator** and press **Enter**.

 Instead of using two commands to get back to the C:\Documents and Settings\Administrator directory, it is easier to use one. Type cd c:\ and press Enter, and then type cd .\documents and settings\administrator and press Enter.

Now, learn how to navigate from one subdirectory to another subdirectory of the same parent.

7. Type **cd desktop** and press **Enter**.

8. Type **cd ..\favorites** and press **Enter**.

 Another (longer) way of moving from one subdirectory to another subdirectory of the same parent is to type cd .. (to get back to the C:\Documents and Settings\Administrator directory) and then type cd c:\documents and settings\administrator\desktop. Press Enter. Next, type cd c:\documents and settings\administrator\favorites and press Enter.

9. Type **exit** and press **Enter** to close the command window.

As you can see, there are several ways to do the same thing using the **CD** command. No single way is better or worse than another, as long as the result is the same. Most people form their preferences based on how much text needs to be typed.

The DIR Command

DIR is used to search for and locate files, determine directory and file sizes and **properties**, and a number of other exploratory tasks. Properties can include details about a file, such as attributes and the dates that changes were made to the file.

DIR   Lists the contents of a directory. Use **/P** or **|MORE** to display a list one screen at a time.

DIR <FILENAME>   Displays the *FILENAME*.

DIR <DRIVE>:\<DIRECTORY>   Lists the contents of the new drive and directory without navigating to the directory itself.

The **DIR** command lists the contents of the directory in which the prompt is currently residing. By default, the prompt displays the current directory. Look again at Figure 2-11 and you will notice that the current directory is C:\Documents and Settings\Administrator, and that the result of the **DIR** command displays the contents of that directory. The first line indicates the drive letter and **volume** that is being listed. Briefly, the volume is the disk partition to which the drive letter has been assigned. When you format a partition, you have the option of assigning the partition a name. By default, Windows 2003 Server does not ask for a partition or volume name during installation, but it does retain an existing name during an upgrade. The second line displays a **volume number**. The volume number is used by the system to keep track of separate partitions and drives. After the files and directories are listed, the total number of files and subdirectories is displayed, along with the disk space occupied by those files. The disk space here (in Figure 2-11, this is 5,771 bytes) is the sum of the files only, and not the subdirectories. Determining the size of an entire directory tree, or all subdirectories, is a topic that you will learn about later in this chapter.

As a system administrator, you need to take note of the contents of the directory shown in Figure 2-11 because it contains the user's profile. An administrator might need to alter or modify the contents of a user's profile by removing icons, altering the desktop, or replacing a corrupted file. Several of the files shown in Figure 2-11 have special system, hidden, archive, and read-only properties that are called **flags** or **attributes**. Each attribute has an on or off condition relative to a particular file. Administrators need to be able to view and manipulate these flags and attributes.

Viewing Hidden Files

As with other commands, options and arguments exist with the **DIR** command that allow you to change the items that are displayed and how they are presented in the command window. It is helpful to note that arguments and options can be combined into a single command.

Recall that options are parts of the syntax that can be added to a command to alter that command's behavior. Options do not change. Arguments are parts of a command syntax in which the user determines the content. For example, **/S** is an option for **DIR**, while an argument is a drive letter or directory, such as C:\Documents and Settings.

Profiles are especially tricky to manage in domain environments because they are often stored both on the desktop and on the network. In any profile directory you will find **system files** and **hidden files**. System files are used exclusively by the operating system to perform specialized functions. The boot.ini file mentioned earlier in this chapter is an example of both a system and a hidden file. Hidden files are files that have been flagged with an attribute to make them invisible to default viewing methods. System and hidden files are usually off limits for a good reason: self-protection. In most cases, you can assume that if a file has been hidden, altering it can be dangerous to system functionality. As an

IT administrator, there are times, however, when you will need to view and modify system and hidden files.

There are several ways to view system and hidden files; one of the most common methods is to use Windows Explorer or My Computer to change the default folder options. Figure 2-12 shows a standard hidden file setting on the left, while on the right the settings allow more user access. Making such changes causes Windows Explorer to display *all* hidden and system files, which can be dangerous for a curious end user.

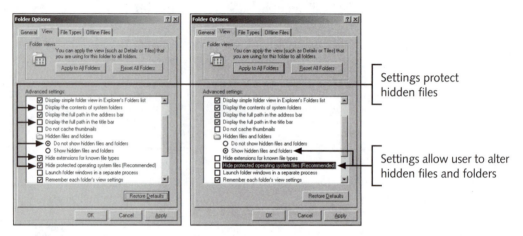

Settings protect hidden files

Settings allow user to alter hidden files and folders

Figure 2-12   Windows Folder Options for hidden and system files

As an administrator, you might be called on to make changes at a user's desktop that require you to view hidden and read-only files. Changing Windows Explorer to view these files lets you accomplish your administrative tasks; you will need to remember to return the file settings back to their defaults (or however the user changed them) after the changes are made. Otherwise, you run the risk of the user crashing his or her computer by tampering with a previously hidden file.

It is much safer to view hidden files within the command window than to change the attributes for all files using Windows Explorer. The following options for the **DIR** command let you view all files from the command line.

DIR /A   Lists a directory's contents, including system and hidden files.

DIR /AD   Lists all directories.

DIR /AR   Lists all read-only files within the directory.

DIR /AH   Lists all hidden files within the directory.

DIR /AS   Lists all system files within the directory.

You will learn how to change file attributes later in this chapter.

Ordering Files

Occasionally, you will need to view the contents of a directory in a particular order. The most frequent reason for sorting a directory's listing is to track down files that are old and have not been accessed recently so that you can identify files for deletion. By default, files are displayed alphabetically, but you might need to sort by reverse alphabetical order (starting with Z), file size, or date. The following commands let you order files using various methods.

DIR /ON   Lists files alphabetically by name. Use /O-N to sort by reverse alphabetical order.

DIR /OS   Lists by smallest file size first. Use /O-S to sort by largest file size first.

DIR /OE   Lists by file extensions alphabetically. Use /O-E to sort by reverse alphabetical order.

DIR /OD   Lists by date and time, from oldest to newest. Use /O-D to sort by newest file first.

DIR /OG   Lists contents of a directory with subdirectories listed first.

Recall that you can combine multiple options in a single command, such as DIR /ON /OS.

Time and Date Stamps

The date and time stamps displayed as a result of the **DIR** command are not the only dates and times associated with a file. Actually, what you see in the **DIR** listing are the date and time that the file was last updated, or written. The command environment provides one option that is used to determine when a file was last accessed or viewed, and another option that shows when a file was originally written. As you will learn in Hands-on Project 2-8, You can access this time and date information using the following commands.

DIR /TA   Lists contents with the date and time the file(s) were last accessed.

DIR /TC   Lists contents with the date and time the file(s) were created.

DIR /TW   Lists contents with the date and time the file(s) were written or updated.

Hands-on Project 2-8

To determine the differences between file creation, modification, and access times:

1. Press and hold **Ctrl** and press **Esc**. Release **Ctrl**. Type **r**, type **cmd**, and press **Enter**.

2. Type **cd .\favorites** and press **Enter**.

3. Type **copy msn.com.url test.txt** and press **Enter**.

4. Type **dir test.txt** and note the time that the file was created.

5. Type **copy msn.com.url>>test.txt** and press **Enter**. You are using the **COPY** command (introduced later in this chapter) to add data to and modify the current test.txt file. Note the time.

6. Immediately type **time** and press **Enter** twice. Make a note of the current time.

7. Type **type test.txt** and press **Enter**. You are using the **TYPE** command to access the test.txt file.

8. Type **dir test.txt /tc** and press **Enter**. This displays the creation date and time, which should be the time that was noted in Step 5. Make a note of this time.

9. Type **dir test.txt /ta** and press **Enter**. This displays the date and time that test.txt was last accessed. This time should be very close to the time that was noted in Step 6.

10. Type **dir test.txt /tw** and press **Enter**. This displays the date and time that test.txt was written, which should be very close to the time that was noted in Step 6.

When a file is being copied, it is also being accessed. After all, it makes sense that to copy something, you must first look at it. If you run DIR MSN.COM.URL /TA, you will notice that the time is the same as that noted in Step 8.

Determining File Ownership

Any multi-user system, whether it consists of multiple users logging in to a single Windows XP machine or network users storing data on a network server, contains files that were created by various people. Sometimes it becomes necessary to determine who created a file to track system usage. More often, you might need to secure data when someone leaves the company. A person who creates a file becomes its **owner**. To be more specific, the account in use at the time that a file is created becomes listed as the owner. File ownership can be determined using the **DIR /Q** command.

DIR /Q   Lists the files within the current directory, along with an additional column indicating file ownership.

DIR <FILENAME> /Q   Lists the owner of *FILENAME*.

As far as Windows Server 2003, XP Pro, or 2000 is concerned, all members of the Administrators group are created equally. `DIR/Q` displays files that are created by a member of the Administrators group as being owned by the Administrators group rather than the individual member.

2

Finding Files

Let's say you need to view, copy, or modify an unknown file. For example, assume that you just downloaded a new program, and you need to first find any documentation or instructions located in the new program directory. After looking for documentation, you would probably want to find the install program to install it properly. You could locate the documentation by searching with wildcards, searching subdirectories, or filtering.

Finding Files Using Wildcards

Assume that you've already downloaded and expanded a compressed file into a directory called C:\toyz. Let's say that you take a quick look at the directory by running **DIR** from the C:\>toyz prompt. Upon finding that there are many files, you need to use wildcards to find a file called "manual". To do this, you enter the following command:

    dir manual.*

Once the file is displayed, and providing its extension is either .txt, .csv, or .tsv, you can view the file using the **TYPE** command, like this:

    type manual.txt

TYPE <*FILENAME*>   Displays the contents of *FILENAME* on the screen.

TYPE <*FILENAME1*> >> <*FILENAME2*>|<*LOCATION*>   Redirects the contents of *FILENAME1* to another file (*FILENAME2*) or specified location, such as a printer port.

If the manual file ends with an extension other than .txt, .csv., or .tsv, you will need to use a different command to view the file. The manual.doc file can be viewed from Wordpad or Microsoft Word, while manual.bat is a batch program that should be executed at the command prompt by typing `manual.bat` and pressing the Enter key.

To continue with this example, you next need to find the installation program. Since most installation programs have an extension of .exe, you will need to use wildcards again to search for all files ending with .exe. This command would be:

    dir *.exe

In this case, you're looking for an installation program, so any file that comes up as install.exe, setup.exe, install.bat, or something similar should be run on the command prompt.

Searching Subdirectories

Recall that **DIR** lists only the contents of the current directory. If you need to look at the contents of subdirectories, you can use the **DIR /S** command to list the subdirectories along with their contents.

C:_
Syntax

DIR /S   Lists the contents of the current directory, all subdirectories, and their contents.

Continuing with our example, assume that your search for an installation program, using the command **dir *.exe**, displayed a "File Not Found" message. To search the entire directory structure of an existing directory, you must change the previous command to read:

```
dir/s *.exe
```

Once again, when you find an appropriate file, type the filename at the command prompt and press Enter to run it.

Filtering File Types

As you may have guessed already, wildcards can also be used to **filter** output from the **DIR** command. A filter is a function that masks specific data, leaving the desired data behind. This is similar to the ordering options described earlier, but it is different in that it displays only files that match the criteria outlined by the wildcards. An added plus is that the directory listing displays the number of filtered files along with the amount of disk space they occupy. In this manner, you can use wildcards to determine how many files of a particular type or name exist within a directory, along with the disk space consumed by the individuals and the group as a whole.

The only difference between locating a specific .exe file using the **DIR /S** command and finding out how many .exe files exist within the directory using a filter is simply how you look at the output. Remember that **DIR** lists all files within a directory, along with a total number of files displayed and the amount of disk space they occupy. Creating the wildcard filter (***.exe** in the example) only changes the data that is displayed—in this case, only. exe files are returned as output.

As mentioned in Table 2-1, .dll files are dynamic link libraries that are used to support various program functionality. To gain a better appreciation of the importance of these support files, in Hands-on Project 2-9 you will determine how many .dll files exist on the C drive, and how much space they occupy.

Hands-on
Project

Hands-on Project 2-9

To use a wildcard filter to determine how many .dll files exist on the system:

1. Open a command window.

2. Type **cd** and press **Enter**. The prompt should now be at the root of the C drive, reading C:\\>.

3. Type **dir/s *.dll** and press **Enter**. It may take a few moments for the command to process.

Once the command prompt is returned (C:\>), you can see that all .dll files are grouped under the directory to which they belong. At the end of each group is a file total and summary of disk space usage. Figure 2-13 shows that at the end of the entire list is another file total and disk usage summary for all .dll files on the entire disk.

```
C:\WINDOWS\system32\cmd.exe                                         _ □ ×

 Directory of C:\WINDOWS\WinSxS\x86_Microsoft.Windows.GdiPlus_6595b64144ccf1df_1
.0.3000.0_x-ww_4A2CA156

07/29/2002  05:40 AM         1,728,512 GdiPlus.dll
               1 File(s)     1,728,512 bytes

 Directory of C:\WINDOWS\WinSxS\x86_Microsoft.Windows.IsolationAutomation.ProxyS
tub_6595b64144ccf1df_1.0.0.0_x-ww_7CFAC880

07/29/2002  05:40 AM             9,216 sxsoaps.dll
               1 File(s)         9,216 bytes

 Directory of C:\WINDOWS\WinSxS\x86_Microsoft.Windows.IsolationAutomation_6595b6
4144ccf1df_1.0.0.0_x-ww_FD9DA872

07/29/2002  05:40 AM            28,160 sxsoa.dll
               1 File(s)        28,160 bytes

 Directory of C:\WINDOWS\WinSxS\x86_Microsoft.Windows.WinHTTP_6595b64144ccf1df_5
.1.0.0.0_x-ww_E0651936

07/29/2002  05:40 AM           330,240 winhttp.dll
               1 File(s)       330,240 bytes

     Total Files Listed:
            2120 File(s)   419,092,779 bytes
               0 Dir(s)    349,016,064 bytes free

C:\>_
```

Figure 2-13   Disk usage for all .dll files

This project is a great opportunity to test the Ctrl+C function.

4. Type **exit** and press **Enter** to close the command window.

Finding Text

At times, you might need to locate files that contain particular words, patterns of words, or a series of characters called **strings**. As an IT professional, you will sometimes need to track down files belonging to a particular program, and one of the best ways to do this is by searching for files that contain the manufacturer or program name. The best way to search for strings in this situation is to use the **FIND** command. **FIND** has several variations.

C:_
Syntax

FIND <*FILENAME*> "*STRING*"   Scans the contents of *FILENAME* and displays lines containing the *STRING*.

FIND <*FILENAME*> "*STRING*" /V   Scans the contents of *FILENAME* and displays lines that do not contain the *STRING*.

FIND <*FILENAME*> "*STRING*" /C   Scans the contents of *FILENAME* and displays the number of lines within the file that contain the *STRING*.

FIND <*FILENAME*> "*STRING*" /N   Scans the contents of *FILENAME* and displays line numbers and data containing the *STRING*.

FIND <*FILENAME*> "*STRING*" /I   Scans the contents of the *FILENAME* for the specified *STRING* in either uppercase or lowercase letters, and displays the data containing the *STRING*.

Most commands accept wildcards instead of filenames, so the **FIND** command can be used to find a string in any file within a listed directory.

Any string that contains a wildcard is called a **regular expression**. Because regular expressions are so powerful, it is possible to search and target not just data, but also patterns of data. A list of applied examples of wildcards and **metacharacters** is shown in Table 2-2. Metacharacters are used to find and hone in on specific instances, placements, and combinations of strings.

Table 2-2   Regular expression wildcards (metacharacters)

Regular expression	Function
m.*soft	Finds a file containing the word Microsoft. Also finds all words that begin with "m" and end with "soft," such as Macrosoft or mentalsoft.
m..soft	Finds a file containing the word Macsoft or Muksoft. Also finds all words beginning with the letter "m," followed by any two letters, and ending in "soft."
^Microsoft	Finds all instances where the word "Microsoft" is at the beginning of a line.
$Microsoft	Finds all instances where the word "Microsoft" is at the end of a line.
[a-t]*	Finds any word that contains the letters "a" through "t".
\$100	Finds the literal $100.
\<Mic	Finds any word that begins with "Mic".
Mic\>	Finds any word that ends with "Mic".

FINDSTR is another text search command, but it is more complex than **FIND**. **FINDSTR** is used most often for locating data within database files, where the string and a number of unknown factors regarding the string are important. In other words, **FINDSTR** can use wildcards in the string itself (regular expressions), whereas **FIND** can only use wildcards in the filenames.

2

FINDSTR *"STRING"* *<FILENAME>*   Finds and displays the entire line(s) containing *STRING* within *FILENAME*.

FINDSTR /B *"STRING"* *<FILENAME>*   Finds and displays the entire line(s) containing *STRING* within *FILENAME* where *STRING* is at the beginning of the line.

FINDSTR *"^STRING"* *<FILENAME>*   A regular expression that performs the same function as the /B option.

FINDSTR /E *"STRING"* *<FILENAME>*   Finds and displays lines containing *STRING* within *FILENAME* where *STRING* is at the end of the line.

FINDSTR *"$STRING"* *<FILENAME>*   A regular expression that performs the same function as the /E option.

FINDSTR /L *"STRING"* *<FILENAME>*   Finds and displays lines containing *STRING* within *FILENAME*. The *STRING* cannot contain any regular expressions.

FINDSTR /C:*STRING* *<FILENAME>*   An alternative to *FINDSTR /L "STRING" <FILENAME>* but does not require quotation marks.

FINDSTR *"\!STRING"* *<FILENAME>*   Finds and displays lines containing *STRING* within *FILENAME* where the character represented by "!" is literal. Used to negate the regular expression characters (, *, ^, $, ., \, *, and) when you want to search for these symbols within a regular expression. An example would be to search for the dollar amount $100, which would be `FINDSTR "$100" *.*` (see Table 2-2).

FINDSTR /S *"STRING"* *<FILENAME>*   Finds and displays lines containing *STRING* within *FILENAME* in the current directory and all subdirectories. Similar to the `/S` option for the `DIR` command.

FINDSTR /I *"STRING"* *<FILENAME>*   Finds and displays lines containing *STRING* within *FILENAME* without regard to uppercase or lowercase letters.

FINDSTR /N *"STRING"* *<FILENAME>*   Finds and displays line numbers and lines containing *STRING* within *FILENAME*.

FINDSTR /M *"STRING"* *<FILENAME>*   Displays *FILENAME*s containing the *STRING*.

FINDSTR /P *"STRING"* *<FILENAME>*   Finds and displays lines containing *STRING* within *FILENAME* where the file(s) do not contain nonprintable characters.

FINDSTR /X *"STRING"* *<FILENAME>*   Finds and displays lines containing *STRING* within *FILENAME*. Used when the *STRING* is intended to search for an entire phrase rather than single words.

Keep in mind the following facts about **FINDSTR** and regular expressions:

- Regular expressions can contain symbols and characters with which you might want to search, such as * or $. If this is the case, use *<CHARACTER>* to change the regularly expressed character to literal.

- When you use **FINDSTR** in conjunction with standard wildcards (not regular expressions), the command will scan and report system and hidden files. Using **FINDSTR** on a hidden file without using wildcards will result in a "File Not Found" message.

- If you receive a message that reads "The system cannot find the file specified," the string may not exist.

- A line of text can be longer than the command window. Lines that are longer than the window are wrapped to enable easier viewing. A literal line of text is created when a **carriage return** (Ctrl+Enter) is generated by the line before it. If you find that the output from **FINDSTR** is difficult to read, use the **/N** option to offset each new result in bold.

Say you want to use **FINDSTR** to locate all files on the system that contain a particular user's name or account. In this situation, **FINDSTR** is locating all files that contain the word "admin" using the following code:

```
findstr /s /i /m "ADMIN" *.*
```

The **/S** option searches the current directory and all subdirectories. The **/I** option ensures that the search will not be case sensitive; without it, the results would only consist of "ADMIN", but not "admin" or "Admin." The **/M** option instructs the system to only display the filenames that match the criteria of the characters "admin."

Now, to evolve this particular command a little bit, you may want to search for all words beginning with "admin"—which would include "adminbob" and "adminjane" as well as "Administrator." The syntax for the command would then change to:

```
findstr /s /i /m "\<ADMIN.*" *.*
```

The **\<** at the beginning of the string instructs the system to search for the characters "admin" at the beginning of every word, while the **.*** at the end of the string places no limit on the number of characters at the end of the word. If it became necessary to search for the characters "admin" followed by only three characters, the command would be:

```
findstr /s /i /m "\<ADMIN..." *.*
```

In this code, each period (.) serves as the individual wildcard for a single character. Changing this command to check once for any word beginning with "admin" at the beginning of a line for a similar command requires the following code:

```
findstr /s /i /m "^ADMIN.*" *.*
```

The carat symbol (^) at the beginning of the string serves two purposes. First, it indicates that the string is a regular expression, which allows the system to search for all words beginning with "admin." Second, the carat further narrows the search to all lines in which the first word begins with "admin."

FINDSTR is a difficult command to understand and master, but it can be useful for administrators who work with databases. For example, it would be convenient to be able to search a customer database for all customers living in a particular region, or those who have purchased a particular item, so that you can target specific marketing campaigns to the customers who are most likely to buy your products. You will learn how to search for strings in Hands-on Project 2-10.

Hands-on Project 2-10

To use **FINDSTR** to search for strings:

1. Open a command window.

2. Type **cd** and press **Enter**. You should now be in the root of the C drive.

3. Type **type boot.ini** and press **Enter**. This displays the contents of the boot.ini file, which is used by the system to choose which operating system to initialize during system startup. Examine the output of the **TYPE** command. This output will serve as the sample data to use with the **FINDSTR** command.

4. Type **findstr /b "time" boot.ini** and press **Enter**. This searches for the character pattern "time" at the beginning of a line within boot.ini. The output should be similar to what you see in Figure 2-14.

```
C:\WINDOWS\system32\cmd.exe                                    _ □ ×
C:\>findstr /b "time" boot.ini
timeout=30

C:\>_
```

Figure 2-14   Using the **FINDSTR** command to find "time"

5. Type **findstr "time" boot.ini** and press **Enter**. This command produces the same output as Step 4. The difference here is that if the word "time" existed in the middle of a line, it would be found using this command. The **/B** option in Step 4 would not have found it because **/B** only searches the first word in each line.

6. Type **findstr "windows" boot.ini** and press **Enter**. This will search for the word "windows" within the boot.ini file. This particular expression did not find any results. Take a look again at the output from Step 3. Notice any characters or spaces that surround the word "windows," as well as any differences between the string that you typed and the word that is in the file.

7. Type **findstr /i "windows" boot.ini** and press **Enter**. The result should be the line that contains the word "windows." **FINDSTR** is literal when it searches for strings; in other words, differences in capitalization in various **FINDSTR** commands will give different results. Using the **/I** option allows **FINDSTR** to search for the string without regard to capitalization of the string.

Now you will do some investigation. You will display the line that states TIMEOUT=30 by finding all lines that end with a 0 character.

8. Type **findstr "$0" boot.ini** and press **Enter**. This doesn't work, and you are returned to the C:\ prompt.

9. Now troubleshoot the problem by typing **findstr "30" boot.ini** and pressing **Enter**. This does work, but you need to find the 0 at the end of the line, not 30.

10. One possible reason that the system returned 30 is that there might be an unseen space after the 0 on this line in boot.ini. Type **findstr /e "0" boot.ini** and press **Enter**. There is no unseen space; otherwise, this command would not display the line that you are looking for. The problem appears only while using a regular expression with the $ argument. Try shifting the expression elsewhere within the string.

11. Type **findstr "0$" boot.ini** and press **Enter**. Only now does the command find the string appropriately.

12. Type **exit** and press **Enter** to close the command window.

MANIPULATING FILES

By now you should have a thorough understanding of what a directory tree looks like, how to navigate between directories, how to find files and text within files, and how to display files and folders within a directory using several different methods. Now you will discover how to make changes to files in order to make modifications to the system. An example of such a modification would be to add an entry to the boot.ini file that causes the system to boot to another partition. In Chapter 3, you will learn about batch files, and how to create and modify groups of commands within a file.

Copying Files

One of the most important tasks a server administrator can perform is a data **backup**. A backup is a process that copies changed or unchanged data to an alternate location. Backups are usually performed for security reasons; in the event that the original data becomes corrupted, lost, or irretrievably deleted, the backup copy is available for use. The **COPY**, **XCOPY**, and **DISKCOPY** commands are used to perform backups. These three commands are the ancestors of today's backup programs. In many ways, these commands are faster and more efficient than their Windows counterparts. Performing data backups using batch programs and automation is covered in Chapter 3. For now, you will learn the basic steps for copying data.

The COPY Command

The **COPY** command is easy to remember and simple to use.

C:_
Syntax

2

COPY <FILENAME1> <DESTINATIONPATH> Copies the original file, *FILENAME1*, into the destination location, *DESTINATIONPATH*.

COPY <FILENAME1> <FILENAME2> Copies the original file, *FILENAME1*, and names it *FILENAME2*. *FILENAME1* and *FILENAME2* can have the same file-name, as long as the destination directory that is included in *FILENAME2* is different from the source directory containing *FILENAME1*.

COPY <FILENAME1> <FILENAME2> /Y Copies the files, and does not warn that you are overwriting any pre-existing files named *FILENAME2*. Without the /Y, the system will warn that you are about to overwrite any existing file with the *FILENAME2* name.

COPY <FILENAME1> <FILENAME2> /-Y Copies the files, and prompts to overwrite any pre-existing files named *FILENAME2*. This is the default setup for **COPY**.

COPY <FILENAME1> <FILENAME2> /Z Copies the files, and restarts a failed copy from the point of failure.

Earlier in this chapter, you used the **HELP** command and redirected the output to a file, help.txt. In Hands-on Project 2-11, you will copy that file to the root of the C drive.

Hands-on Project 2-11

To copy the help.txt file:

1. Open a command window.

2. Type **copy help.txt c:** and press **Enter**. This will copy the help.txt file to the C directory.

3. Normally, you can assume that when the system indicates "1 file(s) copied" that the copy completed successfully. To manually check that the file is in the C directory, type **dir c:\\help.txt** and press **Enter**.

4. Type **exit** and press **Enter** to close the command window.

Filenames can consist of an entire path, such as C:\\Documents and Settings\\Administrator\\filename.tst. Filenames also can contain wildcards. In the event that a wildcard is used in a **COPY** function whose results yield a single file, that file will be copied to the destination file (*FILENAME2*). In the event that a wildcard is used in a **COPY** function whose results yield multiple files, all of those files are copied and appended to the destination file. The downside to this particular function of the command is that the files are copied into the new file in alphabetical order. If you need to copy multiple files into another single file in a specific order, you can use a single **COPY** command.

The following example copies the contents of filez.txt into the file newfile.txt. Then, it does the same for filey.txt and filex.txt, in order.

```
copy filez.txt+filey.txt+filex.txt newfile.txt
```

The **COPY** command has **checkpoint restart**, a feature that allows a failed copy process to be restarted from the point of failure. You probably have had the frustrating experience of an Internet download that failed partway through the download. Instead of picking up where you left off, you had to start all over again. Checkpoint restart is a method of copying data without having to start all over again if the copy fails midway. From an administrative point of view, this feature is valuable when transferring data over a **wide area network (WAN)** where throughput and bandwidth may be relatively low. A WAN is a type of network that is connected over long distances. WAN connections can include dial-up, fiber (optic), T1, 56K, ISDN, DSL, Frame Relay, or other new and emerging technologies.

The XCOPY Command

While it is similar to **COPY** in some ways, the **XCOPY** command is more powerful than **COPY** because it has more features, including the ability to copy subdirectories and hidden files. If you intend to perform backups, **XCOPY** is preferable to **COPY**. Any time you plan on copying more than a handful of files, use **XCOPY** rather than **COPY**.

Understanding the **archive bit** is the key to understanding backups. Every time a file is updated, changed, written, or created, the system flags that file as having been changed by raising a flag called an archive bit. This is similar to raising the flag on a mailbox to indicate that there is mail to be picked up. Several different backup schemes use the archive bit to copy files that have changed, rather than copy an entire directory or volume. This saves time and ultimately costs less money in destination data storage.

XCOPY <FILENAME1> <FILENAME2>   Copies the original file, *FILENAME1*, to destination *FILENAME2*.

XCOPY <FILENAME1> <FILENAME2> /F   Copies files and displays source and destination files.

XCOPY <FILENAMEs> <PATH OR DRIVELETTER:>   Copies multiple files (wildcards assumed) to the destination directory or drive. Does not include system or hidden files. Will prompt to overwrite read-only files.

XCOPY <FILENAMEs> <PATH OR DRIVELETTER:> /H   Copies multiple files to the destination directory or drive and includes hidden and system files. Often used when copying system directories or performing a backup.

XCOPY <FILENAMEs> <PATH OR DRIVELETTER:> /R   Copies multiple files to the destination directory or drive and overwrites read-only files. Often used when copying system directories or performing a backup.

2

XCOPY *<FILENAMEs>* *<PATH OR DRIVELETTER:>* **/C**   Copies multiple files and does not abort if an error occurs.

XCOPY *<FILENAMEs>* *<PATH OR DRIVELETTER:>* **/A**   Copies multiple files whose archive attribute is set to the destination directory or drive. Does not reset the archive bit. Use this command when performing a routine data backup.

XCOPY *<FILENAMEs>* *<PATH OR DRIVELETTER:>* **/M**   Copies multiple files whose archive attribute is set to the destination directory or drive. Resets the archive bit. You can also use the /M option when performing a routine data backup.

XCOPY *<FILENAMEs>* *<PATH OR DRIVELETTER:>* **/U**   Copies multiple files that already exist in the destination to the destination directory or drive.

XCOPY *<FILENAMEs>* *<PATH OR DRIVELETTER:>* **/D**   Copies multiple files whose date and time stamps are more recent than identically named files residing in the destination directory or drive. If one of the files contained in *FILENAMEs* does not exist, that file will also be copied to the destination. Use this command when updating data that resides in an alternate location, or when performing an irregular or occasional data backup.

XCOPY *<FILENAMEs>* *<PATH OR DRIVELETTER:>* **/D:MM-DD-YYYY** Copies multiple files whose date and time stamps are on or after the specified date (MM-DD-YYYY) to the destination directory or drive.

XCOPY *<FILENAMEs>* *<PATH OR DRIVELETTER:>* **/K**   Copies multiple files and their attributes to the destination directory or drive. Use this command when performing network backups.

XCOPY *<FILENAMEs>* *<PATH OR DRIVELETTER:>* **/O**   Copies multiple files, along with their ownership and security access settings, to the destination directory or drive. Use this command when performing network backups.

XCOPY *<FILENAMEs>* *<PATH OR DRIVELETTER:>* **/X**   Copies multiple files, along with their audit settings, to the destination directory or drive. Use the /X option in conjunction with others for routine backups.

XCOPY *<PATH OR DRIVELETTER:>* *<PATH OR DRIVELETTER:>* **/S** Copies an entire directory tree to the destination directory or drive. Data inclusive. Does not include empty directories.

XCOPY *<PATH1>* *<PATH2>* **/T**   Copies the entire directory tree to the destination directory without data. Does not copy empty directories.

XCOPY *<PATH OR DRIVELETTER:>* *<PATH OR DRIVELETTER:>* **/E** Used in conjunction with **/S** or **/T** to include empty directories.

XCOPY *<FILENAMEs>* *<PATH OR DRIVELETTER:>* **/Y**   Copies multiple files to the destination directory or drive. Does not prompt to overwrite existing files.

XCOPY *<FILENAMEs>* *<PATH OR DRIVELETTER:>* **/-Y**   Copies multiple files to the destination directory or drive. Prompts to overwrite existing files. This is the default setting for XCOPY.

XCOPY <FILENAMEs> <PATH OR DRIVELETTER:> /Z   Allows checkpoint restart to occur on a failed XCOPY process.

XCOPY <FILENAMEs> <PATH OR DRIVELETTER:> /EXCLUDE: <FILENAME1>   Copies all files to the destination directory except *FILENAME1*.

As you can see, there are many advanced functions associated with the **XCOPY** command. Most of these are specifically tailored for backups, but many of them can also be used in everyday activities.

As a rule, a file that is in use cannot be copied reliably, so the system refuses to copy it at all, and an error occurs. Any time a file becomes corrupt or cannot be copied, an error occurs, and you will need to copy the file again. When dealing with only a single file this would be a minor annoyance, except for the fact that when an error occurs while copying multiple files, the entire process ends rather than failing on the open file and moving on to the next one. The result is that you have to copy the entire group of files over again to ensure that the job is completed.

Errors that occur during backups are particularly bad, because an entire backup can fail if one user left a document open during a backup period and that file happened to be one of the first files to be copied.

There are several solutions for handling this situation both automatically (within batch files, covered in Chapter 3) and manually. Manually, your **XCOPY** command needs to include the **/C** option to continue copying even when errors occur. **XCOPY** also should include **/Z** to enable checkpoint restart for the failed file. If you are aware that a particular file will fail, or you want to copy all files in a directory except for this single file, you can also use the **/EXCLUDE** option to eliminate the problem altogether.

The following scenario is an example of an **XCOPY** command used to initially back up an entire C drive to a networked Z:\Backups directory:

```
xcopy c:\*.* z:\backups\*.* /s /e /v /h /k /o /x /f /c
>backup.log
```

The various arguments have the following responsibilities:

- The **/S**, **/E**, and **/V** arguments copy the subdirectories, including empty subdirectories, and verify that the process is complete.

- The **/H**, **/K**, **/O**, and **/X** arguments copy hidden and system files, attributes, ownership, security access, and audit settings for the files (an essential aspect of network backups).

- **/F** displays the source and destination files as they are being copied. This is necessary for troubleshooting purposes.

■ The "greater than" character (**>**) redirects the entire output to the backup.log file. If a problem occurs, this file can be scanned to determine the specific troublemaker, making it much easier to solve the problem. The more information that would normally be displayed on the screen (such as source and destination filenames), the more information becomes available in the log file.

■ **/C** continues the copying process despite any errors that may occur.

The DISKCOPY Command

DISKCOPY was designed as a copying tool for floppy disks, which are all but obsolete these days. Consequently, **DISKCOPY** doesn't get much use. **DISKCOPY** copies only removable media, such as ZIP or ORB disks and CD-Rs that have direct-write capabilities. **DISKCOPY** cannot copy data to or from hard disks.

DISKCOPY <DRIVELETTER1> <DRIVELETTER2> /V   Copies the contents of the disk in *DRIVELETTER1* to *DRIVELETTER2* and verifies successful completion.

Old versions of **DISKCOPY** required that two separate devices be present to represent *DRIVELETTER1* and *DRIVELETTER2*. Modern versions of this command allow disks to be copied from the same drive to the same drive by typing the same drive letter for both *DRIVELETTER1* and *DRIVELETTER2*.

Deleting Data

Deleting data in the command window is risky, because there is no easy way to recover it if you change your mind. A couple of measures can help if problems arise. First, Symantec's Norton Utilities has an enhanced recycle bin that can recover files deleted in the command window. Second, the Shadow Copy feature of Windows Server 2003 can recover older versions of files and folders, as long as they are part of a network share or folder. Third, Windows Server 2003's Offline Files and Folders feature can also restore deleted files, but only if they were copied from a network before the file was deleted. No matter what the potential fix, the real solution is to be very careful when deleting files and directories using the command line.

There are four different ways to delete file and directory data at the command prompt: **DEL**, **ERASE**, **RD**, and **REMDIR**. The **DEL** (or **DELETE**—you can type it out if you wish) and **ERASE** commands are essentially identical. The only difference is that **ERASE** allows a list of files to be entered in the command rather than wildcards. **ERASE** is rarely used, so we will not cover its usage in this chapter.

DEL <FILENAME> /F	Deletes the *FILENAME*, including read-only files.
DEL <FILENAME> /S	Deletes the *FILENAME* from all subdirectories.
DEL <FILENAME> /Q	Deletes the *FILENAME* without confirmation.

DEL <*FILENAME*> /A:<*ATTRIBUTES*>   Deletes the specified files based on their attributes. R = read-only files; S = system files; H = hidden files; A = changed files (archive bit on); -R = not read-only files; -S = not system files; -H = not hidden files; -A = unchanged files (archive bit off). Example: `DEL *.* /A:S` deletes all system files in the current directory.

The third and fourth methods of deleting file and directory data are the identical **RD** and **REMDIR** commands. A direct descendant of the UNIX command of the same name, **RD** is used to delete directories, trees, and their files instead of only files, as you would with the **DEL** command. **RD** and **REMDIR** are identical, but since **RD** is more widely used, it is the preferred method of deleting directories and directory trees.

RD <*DIRECTORY*>   Deletes the specified directory. Does not delete the directory if it has files in it. When using a full directory path (for example, C:\Profiles and Settings\Administrator), the last directory in the path is deleted, not the entire tree.

RD <*DIRECTORY*> /S   Deletes the specified *DIRECTORY*, including all files and subdirectories. Prompts for confirmation.

RD <*DIRECTORY*> /S /Q   Deletes the specified *DIRECTORY*, including all files and subdirectories. Does not prompt for confirmation.

The **RD** command does not have an option to delete read-only files. By their nature, read-only files cannot be changed or modified; deleting a read-only file constitutes a significant change, so the **RD** command will not delete a read-only file. By default, the **DEL** command also will not delete read-only files. The solution to deleting an entire tree that contains read-only files is to use the **DEL** command with the **/F** and **/S** options, and then use **RD /S** to finish the job.

Moving Data

The **MOVE** command is used to both move files and rename directories. Unlike the **COPY** command, **MOVE** deletes the source file rather than leaving it intact. Despite its name and purpose, you should not use **MOVE** to move files. The way the system executes the **MOVE** command is to open the file, read it into memory, delete it, and then output the memory to the new file. If an error occurs during this process, there is a strong possibility that the file will be deleted and its data lost irretrievably.

MOVE <*PATH1*>\<*FILENAME1*> <*PATH2*>   Moves the specified file(s) in *FILENAME1* to the location stated in *PATH2*. Will not move a directory tree.

MOVE <*PATH*>\<*DIRECTORYNAME1*> <*DIRECTORYNAME2*>   Renames *DIRECTORYNAME1* in the specified path to the *DIRECTORYNAME2* in the same location.

MOVE does not usually cause problems when moving files on the local machine. Problems can occur, however, when moving data to, from, or between networked drives when a server or network connection goes down. A solution to this problem is to use the **COPY** command to copy the files to their new location and delete the original files. It is an extra step, but it is worth the security. The only time you really need to use **MOVE** instead of **COPY** is when you do not have enough disk space to support an **XCOPY** process or when you need to move data to the same partition or drive letter. In this situation, the physical data isn't moved at all. Instead, the system changes the table of contents on the disk to reflect its new location. Remember, you only need to do this when the source and the destination are on the same drive.

Renaming Files

As you learned in the previous section, changing the name of a directory is done using the **MOVE** command. Doing the same for directories or files is handled with the **RENAME** command. Another version of **RENAME** is **REN**.

RENAME <FILENAME1> <FILENAME2>   Renames *FILENAME1* to *FILENAME2*. For example, `rename hello.txt hello.bak` renames the file hello.txt to hello.bak and eliminates hello.txt altogether.

An alternate path is not available for the destination directory when using **RENAME**. **REN** and **RENAME** are used strictly for renaming files without moving or copying them in any way. If you need to copy *and* rename a file at the same time, use the **COPY** command and simply add a different path to the destination directory.

The following example copies the file xfile located within the C:\Documents and Settings\Administrator directory to yfile within the C:\Documents and Settings\All Users directory.

```
copy c:\documents and settings\administrator\xfile.*
"..\all users\yfile.*"
```

Changing File Attributes

File attributes affect how the file can be used. Each attribute has an on/off condition relative to a particular file. For example, files that are flagged as read-only can only be altered after unflagging the read-only bit. Files that are flagged as archived have changed since the last time a person or program reset the archive bit to 0 (which is the same as unflagging, or setting its status to off or no). Any time a file is altered by the OS or a program, the archive bit is automatically turned on. System files are used to sustain OS functionality and often are flagged as hidden and/or read-only.

As you learned earlier in this chapter, hidden files do not appear in **DIR** output, cannot be copied by **COPY** and **XCOPY** commands, and cannot be seen or viewed within Windows Explorer without special treatment. Despite the fact that most attributes are assigned for good reasons such as security and stability, you may need to change the attributes in order to modify a file, such as you might do when adding an entry to the boot.ini file, which has both system and hidden attributes by default. Changing or flagging the attributes of a file is done using the **ATTRIB** command.

ATTRIB <*FILENAME*>   Displays the attributes associated with the *FILENAME*.

ATTRIB <*FILENAME*> +R   Changes the *FILENAME* attribute to read-only.

ATTRIB <*FILENAME*> -R   Removes the read-only attribute from the *FILENAME*.

ATTRIB <*FILENAME*> +A   Changes the *FILENAME* attribute to archived.

ATTRIB <*FILENAME*> -A   Removes the archive attribute from the *FILENAME*.

ATTRIB <*FILENAME*> +S   Changes the *FILENAME* attribute to system.

ATTRIB <*FILENAME*> -S   Removes the system attribute from the *FILENAME*.

ATTRIB <*FILENAME*> +H   Changes the *FILENAME* attribute to hidden.

ATTRIB <*FILENAME*> -H   Removes the hidden attribute from the *FILENAME*.

ATTRIB <*FILENAME*> <*ANY ATTRIBUTES*> /S /D   Applies the specified attributes to the *FILENAME* in the current directory, and all files in all subdirectories.

ATTRIB <*DIRECTORY*> <*ANY ATTRIBUTES*> /D   Applies the specified attributes to all files within the *DIRECTORY*.

As with any other command option, multiple attributes for a single file can be changed using a single command. Hands-on Project 2-13 teaches you how to change attributes in the appropriate order. In this project, you will make a file read-only, set it to not be a system file and not be hidden, and then restore its original status.

Hands on Project 2-13

To change file attributes:

1. Open a command window.

2. If necessary, type **cd** and press **Enter**.

3. Type **attrib boot.ini** and press **Enter**.

4. Type **attrib boot.ini -s** and press **Enter**. The message shown in Figure 2-15 indicates that the system will not reset the hidden file.

Figure 2-15   Changing file attributes

5. Type **attrib boot.ini –h** and press **Enter**. The message indicates that the system won't reset the system file.

6. Type **attrib boot.ini –s –h** and press **Enter**. No additional output should appear on the screen.

7. Type **attrib boot.ini** and notice that the file is no longer flagged as system or hidden because it doesn't have an S or H listed.

8. Type **attrib boot.ini +r +s +h** and press **Enter**. Again, the lack of system response here indicates success.

9. Confirm that the file is correctly flagged as SHR by typing **attrib boot.ini** and pressing **Enter**.

10. Next, you need to remove the read-only attribute on boot.ini. Do this by typing **attrib boot.ini –r –s –h** and pressing **Enter**.

11. Finally, restore the file to its original attribute status. Type **attrib boot.ini +s +h** and press **Enter**.

12. Type **exit** and press **Enter** to close the command window.

CREATING NEW DATA FILES AND DIRECTORIES

So far, you have learned several ways of viewing and manipulating files and directories within the command window. You are also familiar with methods of creating new files by copying or redirecting existing files. Next you will learn how to create new original directories and files.

Creating Directories

Everybody who uses a computer needs to organize their files into logical groupings. Most people group files by project, date, file type, or some other common theme. Directories are the containers used to hold these groups of files. The command environment provides two commands for creating directories: **MD** and **MKDIR**. These two commands are identical, but **MD** is used more often by IT professionals, and thus we will focus on it rather than **MKDIR**.

MD <DIRECTORY>   Creates the subdirectory *DIRECTORY* in the current directory.

MD ..\<DIRECTORY>   Creates the directory *DIRECTORY* within the parent directory. This new directory is a sister directory to the current directory.

MD \<DIRECTORY>   Creates *DIRECTORY* as a subdirectory of the root.

MD <DIRECTORY1>\<DIRECTORY2>\<DIRECTORY3>   Creates the listed tree of directories.

Directory names and filenames cannot contain backslashes (\).

MD provides various ways of creating directories. For example, the creation of the tree structure that results from md *<directory1>\<directory2>\<directory3>* could also be accomplished using the commands md *<directory1>*, then cd *<directory1>*, md *<directory2>*, cd *<directory2>*, and finally md *<directory3>*.

Using the EDIT Command

Now that you know how to create, modify, copy, move, rename, and delete files and directories, you need to know how to modify the data within the files. The **EDIT** command is used to modify text files in the command window by allowing you to change existing text, create new text, search existing text for specific data, and replace or modify highlighted information within the Edit program.

EDIT   Opens the Edit program.

EDIT <FILENAME>   Opens *FILENAME* using the Edit program.

EDIT <FILENAME> /R   Opens *FILENAME* as read-only using the Edit program.

The **EDIT** command has relatively few options and arguments. Within the Edit program that runs as a result of executing the **EDIT** command, you will find menus for File, Edit, Search, View, Options, and Help functions.

The Edit program and the functions contained within it pose what may be the greatest challenge to working without a mouse. The key to navigating in Edit—in other words, without a mouse—lies in the use of the Alt key, Tab key, and keys for the various letters of the alphabet. Hands-on Project 2-14 introduces you to navigation within Edit.

Hands-on Project 2-14

To use the Edit menu options:

1. Press and hold **Ctrl**, press **Esc**, release **Ctrl**, press **r**, type **cmd**, and press **Enter** to open a command window.

2. Type **edit** and press **Enter**. A blue screen occupies the entire command window. This is the Edit screen, in which text documents, including batch programs, can be created and edited.

3. Hold down **Alt**. Notice that several letters on the menu bar light up. While still holding down the **Alt** key, press **f**. A drop-down menu appears with several options. Release **Alt**. From this menu, you can open, save, or print a file.

4. Press **Esc**, hold down the **Alt** key, and press **e**. Release **Alt**. Another drop-down menu appears. From this menu, you can manipulate highlighted text in an open file.

5. Press **Esc**, hold down the **Alt** key, and press **s**. Release **Alt**. This drop-down menu is used to find and replace specific strings of data.

6. Press **Esc**, hold down the **Alt** key, and press **v**. Release **Alt**. This menu is used to enable simultaneous viewing of two files. The Ctrl+F8 key combination is used to resize the edit window. The Ctrl+F6 key combination is used to switch between two split windows in order to open and manipulate their respective files.

7. Press **Esc**, hold down **Alt**, and press **o**. This menu is used to configure printer and color settings.

8. Press **Esc**, hold down **Alt**, and press **h**. This menu is used to display Edit help, and also to determine which version of Edit is being used. Help is available by pressing F1.

9. Press **Esc**, hold down **Alt**, and press **f**. Use the up and down arrow keys to highlight different entries on the drop-down menu.

10. At any time, use the left and right arrow keys to move to the next drop-down menu item on the menu bar. Press Enter to activate an option from the drop-down menu. Familiarize yourself with this method of navigation.

11. Press **Esc**, hold down **Alt**, and press **f**. Use the highlighted letter keys to select an option from the drop-down menu. Familiarize yourself with this method of navigation by performing the same operation on other menu bar items.

12. Press an hold **Alt**. Press **f**. Release **Alt**. Press **x** to close Edit. If you are prompted to save the file, press **n** for no.

13. Type **exit** and press **Enter** to close the command window.

Creating Files

Within the command environment, you can create new text files of any type. From letters to batch files to lists, files within the command environment are typically created using the **EDIT** command.

The Edit program launches with a blank screen. Into that file you can type text, save text, or change text. The Edit program lacks the formatting features of word processors such as Microsoft Word. While Word and similar programs let you alter a document's fonts and colors, perform sorts, add tables and graphics, and do other appearance-based formatting, Edit only provides basic typing functionality.

Once you have completed typing a file within Edit, you need to save it using the Alt+F key combination, and then pressing the S key. A dialog box appears, asking for a filename and location.

You can also revise existing documents using the **EDIT** command. Typing `edit <filename>` at the command prompt opens the specified file. Figure 2-16 shows the result of typing `edit boot.ini`.

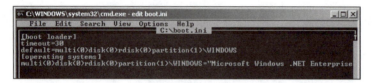

Figure 2-16   Boot.ini shown in the Edit program

As you will learn in Chapter 3, automation through batch files can be a powerful tool. In Hands-on Project 2-15, you learn how to use the Edit program to create a basic batch program that performs a backup of a file.

Hands-on Project 2-15

To make a backup copy of the boot.ini file using the Edit program:

1. Open a command window.

2. Type **edit** and press **Enter**. The Edit program opens.

3. Type **copy c:\boot.ini boot.bak** and press **Enter** to create a new line.

4. Hold down **Alt** and press **f**. Release both keys. This activates the File menu.

5. Press **s**, which displays a Save As dialog box.

6. Type **bootbak.bat** and press the **Enter** key. This saves the file as bootbak.bat.

7. Press and hold **Alt**. Press **f**. Release **Alt**. Press **x**. This returns you to the command prompt.

8. Type **edit bootbak.bat** and press **Enter** to open the bootbak.bat file in the Edit program.

9. Use the arrow keys to change **copy** to **xcopy**.

10. Press and hold **Alt**. Press **f**. Release **Alt**. Press **x**. Edit prompts you to save the file if it has changed since the file was opened.

11. Press **Enter**. You should be returned to the command prompt.

12. Type **exit** and press **Enter** to close the command window.

CHAPTER SUMMARY

In this chapter, you learned how to perform various file and directory manipulation tasks, including printing and navigating without a mouse. You learned about the structure of directories and subdirectories, and how to find, create, list, view, copy, move, delete, manipulate, and edit files within these structures. Searching for data using wildcards and strings was also covered. You can examine a file's characteristics, including its time and date stamp and file attributes. Be sure that you understand these concepts thoroughly, because the rest of this book relies on these basic skills and concepts.

Key, Command, or Key Combination	Function
*	Wildcard: can represent one or more letters, characters, symbols, or numbers in any combination.
?	Wildcard: can represent any single letter, character, symbol, or number.
|MORE	Displays program output one page at a time.
Ctrl+C	Terminates a program from the command window.
Ctrl+C	Copies highlighted text within a text editor.
Ctrl+End	Places the cursor at the end of the document.
Ctrl+Enter	Creates a carriage, or literal, return. Generates a new line.
Ctrl+Home	Places the cursor at the beginning of the document.
Ctrl+V	Pastes copied text.
End	Places the cursor at the end of the line.
Home	Places the cursor at the beginning of the line.
Ins or Insert	Toggles the Insert function. When on, the Insert function allows overwrite.
Shift+arrow key/Home/End	Highlights data within a program.
Tab	Shifts the cursor focus to the next pane or section of the program.

COMMAND SUMMARY

Command	Function
DOSKEY	Enables the system to maintain a list of previously executed commands for recall. Commands can be recalled using the arrow keys.
CLS	Clears the screen.
TREE	Lists the directory structure for the current directory.
CD	Changes a directory.
DIR	Lists directory contents.
TYPE	Displays file contents.
FIND	Locates a search string within one or more files.
FINDSTR	Locates a search string within one or more files. Uses regular expressions.
COPY	Copies files from a source to a destination. Can also rename files within the same directory.
XCOPY	Copies files from source to destination. More powerful than COPY.
DISKCOPY	Copies a removable disk.
DEL	Deletes files.
RD	Deletes a directory.
REMDIR	Deletes a directory.
MOVE	Moves files from a source to a destination.
RENAME	Renames a file.
REN	Renames a file.
ATTRIB	Views and displays file attributes.
MD	Makes a directory. Can also be used to rename a directory.
MKDIR	Makes a directory. Can also be used to rename a directory.
EDIT	A text editing program.

KEY TERMS

archive bit — The bit that, when turned on, indicates that a file has been modified.

attributes — Specialized properties of a file, including read-only, archive, system, and hidden.

back up — The process of copying data for emergency retrieval.

backup — A copy of data that is stored for purposes of file, system, and disaster recovery.

bitmap — A simple picture file.

byte — Eight bits. The basic unit of data.

carriage return — The literal end-of-line marker that generates a new line; it is created using the Ctrl+Enter key combination.

checkpoint restart — A process that enables a failed download to restart at the failed location rather than starting over.

directory tree — A hierarchical view of the directory structure on a hard drive.

extension — The last three letters of a filename preceded by a period. Indicates the type and nature of the file and the programs that use or reference that file.

filter — An option that enables the suppression of certain pieces of data.

flag — An attribute. Used as a verb to refer to the on or yes state of an attribute. For example, "The file is flagged as read-only."

focus — The current location of the cursor. Within Windows, the focus may be indicated by a dotted rectangle around the item of focus.

gigabyte (G) — 1,000 megabytes.

hidden file — A file whose hidden attribute makes it not viewable by standard methods.

kilobyte (K) — 1,024 bytes.

macro — A group of commands or procedures that is assigned a name and executed as a whole.

megabyte (M) — 1,024 kilobytes.

metacharacters — Specialized characters that are used to find patterns of characters specific to regular expressions.

owner — The person who created a file.

pane — An enclosed section of a window.

profile — A directory containing a user's Start menu and desktop icons, My Documents, and other user-specific items, including portions of the registry.

properties — Details of a file, including attributes; creation, access, and modify dates; permissions; and ownership information.

regular expression — A string that allows the usage of wildcards to locate specific pieces of data.

string — A group of characters (symbols, letters, and numbers) used in searching.

system file — A file that is used by the operating system for functionality and maintenance. Usually flagged as a system file.

text file — A document file that contains letters and numbers that can be edited. Text files typically cannot be formatted or include graphic elements.

volume — A drive or partition.

volume number — A number that is assigned to each volume by the system for internal reference.

wide area network (WAN) — A network that is connected by fiber (optic), ISDN, DSL, dial-up, T1, 56K, broadband cable, or other medium that is intended to span large distances.

wildcard — A symbol that is used to represent one or more numeric, symbolic, or alphabetical characters in any combination.

REVIEW QUESTIONS

1. How do you highlight data within a command program?

   a. Hold down the left mouse button and drag.

   b. Use the Ctrl and arrow keys.

   c. Use the Shift and arrow keys.

   d. Use the Alt and arrow keys.

2. What do the Home and End keys do?

   a. Nothing, they are disabled in the command window.

   b. They enable text to be overwritten or inserted.

   c. They scroll displayed text up and down.

   d. They place the cursor at the beginning or end of a line or document.

3. Which key combination is used to copy data?

   a. Ctrl+F7

   b. Ctrl+Enter

   c. Ctrl+C

   d. Ctrl+V

4. What key is used to display a complete list of previously executed commands?

   a. up arrow

   b. down arrow

   c. F7

   d. F8

5. What key is used to select highlighted letters for menu commands?

   a. Tab

   b. Shift

   c. Enter

   d. Alt

6. Which key is used to navigate the drop-down menus from a menu bar? (Choose all that apply.)

   a. Alt

   b. highlighted letters

   c. arrow keys

   d. Ctrl

7. How many bytes are in a gigabyte?

   a. 1,024

   b. 1,024,000

   c. 1,073,741,824

   d. 1,048,576,000

8. Which file extensions can be viewed using the **TYPE** or **EDIT** commands? (Choose all that apply.)

   a. .dll

   b. .csv

   c. .tsv

   d. .sys

9. What is the difference between a wildcard and a metacharacter?

   a. Nothing, they are the same.

   b. Wildcards are used with commands and metacharacters are not.

   c. Wildcards are used within regular expressions and metacharacters are not.

   d. Metcharacters are used within regular expressions and wildcards are not.

10. A directory within a directory within a directory is known as what? (Choose all that apply.)

    a. hierarchical organization

    b. directory structure

    c. tree

    d. It is not possible to store directories within other directories.

11. What command is used to rename a directory?

    a. **MOVE**

    b. **RENDIR**

    c. **DIR /REN**

    d. **CD**

12. The current directory is C:\Documents and Settings\Administrator. What single command can you use to list the contents of the C:\Documents and Settings\All Users directory? (Choose all that apply.)

    a. `cd ..\all users\dir`

    b. `dir "..\all users"`

    c. `dir ..\all users`

    d. `dir c:\documents and settings\all users`

13. What is the most efficient way to view the contents of a hidden file? (Choose all that apply.)

    a. Use the **TYPE** command.

    b. Flag it as not hidden, and then use **TYPE**.

    c. Change the Windows settings for viewing hidden files, and then use **TYPE**.

    d. Use **EDIT**.

14. An employee left your company, and you are responsible for retrieving all of his files on the system. What command lets you locate all of the files that were created by this employee?

    a. `dir *.* /s /a`

    b. `dir *.* /s /q`

    c. `dir *.* /q`

    d. `dir *.* c:\documents and settings\username`

15. You have uninstalled a particular program called Grabit, but the program still seems to launch itself every time the server is started. One way to find the problem is to find all files that were created by the program. Which of the following methods allows you to find all the files created by Grabit? (Choose all that apply.)

    a. `dir *.* /s /<f$>`

    b. `dir grabit.* /s`

    c. `find *.* "grabit" /i`

    d. `findstr *.* "grabit" /i /s`

16. What is a regular expression? (Choose all that apply.)

    a. an expression that uses wildcards to locate files that contain specific text strings

    b. a command that locate files that contain specific text strings

    c. an expression that uses metacharacters to locate files that contain specific text strings

    d. an expression used by metacharacters to locate files that contain specific text strings

17. What command would you use to find files on a hard drive that contain lines starting with the word "copyright"? (Choose all that apply.)

    a. `findstr /b /i /s "copyright"`

    b. `findstr /b /i /s /C:copyright`

    c. `findstr /i /s "^copyright"`

    d. `findstr /i /s "\<copyright"`

18. How do you copy multiple files to a single destination?

    a. Use **COPY** to copy all files with a comma (,) between files.

    b. Use **COPY** to copy and redirect each file.

2

c. Use **COPY** to copy all files using a plus sign (+) between files.

d. Use the **XCOPY** command.

19. Which command is used to make backups?

   a. **SAVE**

   b. **COPY**

   c. **FINDSTR**

   d. **NTBACKUP**

20. Which command is used to delete an entire directory tree?

   a. `del *.* /s`

   b. `rd *.* /s`

   c. `deltree`

   d. `del *.*`

DISCOVERY EXERCISES

1. Use the /? option, which you learned about in Chapter 1, with all the commands mentioned in this chapter. Note that some options are mentioned in the chapter, but are not discussed in detail because they are not frequently used. Choose a command option that is not covered in this chapter and write several paragraphs explaining how it might be used in system administration.

2. Use the appropriate commands to navigate to the Windows directory. Use commands to list all of the contents, with the newest file first. Display the results one page at a time.

3. Find the largest file on the hard drive.

4. In this exercise, you will practice tree navigation.

   a. Use the **TREE** command to choose a subdirectory that is at least three levels removed from the root of the drive.

   b. Write down the full path to that subdirectory.

   c. Use the **CD** command to navigate to the chosen subdirectory using only a single command.

   d. Choose a file in the chosen subdirectory, make a note of its access and modify dates, and copy that file back to the root of the drive without navigating there first.

   e. Navigate back to your original location and make sure the file has been copied successfully. Determine whether the access and modify dates on the copied file have changed.

5. This exercise assumes that you are working within a Windows Server 2003 domain containing at least one member workstation with a drive mapping to a common area on the server. If you are not working in this type of environment, you may need assistance from your instructor to emulate this procedure while logging in locally to a Server 2003 system.

   a. Create a new user account.

   b. Log in to the member workstation as the new user.

   c. Using the **EDIT** command, create a new file called test.txt in a common area on the server.

   d. Log out and log in as the administrator.

   e. Copy the test.txt file to test2.txt. Does the copied file, test2.txt, reflect the original owner (the new user) or the Administrator? What peculiarities did you find in dealing with files owned by the Administrator account?

6. In this exercise, you will search for strings in various combinations.

   a. Search the Web for a flat-text, downloadable dictionary. You can find one at http://wordweb.info/free, or search for one at http://www.downloads.com or http://www.tucows.com.

   b. Randomly choose five letters from the alphabet (try to include two vowels) and use the **FINDSTR** command to determine how many different words can be made from those five letters.

      (*Hint*: To generate results that consist of dictionary words rather than their definitions, search for the five letters at the beginning of a line.)

7. Write an appropriate backup command using **XCOPY** in which only updated files should be copied.

8. Write an explanation of how to use the **EDIT** command to open a file, modify it, and save it.

3

BATCH AND AUTOMATION

> **After reading this chapter and completing the exercises, you will be able to:**
>
> ◆ Create, save, and run a batch program
> ◆ Use conditional statements within a batch program
> ◆ Search for data within files and lists
> ◆ Use variables, parameters, and wildcard parameters within a batch program
> ◆ Prompt the user for input
> ◆ Automate and schedule commands and processes within a batch program

Batch programming is a type of scripting that has been around for decades, with slight modifications and improvements included in each new Microsoft operating system. As you learned in Chapter 1, scripts are text files that perform various commands and functions based on a specific scripting language. Batch programs are simple text files that contain one or more commands. Batch programming is a valuable skill because it enables you to automate just about every command in this book. Throughout this book, you will be using the skills outlined in this chapter to create effective and efficient batch programs for use in day-to-day server, system, and network administration.

Batch-specific commands do have some restrictions. For example, batch programs have limited ability to prompt for user input. Another constraint is that limited logic can be used within batch programs. Within the Windows Server 2003 environment, these limitations are, for the most part, overcome by creating and using scripts. Windows Server 2003 supports **Visual Basic script language**, which is used to create scripts that are run by the **Windows Scripting Host (WSH)**. The WSH is a service that runs in the background and allows these scripts to run (services are special programs that launch automatically; you will learn more about them in later chapters). Visual Basic (VB) scripts are not covered in this book—the topic is worthy of its own course, along with the Visual Basic programming language. VB scripts have a .vbs file extension, and they can be run on the command line using the **CSCRIPT** and **WSCRIPT** commands. You will find various script commands described throughout this book. Most automation tasks can be performed using batch files.

CREATING AND SAVING A BATCH FILE

As you learned in Chapter 2, the **EDIT** command is used to view and modify text files. Text files usually have extensions of .txt, but they can also have extensions of .bat, .cmd, .log, .ini, .vbs, .csv, or .tsv.

Many text files have extensions different from those listed above. Be careful when editing documents with which you are unfamiliar, particularly with Microsoft Word or any other word processor. If you accidentally edit one of these documents, it is possible that the editor program will inadvertently corrupt it. If you are unsure of a given file's format, use the **TYPE** command at the command prompt to learn more about it. If the system beeps at you or what appears on the screen is gibberish, don't make changes to the file.

EDIT <*FILENAME*>.BAT   Opens the specified file for editing.

When you use commands on files, you need to include the filename extension. For this chapter, that extension will always be .bat. The Edit program launched by the **EDIT** command will create a new filename if it cannot find the referenced filename. This can either be an annoyance (in the event that you entered the wrong filename) or a time-saver, because it eliminates the need to name the file when you save it. **Edit** prompts you to save a file when the program is closed (see Figure 3-1), so it is not necessary to do an Alt+F save on the file. However, it's a good idea to save files, simply as a precaution against data loss. Edit will not automatically save a file for you, so it is a good idea to save it occasionally as extra security. Hands-on Project 3-1 provides a quick lesson on using the Edit program.

Hands-on Project 3-1

To use Edit:

1. Open a command window.

2. Create a new file called happy.txt for editing by typing **edit happy.txt** and pressing **Enter**. Edit opens with an empty file.

3. Now, exit the program by holding down **Alt** and pressing **f**. Release **Alt**.

4. Press **x**. This returns you to the command prompt.

5. To determine whether the file happy.txt exists, type **dir happy.txt** and press **Enter**.

6. Notice that the file is not found. This is because the file was not saved. Edit did not prompt you to save it when exiting the program because there were no changes made to the file while Edit was open. Type **edit happy.txt** and press **Enter**.

7. Edit opens with the file happy.txt. Type **happy** and press **Enter**.

8. Now the file contains data to save. Press and hold **Alt** and press **f**. Release **Alt** and press **x** to exit the program.

9. The system prompts you to save the file, as shown in Figure 3-1. Press **Enter** to save it.

3

Figure 3-1 Edit prompts to save before exiting

10. The focus should be back in the command prompt. Type **dir happy.txt** and press **Enter**. The file now exists.

11. Type **exit** and press **Enter** to close the command window.

As you proceed through this chapter, you can assume that all of the chapter's projects are created using **Edit**. A batch file can be edited using Notepad, Wordpad, or Microsoft Word, and you can experiment with these alternative editors. However, the Edit program launched by the **EDIT** command is the primary text editor used throughout this book.

RUNNING A BATCH PROGRAM

To execute a command as a batch routine, the file containing the command must have an extension of .bat or .cmd. Any file with a .bat or .cmd extension can be executed at the command prompt as if it were a command or program.

While a batch routine is running, the user does not see a prompt on the command line—he or she only sees what the batch program is configured to display. The only way to stop a batch program is by using the Ctrl+C key combination. When a batch is executed, it runs each of the commands listed in the file, one by one, in order. Batch programs cannot run more than one command at a time. Batch routines can become complex and difficult to read, so the next section concentrates on how to recognize the specific elements of a batch program.

ELEMENTS OF A BATCH

Batch files, or batches, include several different commands and elements that are exclusive to batches. These elements, which include parameters, variables, REM statement documentation, subroutines, and subprograms, enhance the functionality of a batch program and make your automation tasks easier.

Parameters

Batch programs can be executed with **parameters**. Parameters are the batch equivalents of command options or arguments, and are entered at the command prompt when executing the batch program. Parameters are used within a batch file as customizing elements.

For example, you could use the batch program test.bat to generate user accounts. Instead of running each command for each user, you can use parameters for the usernames. This saves time and effort for the administrator, because he or she can add usernames to the end of the batch file. Figure 3-2 shows the parameters MARY and JANE added to the batch file—a more efficient approach than altering the batch program and repeating the commands for each user.

Figure 3-2   Running the test.bat batch program with parameters

Parameters also enable the batch program to be more versatile because it can be run multiple times with different usernames with the same results. Parameters are referenced internally within the batch routine, usually for commands that require variable user input, such as names or files. Parameters are referenced within a batch file as %1, %2, %3, and so on, according to the order in which they were typed when the batch program was executed on the command line. The test.bat example references only two parameters, but you can include up to 99 in a batch. The test.bat example did not require that the user enter a parameter on the command line. Hands-on Project 3-2 teaches you how to use parameters with a batch file.

Hands-on Project 3-2

To create a simple batch routine that displays a message on the screen using parameters:

1. Open a command window.

2. Type **cd** and press **Enter**.

3. Type **edit test.bat** to create the new batch file.

4. Type **cls**, press **Enter**, and then type **echo Hi there %1 %2**.

5. Press and hold **Alt**, press **f**, release **Alt**, and then press **s** to save the file. Press and hold **Alt**, press **f**, release **Alt**, and then press **x** to exit the program.

6. Type **test** and press **Enter** to run the test.bat file. Notice that the output is "Hi there."

7. Type **test** followed by your first name, and press **Enter**. Notice that the output changes to include your name.

8. Type **test** again, followed by your first and last name (include a space in between). Press **Enter**. The output now includes your first and last name.

9. Type **exit** and press **Enter** to close the command window.

Commands can fail if a parameter is referenced in a batch program that is executed on the command line but the parameter was not entered on the command line when the batch program was run. The following example attempts to copy a file based on parameters entered on the command line that ran the batch program:

```
copy %2 %4
```

In this case, if the batch was executed with no parameter entries on the command line, an error message would occur, because there are no files to copy. There are ways to handle this situation, as you will learn later in the Advanced Batch section of this chapter.

Variables

Batch programs can create and use environmental variables. Recall that variables are memory areas that contain specific information that is referenced by the system for particular functions and tasks. Environmental variables are variables that specifically reference a username, the time, or any piece of information or data that can be used by the system or by a batch program. Environmental variables are created within a batch file using the **SET** command. Within the batch routine, variables are referenced with surrounding percent (%) symbols.

Hands-on Project 3-3 uses the test.bat file from Project 3-2, altering it to include variables so that the file, when run, displays your name and the current time and date. You will create two variables: **FIRSTNAME** and **LASTNAME**. This project also uses two standard environmental variables: **DATE** and **TIME**.

Hands-on Project 3-3

To add variables to a batch:

1. Open a command window. Type **cd** and press **Enter**.

2. Type **edit test.bat** and press **Enter** to open the batch file. Modify the file to read as follows:

```
cls
cd\
```

```
set firstname=%1
set lastname=%2
echo Hi there %1 %2
echo
echo Today is: %date%
echo The time is: %time%
```

3. Press and hold **Alt**, press **f**, release **Alt**, and then press **s** to save test.bat. Next, press and hold **Alt**, press **f**, release **Alt**, and press **x** to exit Edit. At the command prompt, type **test.bat** to run the file. The results should be similar to Figure 3-3. Be sure to include your first and last name.

Figure 3-3 The results of running test.bat

4. From the command prompt, type **set firstname**. Notice that the environment variable still exists even after the batch routine is complete.

5. Close and reopen the command window. Type **set firstname** and press **Enter**. The FIRSTNAME variable no longer exists.

6. Close the command window.

Environmental changes are not retained after the command window in which they are made is closed. File and system changes persist beyond individual command sessions, but environment variables and custom memory settings do not.

Using ECHO to Control What the User Sees

Sometimes you need to display messages on the screen to indicate the status or progress of a batch program. Users typically like to know that the computer is working on something instead of wondering whether a routine has hung or gotten stuck in a loop. It is a good idea to use **ECHO** with time-consuming commands to keep the user informed— even when the routine doesn't really need it.

As you learned by completing projects in previous chapters, the **ECHO** command is used to display messages on the screen. Using **ECHO** by itself displays a blank line. Combining **ECHO** with a message of your choice displays that message. This combination is useful as a status update for any command or activity that the batch program completes.

C:_
Syntax

ECHO *<MESSAGE>*   Displays MESSAGE.

ECHO *ON | OFF*   Displays a command on the screen as it is processing.

@ECHO OFF   Turns command echoes off and does not display any results.

Using **ECHO ON** displays commands that are executed as you would see them if you had executed them manually. Turning **ECHO** off eliminates clutter on the screen as a batch routine executes. Outside of using the **ECHO** command for displaying messages, the only time that you really want to turn **ECHO ON** is when you are troubleshooting a batch routine. The differences between **ECHO ON** and **ECHO OFF** can be seen in Figures 3-4 and 3-5. Figure 3-4 shows **ECHO ON** while a batch program (echo.bat) that searches for **x*.*** and **y*.*** is running. Figure 3-5 shows the same program running with **ECHO OFF.**

Figure 3-4   Using **ECHO ON** with a batch file

Figure 3-5   Using **ECHO OFF** with a batch file

Unfortunately, using **ECHO OFF** in a batch routine still displays the **ECHO OFF** command on the screen, as you can see in Figure 3-6. Anxious end users might question the "echo off" message, so it is a good idea to insert the @ symbol prior to the command, which prevents the **ECHO OFF** command from echoing itself before it turns the **ECHO** feature off.

Figure 3-6   Using **ECHO OFF**

NUL

Even though **@ECHO OFF** suppresses command display, it does not eliminate the normal output from a command, such as the results from a **DIR** or **COPY** command, in which you would see a listing of files or a "file(s) copied" message. Redirecting this output gives your routine a more professional look. The **NUL** command, in combination with **DIR** or **COPY**, eliminates the display of unwanted output.

<COMMAND> >NUL   Eliminates the display of *COMMAND* output.

Any command can be redirected to **NUL**. The result of using **NUL** is that the *COMMAND* shows no status on the screen whatsoever.

TYPE

Another standard method of modifying a batch program to display information on the screen uses the **TYPE** command, which allows you to quickly view the contents of a batch file without modifying it.

TYPE <*FILENAME*> |MORE   Displays *FILENAME* on the screen one screen at a time. Pressing the spacebar displays the next screen.

Hands-on Project 3-4 lets you experiment with the display of program output using **ECHO** and **NUL**. In this project, you use the **ECHO** command within a batch program to display a greeting, along with the date and time. You also copy a file and redirect the output to **NUL**.

Hands-on Project 3-4

To manipulate the display of program output:

1. Open a command window. Type **edit test.bat** and press **Enter** to open the test.bat file in the Edit program.

2. Modify test.bat to read as follows:

```
cls
@echo off
set firstname=%1
set lastname=%2
Echo Hi there %1 %2
echo
echo Today is: %date%
echo The time is: %time%
```

3. Press and hold **Alt**, press **f**, release **Alt**, and then press **s** to save the file. Press and hold **Alt**, press **f**, release **Alt**, and then press **x** to exit the Edit program.

4. Test the results of the batch program by typing **test** followed by your first and last name, and press **Enter**. This runs test.bat with the parameters of your first and last name. The output is much tidier than in the previous examples.

5. At the command prompt, type **edit test.bat** and press **Enter**. Add the following line at the bottom of the file: **copy test.bat %firstname%.bat**. This code copies the test.bat file to another file whose name is the %firstname% environment variable defined earlier in the program.

6. Press and hold **Alt**, press **f**, release **Alt**, and then press **s** to save the file. Press and hold **Alt**, press **f**, release **Alt**, and then press **x** to exit the Edit program.

7. Run the test.bat program by typing **test** followed by your first and last name at the command prompt. Press **Enter**. Notice that the output now includes the message "1 file(s) copied".

8. To remove this message, you need to redirect the output from the **COPY** command to **NUL**. Type **edit test.bat** and press **Enter** again. Modify the last line of test.bat to read **copy test.bat %firstname%.bat >nul**. Press and hold **Alt**, press **f**, release **Alt**, and then press **s** to save the file. Press and hold **Alt**, press **f**, release **Alt**, and then press **x** to exit the Edit program.

9. At the command prompt, type **test** followed by your first and last name, and then press **Enter**. This runs the test.bat program once more. The output from the **COPY** command no longer appears on the screen.

10. Type **exit** and press **Enter** to close the command window.

Logging Batch Events and Status

Automation often occurs when users are not present, so you don't need to display anything during processing. In these cases, it might seem like a good practice to output everything to **NUL** to keep the screen clear of clutter. Unfortunately, if something goes wrong with the batch routine and you have a **NUL** argument in your command, you can't determine what caused the error. In these situations, instead of redirecting to **NUL**, you can redirect to a **log file**. A log file is a simple text file that contains the output results of commands.

Consider the following scenario: A particular employee consistently reports to work late, and your manager needs to document this tardiness to take appropriate disciplinary action. A quick and easy solution is to use the existing test.bat file as part of a **logon script**, since the batch already contains username, date, and time information. Logon scripts, which you learn about in Hands-on Project 3-5, are batch files that execute when the user logs in to the system or domain, and they are assigned from the user account properties.

Hands-on Project 3-5

To create a log from a batch file:

1. Open a command window. Type **edit test.bat** and press **Enter**.
   To create a log, you will replace the test.bat parameters you used in Hands-on Project 3-4 with the system variable USERNAME. This prevents you from having to enter any parameters. Instead, the employee's account name will be displayed. Next, you will redirect output from test.bat to the log.txt file. If log.txt exists, it will be overwritten with a new log.txt. If log.txt does not exist, the system will create it. The **ECHO** date and time commands will also be redirected to the log.txt file. An additional ">" ensures that **ECHO** will append to the existing log.txt file, rather than create a new file. Finally, the log.txt file will be copied to a new file with the username's filename and a .log extension.

2. Modify the test.bat to read as follows:

   ```
   @echo off
   cls
   echo Hi there %username% >C:\log.txt
   echo Today's date is: %date% >>C:\log.txt
   echo The time is: %time% >>C:\log.txt
   copy log.txt %username%.log >nul
   ```

3. Press and hold **Alt**, press **f**, release **Alt**, and then press **s** to save the file. Press and hold **Alt**, press **f**, release **Alt**, and then press **x** to exit the Edit program.

4. At the command prompt, run test.bat by typing **test** followed by your first and last name. Press **Enter**. Notice that nothing appears on the screen. The reason that nothing appears is that all output is being redirected to the log file.

5. At the command prompt, type **dir *.log**. The output should show a log file with the name of the user who is currently logged on.

6. To view the contents of the log file, type **type %username%.log** and press **Enter**. The output of the **TYPE** command should look similar to Figure 3-7.

```
C:\WINDOWS\system32\cmd.exe                                    _ □ X
Hi there Administrator
Today's date is: Wed 09/04/2002
The time is : 5:45:04.06
C:\>dir *.log
 Volume in drive C has no label.
 Volume Serial Number is 5CFB-17F8

 Directory of C:\

09/04/2002  05:45 AM                87 Administrator.log
              1 File(s)            87 bytes
              0 Dir(s)    772,986,880 bytes free

C:\>type administrator.log
Hi there Administrator
Today's date is: Wed 09/04/2002
The time is : 5:45:04.05

C:\>_
```

Figure 3-7   A log file from test.bat

7. To display the **ECHO** commands to the user while creating a log file, type **edit test.bat** and press **Enter**.

8. Position the cursor on the third line, right before the "e" in "echo". Highlight the entire line of code by pressing and holding **Shift** while pressing **End**. Release the keys. Copy the code by pressing and holding the **Alt** key while pressing **e**. Release the keys, and then press **c** to copy the highlighted text.

9. Position the cursor at the beginning of the next line and press **Enter**. This should create a new line.

10. Paste the copied data by pressing and holding **Alt** while pressing **e**. Release the keys and press **p** to paste the copied line into the new line.

11. Repeat Steps 8 through 11 for all lines containing the **ECHO** command, as shown in Figure 3-8.

12. Delete the **>log.txt** and **>>log.txt** code from the new line. Be sure to save the file.

```
C:\WINDOWS\system32\cmd.exe - edit test.bat                    _ □ ×
  File   Edit   Search   View   Options   Help
                                          C:\test.bat
@echo off
cls
echo Hi there %username% >c:\log.txt
echo Hi there %username%
echo
echo Today's date is: %date% >>c:\log.txt
echo Today's date is: %date%
echo The time is : %time% >>c:\log.txt
echo The time is : %time%
copy log.txt %username%.log >nul
```

Figure 3-8   Creating both a log file and screen output

13. Type **exit** and press **Enter** to close the command window.

Batch Documentation Using REM Statements

Batch files can become complex, and troubleshooting or modifying them can quickly get complicated. To help solve this problem, you should always insert remarks preceding or following commands in batch files. **Remarks**, which are made using REM statements, are documentary information that is ignored by the program while the batch routine processes.

REM <*STATEMENT*>   Documentation that does no processing. REM statements are informative for the programmer, but are ignored by the batch.

You should use REM statements often. REM statements can help administrators fixing someone else's batch to make sense of the file. Figure 3-9 shows test.bat with some informational REM statements.

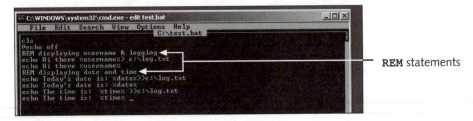

Figure 3-9 Using **REM** statements to document a command's actions

Subroutines and Subprograms

Batch programs are executed line by line, or in a **linear** fashion. However, it is often necessary to jump to a different part of the batch routine to properly run a command or complete a task. Often the target of the jump is a **subroutine**. A subroutine is a collection of commands that performs a specific task, but whose task is only required in certain situations, such as only on Mondays or only when an employee is late. Subroutines also can consist of groups of commands that need to be run repeatedly during the batch program. In these situations, you can use the **GOTO** command.

GOTO <SUBROUTINE>   Jumps to the specified subroutine header and executes commands from that point.

:<ROUTINE>   The destination of the **GOTO** command. All commands after this point will be executed unless another **GOTO** statement directs the operation to another subroutine.

Figure 3-10 contains a flowchart that illustrates a situation in which you might want to use a **GOTO** statement: One user is late, but not all users are late; you want to test to see whether users are late when the batch file runs, and then copy a log file only if they are. You can use **GOTO** to jump to a subroutine at any time within a program. Commands within that subroutine execute, and the process then returns to the origination point and continues running commands from there. Once the main routine has completed, the batch file continues to process any subroutines, in order, until it reaches the end of the file.

Most subroutines handle specialized tasks that are intended for a particular situation; therefore, they should only be executed as a result of a specific yes/no condition. This yes/no decision on whether to process a subroutine is handled by command **logic processing**, which is simply a question that is asked of the system. In Figure 3-10, the test question would be "Is user late?" Logic is also called **conditional processing**, in which the system performs certain commands based upon specifically defined situations. Logic is covered in the Advanced Batch section of this chapter.

In situations where the batch program should skip the subroutine without processing it, you can use **GOTO END** at the end of the main routine or subroutine. **GOTO END** sends processing to the subroutine labeled END, which should be the last line in the batch program. Processing jumps to this last line, and without any other commands following it, the batch program ends. With an appropriate END subroutine tag, processing skips any commands that follow the original **GOTO** statement when the process returns to its origination point. Hands-on Project 3-6 illustrates the **GOTO** command.

3

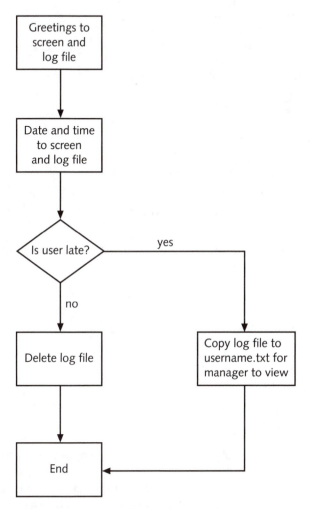

Figure 3-10   A batch program can be used to selectively execute commands

Hands-on Project 3-6

To skip certain commands based on specific data:

    1. Open a command window. Create a new batch file by typing **edit sub.bat**. Press **Enter**.

2. Type the following lines of code:

```
cd\
cls
@echo off
rem greetings
echo hi there %1>log.txt
echo Today's date is: %date%>>log.txt
echo The time is: %time%>>log.txt
rem If Donald is perpetually late, make a log file
 with his name
if %1==Donald goto copylog else delete log.txt
goto end
rem
:copylog
copy C:\log.txt C:\%1.log
:end
```

3. Press and hold **Alt**, press **f**, release **Alt**, and then press **s** to save the sub.bat file. Next, press and hold **Alt**, press **f**, release **Alt**, and press **x** to exit Edit.

4. Now, run the sub.bat program with the JANE parameter to test it. Type **sub Jane** and press **Enter**.

5. Type **dir Jane.log** to see if sub.bat created a log file for Jane. It shouldn't have, because the username was not Donald.

6. Run the sub.bat program with the DONALD parameter to test it again. Type **sub Donald** and press **Enter**.

7. Type **dir Donald.log** to see if sub.bat created a log file for Donald. It should have, because the username was Donald.

8. Type **exit** and press **Enter** to close the command window.

Sometimes a subroutine becomes so large or complex that it is better to make it into a separate batch file and then move processing to that batch file from within the first batch routine. This change in processing focus is referred to as "calling." In this situation, the second batch file is called a **subprogram**. The first batch program uses the **CALL** command to execute the subprogram, along with any appropriate parameters. The subprogram file executes, and then control is returned to the first batch file. The original batch file resumes command execution beginning with the command following the **CALL** statement.

CALL <BATCHFILE>   Executes a subsequent batch routine (subprogram), and resumes command execution once the subprogram commands have been processed.

CALL <BATCHFILE> <PARAMETER1> <PARAMETER2> <PARAMETER3> Executes a subroutine with the specified parameters, and resumes command execution once the specified subprogram commands have been processed.

CALL <BATCHFILE> :<ROUTINE>   Executes only the specific subroutine within the subprogram. Execution of the parent batch routine resumes after the subprogram is completed.

3

Troubleshooting

In addition to their primary uses, **PAUSE**, **ECHO**, and redirection (> and >>) can be used for troubleshooting. You learned about redirection while creating the log files from the previous exercises.

The **PAUSE** command can allow the user to read or examine information at his or her own pace by stopping output until a user presses any key, similar to the way that |**MORE** allows for examination of output with the **TYPE** command, and **/S** for the **DIR** command. However, **PAUSE** is more often used as a strategic placeholder when troubleshooting. If a batch program isn't behaving as expected, you can insert the **PAUSE** command at a critical point, and then the user can press Ctrl+C to see whether the previous command performed as expected (such as **COPY** or **DELETE**). After the offending command has been fixed, **PAUSE** can be removed to re-establish uninterrupted command flow through the program.

PAUSE   Prompts the user to "Press Any Key to Continue..."

The **ECHO** command can be used in the same way that **PAUSE** is without interrupting the flow of the program. Unfortunately, the **ECHO** statement can become misleading if the command preceding it fails, so it is much more beneficial (outside of redirection logging) to simply turn **ECHO** on so that you can track the statements that are being processed, allow the commands to display any errors by not redirecting their output, and insert **PAUSE** statements to pinpoint the problem.

ADVANCED BATCH

You have just learned the basics of batch programming. Several advanced commands can be used to add logic, user input functionality, error handling, and visual appeal to batch programs. These commands include variations of **IF DEFINED**, **CHOICE**, and **IF ERRORLEVEL**.

Logic

Programming **logic** refers to the ability to compare pieces of information and act on the results of the comparison. In Figure 3-10, logic was performed when the answer to the question "Is user late?" was provided. In addition to the simple yes/no processing that logic can provide, you can use specific commands to compare variables, reiteratively search for data, and even pull specific pieces of data out of a file.

Determining Existence of Files and Variables

When a batch file is run on multiple computers, you might want to check for the existence of a variable or a file on the current system, because the existence of certain variables can indicate the status of the system. For example, you can search for the

CLUSTERLOG variable, which does not exist on a Windows XP or nonserver system. If you find CLUSTERLOG, you can conclude that the computer you are searching is not running XP and is not a server. Other variables can be checked to determine which operating system the computer is running. You can add some additional logic to further check for things such as network connectivity by using a logon script to define a particular mapped drive as a variable. If your search shows that the variable does not exist, you can conclude that networking has failed in some way. You can use the **IF DEFINED** command to check for the existence of variables and then perform a specific command if the variable does exist.

IF DEFINED <*VARIABLE*> <*COMMAND*>   Performs *COMMAND* if *VARIABLE* exists.

Finding Files in Batch   You can also use an **IF** statement to determine whether a file exists. This is particularly valuable when you need to determine whether an automated download or copied file has been created successfully.

IF EXIST <*FILENAME*> <*COMMAND*>   Performs *COMMAND* if *FILENAME* exists.

IF EXIST <*FILENAME*> <*COMMAND*> ELSE <*COMMAND*>   Performs the first *COMMAND* if *FILENAME* exists; otherwise, performs the second *COMMAND*.

IF NOT EXIST <*FILENAME*> <*COMMAND*>   Performs *COMMAND* if *FILENAME* does not exist.

IF NOT EXIST <*FILENAME*> <*COMMAND*> ELSE <*COMMAND*>
Performs the first *COMMAND* if *FILENAME* does not exist; performs the second *COMMAND* if *FILENAME* does exist.

You can think of **IF** statements as true/false situations where the command is run only if the **IF** statement is true. All **IF** statements have the ability to execute a command when the **IF** statement is false by adding an **ELSE** statement to the end of the line followed by a command. Adding **ELSE** to the end of an **IF** statement enables the system to execute one command when the **IF** statement is true or execute a different command when the **IF** statement is false.

To understand how the **IF EXIST** command works, consider a modification to sub.bat that causes the batch program to confirm that the log file was copied successfully. Instead of having the system display an error message, the system can display a prompt that allows the user to perform an action. Such a modification would require adding the following code to sub.bat:

```
if not exist c:\%1 echo Notify your administrator that a
login failure has occurred.
```

The results of running sub.bat with the **IF NOT** modification are shown in Figure 3-11, but only when the file copy has failed for the user Donald.

Figure 3-11   Ensuring that the log file copied appropriately within sub.bat

Operators

Operators are symbols or letters that indicate a comparison whose answer is true or false. Operators include equal to, greater than, or less than, and are usually associated with mathematics. Operators are important in batch processing, because batch programs cannot perform arithmetic by adding one number to another, but they can use operators to compare numbers, strings, variables, and other items.

Table 3-1   Operators used in batch logic

%<*VARIABLE1*>%EQU %<*VARIABLE2*>%	*VARIABLE1* is equal to *VARIABLE2*. Can also be represented as ==.
%<*VARIABLE1*>%NEQ %<*VARIABLE2*>%	*VARIABLE1* is not equal to *VARIABLE2*.
%<*VARIABLE1*>%LSS %<*VARIABLE2*>%	*VARIABLE1* is less than *VARIABLE2*.
%<*VARIABLE1*>%LEQ %<*VARIABLE2*>%	*VARIABLE1* is less than or equal to *VARIABLE2*.
%<*VARIABLE1*>%GTR %<*VARIABLE2*>%	*VARIABLE1* is greater than *VARIABLE2*.
%<*VARIABLE1*>%GEQ %<*VARIABLE2*>%	*VARIABLE1* is greater than or equal to *VARIABLE2*.

Table 3-1 refers to variables; however, operators can also be used to compare numbers, strings, or parameters with other numbers, strings, or parameters. For example, it is common to compare a parameter with a generated or pre-existing environment variable in a logon script, which allows the system to determine user group membership and subsequently generate drive mappings appropriate to that membership. In Hands-on Project 3-7, you learn how to compare the words "happy" and "happier" using operators.

Hands-on Project 3-7

To compare strings of data using operators:

1. Open a command window.

2. Type **if happy equ happier echo equal** and press **Enter**.

   The system performs operator comparisons character by character. The words "happy" and "happier" were equal until the fifth character, at which point the character "y" had a greater value than the character "i", even though "happier" contains more characters. Once the system determines that a single character comparison matches the operator request, it discontinues comparing further characters, and performs the command, providing the results match the original **IF** statement. In this case, they don't, so no results are displayed.

3. Type **if happy neq happier echo not equal** and press **Enter**. Since "happy" is not equal to "happier", the words "not equal" appear on the screen.

4. Type **exit** and press **Enter** to close the command window.

Comparing Variables

You can use the comparison operator commands in batch files in the same way that any command can be run from within batch. The true value of comparison comes when performing comparisons on data that may change over time—in other words, when you are comparing variables and parameters, which can change depending on the situation, such as a logged-in username. The **/I** option lets you perform comparisons using variables.

IF /I %<*VARIABLE1*>%==%<*VARIABLE2*>% <*COMMAND*>   Runs *COMMAND* if *VARIABLE1* is equal to *VARIABLE2*.

IF /I %<*VARIABLE1*>%==%<*VARIABLE2*>% <*COMMAND*> ELSE <*COMMAND*>   Runs the first *COMMAND* if *VARIABLE1* is equal to *VARIABLE2*, and also runs the second *COMMAND* if *VARIABLE1* is not equal to *VARIABLE2*.

IF /I %<*VARIABLE1*>% <*OPERATOR*> %<*VARIABLE2*>% <*COMMAND*>   Runs *COMMAND* if *VARIABLE1* compares to *VARIABLE2* according to the operator function. Operators can be one of the following: EQU (equal to), NEQ (not equal to), LSS (less than), LEQ (less than or equal to), GTR (greater than), or GEQ (greater than or equal to).

IF NOT /I %<*VARIABLE1*>% <*OPERATOR*>%<*VARIABLE2*>% <*COMMAND*> ELSE <*COMMAND*>   Runs the first *COMMAND* if *VARIABLE1* does not compare to *VARIABLE2* according to the operator function. Operators can be EQU, NEQ, LSS, LEQ, GTR, or GEQ.

In Hands-on Project 3-8, you will modify the test.bat file you used earlier in this chapter to specifically generate a log file only when a user is late for work. The conditional creation is a practical approach, because in a large environment, log files are only created for accounts that meet certain conditions, and do not consume as much disk space or system resources as would be used if the system were creating log files for every user. In the project, you will test for a login time by an employee and then, if certain conditions are met (that is, if the employee is late), the code will launch a subroutine. In its current version, test.bat is similar to what you see in Figure 3-9. To make test.bat work in the way the flowchart in Figure 3-10 illustrates, a few more commands and modifications need to be made.

Hands-on Project 3-8

To perform tasks based on time:

1. Open a command window.

2. Type **edit test.bat**, press **Enter**, and modify the file as follows:

```
cls
@echo off
echo Hi there %username% >c:\log.txt
echo Today's date is: %date%>>c:\log.txt
echo The time is: %time%>>c:\log.txt
if %time% gtr 09:00:00.00 (goto late)
del log.txt
:late
copy log.txt %username%.log>nul
goto end
:END
```

3. Press and hold **Alt**, press **f**, release **Alt**, and then press **s** to save the test.bat file. Next, press and hold **Alt**, press **f**, release **Alt**, and press **x** to exit Edit.

You may modify the time appropriately to better test the results.

4. Run test.bat by typing **test** and pressing **Enter**.

5. Type **dir %username%.log** and press **Enter**. Notice that the log file is created, even when it is after the specified hour. This is not the intent of the batch program; you need to create the log file only when the user is late. Remember that subroutines return to the point of origin when they are completed; thus, the log file is being created once when the **GOTO** statement runs, and again after it returns. (Note that this step applies only when you are running the project *after* 9:00 a.m.)

6. Type **edit test.bat** and press **Enter**.

7. Change the **IF** statement to read as follows:

```
if %time% gtr 09:00:00.00 (goto late) else (goto end)
```

8. At this point, test.bat should resemble Figure 3-12. Press and hold **Alt**, press **f**, release **Alt**, and then press **s** to save the test.bat file. Next, press and hold **Alt**, press **f**, release **Alt**, and press **x** to exit Edit.

```
C:\WINNT\System32\cmd.exe - edit test.bat                          _□×
   File  Edit  Search  View  Options  Help
                             C:\test.bat
cls
@echo off
echo Hi there %username%> c:\log.txt
echo Today's date is: %date% >>c:\log.txt
echo The time is: %time% >>c:\log.txt
if %time% gtr 09:00:00.00 (goto late) else (goto end)
del log.txt

:late
copy log.txt %username%.log>nul
goto end

:end
```

Figure 3-12   Using **ELSE** to skip the **LATE** subroutine

9. Delete the current log file to obtain proper results. Type **del %username%.log** and press **Enter**.

10. Run test.bat by typing **test** and pressing **Enter**.

11. Type **dir %username%.log** and press **Enter**. Notice that the log file is only created if the current time is later than 9:00 a.m.

12. Change the time in the program to one hour after the current time, then repeat Steps 8 through 11.

13. Type **exit** and press **Enter** to close the command window.

Remember that batch files are linear, and processing will continue to the end of the file, even when you jump to a subprocess or program. Using the **ELSE** statement to jump to the end of the file sidesteps potential problems such as repeating commands unnecessarily or running commands in a situation that is different than the one specified in the original **IF** statement.

Loops

In a program, a **loop** is a command that processes repeatedly based on the true or false condition of certain criteria. In other words, loops are repeating logical operations. In batch files, loops can be used to search for multiple items in a list. This is done by using bogus parameters, more commonly known as **wildcard parameters**, represented in code as %%N. These wildcard parameters are parameters that are used to cycle through the objects in a typed (separated by commas) list or variable, and perform whatever appropriate tasks follow. The **FOR** and **DO** parameters are used together to process loops.

C:_
Syntax

FOR %%N IN (<*LIST*>) DO <*COMMAND*>   Performs *COMMAND* for every item in *LIST*.

FOR %%N IN (<*LIST*>) DO <*COMMAND*> %%N   For each item in *LIST*, *COMMAND* is performed with a parameter of the corresponding item in *LIST*.

FOR %%N IN (<*VARIABLE*>) DO <*COMMAND*>   Performs *COMMAND* for every item in *VARIABLE*.

FOR %%N IN (<*VARIABLE*>) DO <*COMMAND*> %%N   For each item in *VARIABLE*, *COMMAND* is performed with a parameter of that item.

The fact that loops can occur with batch programming does defy the linear nature of batch processing. Consider the following example: Say that you need to create a folder for every user in a group of users. Rather than use the command prompt to issue several commands for each user, you can use a single **FOR** command (either on the command line or within a batch) to perform the same task for each member of the group.

3

 Be sure to note that wildcard parameters are referenced differently within a batch file than they are on the command line: Batch-specific wildcard parameters are %%N, but from the command line, a wildcard parameter is invoked with only a single percent character—%N.

In Hands-on Project 3-9, you will practice looping by using wildcard parameters to create user directories from a list of names.

 ## Hands-on Project 3-9

To use a loop to create user directories:

1. Open a command window.

2. Type **cd** and press **Enter**.

3. Create a new file called makename.bat by typing **edit makename.bat** and pressing **Enter**.

4. Type **for %%N in (jane, jim, mary) do md %%N** and press **Enter**.

 Recall that MD is the command for creating a directory.

5. Press and hold **Alt**, press **f**, and then release **Alt**. Press **x** to close Edit.

6. Press **Enter** to save the file.

7. At the command prompt, type **makename** and press **Enter** to run the batch file. Your screen should look like Figure 3-13.

```
C:\WINDOWS\system32\cmd.exe

C:\>for %n in (Jane, Jim, Mary) do md %n

C:\>md Jane

C:\>md Jim

C:\>md Mary

C:\>
```

Figure 3-13   Using the **FOR** command to loop through a list and run **MD** three times

8. To ensure that the directories were created, type **dir jane*.** and then press **Enter**.

9. Repeat Step 8 for the users Jim and Mary.

Figure 3-14 explains how the system processes the command.

1.	The system translates the command as: For every word in (Jane, Jim, Mary), DO MD for that word.
2.	The system reads the first word, Jane, and temporarily assigns the value Jane to %%N.
3.	The system proceeds to the DO portion of the statement.
4.	The system runs the command MD and replaces %%N with Jane. The end result is MD Jane.
5.	The system reads the second word, Jim, and temporarily assigns the value Jim to %%N.
6.	The system runs the command MD Jim.
7.	The system reads the third word, Mary, and temporarily assigns the value Mary to %%N.
8.	The system runs the command MD Mary.

Figure 3-14   Processing of the loop

You can understand the **FOR** loop if you think of the wildcard parameter as meaning "every object." In other words, the system runs the **FOR** command once for every object in the list, including the commands following **DO**.

Looping can get complex. It helps to remember that the definition of the wildcard parameter (**%%N**) changes every time the **FOR** command processes an object in the list. Additional logic and comparisons can be performed upon these new definitions, using the following command variations:

FOR %%N IN (<*LIST*>) DO IF "<*PARAMETERNUMBER*>"== "%%N" <*COMMAND*>   Compares every object in *LIST* to *PARAMETERNUMBER*. If the two are equal, runs *COMMAND*.

FOR %%N IN (<*VARIABLE*>) DO IF "<*PARAMETERNUMBER*>" =="%%N" <*COMMAND*>   Compares every object in *VARIABLE* to *PARAMETERNUMBER*. If the two are equal, runs *COMMAND*.

FOR %%N IN (<*FILENAME1*>, <*FILENAME2*>) DO IF "<*PARAMETERNUMBER*>"=="%%N" <*COMMAND*>   For every file, runs *COMMAND* if *PARAMETERNUMBER* and the object are equal.

Looping Through Multiple Parameters You can run loops that compare multiple parameters. For example, you might need to check to see if multiple words exist within a file, list, or variable. The first part of this solution would be to place the **FOR** command into a batch file, and use one **FOR** statement for each parameter, like this:

```
for %%N in (<LIST>) do if "%1"=="%%N" <COMMAND>
for %%N in (<LIST>) do if "%2"=="%%N" <COMMAND>
for %%N in (<LIST>) do if "%3"=="%%N" <COMMAND>
```

Even though this might seem like a logical and efficient way to compare multiple parameters, there are two problems with this approach. The first problem is simple style: You are performing the same task three times with only one character difference between each command. The second is practical: If the user ends up only entering one parameter when running the batch program, an error message will occur. You can solve both of these problems by using the **SHIFT** command to process and delete parameters with each iteration of the **FOR** command.

SHIFT   Deletes the contents of the current %1 parameter, and reassigns the %2 parameter as %1.

Remember that when you issue a **GOTO** statement, the process will return to its point of origin providing that the subroutine or subprogram does not jump somewhere else. This is one of the few times where you would use a subroutine that doesn't include a GOTO END in it.

Using the **SHIFT** command, the previous code example would be rewritten as follows:

```
:main
for %%N in (<LIST>) do if "%1"=="%%N" <COMMAND>
shift
goto main
```

Prompting for User Input Using CHOICE

It is possible to create an entire application using only batch programming. This rudimentary programming style leaves out one key element, however: the ability for the user to select or enter information, such as programs to run or variables to create. The **CHOICE** command is available for that purpose.

CHOICE /C <KEYLIST>   Prompts the user to press one of the listed keys. If the user presses a key that is not on *KEYLIST*, the entry is ignored.

CHOICE /C <KEYLIST>/N   Prompts the user to press one of the listed keys, but does not display *KEYLIST*.

CHOICE /C <*KEYLIST*>/T <*TIMEOUT*> /D <*DEFAULTKEY*>   Prompts the user to press one of the listed keys within *TIMEOUT*. If no entry is received, the *DEFAULTKEY* entry is entered by the system.

CHOICE /C <*KEYLIST*>/M "<*PROMPTMSG*>"   Prompts the user to press one of the listed keys, displaying *PROMPTMSG* before the prompt.

Several third-party vendors used to offer many options for allowing user input within batch files in the command environment. Unfortunately, **CHOICE** is the only remaining utility that works with Windows Server 2003. While you may be able to track down some of these older tools, they probably will not work with the command environment because they were created for the original 16-bit DOS environment. Once a user has entered a letter from a **CHOICE** command, the results are sorted out using error handling methods.

Error Handling

Most commands produce what are known as **exit codes**. Exit codes are numbers that are generated by a command when it has completed processing. These numbers indicate status and completion of the command, and are different for every command. As an example, the exit codes associated with the **CHOICE** command are numerically assigned (starting with 1) according to the key list of characters or numbers.

You can use exit codes within batch programs using the **ERRORLEVEL** command, which tests for specific exit codes.

IF ERRORLEVEL <*NUMBER*> <*COMMAND*>   Tests for the specified ERRORLEVEL *NUMBER* and performs *COMMAND*.

IF NOT ERRORLEVEL <*NUMBER*> <*COMMAND*>   Tests for anything but the specified ERRORLEVEL and performs *COMMAND*.

IF ERRORLEVEL <*NUMBER*> <*COMMAND*> ELSE <*COMMAND*>   Tests for the specified ERRORLEVEL and performs the first *COMMAND*. Any other error level will perform the second *COMMAND*.

Hands-on Project 3-10 teaches you how to create a program that enables a user to choose between Notepad, Explorer, and Control Panel.

Hands-on Project 3-10

To use **CHOICE** to create an application:

1. Open a command window. Type **cd** and press **Enter**.

2. Type **edit menu.bat** and press **Enter** to create a new batch file called menu.bat.

3. Type the code indicated in Figure 3-15.

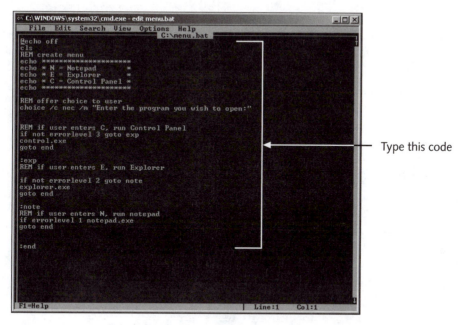

Type this code

Figure 3-15 Creating a program using **CHOICE** and **ERRORLEVEL**

4. Press and hold **Alt**, press **f**, and release **Alt**. Press **x** to exit the program, and press **Enter** when prompted to save.

5. Test to see whether the menu works by typing **menu** and pressing **Enter**. The menu should appear with the prompt.

6. Press **n**. The system prompts you to press any key.

7. Notepad should open. Press ⊠ on the Notepad window to close Notepad.

8. Repeat Steps 5 through 7 using the other menu options (E and C) to ensure that they work.

9. Close the command window.

Unfortunately, outside of the **CHOICE** command, there is no standard for determining error levels or exit codes. You might encounter documentation with some of the more thorough or advanced **HELP** topics available for commands. Because of the lack of error level documentation, it is usually easiest to determine error levels by putting together a batch program that tests for various error levels, and go about forcing different results to generate various error levels. For example, you could run a successful **COPY** command and see if an error level comes up true, as you did in Hands-on Project 3-10. Then, you would run a failed **COPY** command and see if a different error level was generated.

Automating a Batch or Other Program

The true value of batch files is the ability to launch a batch program or regular command without user intervention. This automation allows you to schedule the launch of any command, program, batch, or GUI utility. The **AT** command is responsible for automatic command processing.

AT is most frequently used to launch a tape or backup process. It can also be used to copy files or perform any other command covered in this book. It is also used to run commands and programs on remote computer systems.

AT <TIMEOFDAY> <COMMAND>   Schedules *COMMAND* to occur on the local machine at *TIMEOFDAY*.

AT <TIMEOFDAY> /EVERY:<DAY> <COMMAND>   Schedules *COMMAND* to run at *TIMEOFDAY* every *DAY. DAY* arguments can be M (Monday), T (Tuesday), W (Wednesday), TH (Thursday), F (Friday), S (Saturday), or SU (Sunday) and may be used in combination by listing multiple days separated by a slash (M/T/F) or a comma (M,T,F).

AT <TIMEOFDAY> /EVERY:<DAYOFMONTH> <COMMAND>   Schedules the *COMMAND* to run *TIMEOFDAY* every month on *DAYOFMONTH. DAYOFMONTH* is a number from 1 to 31.

By default, **AT** runs commands and programs in hidden mode, which means that all processing of the automated task is hidden from view during execution. Unless the **/INTERACTIVE** switch is used, all prompts are hidden, and the program will fail. While **AT** works to schedule commands, batch programs, and applications, the automated task may fail, because many programs often require user input. Commands are more often successful with **AT** when they include options and arguments that can eliminate most forms of user intervention. Several GUI programs can also run on the command line that specifically include unattended, automated scheduling. One example is NTBACKUP. You will learn about NTBACKUP in Chapter 4.

The **AT** command works by inserting a scheduled job into the Scheduled Tasks utility within the operating system's System Tools. The value of **AT** is clear once you compare the time required to schedule an event through Scheduled Tasks with the time spent doing the same task using **AT**—the command is much faster than the GUI. **AT**'s ability to process remote scheduling is an added bonus that is not possible with the Scheduled Tasks utility.

3

CHAPTER SUMMARY

This chapter covers the basics of batch programming, including logic processing and user interaction. Many commands and options are used almost exclusively within batch programs. Variables and parameters can be used when executing a batch program. In batches, parameters enable a command within the batch routine to execute with specific information. Logical functions can be included in batch programs to find data, compare data, and recursively search data for specific strings and values. Once a logical command has been initiated, specific commands can be executed depending on the results, enabling an incredible amount of automation and hands-off functionality for many administrative functions. Batch files can also be used to create applications, display information on the screen, and document and log batch process status and updates, all of which allow administrators to enhance the end-user environment as well as troubleshoot automation and system processes.

COMMAND SUMMARY

Command	Function
EDIT	Opens a file for modification.
ECHO	(1) displays a message (2) turns ECHO on or off.
>NUL	Eliminates output.
TYPE	Displays a file.
REM	Documents a line without executing it.
GOTO	Sends the process to a subroutine.
:<ROUTINE>	A subroutine header.
CALL	Sends the process to a subprogram or batch.
PAUSE	Prompts the user to continue.
IF DEFINED	Determines variable existence.
IF EXIST	Determines file existence.
IF	Compares two variables, parameters, or strings and runs a command based on the comparison. Uses operators.
IF ELSE	Compares two variables, parameters, or strings and runs a command based on the comparison. Runs a separate command based on the negative comparison.
FOR IN DO	Determines existence of a single variable, string, parameter, or wildcard parameter within a variable, string, parameter, or wildcard parameter. Performs a command based on the results.
SHIFT	Cycles through multiple parameters. Eliminates the need to perform redundant commands on multiple parameters.
CHOICE	Prompts the user to enter a letter, number, or character.
IF ERRORLEVEL	Performs a command based on exit codes.
AT	Schedules command execution on a local or remote system.

KEY TERMS

conditional processing — A type of process in which certain commands are executed based on specifically defined conditions.

exit codes — Hidden command output that indicates the success, failure, or status of the command.

linear — A method of processing in which the program executes commands line by line.

log file — A simple text file that contains the output results of commands.

logic — The ability to compare or judge two items based on given conditions and to execute commands based on the status of those conditions.

logic processing — A type of command or process that indicates some amount of conditional processing.

logon script — A batch file that executes when the user logs in to a system or domain.

loop — A reiterative process that continues until the specified reiterations have occurred. Within batch, loops reiterate until the end of the file or list has been reached.

operator — Math-based comparison symbols that can be used to compare numbers and characters.

parameter — The batch equivalent of a command option.

remark — A statement that is documentary in nature and is ignored within a batch routine. Represented within batch as REM.

subprogram — A batch program that is executed from within another batch program.

subroutine — A section of a batch, program, or script that is separate from the main processing and is used for processing conditional tasks.

Visual Basic script language — A scripting language supported by Windows Server 2003 that incorporates a subset of the Visual Basic programming language.

wildcard parameter — A type of variable that does not exist outside the bounds of the command that uses it. Wildcard parameters begin as wildcards, but can be temporarily assigned a value within the FOR command.

Windows Scripting Host (WSH) — The Windows Server 2003 service that enables scripts to be executed.

REVIEW QUESTIONS

1. What file extension indicates a batch program?

    a. .exe

    b. .bat

    c. .pif

    d. .cmd

3

2. Which file type(s) can be viewed within the Edit program?

   a. .exe

   b. .exe and .txt

   c. .exe and .bat

   d. .txt and .bat

3. How is the parameter `HELLO` represented within a batch file?

   a. `%HELLO%`

   b. `%1%`

   c. `%1`

   d. `%%1`

4. What command is used to avoid redundancy and errors with parameters?

   a. `GOTO END`

   b. `SHIFT`

   c. `EXIT`

   d. `%%2`

5. Which command converts a parameter into a variable?

   a. `SET <VARIABLENAME>=%<PARAMETER>`

   b. `SET %%<PARAMETER>=<VARIABLENAME>`

   c. `SET %%N==<VARIABLENAME>`

   d. `SET %<PARAMETER>=<VARIABLENAME>`

6. Which command is used to determine the existence of an environment variable?

   a. `IF DEFINED <VARIABLENAME>`

   b. `IF EXIST <VARIABLENAME>`

   c. `IF <VARIABLENAME> EXIST`

   d. `IF <VARIABLENAME>=1`

7. Which command would be used to eliminate output from a batch program?

   a. `ECHO ON` and `>NUL`

   b. `ECHO OFF` and `>NUL`

   c. `@ECHO OFF` and `>NUL`

   d. `@ECHO ON` and `>NUL`

8. What is the difference between a subroutine and a subprogram?

  a. A subroutine is code within the batch program that calls it; a subprogram is a separate batch program.

  b. A subprogram is code within the batch program that calls it; a subroutine is a separate batch program.

  c. A subroutine uses the **GOTO** command; a subprogram uses the **CALL** command.

  d. A subprogram uses the **GOTO** command; a subroutine uses the **CALL** command.

9. Which commands are used for conditional processing?

  a. **CASE** and **WHEN**

  b. **IF** and **DO/WHILE**

  c. **IF** and **THEN**

  d. **FOR** and **WHILE**

10. Which commands involve user input?

  a. **WAIT** and **CALL**

  b. **PAUSE** and **CHOICE**

  c. **PROMPT** and **AT**

  d. **CHOICE** and **WAIT**

11. Operators only work for numbers.

  a. true

  b. false

12. Which of the following can be a valid command?

  a. **IF ELSE IF ELSE IF**

  b. **DO WHILE IF ELSE**

  c. **FOR IN DO IF ELSE**

  d. **FOR IN DO FOR IN DO IF ELSE**

13. Which of the following are standard environment variables?

  a. **%GROUP%** and **%DIRECTORY%**

  b. **%PATH%** and **%ADMINISTRATOR%**

  c. **%USERNAME%** and **%TIME%**

  d. **%TIME%** and **%SYSTEM%**

14. How can you determine group membership within a batch program?

  a. Use the **FOR IN DO** command in a loop.

  b. Use the **%GROUP%** variable with the **FOR** command.

  c. Use the **ISMEMBER** command.

  d. Create a text file list of the members with the **FOR** command.

15. Which of the following commands runs the file cclog.bat every night at midnight?

    a. `AT 24:00 CCLOG.BAT`

    b. `AT 12:00AM CCLOG.BAT`

    c. `AT 12:00PM CCLOG.BAT`

    d. `AT 12:00AM CCLOG.BAT /EVERY:M/T/W/TH/F/S/SU CCLOG.BAT`

16. Which batch command searches for the word "james?"

    a. `for %N in (mary, james, john) do if %N=james echo hit`

    b. `for %%N in (mary, james, john) do if %%N=james echo hit`

    c. `for %%N in (names.log) do if %%N=james echo hit`

    d. `for %%N in (names.txt) do if %N=james echo hit`

17. Which of the following commands runs at the command prompt?

    a. `for %N in (mary, james, john) do if %N=james echo hit`

    b. `for %%N in (mary, james, john) do if %%N=james echo hit`

    c. `for %%N in (names.txt) do if %%N=james echo hit`

    d. `for %%N in (names.txt) do if %N=james echo hit`

18. Which of the following commands makes directories for Mary, James, and John?

    a. `for %N in (mary, james, john) do md %N`

    b. `mdname.bat mary james john; mdname.bat=md %1; md%2; md %3`

    c. `mdname.bat; mdname.bat= for %%N in (mary, james, john) do md %%N`

    d. `mdname.bat mary james john; mdname.bat=md %1; goto shift; md %1; :shift; shift`

19. Which of the following is used when creating a log?

    a. `REM`

    b. `<`

    c. `>`

    d. `<<`

20. Which command is a looping command?

    a. `FOR`

    b. `CASE`

    c. `IF`

    d. `DO`

DISCOVERY EXERCISES

1. Modify the test.bat file that you used in this chapter so that it is a logon script for the currently logged-on user, with the log files in the same place.

    a. Start by creating a share (using Windows Explorer) called NETLOGON with the appropriate access and copy test.bat into that location. Windows Server 2003 differs from Windows 2000 in that default share permissions are Everyone/Read, so you need to change the permissions to Everyone/Change or Everyone/Full Control. Domain controllers will already have a NETLOGON share with the appropriate permissions. For the time being, change permissions using Windows Explorer.

    b. After test.bat is modified, you need to assign it as a logon script. Open Local Users and Groups by clicking the Start menu, right-clicking My Computer, clicking Manage, and highlighting the Local Users and Groups snap-in utility from the Computer Management MMC (Microsoft Management Console). This step assumes that you are working on a stand-alone, non–Active Directory server.

    If the server is a domain controller, you need to do the following steps from within the Start menu "Administrative Tools" AD Users and Computers: Open the user account in question by double-clicking it. Add the test.bat to the logon script line, and log on as the user and see if the batch file runs when logon is complete. If it doesn't work, try a few troubleshooting methods: Run test.bat from its new location using Windows Explorer; run it from the command line using \\<SERVERNAME>\ NETLOGON\TEST.BAT; determine if the script runs when you log on by inserting a PAUSE or two to keep the window open.

2. If you applied the previous exercise for all user accounts on the system or network in a setting where employees all start work at the same time, your script might encounter some problems. What are some problems that might occur?

3. How can you modify Discovery Exercise 1 to maintain a running log over the course of several days?

4. Determine the error levels for common commands such as COPY and DIR. This can be done by creating a batch file that performs a command, and tests for different error levels with GOTO statements to subroutines that will display the appropriate results. You can then induce successes and failures by altering the parameters of the batch program. Remember that there are no operators with error levels. The test statements should be IF ERROR LEVEL <#> GOTO <SUB>.

UNIT
2

COMPUTER
ADMINISTRATION

4

SYSTEM ADMINISTRATION

After reading this chapter and completing the exercises, you will be able to:

- ◆ Perform power management tasks
- ◆ View and modify the registry
- ◆ Perform page file configuration tasks
- ◆ View and modify services
- ◆ Manage tasks and processes
- ◆ Create and perform data backups
- ◆ Monitor and optimize a system

You might be surprised to learn how many administrative functions are available from the command window. Other than reasons mentioned in previous chapters—including the advanced features of commands, the lack of GUI equivalents, speed, and so on—there is one more very important reason for using commands: When a system is failing, sometimes the command window is the only thing that works. If you can master the command window, you could save yourself hours, if not days, of additional recovery work. This chapter focuses on server-specific commands that are available for administration. Subsequent chapters will look at type-specific administration such as disk administration, networking, and Active Directory.

Viewing What Is Installed on a System

Server administration can be a challenging and intimidating task, even with the GUI administration tools available within Windows. Microsoft reduces, if not eliminates, many administrative tasks by automatically configuring certain features. Automatic configuration doesn't necessarily mean that these items need any less attention. Features such as Plug and Play, which allows a system to automatically detect new devices and assigns drivers, can become troublesome when Windows incorrectly implements these changes. When it comes time to troubleshoot, less knowledgeable administrators often neglect to consider some of these unseen factors, such as the results from Plug and Play, simply because they lack experience.

A well-trained and thorough systems expert is aware of all server components and their OS functions—whether they were configured automatically by the system or manually by another administrator. One of the first steps toward gaining this knowledge is to run a few commands that display system information appropriately. **SYSTEMINFO** and **DRIVERQUERY** are two commands that provide this insight.

SYSTEMINFO   Displays system information.

SYSTEMINFO /S <COMPUTERNAME> /U <USERNAME> /P <PASSWORD>   Displays system information for the remote computer specified.

SYSTEMINFO /FO TABLE|LIST|CSV /NH   Displays system information in the specified format (table, list, or comma delimited), with no header information.

Figure 4-1 shows the results of running **SYSTEMINFO**. From looking at Figure 4-1, it appears that **SYSTEMINFO** doesn't provide much detail in the information it presents. It does, however, provide more information than you might expect, along with some data that you can't find anywhere else. Running **SYSTEMINFO** provides the following information:

- **OS Name and Version**—Service packs show up as part of the OS version; therefore, **SYSTEMINFO** provides a quick and easy way to determine whether a server has been updated appropriately.

- **OS Configuration**—The OS configuration quickly tells you whether the server is a domain controller, domain member server, or standalone system.

- **OS Build Type**—Quickly tells you whether the system has multiple processors installed, and whether they are being utilized.

- **Processor(s)**—Indicates the approximate CPU speed.

- **BIOS Version**—The BIOS is a part of the OS that tracks installed hardware and performs essential startup functions. The BIOS version can indicate the features of these functions, including the ability to boot from a CD, boot to the network, or USB functionality.

Figure 4-1   The result of running **SYSTEMINFO**

4

- **Total/Available Physical Memory**—Gives information about the installed RAM and how much of it is being used. Unlike comparable GUI tools, **SYSTEMINFO** shows memory and page file usage without eating away at valuable system performance, especially when used at peak and quiet times.

- **Page File: Max Size/Available/In Use**—Displays a quick analysis of your page file capacity and size. The page file is a file located on the hard disk that acts as a RAM extension. The OS and the programs running on it use the page file to temporarily store data that would otherwise not fit in RAM. If the Page File In Use is approaching the Max Size, you may need to increase the size, increase RAM, or move the page file to another disk.

- **Page File Location(s)**—Indicates the location of the page file. This is particularly valuable if you are running a server with multiple hard disks. The physical location of the page file can have an impact on system performance. Page files generate a lot of hard disk activity, and it is a good idea to place them on a separate disk from the partition containing the system and boot files. To further increase efficiency, you may consider splitting the page file across multiple hard disks to evenly distribute the load across all disks.

- **Domain/Logon Server**—Displays the location of the system within the network hierarchy.

- **Hotfix(es)**—Lists the service packs and patches that have been applied to the system, and also lists their Microsoft article numbers. You can take the hotfix number (in Figure 4-1, it is Q147222), go to www.microsoft.com, and enter it as a search parameter. The resulting Technet article describes the purpose of the hotfix.

The **SYSTEMINFO** command can be a source of baseline and general system information that you can use as a reference. The information provided by the command is essential in the event of a system rebuild.

In Hands-on Project 4-1, you will learn how to use **SYSTEMINFO** to gather information about your server and save that information to a file.

Hands-on Project 4-1

To gather system information:

1. Open a command window.

2. Type **systeminfo** and press **Enter**. The results should be similar to Figure 4-2.

```
C:\WINDOWS\system32\cmd.exe                                          _ □ ×
System Model:                 N/A
System Type:                  X86-based PC
Processor(s):                 1 Processor(s) Installed.
                              [01]: x86 Family 6 Model 4 Stepping 2 AuthenticAMD ~8
48 Mhz
BIOS Version:                 PhoenixBIOS 4.0 Release 6.0
Windows Directory:            C:\WINDOWS
System Directory:             C:\WINDOWS\system32
Boot Device:                  \Device\HarddiskDmVolumes\MachineDg0\Volume1
System Locale:                en-us;English (United States)
Input Locale:                 en-us;English (United States)
Time Zone:                    (GMT-07:00) Arizona
Total Physical Memory:        128 MB
Available Physical Memory:    40 MB
Page File: Max Size:          447 MB
Page File: Available:         270 MB
Page File: In Use:            177 MB
Page File Location(s):        C:\pagefile.sys
Domain:                       AVIANWORKS
Logon Server:                 \\MACHINE
Hotfix(s):                    1 Hotfix(s) Installed.
                              [01]: Q147222
NetWork Card(s):              1 NIC(s) Installed.
                              [01]: AMD PCNET Family PCI Ethernet Adapter
                                    Connection Name: Local Area Connection
                                    DHCP Enabled:     No
                                    IP address(es)
                                    [01]: 192.168.123.67

C:\Documents and Settings\Administrator.MACHINE>
```

Figure 4-2   Using **SYSTEMINFO** to view system information

3. Type **cd** and press **Enter** to navigate to your system's root drive.

   To create a file containing the **SYSTEMINFO** information, you need to run the command again with redirection to a file.

4. Type **systeminfo>sys.txt** and press **Enter**.

5. Type **type sys.txt** and press **Enter** to view the sys.txt file. The results should be similar to Figure 4-2.

6. Type **exit** and press **Enter** to close the command window.

As a Windows Server 2003 expert, you will need to be familiar with the difference between a system rebuild and a system restore. A system rebuild becomes necessary when, for some reason or another, something goes wrong with the server and the backup methods do not work properly. Normally, if something renders a server inoperable, a system restore (usually a tape restore) becomes necessary. A tape restore can fail for several reasons, including tape drive failure, tape failure, inappropriate backups, or simply because the backups didn't run properly. If the tape restore fails to solve the problem, the next step on the road to recovery is a system rebuild. A system rebuild requires that you reinstall the OS, applications, and any remaining data with as little loss as possible. **SYSTEMINFO**, when run regularly, assists you in the rebuilding process by helping you keep track of the system updates and hotfixes that have been applied to the system.

4

DRIVERQUERY is another command that documents the elements that are currently on the server. Specifically, the command lists drivers on the system and shows details about them. A **driver** is a piece of software that is used to bridge the gap between the operating system and a piece of hardware and allows the OS to communicate with the device using standardized protocols. Most of the drivers you encounter are system-generated drivers that are used to handle generic devices such as floppy drives and hard disk drives. You cannot make driver changes with **DRIVERQUERY**, but the command can provide you with a full list of drivers that are currently installed.

DRIVERQUERY   Displays a table containing all of the loaded drivers on a system.

DRIVERQUERY /S <COMPUTERNAME> /U <USERNAME> /P <PASSWORD>   Displays a driver list for the remote computer specified.

DRIVERQUERY /FO TABLE|LIST|CSV /NH   Displays the current drivers in the specified format (table, list, or comma delimited) with no header information.

DRIVERQUERY /V   Displays information about system drivers.

DRIVERQUERY /SI   Displays information about signed drivers.

Figure 4-3 shows the result of running **DRIVERQUERY**. The Display Name heading shown in Figure 4-3 indicates what many of the drivers do. While many drivers are associated with hardware devices (such as Cdrom for the CD and Fdc for the floppy disk), many are not associated with hardware. Sometimes more than one driver is needed to handle specific tasks associated with OS-to-device communications.

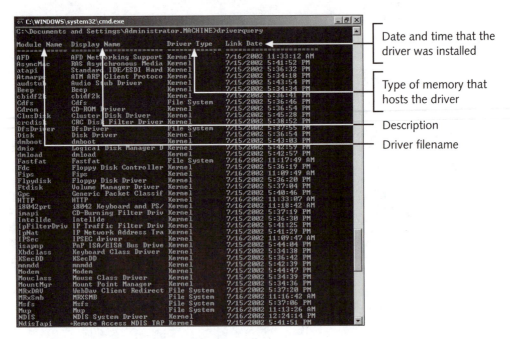

Figure 4-3 DRIVERQUERY output

Microsoft uses drivers in a similar way to add enhancements in communications with the devices, even when the enhancement appears to be completely software-based. Consider DfsDriver shown in Figure 4-3. DFS (Distributed File System) is a server feature that allows shared server data to be distributed and stored on separate networked machines. In a DFS-configured server, the OS (through Windows Explorer, My Computer) still communicates with a DFS-configured system as though it were communicating with any other hard drive. DfsDriver is responsible for handling the DFS-specific tasks that make this possible (and transparent) from the point of view of the user (and other parts of the OS).

POWER MANAGEMENT

Until a few years ago, only users of laptop computers needed to be concerned with the amount of electricity consumed by their computers. In locations outside of the United States, where power restrictions and guidelines are in place, power has been a concern for all types of computer equipment. Throughout the computer industry, power consumption and management are receiving scrutiny as both hardware and software issues. This focus brings attention to the power management feature of Windows Server 2003.

From a hardware perspective, power management has two standards: APM and ACPI. **Advanced Power Management (APM)** is a hardware standard that allows the BIOS

4

to shut off or suspend power to certain high-use components when a preconfigured state (such as non-use) has been achieved. **Advanced Computer and Power Interface (ACPI)** is a newer power standard that allows the operating system to fully control the power status (on or off) of various components on the system. Both of these standards reside with the hardware, and particularly in the BIOS. Most current servers are ACPI compliant, which allows administrators to craft flexible power management schemes.

Power management within Windows Server 2003 is divided into **power schemes**. These schemes represent a particular state at which the computer might require a different power configuration. Power management within the Windows Server 2003 GUI world can be viewed from the Power Options item within Control Panel. By default, Windows Server 2003 defines the following schemes:

- **Home/Office Desk**—Turns off the monitor after 20 minutes of user inactivity.

- **Portable/Laptop**—Turns off the monitor after 15 minutes of user inactivity and turns off the hard disks after 30 minutes.

- **Presentation**—Never turns anything off.

- **Always On**—Turns off the monitor after 20 minutes of user inactivity.

- **Minimal Power Management**—Turns off the monitor after 15 minutes of user inactivity.

- **Max Battery**—Turns off the monitor after 15 minutes of user inactivity.

Most desktop systems consider the Home/Office Desk and Always On schemes to be identical. The purpose of the Portable/Laptop power scheme should be self-explanatory: Laptop batteries usually only work for a few hours before requiring a charge, so it may be wise to leave this particular configuration alone. From the Control Panel, you have the ability to define the current power scheme. Laptop systems automatically detect the different power schemes of the system: unplugged with the battery on = Portable/Laptop; plugged in or docked = Home/Office Desk; plugged in with an external monitor = Presentation.

The **POWERCFG** command enables you to configure the power settings for a system from the command line. Additionally, **POWERCFG** has the ability to distinguish between power received in alternating current (AC, which is from a wall outlet) and power received in direct current (DC, which is from batteries). This allows you to configure one power scheme for standard power and one for battery backup.

POWERCFG /LIST   Displays a list of the current power schemes.

POWERCFG /QUERY <SCHEME>   Displays the power configuration associated with the specified scheme.

POWERCFG /SETACTIVE <SCHEME>   Assigns the specified scheme as the current scheme. The system will then associate the current status with that particular scheme.

POWERCFG /CREATE <*SCHEME*>   Creates a blank power configuration scheme and assigns it the specified scheme name.

POWERCFG /CHANGE <*SCHEME*> /MONITOR-TIMEOUT-*AC|DC* **<*MINUTES*>**   Shuts down the monitor at the specified time (the designated amount of elapsed time) for the specified scheme under either AC or DC power.

POWERCFG /CHANGE <*SCHEME*> /DISK-TIMEOUT-*AC|DC* **<*MINUTES*>**   Shuts down the hard disks at the specified time for the specified scheme under either AC or DC power.

POWERCFG /CHANGE <*SCHEME*> /HIBERNATE-TIMEOUT-*AC|DC* **<*MINUTES*>**   Hibernates the system at the specified time for the specified scheme under either AC or DC power.

POWERCFG /CHANGE <*SCHEME*> /PROCESSOR-THROTTLE-*AC|DC* *NONE|CONSTANT|DEGRADE|ADAPTIVE*   Alters the processor performance based on the specified throttle type.

POWERCFG /EXPORT <*SCHEME*> /F <*FILENAME*>   Exports the specified scheme to the specified file.

POWERCFG /IMPORT <*SCHEME*> /F <*FILENAME*>   Imports the specified scheme from the specified file.

Hibernation is a suspended state of operation in which the active configuration is stored on the hard disk, and the system is powered off. As shown in Figure 4-4, the **/HIBERNATE** option is available to trigger hibernation in certain circumstances. Hibernation can cause problems in proprietary and laptop systems that are not completely ACPI-compliant. For example, partially ACPI-compliant systems tend to be unable to fully recover from a hibernation state, sometimes losing mouse or other peripheral equipment functionality. By default, hibernation is disabled, and it is a good idea to leave it that way until you test it or check the hardware system documentation to determine if it is fully supported. Hibernation-related problems occur because it doesn't take much to make a system hibernate, but if ACPI is not fully supported by the hardware, the system may never fully be able to power up. Instead, if it is truly necessary to shut down components when they are not in use, you would be better off changing the power scheme to shut down the components individually without changing the system state through hibernation.

It may be easy to shrug off power management as an issue of money when you know that your company can afford the power bill. While this may be the case, your greater concern should be in the realm of system survival during a power outage.

```
C:\WINDOWS\system32\cmd.exe                                          _ □ ×

POWERCFG [/LIST | /QUERY [name] | /CREATE name | /DELETE name |
         /SETACTIVE name | /CHANGE name settings |
    ►    /HIBERNATE [ON|OFF] | /EXPORT name [/FILE filename] |
/?]      /IMPORT name [/FILE filename] | /GLOBALPOWERFLAG [ON|OFF] /OPTION:FLAG |

Description:
    This command line tool enables an administrator to control
    the power settings on a system.

Parameter List:
    /LIST, /L        Lists the names of existing power schemes.
    /QUERY, /Q       Displays the configuration of the specified power scheme.
                     If no name is specified, the configuration of the currently
                     active power scheme is displayed.
    /CREATE, /C      Creates a power scheme with the specified name.  The new
                     scheme is created with the properties of the currently
                     active scheme.
    /DELETE, /D      Deletes the power scheme with the specified name.
    /SETACTIVE, /S   Makes the power scheme with the specified name active.
    /CHANGE, /X      Changes settings of the specified power scheme. Additional
                     switches specify the changes as follows:
                         /monitor-timeout-ac <minutes>
                         /monitor-timeout-dc <minutes>
```

/HIBERNATE option

Figure 4-4 POWERCFG options and arguments

One of the first disaster prevention items that your company should purchase is a **battery backup** or **uninterruptible power supply (UPS)** unit. A battery backup is a heavy box that is full of batteries. It is plugged into an electrical outlet, and the server and any other necessary equipment are plugged into the battery backup. The battery protects against power surges and brownouts, and also provides a constant (albeit limited) power source in the event of a power failure. The overriding purpose of a battery backup is to provide enough power to a server or system to safely shut it down without losing data.

Each battery backup unit is rated to provide a certain amount of power over a certain period of time, usually less than a half hour, depending on the size and capacity of the battery and the power needs of the equipment that it supports. Although the term UPS is often synonymous with battery backup, there are other solutions for power supplies, depending on the number of systems and the amount of power required. Some batteries are capable of handling only a small PC, others are rated for one or more servers, and other power generator devices, such as an external diesel engine, are rated to support an entire data center for the duration of the diesel supply. If, for example, a battery is capable of handling a server for 15 minutes, adding a monitor to that battery will shorten the time to approximately 8 minutes. Additional equipment, such as a modem, router, or printer (particularly a laser printer), will further decrease the time that the battery can provide power to all of these items. An adequately configured power scheme can maximize available battery time, and helps reduce electricity costs.

Using **POWERCFG**, you can configure automatic power-shutoff or hibernation for a server's most power-hungry components: the monitor, hard disks, and processor. **POWERCFG** also can tell when the system is running on UPS battery power or on the normal power grid. This is differentiated by the *AC|DC* timeout values, which you learned about in the syntax examples for the **POWERCFG** command. This feature is not available from within the Control Panel, Power Options GUI applet. This particular option allows you to further configure your standard server's Always On (or other preferred) scheme to include a monitor and hard disk shutdown almost as soon as the DC power is activated.

You can force the CPU to slow itself down in the interest of saving electricity. Forcing the CPU to change speeds is called **CPU throttling**. Windows Server 2003 supports four different ways to throttle the CPU:

- **None**—Allows the CPU to function at peak performance.

- **Constant**—Forces the CPU to function at its lowest performance state without being off.

- **Degrade**—Varies the CPU performance based on the battery life.

- **Adaptive**—Varies the CPU performance based on the OS and application demands made on the unit.

REGISTRY

Other than the hardware, the **registry** is the single most vital component of the server. The registry is a database that contains every setting, pointer, configuration, profile, and policy that exist on a system. Everything that exists on a system, including usernames, desktop settings, icons, programs, drivers, and services, is in the registry. When you install applications, they will typically add settings and configuration information to the registry. The amount and importance of the data within the registry makes it not only the single most *important* object in the OS, but also the most *dangerous* item on the server.

Because of its importance, you should always remember the consequences of altering the registry. Part of any system administrator's job requires registry modification, but most registry changes can actually be made through changes in the Control Panel. Viewing and changing the registry itself must be done with great care and consideration. Put bluntly: If you mess it up, you could lose your job. While unemployment may not always result from such tinkering, keep in mind that you could easily destroy a server by modifying the registry, and you might not know it until the next time a restart becomes necessary. While system, tape, and registry backups can rectify problems when they occur, it is far better to proceed cautiously and avoid the problem entirely.

Because the registry is essentially the source of all information on the server, it is sometimes necessary to look at or modify parts of the registry to gather information about system settings (such as which programs automatically start) or fix problems (such as a recently installed program that has caused trouble). The registry is divided into five different sections, called **hives**, which are stored in two main files and a few smaller files. An entry within a hive that contains subentries is called a **key**. When the system is powered on, there are only three hives: HKEY_LOCAL_MACHINE (HKLM), HKEY_CLASSES_ROOT (HKCR), and HKEY_USERS (HKU). The HKCR hive contains driver and system classes and is rarely changed. HKLM and HKU, however, are a different story. HKLM contains system and hardware information and settings. HKU contains user profiles and settings. When a system has booted, HKLM splits into two pieces, with a smaller piece consisting of the current hardware configuration. This smaller piece is then loaded into memory and becomes a fourth hive called HKEY_CURRENT_CONFIG (HKCC). When the user logs in, HKU splits into two pieces, with the smaller piece containing data specific to that user. This smaller piece is similarly loaded into memory and becomes the fifth hive, called HKEY_CURRENT_USER (HKCU).

REGEDIT is a GUI program used to view and modify the registry. There is no command that allows you to view the entire registry in a manner that is comprehensive, so before proceeding, you should type REGEDIT from the Run line to open the registry editor, look at the registry, and become familiar with its contents, shown in Figure 4-5. You may notice that many of the **registry keys** are similar between hives. These similarities result from the split that was mentioned in the previous paragraph. When a user logs out of the system, changes that were made to HKCU are re-integrated into HKU. When a new user logs in to the system, HKCU is newly created with HKU information specifically for that user. When the system is rebooted, HKCC is similarly reabsorbed into HKLM.

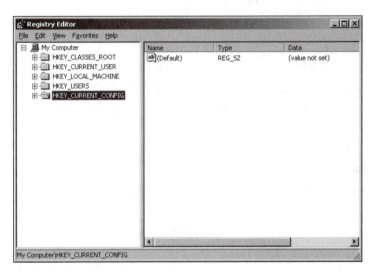

Figure 4-5 Basic registry structure

Each key contains **registry values** and/or **subkeys**. A registry value is an entry that contains specific information. A subkey is a key that exists as part of another key. Entries can have one of five data types: REG_SZ, REG_BINARY, REG_DWORD, REG_MULTI_SZ, or REG_EXPAND_SZ. You will rarely be called upon to create a new value, but in the course of troubleshooting or program installation, it might become necessary. If a new value is required, the data type is irrelevant. This is mainly because the only two human-readable data types are REG_SZ and REG_BINARY, where REG_SZ contains string, pointer, or path data, and REG_BINARY contains on/off switches: 0 for off, and 1 for on. Every other type is stored in hexadecimal format, according to strict rules that are beyond the scope of this text.

Automatic Program Launch Within the Registry

As an administrator, most of the work you will do in the registry will involve applications that automatically start when the user logs in. There are three places that an application can start without user intervention: the Startup folder that resides in the Programs item within the Start menu, Services (which are covered later in this chapter), and the registry. Many installation routines start applications automatically using the registry rather than the Startup folder for several reasons. Most frequently, autostart occurs because there is no reason to clutter the Startup folder with the icon and potentially confuse the user. Another reason deals with safety: Vital programs such as antivirus applications are frequently in the registry. The final reason, and perhaps the most vital to the average administrator, deals with the fact that the registry is an out-of-the-way place for a virus to hide, ensuring its longevity and self-propagation. Frequently, virus programs will not only autostart themselves in the registry, but also give themselves innocuous filenames that sound suspiciously systemlike.

Learn and memorize the registry location and steps of Hands-on Project 4-2. You should become familiar with all of the system-essential programs that autostart within the registry so that you can recognize a bogus one when it comes along.

To become more familiar with the registry, you will use **REGEDIT** to learn which programs start automatically when the user logs in to the system.

Hands-on Project 4-2

To find autostarting programs:

1. Press the **Start** button ![Start], click **Run**, and type **regedit** on the Run line. Press **Enter**.

2. Click the **+** symbol next to HKEY_LOCAL_MACHINE.

3. Scroll down and click the **+** symbol next to SOFTWARE.

4. Scroll down and click the **+** symbol next to Microsoft.

5. Scroll down and click the **+** symbol next to Windows.

6. Scroll down and click the **+** symbol next to CurrentVersion.

7. Scroll down and highlight the entry labeled **Run**.

   Take note of all the entries listed in the right pane. A default standalone Windows Server 2003 server should only have the (default) entry.

8. Right-click the **right pane**, and select **New**. A pop-up menu opens.

9. Select **String Value** from the pop-up menu.

10. A new entry appears with the title New Value #1 highlighted, as shown in Figure 4-6. Type **Notepad** over the New Value #1 text and press **Enter**.

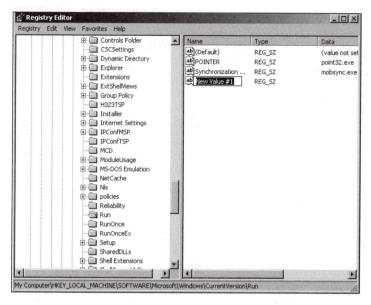

Figure 4-6 Creating a new registry entry using **REGEDIT**

11. Double-click **Notepad**, and in the Value data, type **notepad.exe**.

12. Click **OK** to close the entry.

13. Open the **RunOnce** and **RunOnceEx** folders in the left pane and examine their contents. These can harbor viruses. They are usually empty; installation routines often require a reboot before completing installation. Installation routines will place any leftover tasks that need to be performed after a reboot and automatically removed after the reboot in the RunOnce and RunOnceEx folders. To test that the changes worked, you will need to logoff and logon again.

14. Click ▒**Start**.

15. Click the **Log Off** 🔑 button.

16. The Log Off Windows dialog box opens. Press **Enter**.

17. Press **Ctrl+Alt+Del** to log in again.

18. Type your password and press **Enter**. Notice that Notepad automatically starts.

19. You will need to run **REGEDIT** again. Click ▒**Start**. Select **Run**, type **regedit**, and then press **Enter**.

20. Repeat Steps 2 through 7.

21. In the right pane, select the Notepad entry and press **Delete**. Click **Yes** to confirm the deletion.

22. Right-click the right pane, and select **New**. A pop-up menu opens.

23. Select **String Value** from the pop-up menu.

24. A new entry appears with the title New Value #1 highlighted. Type **cmd** over the New Value #1 text and press **Enter**. This automatically launches a command window every time a user logs off or reboots.

25. Press **Enter** to open the Registry Entry dialog box. Type **cmd** in the Value data text box, and then press **OK**. This change opens a command window automatically every time the user launches Windows.

26. Click the **Close** button ▣ to close **REGEDIT**. The next time you logoff or reboot, the command window will automatically open.

Looking at the Registry

From a command perspective, it is difficult to learn and understand the registry. Instead, you should consider **REGEDIT** your primary method of viewing the registry. Use the registry commands in this section for quick modification and information gathering in situations in which you know exactly what you are looking for. While you can't view the entire registry at the command prompt, it is possible to view the contents of an entire hive. The **REG QUERY** command, when used with various options, lets you view hives or run a query in several ways.

REG QUERY <*KEYORHIVENAME*>   Displays the entries and first-level subkeys for the specified key or hive.

REG QUERY \\<*COMPUTER*>\<*KEYORHIVENAME*>   Displays the entries and first-level subkeys for the specified key or hive.

REG QUERY <*KEYORHIVENAME*> /S   Displays the entries and subkeys for the specified key or hive, including the entire subtree structure.

REG QUERY <*KEYNAME*> /V <*ENTRY*>   Displays the specified entry data that is located in the *KEYNAME*.

You don't need to type out the entire hive name when the hive is entered as the keyname. Instead, the appropriate abbreviations can be used, as specified in Table 4-1.

Table 4-1   Hive name abbreviations

Abbreviation	Full hive name
HKCC	HKEY_CURRENT_CONFIG
HKLM	HKEY_LOCAL_MACHINE
HKCR	HKEY_CLASSES_ROOT
HKU	HKEY_USERS
HKCU	HKEY_CURRENTUSER

If you were to run a query on HKCC, you would see a screen resembling Figure 4-7.

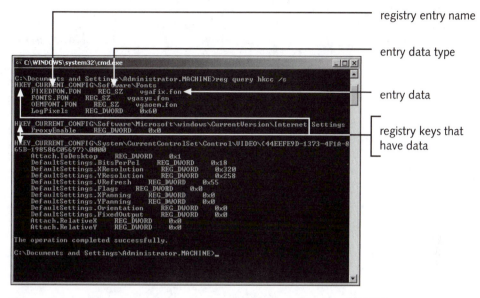

Figure 4-7   Using **REG QUERY** to determine the contents of HKCC

Determining the contents of the Run entry in the registry is straightforward and faster than performing the same task through the GUI utility, as you will learn in Hands-on Project 4-3.

Hands-on Project 4-3

To query the Run entry within the registry:

1. Open a command window.

2. At the command prompt, type **reg query hklm\software\microsoft\ windows\currentversion\run** and press **Enter**.

3. You will see the same entries that you saw in Hands-on Project 4-2, including the new one labeled CMD.

4. Type **exit** and press **Enter** to close the command window.

Manipulating the Registry

Usually, the best way to make registry changes is to use **REGEDIT**. Programmers and application installation routines often make registry changes either through routine scripts or through .reg files, which are small text files containing a registry entry. Files with a .reg extension behave similarly to batch files in that they can be executed from the command line and are text files, but they contain no commands. Instead, they are created by an administrator specifically for the registry and contain only registry keys and entries. Discovery Exercise 3 at the end of this chapter deals specifically with .reg files.

Bearing in mind that an incorrect or flawed registry entry can bring a server to its knees, you should get in the habit of backing up the keys and hives that are being modified or changed. It is a very good idea to make backup copies of the registry every chance you get. As you will learn later in this chapter, running a tape backup program will back up the registry. However, maintaining a copy of the registry elsewhere on the hard disk may save you from performing a partial tape restore (which can be time consuming) when the only problem is a bad registry key or entry. The **REG COPY**, **REG EXPORT**, **REG IMPORT**, **REG SAVE**, and **REG RESTORE** commands let you manipulate registry contents.

REG COPY <*SOURCEKEY*> <*DESTINATIONKEY*> /S /F   Copies the contents of the *SOURCEKEY* into a new *DESTINATIONKEY* within the registry.

REG EXPORT <*KEYORHIVENAME*> <*FILENAME*>   Exports the contents of the specified hive or key into the *FILENAME*. Used to export hives and keys to other servers.

REG IMPORT <*FILENAME*>   Imports the contents of the *FILENAME* into the registry.

REG SAVE <*KEYORHIVENAME*> <*FILENAME*>   Performs the same action as REG EXPORT, only with a file format that is not transferable to a different system.

REG RESTORE <*FILENAME*>   Performs the same action as REG IMPORT but must be performed on the same system that the REG SAVE file was created on.

The correct command to use when importing or exporting files may not be obvious, since the **REG EXPORT** and **REG SAVE** commands are so similar. You should only use the **REG SAVE** command when you are sure that the backup data will be restored on the same system. If there is any chance that the server will be entirely rebuilt, or the hive/key will be integrated into a different server, then **REG EXPORT** or **REG IMPORT** should be used. To eliminate the risk of data loss, you can place both commands into a batch file, and automate the batch routine with the **AT** command.

PAGE FILE OPTIMIZATION

A **page file** is a file that is used by the operating system or application to handle memory needs that exceed the physical RAM on the system. Essentially, a page file is an annex or overflow area for RAM. In recent years, Microsoft has been using a method of RAM data prioritization that takes advantage of the page file as not just a memory overflow area, but also a temporary storage location for data that is used infrequently or that is not important to the system—data that would otherwise be in RAM. A page file (also known as a **swap file**) is required by Windows Server 2003 and should be optimized for the best performance of the system.

Every system contains at least one page file. Because the page file acts as a copy of RAM, the system refers to the data within the page file as if it were RAM, with no consideration for the limitations of the physical hard disk speed and data transfer speed. This means that the page file is, at best, frequently referenced, and at worst, a serious detriment to the performance of the server. To optimize the performance of the page file and the system, you need to first take a look at the current configuration of the page file using the **PAGEFILECONFIG /QUERY** command, as shown in Figure 4-8.

 You might receive an error warning regarding cscript when you run the **PAGEFILECONFIG /QUERY** command. Pagefileconfig is a Visual Basic script, not an .exe file. To run the command, either follow the steps described in the dialog box or run **CSCRIPT PAGEFILECONFIG**.

```
C:\WINDOWS\system32\cmd.exe                                          _□×

C:\Documents and Settings\Administrator.MACHINE>pagefileconfig /query
Microsoft (R) Windows Script Host Version 5.6
Copyright (C) Microsoft Corporation 1996-2001. All rights reserved.

Host Name:              MACHINE
Drive/Volume:           C:
Volume Label:           N/A
Location\File Name:     C:\pagefile.sys
Initial Size:           192 MB
Maximum Size:           384 MB
Current Size:           192 MB
Total Free Space:       926 MB

Host Name:                              MACHINE
Total (All Drives): Minimum Size:           2 MB
Total (All Drives): Recommended Size:      190 MB
Total (All Drives): Currently Allocated:   192 MB

C:\Documents and Settings\Administrator.MACHINE>_
```

Figure 4-8   The current page file configuration

PAGEFILECONFIG /QUERY   Displays the current page file configuration.

PAGEFILECONFIG /QUERY /S <COMPUTERNAME> /U <USERNAME> /P <PASSWORD>   Displays the page file configuration on the specified remote computer using the *USERNAME* and *PASSWORD* provided.

PAGEFILECONFIG /QUERY /FO *TABLE|LIST|CSV*   Displays the page file configuration in the specified format (table, list, or comma delimited). This is ideal for documentation purposes when used with redirection.

Changing the Page File Configuration

By default, Windows Server 2003 installs the page file on the partition or volume where the system (\Windows) directory resides. Considering that this particular directory is bound to have a significant amount of disk-processing activity, it is a good idea to move the page file to a separate disk (a physical disk, not necessarily a partition or volume). Moving the page file reduces the amount of work the physical drive heads must do to keep up with the demands of the system. The following versions of the **PAGEFILE-CONFIG** command let you manipulate the page file.

PAGEFILECONFIG /CHANGE /I <*INITIALSIZE*> /M <*MAXSIZE*> /VO <*DRIVELETTER*>:   Changes the existing page file to the specified initial size and maximum size for the specified drive.

PAGEFILECONFIG /CHANGE /S <*COMPUTERNAME*> /U <*USERNAME*> /P <*PASSWORD*> /I <*INITIALSIZE*> /M <*MAXSIZE*> /VO <*DRIVELETTER*>:   Changes the existing page file on the remote computer to the specified initial size and maximum size for the specified drive.

Windows Server 2003 automatically determines the optimal size for the page file. This is done through a complex calculation that considers factors such as RAM, hard disk space, user accounts, and services. The page file begins at a specified initial size, and it automatically grows when the need arises. Once a page file has grown, it does not correspondingly shrink in size when the need for it no longer exists.

Generally, if you intend to manually adjust the size of the page file, as shown in Figure 4-9, you should set the initial size somewhere between 1.5 and 3 times the currently installed RAM. For example, if your server is running with a large amount of RAM (say, over 1 GB), the initial page file size should be around 512 MB with a maximum of 1 to 1.5 GB. The reasoning behind this is simple: A system with less RAM is more likely to rely heavily on its page file (and corresponding size) than a system with more RAM. Don't get the impression, however, that a page file is not necessary for a system with plenty of RAM. As mentioned earlier, Windows Server 2003 prioritizes RAM data and requires the page file for overall system performance and functionality.

```
C:\WINDOWS\system32\cmd.exe

Host Name:              MACHINE
Drive/Volume:           C:
Volume Label:           N/A
Location\File Name:     C:\pagefile.sys
Initial Size:           192 MB
Maximum Size:           384 MB
Current Size:           192 MB
Total Free Space:       926 MB

Host Name:                              MACHINE
Total (All Drives): Minimum Size:       2 MB
Total (All Drives): Recommended Size:   190 MB
Total (All Drives): Currently Allocated: 192 MB

C:\Documents and Settings\Administrator.MACHINE>pagefileconfig /change /i 200 /v
o c:
Microsoft (R) Windows Script Host Version 5.6
Copyright (C) Microsoft Corporation 1996-2001. All rights reserved.

SUCCESS: The initial size for the paging file on 'C:' was changed from
        192 MB to 200 MB.
Restart the computer for these changes to take effect.

C:\Documents and Settings\Administrator.MACHINE>
```

Figure 4-9   Changing the size of the page file

Moving Page Files

If your system has two hard disks, it is a good idea to store the page file on the disk that does not contain the system files. If you have more than two disks installed, you can further enhance performance by splitting a single page file across multiple disks, therefore increasing the page file I/O by splitting the chores across each disk. Various **PAGEFILE** commands let you create, delete, and move the page file.

PAGEFILECONFIG CREATE /I _<INITIALSIZE>_ /M _<MAXSIZE>_ /VO _<DRIVELETTER1>_: /VO _<DRIVELETTER2>_: Configures a page file with the specified initial size and maximum size. At least one volume (/VO) is required. The page file will be split across the number of /VO entries that are specified.

PAGEFILECONFIG CREATE /S _<COMPUTERNAME>_ /U _<USERNAME>_ /P _<PASSWORD>_ /I _<INITIALSIZE>_ /M _<MAXSIZE>_ /VO _<DRIVELETTER1>_: /VO _<DRIVELETTER2>_: Same as the above command, but this version runs on a remote computer.

PAGEFILECONFIG DELETE /VO _<DRIVELETTER1>_: /VO _<DRIVELETTER2>_: Deletes the page file located on one or more disks.

PAGEFILECONFIG DELETE /S _<COMPUTERNAME>_ /U _<USERNAME>_ /P _<PASSWORD>_ /VO _<DRIVELETTER1>_: /VO _<DRIVELETTER2>_: Deletes the page file located on one or more disks on a remote system.

SERVICES

Services are among the few programs that can automatically start when the system boots. Services are programs that stay in the background, monitor the environment for certain events, and once those events occur, they perform specific tasks. There are more than 80 services installed with Windows Server 2003. Many of these services are associated with user logins, authentication, networking, Internet Information Server, and other applications that might be installed, such as Domain Name System and Dynamic Host Control Protocol.

Services are unique in that they start as soon as the server is running, and not when a user logs on, as with other programs that start at system boot, such as the Run entry and the Startup folder. Services do not require a user to login. You may have noticed that you can log on to a domain or access network data on a server when nobody is logged on to that server. This situation results from a handful of services that handle basic system services, such as network access, without requiring an active logon. One of the reasons that services don't require an active logon is that services run with the elevated privileges of a Service account. Many server-specific applications install services to complete specific tasks independent of the current logon, such as antivirus and backup programs.

Finding Information on a Service

The best way to become more acquainted with services is to look at the Windows utility for services. This can be done through the Start menu by clicking All Programs, Administrative Tools, and then Services. You can also access this information by opening the Start menu, right-clicking My Computer, and selecting Manage. It is a good idea to spend some time in the GUI application and learn about the standard services and what they do. This is an advantage of Windows Server 2003 over Windows 2000: MMC (when displayed with the Extended tab) displays the description when the service is highlighted.

Service names come in two parts. The display name is what you see with the MMC snap-in. The actual name of the service is called the keyname, which is what you will use with the **SC** command.

SC QUERY   Displays a list of all of the services on the local machine.

SC GETKEYNAME <*DISPLAYNAME*>   Returns the formal service name for the key *DISPLAYNAME*.

SC QUERY <*KEYNAME*>   Displays the entries associated with the specified *KEYNAME*.

SC ENUMDEPEND <*KEYNAME*>   Displays the services that depend on the *KEYNAME*.

Many services rely on other services to function. Two examples of this relationship can be found in the Workstation and Net Logon services. The Net Logon service handles user logons and authentication, which may be associated with the user lists that are stored on a domain controller or other server. The Workstation service handles client networking to other servers. Since server authentication (security logon) may be coming from a networked computer, the Net Logon service requires that the Workstation service be functioning to provide permission to access the local system. Put simply: If the Workstation service is not running, the Net Logon service will not work either. Inter-service dependencies, such as the one between the Net Logon and Workstation services, always apply—even with systems that do not reside on an active network. Figure 4-10 shows a full accounting of the Workstation service, including its dependencies.

```
C:\WINDOWS\system32\cmd.exe                                          _ 8 x

C:\>sc getkeyname workstation
[SC] GetServiceKeyName SUCCESS
Name = lanmanworkstation

C:\>sc query lanmanworkstation

SERVICE_NAME: lanmanworkstation
        TYPE               : 20   WIN32_SHARE_PROCESS
        STATE              : 4    RUNNING
                                  (STOPPABLE, PAUSABLE, ACCEPTS_SHUTDOWN)
        WIN32_EXIT_CODE    : 0    (0x0)
        SERVICE_EXIT_CODE  : 0    (0x0)
        CHECKPOINT         : 0x0
        WAIT_HINT          : 0x0

C:\>sc enumdepend lanmanworkstation
[SC] EnumDependentServices: entriesread = 5

SERVICE_NAME: RpcLocator
DISPLAY_NAME: Remote Procedure Call (RPC) Locator
        TYPE               : 10   WIN32_OWN_PROCESS
        STATE              : 1    STOPPED
                                  (NOT_STOPPABLE, NOT_PAUSABLE, IGNORES_SHUTDOWN))

        WIN32_EXIT_CODE    : 1077 (0x435)
        SERVICE_EXIT_CODE  : 0    (0x0)
        CHECKPOINT         : 0x0
        WAIT_HINT          : 0x0

SERVICE_NAME: Netlogon
DISPLAY_NAME: Net Logon
        TYPE               : 20   WIN32_SHARE_PROCESS
        STATE              : 1    STOPPED
                                  (NOT_STOPPABLE, NOT_PAUSABLE, IGNORES_SHUTDOWN))

        WIN32_EXIT_CODE    : 1077 (0x435)
        SERVICE_EXIT_CODE  : 0    (0x0)
        CHECKPOINT         : 0x0
        WAIT_HINT          : 0x0

SERVICE_NAME: Messenger
DISPLAY_NAME: Messenger
        TYPE               : 20   WIN32_SHARE_PROCESS
        STATE              : 1    STOPPED
                                  (NOT_STOPPABLE, NOT_PAUSABLE, IGNORES_SHUTDOWN))
```

Figure 4-10   The Workstation service and its dependencies

Starting and Stopping a Service

When troubleshooting a performance problem, you may need to stop a service or change its startup specifications. **SC START**, **SC STOP**, **SC PAUSE**, and **SC CONTINUE** let you make service adjustments.

C:_
Syntax

SC START *<KEYNAME>*   Starts the service.
SC STOP *<KEYNAME>*   Stops the service.
SC PAUSE *<KEYNAME>*   Pauses the service.
SC CONTINUE *<KEYNAME>*   Restores the service after it has been paused.

When a service is stopped, it ceases performing all tasks, shuts itself down, and removes itself from memory. Starting a service reloads a service into memory, and the system begins executing the tasks that it was designed to perform. When a service is paused, it similarly stops performing tasks, but does not remove itself from memory. Troubleshooting service problems may require stopping the service rather than pausing it. Pausing a service is usually done only when service functionality needs to be disabled for a period of time.

SC CONFIG <*SERVICENAME*> START=*BOOT* | *SYSTEM* | *AUTO* | *DEMAND* | *DISABLED* Configures the specified service to start on boot, when the system kernel is loaded, automatically without logon, manually, or not at all.

In Hands-on Project 4-4, you will learn how to use **SC** to determine what services are running on the server and to identify dependencies between services.

Hands-on Project 4-4

To use **SC**:

1. Open a command window.

2. Type **sc query** and press **Enter**. The results will scroll for a few moments while the system lists all of the services that are installed.

3. Type **sc getkeyname "workstation"** and press **Enter**. Notice that the results indicate that the keyname for the Workstation service is "lanmanworkstation". You will need this keyname for all other **SC** commands.

4. Type **sc enumdepend lanmanworkstation** and press **Enter**. Several services are displayed, including Net Logon and the computer browser.

5. Close the command window by typing **exit** and pressing **Enter**.

Services have only two ways of starting: automatically when the server boots and manually when a user starts the service. A service that has been disabled will not start automatically or manually. Once you have disabled a service, you must first enable it, and then set the start type to automatic or manual.

Many device drivers are disguised as services, but device drivers have only two startup types: boot and system. From an administrative perspective, there is little or no difference between startup types. From the systems point of view, a device driver service that is required for boot should start up at boot. Otherwise, the system startup should be sufficient.

Converting a Program into a Service

You may want an application to run without the benefit of an active logon; in other words, you might want it to run automatically with a specified launch setup. You can tailor this setup by converting the application to a service using **SC CREATE**. The application can be any executable file: .bat, .com, or .exe.

SC CREATE <*KEYNAME*> BINPATH= <*EXEFILE*> TYPE= SHARE START= AUTO Instructs the system to start the program (*EXEFILE*) as a service without requiring an active logon.

Figure 4-11 shows an example of using **SC CREATE**.

Figure 4-11 Using **SC CREATE** to create a service

Next, you will learn about the most important and frequently used options for services. There are many additional configuration options for services, both within the GUI MMC and at the command prompt.

Task Manager

Task Manager is a GUI tool that is used to display and control active **processes** and tasks, as well as network connections and CPU and memory utilization. Task Manager is normally accessed by pressing Ctrl+Alt+Del and navigating to the Task Manager button. The Task Manager processes are subprograms that are executed by a parent program. Five tabs reside in the Task Manager window: Applications, Processes, Performance, Networking, and Users. Their purposes are described below:

- **Applications**—Displays current programs that are running.

- **Processes**—Displays all subprograms, services, applications, and tasks that are currently running. All currently running applications are represented as one or more component processes.

- **Performance**—Displays performance graphs for CPU and memory utilization.

- **Networking**—Displays a performance graph for networking bandwidth and utilization, along with a list of all installed LAN adapters.

- **Users**—Displays a list of all locally logged-on, remote-access, terminal-server, and LAN-access clients.

The command prompt equivalents of these items are covered throughout this book. Users and user status is covered in Chapter 6, networking is covered in Chapter 8, and performance monitoring is covered later in this chapter. The Applications and Processes tabs are covered in the next section of this chapter.

The TASKLIST Command

The **TASKLIST** command is used to display all of the current tasks (or processes) on the system. The displayed list includes all system processes, programs, subprograms, and services that are currently running on the server.

TASKLIST   Displays all the current processes on the system.

TASKLIST /S <COMPUTER> /U <USERNAME> /P <PASSWORD>
Displays all processes currently running on the remote system.

TASKLIST /FO *TABLE|LIST|CSV* /NH   Displays all processes in either table, list, or comma-delimited format. Used primarily with redirection to a file.

Figure 4-12 shows an example of using **TASKLIST** to display current processes. The tasks displayed in Figure 4-12 include the filename of the command or executable file, which is called the Image Name. PID is the Process ID number, which increments for every new process or task that is added to the list. Session Name and Session # indicate the process origin: If Console is listed, the task was spawned locally (either from the system or from a logged-on user); if something other than Console is listed, the task was created by a networked user. Mem Usage displays the amount of total RAM and page file memory that is being used by the task, and is particularly valuable in determining tasks and programs that cause system slowdown and performance issues.

```
 C:\WINDOWS\system32\cmd.exe                                    _ □ X

C:\>tasklist

Image Name                    PID Session Name    Session#  Mem Usage
========================= ======= ============== ========= ============
System Idle Process             0 Console                0         16 K
System                          4 Console                0        212 K
smss.exe                      404 Console                0        456 K
csrss.exe                     452 Console                0      3,632 K
winlogon.exe                  476 Console                0      3,396 K
services.exe                  520 Console                0      8,348 K
lsass.exe                     532 Console                0      7,296 K
svchost.exe                   708 Console                0      2,468 K
svchost.exe                   760 Console                0      3,380 K
svchost.exe                   880 Console                0      3,244 K
svchost.exe                   960 Console                0      1,612 K
svchost.exe                   972 Console                0     14,756 K
spoolsv.exe                  1136 Console                0      3,104 K
msdtc.exe                    1188 Console                0      3,660 K
certsrv.exe                  1280 Console                0      8,616 K
dns.exe                      1312 Console                0      3,672 K
llssrv.exe                   1384 Console                0      2,536 K
ntfrs.exe                    1400 Console                0        300 K
svchost.exe                  1508 Console                0      1,032 K
VMwareService.exe            1560 Console                0      1,184 K
dfssvc.exe                   1624 Console                0      3,068 K
explorer.exe                  248 Console                0     11,496 K
VMwareTray.exe                336 Console                0      1,844 K
cmd.exe                       344 Console                0      2,836 K
svchost.exe                   456 Console                0      3,248 K
HelpCtr.exe                  1392 Console                0     16,552 K
HelpSvc.exe                  1644 Console                0      9,276 K
HelpHost.exe                 1904 Console                0      5,528 K
wuauclt.exe                  1988 Console                0      2,924 K
tasklist.exe                 2892 Console                0      2,888 K
wmiprvse.exe                 2928 Console                0      4,180 K
```

Figure 4-12   Using **TASKLIST** to display all running tasks

Within the Task Manager GUI tool, you can easily determine an application's primary running process by right-clicking the application and selecting the Go To Process option from the pop-up menu. The command equivalent of Task Manager, **TASKLIST**, deals strictly with processes, so it is a good idea to become familiar with an application's associated processes before attempting any **TASKLIST** manipulation.

Several command options are available with the **TASKLIST** command. Many of these are beyond the scope of what you may need as an administrator. The following commands can be specifically used to focus on specific problem processes and applications.

TASKLIST /FI "STATUS *EQ | NE RUNNING | NOT RESPONDING | UNKNOWN*" Displays a list of all processes matching the criteria (equal or not equal) of *RUNNING*, *NOT RESPONDING*, or *UNKNOWN*.

TASKLIST /FI "SERVICES *EQ | NE <KEYNAME>*" Displays a list of processes that are associated with a service where SERVICES are either equal (*EQ*) or not equal (*NE*) to the keyname.

TASKLIST /FI "WINDOWTITLE *EQ | NE <WINDOWNAME>*" Displays a list of processes that are associated with a particular application's window where the WINDOWTITLE is either equal (*EQ*) or not equal (*NE*) to the *WINDOWNAME*.

4

For the average daily routine, you will not need to use **TASKLIST** at the command prompt. Task Manager is capable of handling most situations. The capabilities of Task Manager really shine when you find yourself in a crisis, such as when the system won't boot fully and the only application that you can access is Task Manager, using the Ctrl+Alt+Del key combination. In this situation, you can use Task Manager to spawn a command window and then identify and solve the problem using commands covered in this book. Remember that many problems are registry-related; this approach is a way to restore a copied backup of the registry. Many less knowledgeable (yet capable) administrators resort to performing a system rebuild and tape restore from this point.

Stopping a Task Manager Process

From the command prompt, it may be necessary to stop a process so that you can restore order to the system. Stopping a process or application with Task Manager can forestall a complete system hang-up, and the same can be done from the command prompt with greater reliability. Task Manager is a process in and of itself, and if the system is on its way to failure, the command prompt can sometimes shut off an offending process; performing such an operation with Task Manager can be too late if Task Manager has already fallen into the void. Variations on the **TASKKILL** command let you stop processes.

TASKKILL /IM *<PROCESSNAME>* Stops the *PROCESSNAME*.

TASKKILL /S *<COMPUTER>* /U *<USERNAME>* /P *<PASSWORD>* /IM *<PROCESSNAME>* Stops the *PROCESSNAME* on the remote computer.

TASKKILL /FI "STATUS *EQ | NE RUNNING | NOT RESPONDING*" Stops any process that matches the criteria (equal/not equal) of *RUNNING* or *NOT RESPONDING*.

TASKKILL /FI "SERVICES *EQ | NE <KEYNAME>*" Stops all tasks associated with the specified service name.

TASKKILL /FI "WINDOWTITLE *EQ | NE <WINDOWNAME>*" Stops all processes associated with the specified application window (*WINDOWNAME*).

A great example of using the **TASKKILL** command is to close an application. Figure 4–13 shows **TASKKILL** being used to terminate a Notepad window. Notice that spaces are included in the window title. You will practice using **TASKKILL** in Hands–on Project 4–5. In this project, you will learn how to terminate a running task (in this case, notepad.exe) from the command line.

```
C:\WINDOWS\system32\cmd.exe                                          _ □ ×

C:\>taskkill /fi "windowtitle eq Untitled - Notepad"
SUCCESS: Sent termination signal to the process with PID 2980.

C:\>
```

Figure 4-13   Using **TASKKILL**

Hands-on Project 4-5

To use **TASKKILL** to close a Notepad window:

1. Open a command window.

2. Type **notepad.exe** and press **Enter**. This will open a Notepad window. Notice that the window title (on the blue bar at the top of the window) is "Untitled – Notepad."

3. Press and hold **Alt** while pressing **Tab** to shift the focus to the command window.

4. Type **taskkill /fi "windowtitle eq Untitled – Notepad"** and press **Enter**. The Notepad window should disappear.

5. Type **exit** and press **Enter** to close the command window.

DATA BACKUP

Data backup was discussed briefly in Chapter 2, where you learned about using the **COPY** and **XCOPY** commands in a batch program to back up data. The NTBACKUP utility can be used to perform system backups in both GUI and command environments. NTBACKUP is one of the few programs that acts as both a command and a GUI utility. The only difference between the two is that running NTBACKUP at the command prompt or on the Run line launches the GUI tool, while running NTBACKUP with additional command options executes the program from the command line with those command options included. Before you learn the details of NTBACKUP, you should learn some details associated with data and system backup.

Backing up a server should be a relatively easy task to accomplish. After all, all there is to it is copying data from the hard disk to another hard disk or tape, right? Wrong. There are several factors to consider. First and foremost, you need to consider the nature of the data: If a file is currently being used by an application or process, it cannot be thoroughly or reliably copied by another process because parts of the data may change before the file copy has completed. This effectively renders a thorough and complete **XCOPY** command for the entire system useless, due to the risk of not having a complete or thorough copy. This does not mean that **XCOPY** is useless; it just means that the files that are copied must not be used. **XCOPY** is a good command for copying general data, but not for system or OS information, since those files are often in use all the time.

To solve the problem with in-use files, you need to use a backup program such as Backup Exec, NTBACKUP, and others that have the ability to back up system files that are in use. This capability is a big advantage over the features of the **XCOPY** command.

 Most backup programs automatically support open system-file backups. However, many do not support backups for third-party applications that may make up the core of your backup concerns. The best backup applications include support for some e-mail and database applications. Most of the backup programs allow you to install an add-on specific to the application, such as Exchange or SQL Server. These add-ons ensure that your databases are properly backed up despite being open, functioning, and in use nearly all the time.

Backup programs also have the added feature of backing up an object called the **system state**. The system state is a group of files that comprise the system. The system state is unique and irreplaceable OS system data. The system state includes the registry, Active Directory database (with domain controllers), and a few other specialized files. While you can make backups of the registry using the **REG**, **REGEDIT**, or **XCOPY** command on the specific files (such as user.dat or system.dat), other important OS files, such as those containing usernames and passwords, cannot be reliably copied by means other than a backup program.

Another feature of most backup programs involves automation. Specific files are selected by the administrator for backup because it may be necessary to segment data backups for organizational purposes. In other cases, you may opt to back up a specific file or folder rather than the whole system. Files that are selected for backup can be saved as **backup jobs**. A job is a list of files that need to be backed up, not the backup itself. A backup program such as NTBACKUP can back up specific files that are selected immediately, or it can back up selected files whose locations have been saved as a backup job. These options allow for a diverse set of files to be backed up without repeated file selection.

A backup program also can take advantage of a file's archive bit to allow more flexibility in how data is backed up. Recall that when a file is changed or modified, its archive bit (the archive attribute) is turned on. As a result of this archive bit modification, there are five different ways of backing up data with NTBACKUP and other backup programs: **normal backup**, **incremental backup**, **differential backup**, and **daily backup**.

- **Normal backup**—Backs up the selected files and folders, and turns off the archive bit for files that are backed up.

- **Copy backup**—Backs up the selected files and folders, and does not turn off the archive bit for files that are backed up.

- **Incremental backup**—Backs up selected files and folders, but only those that have been created or modified since the last incremental or normal backup. It turns off the archive bit for files that are backed up.

- **Differential backup**—Backs up selected files and folders, but only those that have been created or modified since the last incremental or normal backup. It does not turn off the archive bit.

- **Daily backup**—Backs up selected files and folders, but only those that have been created or modified that day. It backs up files whose archive bit is on, and whose modification date is that day.

Server administrators traditionally run server backups to an external tape device. The reasoning behind this is that tapes can be removed and stored offsite for an added level of protection against a physical disaster such as a fire or flood. In the event that the server is physically unavailable, tape backups can be retrieved from their storage location. The backup is then restored onto different equipment, contributing to **business continuity**. Business continuity is the survival of a business in the face of events that would otherwise put a company out of business. This concept only works with a well-planned and well practiced disaster recovery program.

Another advantage to tape backup lies in the ability to archive data. A business may choose to archive information in hard-copy format, which costs money in paper, boxes, and storage space, or it may accomplish the same goal by storing the source data on tape. Depending on how tapes are rotated and reused, it is possible to archive specific data for years.

Tape Backup Limitations

Tape backups can have some serious setbacks. Tapes can be reused in the same way that an audiotape or videocassette can be rerecorded, but eventually they wear out. Because you are likely to view the contents of a tape only in an emergency, the chance of you knowing that a tape is corrupt is low. Backup programs have safety measures that verify that data has been backed up successfully, but these measures only guarantee that the data has been backed up onto a tape; they do not guarantee that the tape will function when it is most needed, which could be months or years later.

Another detriment of tape backup is its cost. Tape media is expensive. Generally, the greater the capacity of the tape, the more expensive it is. Tape manufacturers understand the demands that may one day be placed on their products, and they continually strive to improve the quality and capacity of their tapes and tape drives. Consequently, manufacturers can require premium prices for their products.

Lastly, any tape activity takes a long time. It can take upward of 45 minutes for a tape drive to determine the contents of a tape, and hours (if not days) to perform a full restore of a fully loaded server.

With all of these complications, many companies are implementing advanced technologies that centralize tape backup by allowing individual servers to back up to a centralized network location. This approach reduces costs of tape devices and tapes, and also eliminates the time factor in many cases, because tape backup operations are usually scheduled in the evening hours, when fewer files are likely to be opened by both the system and users, resulting in a more reliable and stable backup. A tape backup that would normally take all night might be completed in just an hour or two when the data is stored on a networked device because data transfer speeds over the network are much faster than those between the server and any tape drive. Once all servers are backed up in this manner, tape backup from the central location can proceed without an administrator having to worry about a backup interfering with prime-time server usage. The networked storage device can be a hard disk on another system, disk space on a mainframe or minicomputer, or simple network storage device. This type of backup is called **remote storage**. There are several different types of remote storage, and implementation can range from quick and easy to complex and expensive. Since remote storage is not covered from a command perspective outside of the standard NTBACKUP capabilities, it is not covered in this book.

With or without remote storage implemented, tape backup should be specified somewhere within the backup plan to include off-site storage and archiving capabilities. The additional advantages in disaster recovery and business continuity justify a concept called **tape rotation**, a method of labeling and recycling tape media. In tape rotation, several tapes are used and reused in such a way that one or more tapes can be stored off-site for safekeeping. Ultimately, tape rotation can reduce the overall cost of tape media, reduce backup time, and reduce the time necessary to perform a restore by performing partial backups based on changes to the data. When coupled with a specific backup type (such as incremental or differential backups), tape rotation provides the best cost-to-benefit ratio for an organization.

Backup Frequency and Timing

You may be wondering why a normal backup of all system and system state data isn't performed every night. The reason is simple: Tape backups take a long time, and you don't want a tape backup running when users are accessing data on the server. Despite manufacturers' claims that backup programs will safely back up open files, they can only do so with system files, and cannot always do so with normal user data files. Open user files usually will not be successfully backed up. This is why it is best to automate tape backups (using the **AT** command or Task Scheduler) in the evenings.

Because of the inaccuracy of open file backups, your goal as an administrator should be to reduce the possibility of an active user file encountering a backup routine by ensuring that the backup does not continue through the night into regular working hours. Since a normal backup of all files on a server (also called a **full backup**) takes a very long time, there's a good chance that the backup will overlap with normal working hours. Couple that with the likelihood that a full backup will consume more than one tape (a tape **backup pool** is a single backup that spans multiple tapes) and require a person to change tapes when the backup runs (inevitably, tapes need to be changed in the middle of the night) and the associated costs, full backups are usually scheduled weekly or monthly.

 Tape backup devices that can handle more than one tape are available. This can eliminate the need for manual intervention with tape pools. Unfortunately, these devices are expensive. The frugal way of avoiding a midnight trip to the office is to back up to a remote computer's hard disk, and then transfer that data to tape during normal office hours.

Now that you are familiar with some of the issues associated with performing backups, you need to learn how to use the backup utility that comes with Windows Server 2003: NTBACKUP.

Working With NTBACKUP

The best way to handle data backups using NTBACKUP is to first use the GUI version of NTBACKUP to select files, create jobs, designate tape or media pools if necessary, and then automate the process by creating a schedule within NTBACKUP. The utility creates an automated task that is viewable from the Start menu by clicking All Programs, Accessories, System Tools, and Scheduled Tasks, or with the **AT** command. The automated task is performed at a hidden command prompt, and contains all of the options and switches that are appropriate for the configuration you selected. The properties of the item in Scheduled Tasks will display the NTBACKUP command with these options. As shown in Figure 4-14, the entire command, which is listed on the Run line, can be copied and pasted into a batch file or the command prompt. Using the NTBACKUP command in such a way enables you to perform tasks before and after the NTBACKUP process.

As an example, assume that every evening your system downloads data from another server on the Internet. You don't want the backup routine to interfere with this download, so you place both the download process and the NTBACKUP command into a batch program, and then schedule it to occur every night using **AT**. This allows the backup routine to begin only *after* the previous download is complete.

There are several reasons for placing the NTBACKUP command in a batch file. First, NTBACKUP cannot back up nonsystem files that are in use. Many other backup applications also do not have this functionality (although you can add it for a price). An easy way to back up running programs is to use the commands **SC** or **TASKKILL** to stop the running applications and services, run NTBACKUP, and then use **SC** to restart the services once the backup is complete. This start-and-stop approach ensures the best possible backup available. Running **SC** and **TASKKILL** to stop services and programs before running NTBACKUP is the perfect reason to use a batch file, which can then be automated using **AT** or the Scheduled Tasks Windows tool.

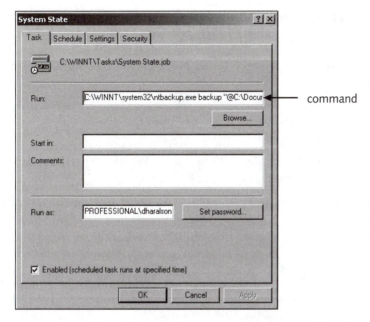

command

Figure 4-14   The NTBACKUP command as generated by the NTBACKUP GUI program

It is possible to use NTBACKUP completely from the command prompt. Unfortunately, the command options and arguments are numerous and complex. It is much easier and faster to use the GUI form of NTBACKUP to select the files for backup, and schedule a backup task that will build the command exactly how you want, rather than risk repeated backup failures by experimenting from scratch at the command prompt.

Hands-on Project 4-6 walks you through the process of building an NTBACKUP command that can be pasted into a batch file or on the command line.

Hands-on Project 4-6

To build an NTBACKUP command using NTBACKUP and Scheduled Tasks:

1. Click the **Start** button ![Start]. Click **Run**. On the Run line, type **ntbackup** and press **Enter**.

2. The first time you run NTBACKUP, a wizard opens. Clear the Always start in wizard mode checkbox, click **Cancel** to close the Wizard, and then click the **Backup** tab.

3. Click the checkbox next to **System State** in the left pane beneath My Computer. A check mark appears in the box.

4. Click **Job** on the menu bar, and then click **Save Selections** from the drop-down menu.

5. In the File name text box, type **systemstate** and click **Save**.

6. Click the **Schedule Jobs** tab.

7. Double-click a date that is sometime in the future. Click **Yes** to start the wizard.

8. The Backup Wizard opens. Click the **Next** button twice. The system state will already be selected.

9. Ensure that the location to save the backup contains C:\ and that the name of the backup is "Systemstate." Click the **Next** button.

10. The Type of Backup window appears, with a default of Normal. Click the **Next** button again, and select the option to **Verify data after backup**. A check mark appears in the box.

11. Click the **Next** button, and select the option to **Replace the existing backups**.

12. Click the **Next** button, and type **state** in the entry labeled Job Name. Click the **Next** button.

13. The system now displays the current username and blank fields in which you can enter the appropriate password. Type the password, press **Tab**, type the password again, and click the **OK** button.

In a business setting, you would probably create a specific user account for the tape backup. This account should be made a member of the Backup Operators group so that it has the appropriate access to back up all of the selected files.

14. Click the **Finish** button, and close NTBACKUP by clicking the **Close** button [X].

15. Click [Start], point to **All Programs**, point to **Accessories**, point to **System Tools**, and then click **Scheduled Tasks**.

16. Double-click the **State** entry.

17. By default, the contents of the Run entry should be highlighted. Press and hold **Ctrl**. Press **c**. Release **Ctrl**.

18. Click the **Cancel** button and close Scheduled Tasks by clicking [X].

19. Open a command window.

20. Right-click the **command window title bar**, point to **Edit**, and point to **Paste**.

21. Your screen should like Figure 4-15. What you see is the command that was generated by NTBACKUP for the Scheduled Task called State. You can use this command on the command line or paste it into a batch file to run it with other commands.

Figure 4-15   Using the NTBACKUP GUI to back up the system state to the C drive with appropriate settings

22. Press **Enter** to start the backup process.

23. Close the command window by typing **exit** and pressing **Enter**.

MONITORING AND OPTIMIZATION

Monitoring and **optimization** are important parts of system administration. Monitoring is a process in which a system is regularly checked for problems in normal system operations. Optimization is the process of fine-tuning a system's performance to its optimal capacity. When a system begins to slow down or behave erratically, programs such as Event Viewer and Performance Monitor are used to determine exactly where the problem is by monitoring specific aspects of the system. Event Viewer is a utility that tracks application and system messages, alerts, and errors. The Performance tool (also known as Performance Monitor) is used to monitor ongoing activities in specific areas of hardware and software performance. Once potential issues are targeted using these tools, you can perform maintenance or preventative tasks to alleviate or eliminate the symptoms that are displayed by Event Viewer and the Performance tool. You learn about Event Viewer in the next section.

Event Viewer

From a command-line perspective, there is little need for monitoring and optimization because most tasks are easily and quickly done by using the GUIs for Event Viewer and Performance Monitor. There are times, however, where you may wish to create an event message, using the **EVENTCREATE** command, that appears as the result of an action that occurs in a batch routine. In such a situation, you could print the log results from the batch routine, and place an entry in Event Viewer for the sake of system tracking.

EVENTCREATE /L APPLICATION /SO <ADMINISTRATOR or APPLICATION NAME> /T ERROR|WARNING|INFORMATION /ID <EVENT ID> /D <DESCRIPTION>   Creates an event in Event Viewer's application log with *ADMINISTRATOR* or *APPLICATION NAME* as the title, an event type of *ERROR, WARNING,* or *INFORMATION*, the specified *EVENT ID*, and the *DESCRIPTION*.

Hands-on Project 4-7 teaches you how to create an event in the application log. In this project, the event will state a simple message. In an administrative situation, you would change this message to be anything appropriate to the situation, such as "FTP transfer complete" or "batch failure."

Hands-on Project 4-7

To use **EVENTCREATE** to generate an event in the application log:

1. Open a command window.

2. Type **eventcreate /l application /so administrator /t information /id 999 /d "hi there"** and press **Enter**. The **/l** switch places the event in the application log. The **/so** switch places the event on behalf of the administrator. The **/t** option generates an information event (as opposed to an error or warning event), and the **/id** switch assigns the event an ID of 999.

3. A success message should appear on the screen. To ensure that the event is in Event Viewer, type **eventvwr** and press **Enter**.

You can also access Event Viewer using the Start menu by clicking All Programs, Administrative Tools, Event Viewer.

4. Click **Application** in the left pane. By default, the application log is displayed. The first event in the right pane should show the event that you just created. Notice that the source shows administrator.

5. Double-click the event whose source is administrator. As shown in Figure 4-16, the event shows a description of "hi there."

6. Close the Event Properties window by clicking its **Close** button $\boxed{\mathbf{X}}$, then close Event Viewer by clicking.

7. Click the command window, type **exit**, and press **Enter** to close it.

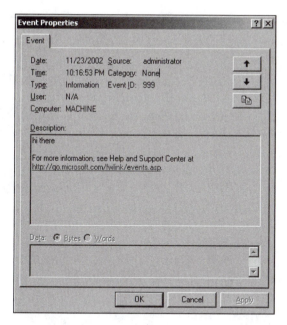

Figure 4-16   An event created using **EVENTCREATE**

ADDITIONAL COMMANDS

Several administrative commands and tools do not fall under any standard categories. These items include the boot.ini file, the **BOOTCFG** command, and the **INUSE** command. These three items are covered in this section.

The Boot.ini File

The boot.ini file is an important system file that the system uses to determine which hard disks, partitions, and operating systems will be booted. If only one OS or boot partition exists on a system, boot.ini automatically defaults to this OS and the boot.ini startup menu does not appear on the monitor. If more than one OS has been installed on the server, the contents of the boot.ini file appear on the screen during the server's boot process, and the user is given the choice of operating systems with which to boot. You can view the boot.ini startup menu by pressing F10 during the boot process.

The BOOTCFG Command

The **BOOTCFG** command is used to modify the boot.ini file. Generally, you can modify boot.ini manually by changing the file's hidden attribute to "not hidden" and using the Edit program to make any necessary changes. The boot.ini file is located in the root of the C drive. Using **BOOTCFG**, you can view and modify boot.ini without having to remove or reset attributes. **BOOTCFG** can also be used to view and modify boot.ini files on remote systems. This is handy for the average network administrator, as there is no GUI equivalent for this particular function. Several options are available for **BOOTCFG**.

BOOTCFG /QUERY   Displays the boot and OS sections of the boot.ini file.

BOOTCFG /QUERY /S <COMPUTER> /U <USERNAME> /P <PASSWORD>   Displays the boot and OS sections of boot.ini on a remote computer.

BOOTCFG /DEFAULT /ID <OPERATING SYSTEM NUMBER>   Sets the default operating system (the line number of the OS shown in **BOOTCFG /QUERY**) with which the system boots.

BOOTCFG /TIMEOUT <SECONDS>   Sets the amount of time the system will wait before automatically selecting the default OS.

The INUSE Command

Files become corrupt—that is an unavoidable truth. Normally, replacing a corrupt file is the simple matter of replacing a bad file with a good file. The same is not so easy for system files or files that are corrupt, but are still in use by the system or an application. Any attempt at copying or deleting these files results in an error message stating that the file is in use by another process. The solution for this particular problem lies with the **INUSE** command. **INUSE** is used to replace a bad file with a good file without disrupting service or functionality. There is no GUI equivalent for the **INUSE** command.

INUSE <REPLACEMENTFILE> <CORRUPTFILE>   Replaces the *CORRUPTFILE* with the *REPLACEMENTFILE*.

CHAPTER SUMMARY

In this chapter, you learned about several ways to administer systems from the command window. You can use several commands to determine and document the physical contents of the server and the software that is installed on it. GUI counterparts of these commands do not allow you to document and list a full inventory of the server's contents.

You can modify several configuration options from the command line, including power configuration, registry modification, running services, tasks, and data backup. These modification commands allow for automation of the functions, and also are valuable in emergency situations when the GUI interface for Windows Server 2003 is unavailable: you can boot to a command prompt during boot. In situations when the main interface locks up, you can open a command window from the Task Manager.

COMMAND SUMMARY

Command	Function
SYSTEMINFO	Displays system information.
DRIVERQUERY	Displays a list of installed drivers.
POWERCFG	Displays, creates, and modifies power schemes.
REG QUERY	Displays registry hives or keys.
REG COPY	Copies a source key to a destination key within the registry.
REG EXPORT	Exports a registry hive or key to a file.
REG IMPORT	Imports a registry hive or key from a file.
REG SAVE	Saves a registry hive or key to a file.
REG RESTORE	Restores a registry hive or key from a file that was saved on the same system.
PAGEFILECONFIG QUERY	Displays the current page file configuration.
PAGEFILECONFIG CHANGE	Modifies existing page files.
PAGEFILECONFIG CREATE	Creates a page file.
PAGEFILECONFIG DELETE	Deletes a page file.
SC QUERY	Displays a list of services.
SC GETKEYNAME	Retrieves the keyname for a service based on its display name.
SC ENUMDEPEND	Displays upstream and downstream dependent services.
SC START	Starts a service.
SC STOP	Stops a service and unloads it from memory.
SC PAUSE	Pauses a service.
SC CONTINUE	Un-pauses a service.
SC CONFIG	Configures an existing service.
SC CREATE	Creates a service from a program.
TASKLIST	Displays a list of all running tasks and processes.
TASKKILL	Terminates a task or process.
NTBACKUP	Data backup utility and command.
EVENTCREATE	Creates an event within Event Viewer.
BOOTCFG	Views and changes configuration for the boot.ini file.
INUSE	Allows a system file to be replaced without interfering with normal system operations.

4

Key Terms

ACPI (advanced computer and power interface) — A power standard that allows the OS to fully control the power status (on or off) of hardware components on the system.

APM (advanced power management) — A power standard that allows the BIOS to shut off or suspend power to certain components.

backup job — A list of files and folders that is referenced during a backup procedure.

backup pool — A backup that consumes more than one tape.

battery backup — An external battery power source.

business continuity — The idea or concept of being able to continue business when disaster strikes, specifically when the office building has been destroyed or is otherwise uninhabitable.

copy backup — A backup type that copies selected files and does not reset the archive bit.

CPU throttling — A procedure that allows the CPU to change its performance based on power needs.

daily backup — A backup type that copies selected files and folders that have been created or modified that day.

differential backup — A backup type that copies selected files and folders that have been created or modified since the last incremental or normal backup. Does not reset the archive bit.

driver — A software program that allows the OS or application to communicate and interface with a specific hardware component.

full backup — A normal backup of all files on a server.

hibernation — A process in which current settings are stored on the hard disk, and the system is powered off. When the system is powered on again, the current settings are restored.

hive — The primary or first-level section (key) in the registry. There are five hives in the registry: HKLM, HKCC, HKU, HKCR, and HKCU.

incremental backup — A backup type that copies selected files and folders that have been created or modified since the last incremental or normal backup. Resets the archive bit.

key — An entry within a hive that contains subentries.

monitoring — Checking a system for problems in normal operations.

normal backup — A backup type that copies selected files and resets the archive bit.

optimization — The process of fine-tuning a system's performance to its optimal capacity.

page file — A file that is used by the OS as supplemental RAM.

power scheme — A power configuration that is based on a specific system state.

process — One or more tasks that are performed on behalf of an application.

registry — A system database that contains system and application settings.

registry key — Any entry that exists within a hive that contains subentries or subkeys.

registry value — A registry entry that contains specific information.

remote storage — Backup data storage that is remote to the server.

service — An automated background program that performs actions based on specific events.

subkey — A key that exists as part of another key.

swap file — A page file.

system state — A backup term specifically referring to system-specific files, including the registry and Active Directory database.

tape rotation — A method of recycling and reusing backup tapes for archive and cost-saving purposes.

uninterruptible power supply (UPS) — Another term for a battery backup.

4

REVIEW QUESTIONS

1. What command is used to determine system information?

   a. **POWERCFG**

   b. **DRIVERQUERY**

   c. **SYSTEMINFO**

   d. **PAGEFILECONFIG**

2. Which commands can be used to determine the OS version? (Choose all that apply.)

   a. **SYSTEMINFO**

   b. **DIR**

   c. **OSID**

   d. **VER**

3. ACPI is older than APM.

   a. True

   b. False

4. A UPS's backup power is based on which of the following factors? (Choose all that apply.)

   a. the length of time the power is out

   b. the capacity of the battery

   c. the number of devices that are attached to the UPS

   d. the amount of time it takes to shut off the system

5. Assume that you need to change the power configuration of your server to cause the CPU to consume less power when the system is running on battery power. Which CPU throttling method should you use?

   a. Adaptive

   b. Constant

   c. Degrade

   d. None of the above

6. How can you automatically run a batch program that copies certain files every time the server boots?

   a. Place a link to the batch file into the Startup folder.

   b. Place an entry in the RUN key for the batch file.

   c. Place an entry in the RUNONCE key for the batch file.

   d. Create a service from the batch file.

7. How can you automatically run a batch program that copies specific files every time a certain person logs in to the system?

   a. Place a link to the batch file into the Startup folder.

   b. Place an entry in the RUN key for the batch file.

   c. Run the batch file as part of a login script.

   d. Create a service from the batch file.

8. Which of the following registry hives contains user-specific data? (Choose all that apply.)

   a. HKLM

   b. HKU

   c. HKCU

   d. HKCC

9. Which of the following registry hives contains all hardware profile information? (Select all that apply.)

   a. HKLM

   b. HKCC

   c. HKU

   d. HKCU

10. Which registry data type contains string, pointer, or path data?

    a. REG_EXPAND_SZ

    b. REG_SZ

    c. REG_DWORD

    d. REG_BINARY

11. What is the syntax for determining the contents of the HKEY_LOCAL_MACHINE hive on a remote computer with the name SUPERMAN?

   a. **REG QUERY \\SUPERMAN\HKLM /S**

   b. **REG QUERY \\SUPERMAN\HKEY_LOCAL_MACHINE /S**

   c. **REG QUERY \\SUPERMAN\HKLM**

   d. **REG QUERY \\SUPERMAN\HKEY_LOCAL_MACHINE**

12. What process or command lets you determine the current page file configuration on a remote server with the name SUPERMAN?

   a. My Computer/Properties

   b. **PAGEFILECONFIG QUERY**

   c. **PAGEFILECONFIG \\SUPERMAN**

   d. **PAGEFILECONFIG QUERY /S SUPERMAN**

13. Which command is used to display information about the Workstation service?

   a. **SC QUERY**

   b. **SC QUERY WORKSTATION**

   c. **SC QUERY GETKEYNAME WORKSTATION**

   d. **SC QUERY LANMANWORKSTATION**

14. Which command is used to display all currently running services on the system?

   a. **SC QUERY**

   b. **TASKLIST**

   c. **TASKLIST /FI "SERVICES NE 0"**

   d. **SC QUERY SERVICES**

15. Which command(s) can be used to perform a tape backup? (Choose all that apply.)

   a. NTBACKUP

   b. **XCOPY**

   c. **COPY**

   d. **MOVE**

16. Which backup type consumes the most tapes over the course of a week?

   a. normal backup

   b. copy backup

   c. incremental backup

   d. differential backup

17. What can you do to ensure that a nightly backup process does not run into regular business hours?

    a. Implement a tape rotation scheme.

    b. Ensure that the data does not consume more than one tape.

    c. Implement a remote storage method.

    d. Back up to a hard disk.

18. Which utility is used to view error messages that are produced by the system?

    a. Monitoring

    b. Event Viewer

    c. Task Manager

    d. Performance Monitor

19. The system file system.dll has become corrupt. You need to replace it with the one on the installation disk. Which of the following is the best restore option?

    a. Use the **COPY** command to copy the file.

    b. Use the **INUSE** command to replace the copied file.

    c. Boot to a floppy and use the **COPY** command to copy the file.

    d. Boot to the installation CD and choose the Repair option.

20. You recently installed Windows Me on a partition of your computer. How can you configure that OS to boot automatically when the system starts?

    a. Use **FDISK** to configure the partition as the active partition.

    b. Change the attributes of the boot.ini file with the **EDIT** command.

    c. Use the **BOOTCFG /DEFAULT** command to change the boot system.

    d. Edit the boot.ini file using the **EDLIN** command.

DISCOVERY EXERCISES

1. Research use of the **PRNPORT** command to create, delete, and list TCP/IP printer ports.

2. Determine the contents of the Run entry in the registry.

3. Registry entries can be generated using .reg files, which are text files that insert or replace existing registry entries with its contents when it is double-clicked or run from the command or Run line. There are several .reg files located in Windows Server 2003. Use one as a template for creating a new entry in the RUN key to open notepad.exe when the system starts or a user logs on. (*Hint*: Investigate the .reg file documentation on the Microsoft Web site.)

4. Use the .reg file created in Discovery Exercise 3, and use a batch routine to implement the notepad.exe entry for every system on the network. There are several different ways to do this. Which methods rely on the networked systems to process the necessary commands? Which methods work only once and not for new computers or users on the network? Which methods rely on server processing more than on the client?

5. How would you automate the process of stopping a service, running a backup, and starting a service without the benefit of an active login?

6. Do some research on the available UPS devices on the market. You will find that many of them come with applications that can help you with your power management and disaster recovery/prevention program. In particular, some batteries can be configured with a serial port that connects to the server. When configured properly, the serial port can order the safe shutdown of the server either when the main power grid is off for a specified amount of time or when an administrator remotely gives the instruction to do so. This is not only convenient, but it is a benefit for the system administrator who is handling administration tasks remotely, as this person no longer needs to come into the office to shut down the server when the power is out and restart it again once the power returns.

5

DISK AND DATA MANAGEMENT

After reading this chapter and completing the exercises, you will be able to:

♦ Diagnose and fix physical disk problems and disk fragmentation issues

♦ Understand the differences between basic disks and dynamic disks

♦ Create partitions and volumes

♦ Create extended, spanned, mirrored, striped, and RAID 5 volumes

♦ Format disks

♦ Implement disk quotas

♦ Compress and decompress files

♦ Encrypt files

This chapter covers a wide range of disk and data management functions that you can perform on the command line. Although most of these commands have GUI counterparts, many do not. Most of these commands give you insight into how a system handles data and a view of the hard disks on which the data is stored.

MANAGING DISKS AND DRIVES

Most disk management functions occur from the Disk Management section of the Computer Management GUI within Windows. Disk management involves the formatting and structure of disks and drives. The health and structure of the data that resides on these drives are easily handled by functions within Windows Explorer or My Computer, such as Scandisk or Defrag. Scandisk is a GUI utility that scans the data on a drive and locates and fixes corruptions. Defrag, another GUI utility, restructures the data on a drive in a way that speeds up the process of reading and writing data. Most of these disk and data management tasks can be completed in the command window, as well.

Disk Condition and Viability

In general, data can be stored either in memory (RAM) or on a disk. RAM is volatile, meaning that the data stored on it is lost when the server is powered down. Consequently, users need a nonvolatile means of storing data; disks provide such stability.

Several different types of nonvolatile memory, or **disks**, are available to store data. Among these storage media are floppy disks, Zip disks, CD-ROMs, and hard disks. Hard disks, in particular, are considered permanent data media, because they are not portable or removable and their long-term usage often requires certain maintenance tasks to ensure their continued and successful functionality. Several functions dealing with the health and status of hard disks can be performed or automated within batch files to protect against potential problems that disks may encounter. Disk problems are described in the next sections.

Physical Disk Problems

A hard disk usually does not have errors when it is brand new. Hard disks are magnetic media, and the drive heads manipulate the magnetic bits in order to create patterns of data. Over time these magnetic bits can demagnetize, causing problems on a drive. You can use the **CHKDSK** command to scan a specific volume, partition, or assigned drive for physical errors on the disk. **CHKDSK** will scan the entire drive for magnetic and surface viability. In other words, **CHKDSK** finds problems with the surfaces of the drive, and appropriately flags those problems so that in the future, the system doesn't attempt to read or write data on those places.

CHKDSK <DRIVELETTER>:   Scans *DRIVELETTER* for physical disk problems.

CHKDSK <DRIVELETTER>: /F   Scans *DRIVELETTER* for and fixes physical disk problems.

CHKDSK <DRIVELETTER>: /V   Scans *DRIVELETTER* for physical disk problems and reports file-by-file progress to the screen.

CHKDSK <DRIVELETTER>: /R   Scans DRIVELETTER for physical disk errors and recovers readable data.

CHKDSK <DRIVELETTER>: /X   Powers off the drive, and then scans *DRIVELETTER* for physical disk errors.

When a system has been turned off without a proper shutdown procedure, the system sometimes automatically runs **CHKDSK** before even booting the OS. There are several reasons for this. First, when a power loss occurs, any write processes are immediately abandoned, and the drive heads retract as the drive spins down. These abandoned write processes can lead to file corruption, including system files necessary for startup. This potential for corruption is the primary reason it's not a good idea to power off a server without properly shutting it down first. In situations where **CHKDSK** does not run automatically, you should run **CHKDSK** to try to fix any problems caused by the abnormal shutdown as soon as the system powers on. **CHKDSK** cannot solve or scan any system file corruptions, but it can detect problems with other files on the disk.

The reason that **CHKDSK** should run before the rest of the operating system loads is related to the previous corruption issue. **CHKDSK** requires exclusive usage while it is attempting to fix errors. In other words, **CHKDSK** requires that no other programs or processes access a file that it is checking. Even when a server doesn't appear to be doing anything, you can be sure that it is. Windows Server 2003 is always advertising services, updating system files, and performing other server-related tasks. These system files are not normally available to programs such as **CHKDSK**, because of the exclusive usage requirement: They're already being used by the system. Therefore, **CHKDSK** can be executed manually, but to ensure that the system files are scanned and fixed, it must be run before the OS loads—and before these server tasks begin running—to attempt to fix damaged system files before they are loaded and become unavailable.

You can use **CHKDSK /F** to fix problems manually on a hard disk. If the drive contains system files, you will only be able to run **CHKDSK** without options. Running **CHKDSK /F** on a system drive prompts you to schedule **CHKDSK** to run at the next boot cycle.

CHKNTFS is a control program that is used to help automate **CHKDSK**. You can use it to schedule **CHKDSK** to run on the next reboot, but it can also determine which disks to scan and can set a countdown timer for canceling the process.

CHKNTFS <DRIVELETTER>:   Displays the status of whether CHKDSK runs automatically when the system boots.

CHKNTFS <DRIVELETTER>: /T:<SECONDS>   When the system reboots, the system displays a countdown to cancel the CHKDSK operation before it begins. /T sets the countdown timer.

CHKNTFS /X <DRIVELETTER>:   Excludes the specified DRIVELETTER from the CHKDSK process.

CHKNTFS <DRIVELETTER>: /C   Sets DRIVELETTER to be scanned when the system reboots.

The easiest way to schedule **CHKDSK** to run automatically at reboot is to run **CHKDSK /F** at the command prompt. Hands-on Project 5-1 teaches you how to do this. Then, you will use **CHKNTFS** to change the countdown timer, and test your results.

Hands-on Project 5-1

To schedule **CHKDSK** at reboot:

1. Open a command window.

2. At the prompt, type **chkdsk /f c:**. You will be prompted to schedule **CHKDSK** for the next system restart. Press **Y** and press **Enter**.

3. Type **chkntfs /t:45** and press **Enter**. This sets the countdown timer for the **CHKDSK** at reboot to 45 seconds.

4. Click the **Start** button ![Start], and then click the **Shut Down** button ⏻. In the Comment section of the Shut Down Windows dialog box, type **chkntfs test** and click **OK**. When the server restarts, the system begins to run **CHKDSK** before the system files are loaded. Your screen should look like Figure 5-1. Your system message may be different, depending on the OS you are running.

```
Checking file system on C:
The type of the file system is NTFS.
Volume label is Simple.

One of your disks needs to be checked for consistency. You
may cancel the disk check, but it is strongly recommended
that you continue.
Windows will now check the disk.

CHKDSK is verifying files (stage 1 of 3)...
File verification completed.
CHKDSK is verifying indexes (stage 2 of 3)...
1 percent completed.
```

Figure 5-1   CHKDSK at boot

Fragmentation

Fragmentation is the splitting and distribution of a file in multiple locations on a disk. Fragmentation is caused by limitations in the space available for a file to increase in size. To understand fragmentation, imagine that a brand new hard disk has a file called Corpy written onto it. Corpy is the first file on the disk and subsequently occupies the outermost area of the disk. Another file, called Machine, is also written onto the disk, right next to Corpy. In the interest of efficiency, the system places these two files as close as possible to the outer edge of the disk, as shown in the second part of Figure 5-2. The Corpy file is subsequently edited, and the file size increases. Since it is bound on one side by the outer edge of the disk and the other side by the Machine file, there is no room for Corpy to increase, so the portion of the file that does not fit in the space originally occupied by Corpy is physically placed as nearby as possible. In this case, it would be on the other side of the Machine file, as shown in the third part of Figure 5-2.

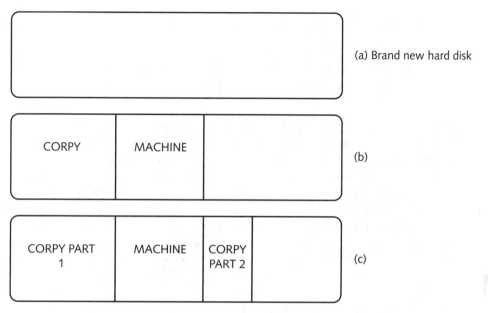

Figure 5-2   How data is written

When fragmentation occurs over time and with many files, problems can occur because the drive heads need to travel farther to read any single complete file. Server processing can slow to a crawl and launch into **disk thrash** when this happens on a large scale. Disk thrash occurs when files on a hard disk become so fragmented and scattered that the drive heads have to work overtime to gather all of the pieces of any given file, even when the system is apparently at rest. You can tell when disk thrash happens because you can hear the hard disk working constantly for at least 2 seconds.

In this case, the resolution to the disk thrash situation would be to temporarily store the Corpy and Machine files somewhere else, and then write them to the disk contiguously, so that the Corpy file is no longer split into two pieces. The process of consolidating data and files is called defragmentation. Defragmentation is accomplished by using the **DEFRAG** command.

Hard disk heads move back and forth along the surface of the platters; therefore, the closer a file is to the beginning of the disk, the less the drive heads need to move to work with that file. System files are usually placed at the outer regions of the disk because their frequent usage justifies the valuable real estate in time saved.

DEFRAG <DRIVELETTER>: /A   Runs an analysis on *DRIVELETTER* and determines whether the drive needs to be defragmented.

DEFRAG <DRIVELETTER>: /A /V   Same as above, but displays detailed status as it runs the analysis.

Syntax **DEFRAG <*DRIVELETTER*>: /V**   Defragments the drive and displays detailed results.

DEFRAG <*DRIVELETTER*>: /F   Defragments the drive only when free disk space is approaching 15 percent of total disk capacity.

Notice that the **DEFRAG <DRIVELETTER>: /F** option defragments the drive when disk space usage is approaching 15 percent. This option is available for two reasons. First, **DEFRAG** requires at least 15 percent of disk capacity. If less capacity is available, you will need to move data off the drive to run the program. The second reason this option is available is a cautionary measure—you need to be sure that you run **DEFRAG** on occasion. When placed at the end of a login script, in the registry, or in the Startup folder, **DEFRAG** allows you to defragment the drive when free disk space is low, but not every time the system starts, which ensures that the drive is automatically defragmented but is not defragmented when it isn't necessary to do so. **DEFRAG** is a time-consuming program that shouldn't be run every day, but should be executed regularly to enhance performance.

 DEFRAG frees up some disk space when it is run—an added bonus.

Restoring Data from Bad Disk Areas

When **CHKDSK** encounters a problem with the disk, data frequently occupies the space where the problem occurred. **CHKDSK** will mark the problem spot on a drive by flagging it as unusable in the same way that a road sign would mark a pothole in the road. Unfortunately, any data that was stuck in the bad spot must be removed and repaired. **CHKDSK** digs out the data and converts it to a file with a .chk extension.

When a piece of data falls into a bad spot and is recovered, you can't be certain that it has been *fully* recovered, because it is possible that an entire file was caught in that same bad spot. As a result, it is possible to have an entire file become corrupted because of one small portion that was originally written to a bad spot on the drive. **CHKDSK** does not piece together the files that it recovers from these bad disk locations. With older versions of programs, it was sometimes possible to manually recover the data in .chk files, but nowadays that is becoming more and more difficult because the raw data contained in .chk files is rarely in a readable text format. Third-party utilities, such as Norton Utilities, do a better job of recovering data in .chk files, but only when they are the tools originally used to restore the data from the bad spot.

The use of **CHKDSK** and repair utilities does not guarantee that the data removed from the bad disk area can be recovered and used. Quite often, this data is a small part of a larger file, which then becomes corrupted by association. The **RECOVER** command can piece together the original file in a way that sometimes fills in the missing pieces, allowing the file to work properly.

RECOVER <*DRIVELETTER*>:\<*PATH*>\<*FILENAME*> Attempts to recover a file (*FILENAME*) that has been corrupted by a physical disk problem (or other corruption).

Use the **RECOVER** command after running **CHKDSK** when you notice that a particular file has become corrupted or unreadable. This usually only works with data that is not in a system file. You can determine when a corruption has occurred when you attempt to open a file and it is unreadable or unusable by the application. Corrupted system files that are in use are more difficult to recover than files not in use, because in-use files are locked by the system. In these situations, you will need to use the **INUSE** command, described in Chapter 4.

Disks and Drives

A **drive** is all or part of a disk that has been assigned a drive letter and has been formatted. For example, the primary drive of most computers is designated as the C drive. Additional drives can be formatted on the same hard disk as the C drive and assigned names such as D drive, F drive, and so on.

A physical hard disk is automatically recognized by the system as a hard disk, but it is unusable until it has been formatted, or prepared to use data, as you will learn later in this chapter. Once a disk is ready, it can then be considered a drive. The **DISKPART** command can be used to determine the current status of a disk, as well as its availability for regular usage. **DISKPART** is a powerful command, because it can perform nearly every task that is available in the Windows Disk Management tool (which you access by right-clicking My Computer, selecting Manage, and then clicking Disk Manager). Most of this chapter focuses on the specific tasks that **DISKPART** can perform while introducing you to the capabilities of Windows Server 2003's disk administration capabilities.

Several commands operate by creating separate command environments for themselves. These commands usually require too many options and arguments to be feasible for execution on a single command line, so a special environment is created for that command in which only specific commands can be executed. **DISKPART** is one of these commands, and its environment is complete with options and subentries that assist in navigation and task completion. Generally, you can launch this specialized environment by simply typing the command name in a command window. The prompt changes and you can type ? or /? to view a list of further options for the command. Figure 5-3 shows a listing of options for **DISKPART**. These syntax versions are described below.

As described above, executing a **DISKPART** command requires two steps. First, you type **DISKPART** on the command line and press Enter, which launches the special **DISKPART** environment. Then, you type the various commands available for **DISKPART**, which are listed below.

```
C:\WINDOWS\system32\cmd.exe - diskpart                              _□×

DISKPART> /?

Microsoft DiskPart version 5.2.3663
ADD       - Add a mirror to a simple volume.
ACTIVE    - Marks the current basic partition as an active boot partition.
ASSIGN    - Assign a drive letter or mount point to the selected volume.
BREAK     - Break a mirror set.
CLEAN     - Clear the configuration information, or all information, off the
            disk.
CONVERT   - Converts between different disk formats.
CREATE    - Create a volume or partition.
DELETE    - Delete an object.
DETAIL    - Provide details about an object.
EXIT      - Exit DiskPart
EXTEND    - Extend a volume.
HELP      - Prints a list of commands.
IMPORT    - Imports a disk group.
INACTIVE  - Marks the current basic partition as an inactive partition.
LIST      - Prints out a list of objects.
ONLINE    - Online a disk that is currently marked as offline.
REM       - Does nothing. Used to comment scripts.
REMOVE    - Remove a drive letter or mount point assignment.
REPAIR    - Repair a RAID-5 volume.
RESCAN    - Rescan the computer looking for disks and volumes.
RETAIN    - Place a retainer partition under a simple volume.
SELECT    - Move the focus to an object.

DISKPART> list disk

  Disk ###  Status      Size     Free     Dyn  Gpt

  Disk 0    Online      4095 MB  1994 MB   *
  Disk 1    Online      1023 MB   923 MB   *
  Disk 2    Online      1023 MB   923 MB   *
  Disk M0   Missing        0 B      0 B    *

DISKPART> _
```

Figure 5-3   `DISKPART` commands

LIST DISK   Lists the physical disks installed on a server. The currently selected disk appears with an asterisk (*) to the left of the entry.

SELECT DISK <DISKNUMBER>   Selects the disk on which subsequent commands will be performed. *DISKNUMBER* is obtained from the LIST DISK command.

CLEAN   Removes all data and information from a drive.

DELETE DISK   Deletes the selected disk. Applies to an entire disk—not a drive, partition, or volume.

DETAIL DISK   Displays disk information, including type, ID, and volume information.

ONLINE   Attempts to mount and bring the selected disk online.

RESCAN   Scans the systems disk configuration to reflect any changes.

Hands-on Project 5-2 teaches you how to use **DISKPART** to list all of the disks on a server and also to display detailed information about the current drive.

Hands-on Project 5-2

To determine the current disk configuration:

1. Open a command window.

2. Type **diskpart** and press **Enter**. The system will initialize the **DISKPART** environment and the prompt will change to read "DISKPART>." At this point, only **DISKPART** commands will function in the window.

3. To view the disks that are installed on the system, type **list disk** and press **Enter**. `DISKPART` displays a list of the installed disks, along with a disk number, its status, size, and the amount of free space available on that disk.

4. To view more detailed information about a disk, you must first select that disk. Type **select disk 0** and press **Enter**. This should select the first disk in the list that was displayed by the `LIST DISK` command.

5. Type **detail disk** and press **Enter**. This displays detailed information about disk 0, including its volumes/partitions, assigned drive letters, format type, size, and status.

6. Type **exit** and press **Enter** to leave the `DISKPART` environment. You should now be in the standard command prompt.

7. Type **exit** and press **Enter** to close the command window.

Next, you will learn about basic disks and partitions. Then, dynamic disks and volumes are introduced. Familiarity with these concepts is required to understand the overall disk management scheme within Windows Server 2003.

Basic Disks and Partitions

A **basic disk** is a Microsoft term for a disk that has been divided into partitions and formatted with either the FAT, FAT32, or NTFS file system, which are all described later in this chapter. Basic disks contain **partitions**. A partition is part or all of a disk that has been divided for eventual use, formatting, and drive letter assignment. Basic disks have two types of partitions: **primary** and **extended**. A primary partition can be used to boot an OS, and there can be no more than four primary partitions per disk—three primary partitions and one extended partition. Primary partitions are formatted and assigned drive letters. An extended partition is not bootable, there can be only one per disk, and it cannot be formatted. Instead, an extended partition can host **logical drives**, which in turn can be formatted and assigned drive letters. Logical drives exist only on extended partitions. The number of logical drives that can exist on a system is limited only by the letters of the alphabet that can be assigned to them, excluding the drive letters that already exist on the system.

Figure 5-4 shows the Windows Disk Management MMC view of a basic disk with a primary partition, extended partition, and two logical drives. What you see in the Disk Management GUI can all be accomplished from the command line using `DISKPART` commands. The following `DISKPART` commands are specific to partition management. Using these commands, you can create, delete, and modify disk partitions, as well as mark a primary partition as active so that the system will boot to that partition.

Figure 5-4   The Disk Management console

To access Disk Management, right-click My Computer, select Manage, and then select Disk Management from the left pane.

CREATE PARTITION PRIMARY SIZE=<*PARTITIONSIZE*>   Creates a primary partition of *PARTITIONSIZE* with the size in megabytes.

CREATE PARTITION EXTENDED SIZE=<*PARTITIONSIZE*>   Creates an extended partition of *PARTITIONSIZE* with the size in megabytes.

CREATE PARTITION LOGICAL SIZE=<*PARTITIONSIZE*>   Creates a logical drive based on an existing extended partition.

LIST PARTITION   Lists all partitions on the specified disk.

SELECT PARTITION <*PARTITIONNUMBER*>   Selects a partition for subsequent partition-related commands. *PARTITIONNUMBER* comes from the LIST PARTITION command.

DELETE PARTITION   Deletes the specified partition.

DETAIL PARTITION   Lists details on the specified partition, including volume number, drive letter, drive label, file system format, type, size, and status.

ACTIVE   Mounts the specified partition.

INACTIVE   Dismounts the specified partition.

ASSIGN LETTER=<*DRIVELETTER*>   Assigns a drive letter to the specified partition.

Hands-on Project 5-3 teaches you how to create partitions. You must first select a disk before attempting to create partitions. Not doing so could result in creating partitions on the wrong disk. Similarly, you must select a partition before any commands are performed on it, such as **DELETE PARTITION**, **DETAIL PARTITION**, **ACTIVE**, or **INACTIVE**. In this project, you will learn how to create primary and extended partitions as well as logical drives. To complete this project, you will need a blank hard disk. You can modify the partition sizes to suit your particular situation.

DISKPART is a very powerful command and, if used inappropriately, can completely eliminate the operating system. Use care to ensure that you are working on a test or laboratory server, that the system has at least two hard disks installed, and that one of the disks is blank.

Hands-on Project 5-3

To create and delete partitions:

1. Open a command window.

2. At the command prompt, type **diskpart** and press **Enter** to launch the **DISKPART** command.

3. Type **list disk** and press **Enter**. This displays a list of all hard disks that are installed on the server.

4. Notice that each disk is labeled with a number, beginning with zero (0). Assuming that your blank disk is disk 1, you need to select this disk to perform further tasks on it. Type **select disk 1** and press **Enter**.

5. Type **detail disk** and press **Enter** to confirm that there are no partitions.

6. To create a primary partition whose size is 200 MB, type **create partition primary size=200** and press **Enter**.

7. Type **create partition logical size=20** and press **Enter**. This command generates an error, because logical disks must be created from extended partitions.

8. To create an extended partition to house a logical partition, type **create partition extended size=200** and press **Enter**.

9. Now, create a logical partition by typing **create partition logical size=20** and pressing **Enter**.

10. Repeat Step 9 until the system is unable to create any more logical partitions due to the extended partition size limitation.

11. Type **detail disk** and press **Enter** to view information about the disk. Notice that the partitions are all shown as VOLUME NNN. These are partitions and not actual volumes. Because **DISKPART** is used in overall disk administration, the column label indicates volumes even when partitions are present.

12. Type **list partition** and press **Enter** to display a list of the partitions on the selected disk. The partition numbers listed here are what you will use to select a partition. Notice that the selected partition is the last one that was created.

13. Type **select partition 5** and press **Enter**. This selects the fifth partition so that you can delete it.

14. Delete the partition by typing **delete partition** and pressing **Enter**.

15. Type **list partition** and press **Enter** to display the partition list again. Notice that the original partition 5 was deleted, and all subsequent partitions were renumbered. Also notice that the offset column displays the location of the partition relative to the beginning of the disk.

16. Type **select partition 5** and press **Enter** to select the newly numbered partition.

5

17. To assign a drive letter to partition 5, type **assign letter=t** and press **Enter**.

18. Type **detail partition** and press **Enter**. The partition information for partition 5 appears. Notice that the partition now has a drive letter assigned to it.

19. Use Disk Management (right-click **My Computer**, click **Manage**, and then click **Disk Management**) to see what you have accomplished. Your screen should look like Figure 5-5. Using **DISKPART** commands to create partitions is much faster and provides more control than performing the same tasks using Disk Management.

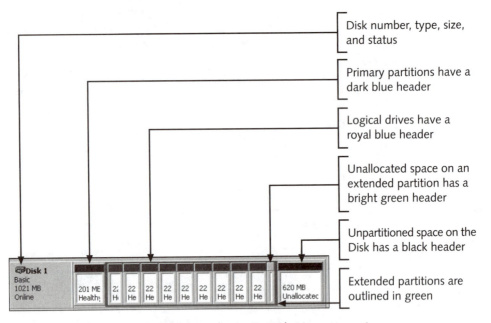

Figure 5-5 The partitioned drive as shown in Disk Management

20. Return to the command prompt. Type **exit** and press **Enter** to leave the **DISKPART** environment. Type **exit** and press **Enter** again to close the command window.

 Providing the disk was blank, you may run **DISKPART** again, then run **SELECT DISK 1**, and then run **CLEAN** to remove all partitions and return the disk to the same state that it was at the beginning of the project.

Dynamic Disks and Volumes

Dynamic disks are different from basic disks in that dynamic disks offer more features. Dynamic disks can perform nearly any disk management task without requiring a system reboot, which you need to do when there are many partition changes on a basic disk.

Dynamic disks contain **volumes**, which are simply the dynamic disk equivalent of partitions. All volumes can be labeled, formatted, and have drive letters assigned to them. One of the additional features that is available with dynamic disks and volumes is the ability to have an unlabeled volume in use in the same way as a drive is used, without a drive letter. You will learn about this feature later in this chapter.

Earlier you learned about the **DISKPART** commands that can be used with basic disks. The following **DISKPART** commands are used to manage dynamic disks and correlate directly to their basic disk counterparts. The **VOLUME** included in each syntax version indicates that the command is being used on a dynamic disk and not a basic disk.

5

LIST VOLUME   Lists volumes on the specified disk.

SELECT VOLUME <VOLUMENUMBER>   Selects the *VOLUMENUMBER* that was listed in the LIST VOLUME command.

DELETE VOLUME   Deletes the selected volume.

DETAIL VOLUME   Displays statistics for the selected volume, including number, drive letter, label, format type, volume type, and size.

ASSIGN LETTER=<DRIVELETTER>   Assigns a drive letter to the selected volume.

Converting Basic and Dynamic Disks

Prior to the introduction of Windows 2000, all hard disks were basic disks (although the term "basic disk" was not used to describe the disks, since such distinction was not necessary). However, Windows 2000 introduced dynamic disks. Windows Server 2003 also initializes new disks as basic disks. To enable some of the advanced features of dynamic disks, particularly the volume types described later in this chapter, you need to convert existing basic disks to dynamic disks. Fortunately, the following two commands will perform these conversions without losing data that already exists on the disk.

Windows 2000, XP, and Server 2003 are the only operating systems that support both basic and dynamic disks. All other Windows platforms only support basic disks. Any disk that hosts an older version of Windows, or any other OS, should never be converted to a dynamic disk.

CONVERT BASIC   Converts the selected dynamic disk to a basic disk. This will only succeed if the disk has no volumes or data on it.

CONVERT DYNAMIC   Converts the selected basic disk to a dynamic disk. At least 1 MB of free space must be available on the selected disk.

While any basic disk can be converted to a dynamic disk at any time, the reverse is not true. A dynamic disk can only be converted to a basic disk when it is completely devoid of volumes and data. However, because servers should use dynamic disks for the volume features and capabilities described in the next section, this limitation should never be a problem.

Volume Types

Dynamic disks can have one of several types of volumes. The different dynamic disk volume types include simple, extended, spanned, mirrored, striped, and RAID 5. The various dynamic disk volume types give you some idea of the full range of features available with dynamic disks.

 Many of these volume types exist for basic disks on systems running Windows NT, and are maintained as basic disks when upgrading the OS to Windows 2000 or Server 2003. However, dynamic disk features will not be available to such disks.

Simple Volumes   A **simple volume** is the default volume type for dynamic disks and is the basic disk equivalent of a primary partition. There is no equivalent for an extended partition. You can create a simple volume using the following command.

 DISKPART | CREATE VOLUME SIMPLE SIZE=<*VOLUMESIZE*>   Creates a simple volume of *VOLUMESIZE* in megabytes.

Extended Volumes   When a simple volume is created, and at some time later requires more disk space, it is converted to an extended volume. An **extended volume** is a simple volume that has outgrown its size limitations and becomes extended to another unallocated section of the same disk. You can create an extended volume using the following **DISKPART** command.

 EXTEND DISK=<*DISKNUMBER*> SIZE=<*SIZE*>   Extends a selected volume *DISKNUMBER* to add the *SIZE* in megabytes. Unallocated free space must exist on the disk.

Hands-on Project 5-4 teaches you how to extend a simple volume, changing it to an extended volume.

 ## Hands-on Project 5-4

To extend a basic volume:

1. Open a command window. At the command prompt, type **diskpart** and press **Enter** to initialize the **DISKPART** environment.

2. Type **list disk** and press **Enter** to display all disks on the system.

3. Type **select disk 1** and press **Enter** to select the blank disk. If the blank disk on your server is not disk 1, replace the 1 in this step with the appropriate disk number shown in the **LIST DISK** results.

4. Assuming disk 1 is still a basic disk, you will need to convert it to a dynamic disk before proceeding. Type **convert dynamic** and press **Enter**.

5. Now that the disk is dynamic, you need to create a simple volume that can later be extended. Type **create volume simple size=100** and press **Enter**.

6. Type **detail disk** and press **Enter** to list the new volume.

7. To extend the volume, it must first be selected. If the volume number is 1, type **select volume 1** and press **Enter**. If the volume number is not 1, replace 1 with the number that appeared after you completed Step 6.

8. To display information about this volume, type **detail volume** and press **Enter**. The results should be similar to Figure 5-6.

Figure 5-6 DETAIL DISK and DETAIL VOLUME results

9. Type **extend disk=1 size=100** and press **Enter** to extend the selected volume on disk 1 by an extra 100 megabytes.

10. Type **exit** and press **Enter** to exit the **DISKPART** environment. Type **exit** again and press **Enter** to close the command window.

Spanned Volumes Similar to an extended volume, **spanned volume** is a primary volume that has consumed the entire disk and needs to be extended to another disk. The only difference between turning a simple disk into an extended disk and turning an extended disk into a spanned disk is changing the **DISKPART EXTEND DISK** command to reflect a separate disk number. You could accomplish this using the steps outlined in Hands-on Project 5-4, but instead of using the command EXTEND DISK=1 SIZE=100, as you did in Step 9 of the project, you would need to change the command to read:

```
EXTEND DISK=2 SIZE=100
```

Running the **DISKPART DETAIL DISK** command on an extended disk shows a volume type of spanned, and the **DISKPART DETAIL VOLUME** command lists both disks.

Figure 5-7 shows the results of running the **DETAIL VOLUME** command (within **DISKPART**) on an extended disk.

Figure 5-7 An extended disk results in a spanned volume

Mirrored Volumes A **mirrored volume** is a simple volume that has been copied and is constantly updated to another disk. **Mirroring** is one of the several types of **disk fault tolerance** supported by Windows Server 2003. (Another term for mirroring is **RAID 1**.) **Disk fault tolerance (DFT)** is a technological concept that allows a server to sustain a drive failure without resulting in overall system failure. The server can do this by maintaining copies of the data in different ways that allow the data to be recompiled and retrieved when a given drive fails. Mirroring is a simple example of DFT because it copies all of the data on one volume to another volume on a separate disk. Additional fault tolerance can be added by attaching each disk to a separate disk controller, which ensures that a single controller failure can be sustained in addition to a disk failure. This dual-controller technology is called **duplexing**. Mirroring and duplexing enable the system to function if one of the two disks (the simple volume or its mirrored duplicate) or controllers fails. The system does so by simply reverting to the healthy mirrored partner. The following commands let you mirror a simple volume.

ADD DISK=<*DISKNUMBER*> Adds a mirror to the specified volume, where *DISKNUMBER* is the number of the second disk.

BREAK DISK=<*DISKNUMBER*> Breaks a mirrored volume into two separate simple volumes. *DISKNUMBER* is the disk that does not belong to the selected volume.

BREAK DISK=<*DISKNUMBER*> /NOKEEP Same as the previous command, but deletes the currently selected simple volume and retains only one half of the mirror.

If one disk in a mirrored volume fails, you can easily restore a mirror using **DISKPART** commands: Use the **BREAK DISK** command to break the mirror, replace the disk, and then use **ADD DISK** again to re-establish the mirror.

As you work with the more advanced aspects of **DISKPART**, it is a good idea to get into the habit of checking which disks and volumes are selected by using the **LIST DISK**, **DETAIL**

DISK, **LIST VOLUME**, and **DETAIL VOLUME** versions of the **DISKPART** command. This can prevent you from creating a mirror from the wrong partition. Hands-on Project 5-5 gives you practice with these commands as you learn how to create a mirrored disk.

This project assumes that you have a server with two extra disks installed for a total of three disks, with the further assumption that disk 1 is the second disk on the system and disk 2 is the third. The two extra disks (disk 1 and 2) should be blank and unformatted.

> You might not be able to use a system with enough hard disks to complete this exercise. If this is the case, you should review the project anyway, because it contains information that is essential for creating a mirrored volume.

Hands-on Project 5-5

To create a mirrored disk:

1. Open a command window. At the command prompt, type **diskpart** and press **Enter**.

2. Type **select disk 1** to select the first blank disk and press **Enter**.

3. Type **clean** and press **Enter** to clear any old partitions or volumes from disk 1.

4. Since the configuration information has been cleared from disk 1, you need to reconvert it to a dynamic disk. Type **convert dynamic** and press **Enter** to convert the disk to a dynamic disk.

5. Type **detail disk** and press **Enter**. The results should indicate that there are no volumes on the disk.

6. Repeat Steps 2 through 5 for disk 2.

7. Now, you need to create a simple volume, but before doing so, type **select disk 1** and press **Enter**.

8. To create the new volume, type **create volume simple size=100** and press **Enter**.

9. Type **detail disk** and press **Enter** to make sure that the volume has been created. Make a note of the volume number.

10. Creating a mirrored volume requires that the volume that will be mirrored is selected. Type **select volume** followed by the volume number from Step 9, then press **Enter**.

11. Type **add disk=2** and press **Enter** to create the mirror (2 is the number of the disk that will contain the mirrored volume). In most business settings, volume 1 would probably have data on it prior to mirroring. When the mirror is configured, all data on disk 1 must be synchronized to disk 2. The more data that exists on disk 1, the longer it takes for the **ADD DISK** process to complete.

12. Type **list volume** and press **Enter**. Notice that the volume type is now Mirror, as shown in Figure 5-8.

Figure 5-8 LIST VOLUME results

13. Type **assign letter=m** and press **Enter**.

14. Type **exit** and press **Enter** to leave the **DISKPART** environment.

15. Type **format m: /fs:ntfs** and press **Enter**, which applies NTFS formatting to the drive. Press **Y** and press **Enter** to proceed with the format.

16. When prompted for the label, type **mirror** and press **Enter**.

17. Look at the Disk Management window. Your screen should look like Figure 5-9, which shows the same mirrored volume M on both disks 1 and 2.

Figure 5-9 Disk management displays the mirrored volume

Striped Volumes In striping, a simple volume's data has been evenly distributed across three or more disks. Such volumes are known as striped volumes or RAID 0 volumes. Striping is used primarily to increase drive efficiency, since having more than one drive performing a single task will complete the task faster.

One significant issue with striping is that it is not fault tolerant. If one disk in the striped volume fails, then all of the data for the whole volume, including data on healthy disks, is rendered useless. Striping is generally used in situations requiring super-fast disk speeds because disk input and output is faster for striping than for a single disk. The following **DISKPART** command is used to create striped disks.

CREATE VOLUME STRIPE SIZE=<SPACEPERDISK> DISK= <DISKNUMBER1>, <DISKNUMBER2>, <DISKNUMBER3> Creates a stripe set whose width is *SPACEPERDISK* across each of the listed disks.

Calculating the available disk space for a striped volume is relatively easy: You need to determine the amount of space required, and divide that by the number of disks you want to stripe the data across. The resulting number should be entered as *SPACEPERDISK*. Note that creating a striped volume must occur before data is placed on the volume. Unlike mirroring, striping must be configured before data is placed on the disk. Next, learn about RAID 5 volumes, which also require configuration prior to data placement.

RAID 5 Volumes RAID 5, or **striping with parity**, is a fault-tolerant volume that stripes data across three or more drives and adds parity. Parity is a small amount of extra data that allows the system to reconstruct missing data in the event that a single drive fails. The general concept of how a RAID 5 volume's stripes are configured is shown in Figure 5-10. The parity in RAID 5 allows a system to sustain a single drive failure. The system uses the parity information to calculate the missing data on the fly until a replacement disk can be installed.

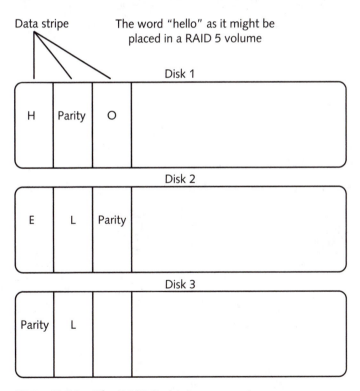

Figure 5-10 The RAID 5 striping concept

In the system administration industry, mirroring, striping, and RAID 5 all are assumed to exist on volumes in which the volume consumes the entire disk. As you learned in Hands-on Project 5-5, this isn't always the case when creating a mirror. Administrators prefer to have these types of volumes consume the entire disk because any failures will constitute the loss of any remaining data on the drive.

Figure 5-11 shows a fully configured Windows Server 2003 disk configuration within Disk Management, including simple, extended, spanned, striped, mirrored, and RAID 5 volumes. Several of the Hands-on Projects in this chapter configure these volumes individually.

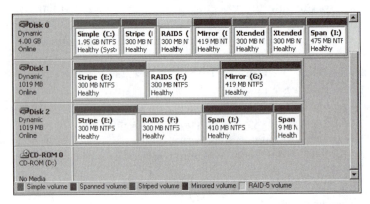

Figure 5-11   Disk Management displays a server configured with mirrored, extended, spanned, striped, and RAID 5 volumes

The following **DISKPART** commands let you create RAID 5 volumes.

**CREATE VOLUME RAID SIZE=<SPACEPERDISK>
DISK=<DISKNUMBER1>, <DISKNUMBER2>, <DISKNUMBER3>**   Creates a RAID 5 volume whose width is *SPACEPERDISK* across the specified disks.

REPAIR DISK=<REPLACEDDISKNUMBER>   Repairs a failed and replaced RAID disk.

A RAID volume appears in **LIST DISK** and **DETAIL DISK** command output as RAID 5. Calculating the space per disk for a RAID volume is a bit trickier than for a striped volume. First, you must figure out how much disk space you will need. Then, figure out how many drives you have to work with. Subtract one from the number of drives you have to allow room for the parity data, and divide the amount of disk space you need by this number (number of drives - 1). The result is the space per disk.

If one of the disks in the RAID 5 volume fails, running the **DISKPART** command **LIST DISK** displays the failed disk with a "missing" status. A disk status of "missing" appears any time a spanned, striped, mirrored, or RAID 5 volume is broken. Additionally, a **DISKPART DETAIL DISK** command run on one of the remaining drives will display a

"Failed RD" status for the RAID volume. You can quickly track down the missing or failed disk by running **DETAIL DISK** on all of the applicable disks in the RAID 5 array.

Fixing a failed RAID 5 volume is relatively easy: You just need to physically remove the failed disk, replace it with a new one, and then run the **DISKPART** command **CONVERT DYNAMIC** on the disk, run **SELECT DISK** for the RAID volume, and then run **REPAIR DISK**. A subsequent **LIST VOLUME** command executed after this process shows a status of "Healthy."

Creating a RAID 5 volume is an involved process, as you will see in Hands-on Project 5-6. First, this project assumes that you have three disks installed on the server, with some unallocated space on each of them. It is best to start with blank disks, but that is not always possible. As long as you have three disks, with at least 100 MB of unallocated space available on disk 0, you will be able to complete the project. Otherwise, you may need to modify the steps to suit your environment. Ask your instructor for assistance in modifying the project, if necessary.

Hands-on Project 5-6

To create a RAID 5 volume, simulate a drive failure, and repair the RAID volume:

1. Open a command window.

2. Type **diskpart** and press **Enter**.

3. To make sure that disks 0, 1, and 2 have at least 100 megabytes of unallocated space, type **list disk** and press **Enter**.

 You might need to convert all disks to dynamic using the **Convert Dynamic** command.

4. Type **create volume raid size=100 disk=0,1,2** and press **Enter**. This creates a RAID volume with 200 MB of available space, with 100 MB of that for parity information.

5. Type **list volume** and press **Enter** and notice that the new volume is RAID 5.

6. The new volume should be volume 1. Type **select volume 1** and press **Enter**.

7. Type **detail volume** and press **Enter** to display the disks that volume 1 occupies.

8. Simulate a failure on disk 1 by typing **select disk 1** and pressing **Enter**.

9. Type **clean** and press **Enter** to remove the configuration information from the disk. The system now assumes that the disk has failed.

10. Type **list disk** and press **Enter**. Notice that there is a new disk, M0, on the list. This is a bogus entry: Once you ran the **CLEAN** command on disk 1, the disk had no configuration information stating that it was ever part of a RAID

array. The system, however, retained this information; even though the server cannot find the target disk, it still maintains an entry for it.

11. Type **list volume** and press **Enter**. Volume 1 now displays as "Failed Rd."

12. The **CLEAN** command also simulated installing a new disk, and new disks, by nature, are not dynamic, so the new disk needs to be selected and converted. Type **select disk 1** and press **Enter**.

13. Convert the disk to dynamic by typing **CONVERT DYNAMIC** and pressing **Enter**.

14. Since volume 1 is the RAID 5 volume that failed, you must now select that volume to repair it. Type **select volume 1** and press **Enter**.

15. Type **repair disk=1** and press **Enter** to repair the RAID volume.

16. Type **detail volume** and press **Enter** to check that the former disk 1 is intact again. If data was actually on the RAID volume to begin with, it would take some time for the system to replace the missing data during the **REPAIR DISK** process.

17. Type **list volume** and press **Enter**. Volume 1 should now show a status of "Healthy." Your results should be similar to Figure 5-12, which shows the results of Steps 14 through 17.

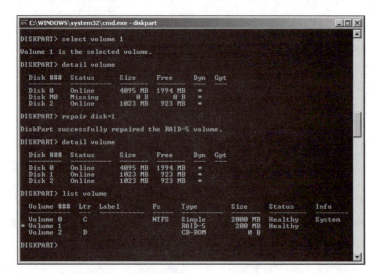

Figure 5-12   Repairing a failed RAID 5 volume

The **boot drive**, which is the disk and drive that contain the operating system, can reside on mirrored volumes, but not on extended, spanned, striped, or RAID 5 volumes. The reason for this is simple: Because the disks are configured by the operating system, these volume types do not exist until after the OS is loaded, which means that the boot drive must be readable without the OS. Mirrored volumes maintain one exact copy of the volume on a separate disk, meaning that each disk is readable without the OS being present.

Moving Dynamic Disks

One further advantage of dynamic disks is that you can move them from server to server without reconfiguring them. While it has always been possible to move a single disk from one system to another, what makes dynamic disks unique is that you can move a mirrored, striped, or RAID 5 volume to another computer without losing data or reconfiguring the volume. The **IMPORT** command lets you move dynamic disks.

IMPORT   Integrates another system's volume into the current server without reconfiguring the volume or losing the data.

If you need to move a RAID, striped, or mirrored volume from one server to another, the procedure is as follows:

1. Physically remove the disks from the source server.
2. Install the disks onto the destination server.
3. Run the **DISKPART** command **LIST DISK**. The new disks will be listed with a status of "Foreign."
4. Use the **SELECT** command to select one of the recently installed disks, preferably the primary, or lead, disk if you are importing a striped or RAID 5 volume.
5. Run the **DISKPART** command **IMPORT**.

That's it! The volume will be integrated into the current configuration.

Formatting FAT, FAT32, and NTFS

Once you have created partitions or volumes and assigned drive letters using **DISKPART**, you need to format these elements so that data can be placed on them. A **format** is a way of preparing a disk to receive and use data. There are three format types used in Windows systems today: FAT, FAT32, and NTFS. **FAT (File Allocation Table)** provides a minimal level of disk security and protection, but it does do the job. **FAT32**, described below, provides more features than FAT. **NTFS (New Technology File System)** provides an even higher level of security and protection, and therefore is more appropriate for the heavy-duty usage that a server regularly performs.

You can safely assume that NTFS is the preferred format for Windows Server 2003. The primary reason for this is that NTFS offers additional security. The secondary reason is that dynamic disks must be formatted NTFS. Outside of a server application, NTFS is more flexible than FAT or FAT32 (discussed in the next paragraph) because it supports additional information and properties for the files it stores. These properties include additional security in the form of user permissions, which allow and deny specific user account access to selected files. NTFS also is generally a more stable, less corruptible, and less fragmented disk format than either FAT or FAT32.

Although NTFS is the most ubiquitous disk format, you should know a bit about FAT and FAT32 as well. FAT, the format that was originally introduced with DOS, supports eight-character filenames with three-character extensions. It does not have as much security as NTFS, but it does run faster because it doesn't maintain as much overhead. There are limitations on FAT disk, partition, and drive sizes (2 GB), which can become annoying very quickly.

FAT32 is an intermediate format that was created by Microsoft to resolve some of the glaring issues with FAT, namely the restrictions on filename and drive size. FAT32 was introduced with the second release of Windows 95.

FORMAT is the command you use to manage the process of formatting disks. Before you embark on any format process, you should be aware that the **FORMAT** command completely erases any data that exists on a drive. Recall that a disk is a physical disk, but a drive has a letter attached to it. Formatting a drive erases all of the data on the *drive*, but it won't touch any data that exists on other volumes on the same *disk*.

FORMAT <*DRIVELETTER*>: /FS:*NTFS*|*FAT*|*FAT32* /V:<*LABEL*>   Formats *DRIVELETTER* as NTFS, FAT, or FAT32 and adds a label of *LABEL* to the drive.

An example of formatting the J drive for NTFS is as follows:

```
FORMAT J: /FS:NTFS
```

All disks have disk labels. A disk label is a name for the disk that can be applied at any time. If a disk label is not applied by the user during the format process, the system will create a default label with the name NEW VOLUME, even if the disk is not dynamic. Do not assume that a label that includes the word "volume" means that the drive necessarily is a volume or dynamic disk.

LABEL <*DRIVELETTER*>: <*LABEL*>   Adds a *LABEL* to the *DRIVELETTER*.

When Microsoft introduced NTFS, administrators needed a way for FAT-formatted drives to be recognized by NTFS without requiring formatting of the FAT drive (subsequently losing all the data they contained). The **CONVERT** command accomplishes this. **CONVERT** offers a few new features available only with Windows Server 2003: **/CVTAREA**, **/NOSECURITY**, and **/X**, which are described below.

CONVERT <*DRIVELETTER*>: /FS:NTFS   Converts the format to NTFS for *DRIVELETTER*.

CONVERT <*DRIVELETTER*>: /FS:NTFS /CVTAREA:<*FILENAME*>
Converts *DRIVERLETTER*'s format to NTFS and places the new system files at the beginning of the drive.

CONVERT <*DRIVELETTER*>: /FS:NTFS /NOSECURITY   Converts *DRIVELETTER*'s format to NTFS and nullifies all security settings.

CONVERT <*DRIVELETTER*>: /FS:NTFS /X   Dismounts the drive prior to converting the format to NTFS.

Recall that the more often a file is accessed, the closer it ideally should be placed to the beginning of the drive in order to decrease the amount of time it takes to read that file. When a drive is formatted, certain system files are placed at the beginning of the drive for exactly this reason. Unfortunately, in versions of Windows prior to Windows Server 2003, the **CONVERT** command has been unable to place the new NTFS system files at the beginning of the disk because that space was already occupied by other files that needed to be retained. The result was that a converted NTFS drive would perform a bit slower than a formatted counterpart. Windows Server 2003 fixed that with the **/CVTAREA:<*FILENAME*>** option of the **CONVERT** command.

The **/CVTAREA:<*FILENAME*>** option works by moving existing files to a temporary location while the underlying part of the drive is reformatted (this idea is illustrated in Figure 5-13), replacing the files, and then moving on and doing the same thing for the next section of drive. Instead of moving the FAT system files, the command deletes them, and subsequent regular files are placed in the location of old system files. With the **/CVTAREA** option, **CONVERT** looks out for the listed filename and places it in the beginning of the disk as a placeholder instead of placing regular files in the same location. When the drive is converted to NTFS, **CONVERT** deletes the **/CVTAREA** file and replaces it with the newly completed system files.

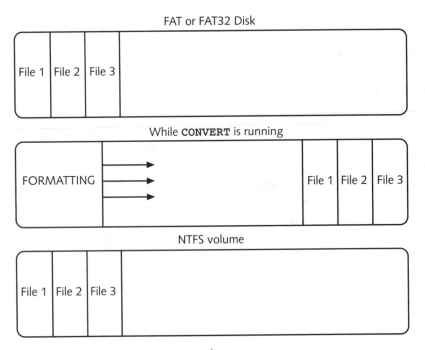

Figure 5-13   How **/CVTAREA** works

FAT and FAT32 formats have some security capabilities associated with network shares. Network shares are folders that have been configured for network access. Network shares contain permissions that are lists of user accounts that show the level of access the account has been granted for the share. Permissions are essential for restricting specific users to only the file access (whether they may read, change, or perform other functions on files) that they require. The permissions associated with shares residing on FAT or FAT32 partitions are different from share permissions found on a Windows Server 2003 system running on an NTFS-formatted disk. The **CONVERT** command attempts to map the FAT share permissions to the appropriate equivalent for Windows Server 2003. Unfortunately, sometimes the result is not really what you were anticipating. Instead of finding and fixing all of the potential translation results, you can use the **/NOSECURITY** option, in which **CONVERT** changes all share permissions to "Full control."

Finally, **CONVERT** can dismount the drive prior to starting the conversion process. Dismounting the drive means that the hard disk is not available for standard local or network functions. In this manner, **CONVERT** is similar to **CHKDSK** in that it requires exclusive access to the drive, but **CONVERT** is not available as an automated boot process. Instead, you can use the **CONVERT <DRIVELETTER>: /FS:NTFS /X** command to dismount the drive and automatically ensure that no process or application is using the drive while the **CONVERT** process takes place.

The **FSUTIL** Command

FSUTIL is a command that is used to perform just about every other disk administration task that you might want to perform using the Disk Management MMC. It has many additional features that are not available anywhere else. These tasks range from dismounting a drive, which removes it from standard access, to displaying NTFS statistics on a given drive.

FSUTIL requires that all options be typed on the same line. Typing **FSUTIL** on the command line displays all of the second-level options for the **FSUTIL** command. One of these second-level options is **FSINFO**. Typing **FSUTIL FSINFO** displays all of the third-level options. One of these third-level options is **VOLUMEINFO**. Typing **FSUTIL FSINFO VOLUMEINFO** displays the fourth-level options, and so on. Fortunately, you can use **DOSKEY**, which you learned about in Chapter 1, to avoid having to type these commands over and over again.

FSUTIL DIRTY   Allows the disk to be marked as corrupt, even if it is not.

FSUTIL FSINFO VOLUMEINFO <*DRIVELETTER*>:   Displays volume information, including support capabilities.

FSUTIL FSINFO NTFSINFO <*DRIVELETTER*>:   Displays NTFS statistics on the drive.

FSUTIL VOLUME DISMOUNT <*DRIVELETTER*>:   Dismounts the volume.

FSUTIL VOLUME DISKFREE <*DRIVELETTER*>:   Displays the amount of free disk space on the drive.

Disk Quotas

NTFS can restrict and monitor network user disk space usage. Specific limitations on disk space are known as **disk quotas**. Disk quotas are imposed on a volume-by-volume basis for all users who access the volume. Using disk quotas, an administrator can place a limit on how much space a user can consume, and you can either warn them that they are exceeding their limit, or simply prohibit them from exceeding their limit. What's more, you can generate event log entries for any offenders. Disk quotas are managed on the command line using the **FSUTIL** command.

Be aware that if you configure a quota after a user has exceeded that quota, the newly applied quota will not function for that user.

FSUTIL QUOTA QUERY <*DRIVELETTER*>:   Displays quota status and configuration for *DRIVELETTER*.

FSUTIL QUOTA TRACK <*DRIVELETTER*>:   Enables and tracks disk usage on *DRIVELETTER*.

FSUTIL QUOTA DISABLE <*DRIVELETTER*>:   Disables tracking and enforcement of disk quotas on *DRIVELETTER*.

FSUTIL QUOTA ENFORCE <*DRIVELETTER*>:   Restricts users from adding more disk space once the quota has been met. If quotas are not enforced, violations generate a warning to the user and also generate an event log entry.

FSUTIL QUOTA VIOLATIONS <*DRIVELETTER*>:   Displays a report of all quota violations.

FSUTIL QUOTA MODIFY <*DRIVELETTER*>: <*WARNINGSPACE*> <*MAXDISKSPACE*> <*USERNAME* or *GROUPNAME*>   Sets the quota limit for the volume. Users would be warned about reaching their limit and would be alerted to the maximum disk space limit.

Hands-on Project 5-7 lets you practice with disk quotas. This project involves three major steps: assigning a drive letter for the RAID 5 volume that you created in Hands-on Project 5-6, formatting it, and then enabling disk quotas. You will manage all of these tasks from the command window.

Hands-on Project 5-7

To format and enable disk quotas:

Assign a Drive Letter

1. The first thing to do is use **DISKPART** to assign a drive letter for the RAID volume. Type **diskpart** and press **Enter**.

2. Type **list volume** and press **Enter**. Note the volume number for the RAID 5 volume.

3. Type **select volume 1** and press **Enter**. (Note: If your volume number is not 1, use the same volume number as you used in Hands-on Project 5-6.)

4. To assign the drive letter, type **assign letter=r** and press **Enter**.

5. Type **list volume** and press **Enter** again to ensure that the correct drive letter has been assigned.

6. Type **exit** and press **Enter** to exit the **DISKPART** environment.

Format the Drive

7. There are ways of performing tasks without having a drive letter; however, they usually require additional data entry, so it is much easier to assign a drive

letter first. Before disk quotas can be enabled, the volume must be NTFS, so type **format r: /fs:ntfs** and press **Enter**.

8. When you are prompted, proceed with the format, and label the volume by typing **label r: raid5quota** and pressing **Enter**.

Enable Quotas

9. Type **fsutil quota query r:** and press **Enter**. This command reports that quotas are not enabled on the R drive.

10. Type **fsutil quota modify r: 25 30 everyone** and press **Enter**. This will configure quotas for the local group Everyone so that all users will receive a warning when they reach 25 MB in space, and they will have an absolute limit of 30 MB per user.

11. Type **fsutil quota enforce r:** and press **Enter** to turn on disk quotas with the specifications listed in Step 10.

12. Disk quotas are enabled for drive R; to log quota violations, type **fsutil quota track r:** and press **Enter**.

13. Type **fsutil quota query r:** and press **Enter**. The command should show that the user group Everyone is being monitored.

14. Type **fsutil quota modify r: 40 50 administrator** and press **Enter**. This will configure an additional quota entry for the administrator, specifying that the account will receive a warning at 40 MB with a limit at 50 MB.

15. Type **fsutil quota query r:** and press **Enter** to display the quota information on the screen. See Figure 5-14.

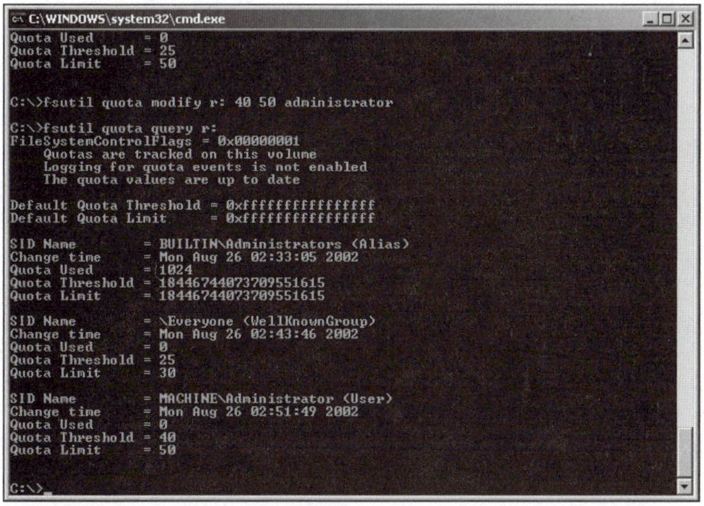

Figure 5-14   Viewing the current quota settings

COMPRESSION AND ENCRYPTION

Compression is a technology that enables a system to remove redundant space from a file, resulting in a smaller file size. Compression can be applied to any type of data, including an entire hard disk. **Encryption** uses algorithms to diffuse and scramble data in such a manner that it is not readable without being unencrypted. While compression and encryption technologies have been available for many years, it was only with the introduction of Windows 2000 that both technologies became integrated options on NTFS volumes.

Compression

There are essentially two different types of compression: **file compression** and **drive compression**. File compression is applied to one or more specific files, while drive compression is applied to an entire disk. While file compression requires manual intervention to compress file data, drive compression automatically compresses any data that resides on the drive. File compression requires decompression prior to usage, while disk compression decompresses data automatically when necessary. File compression has existed for decades in the form of PKZip, WinZip, and other programs that provide easy file compression and transport. Drive compression has also existed for many years. Doublespace and similar programs compress hard disks for usage. File compression within the Microsoft world hasn't changed very much for several years. Disk compression, however, has.

Compressing Files

The **COMPACT** command is used to compress files and folders residing on an NTFS-formatted partition or volume into a smaller disk size. Unlike compression programs such as WinZip, **COMPACT** does not compress multiple files into a new archive file.

COMPACT /C <FILENAME>	Compresses *FILENAME*.
COMPACT /U <FILENAME>	Extracts *FILENAME*.
COMPACT /C /S:<DIRECTORY> Compresses *DIRECTORY* and all its subdirectories.	
COMPACT /U /S:<DIRECTORY> Extracts *DIRECTORY* and all its subdirectories.	
COMPACT /U /F <FILENAME> Forces extraction of *FILENAME* and is used to fully decompress a partially decompressed file.	

Decompressing Distribution Files

Since the launch of Windows 95, the majority of Microsoft programs use compressed .cab files for program installation. These .cab files are **distribution files**. Outside of program installation, distribution files are rarely used, but they can become valuable if you can extract a particular file from the distribution file in order to replace a corrupted file that is already installed on the system. These .cab files contain several compressed files, and are used by installer programs to install an application. You can install the OS from those .cab files by running whatever setup or install executable file resides in that directory.

The **EXPAND** command can be used to extract one or more files from a .cab file. This is most often used when one or more installed files have become corrupt, and the program or OS will not function correctly. In certain situations, you might want to extract a specific file from a .cab, rather than reinstall the program or OS. Such occasions include when you have corrupted DLLs, system files, or even device drivers.

EXPAND can also be used to extract individual files whose extension ends with an underscore. These types of files are also called distribution files.

EXPAND -R <DISTRIBUTION FILE> <DESTINATION FILE>   Extracts *DISTRIBUTION FILE* and renames it *DESTINATION FILE*.

EXPAND -D <CABFILE>   Displays a list of the .cab file contents.

EXPAND <CABFILE> <DESTINATIONDIR>   Extracts the contents of the .cab file into the *DESTINATIONDIR* directory. If *DESTINATIONDIR* is empty, files will be extracted and placed in the current directory.

EXPAND <CABFILE> -F:<FILENAME> <DESTINATION FILE or DIRECTORY>   Extracts *FILENAME* from the .cab file and places it into *DESTINATION FILE* or *DIRECTORY*.

Disk Compression

You can perform disk compression on any NTFS volume on a server. Again, the difference between file compression and disk compression is that file compression requires that each file be manually compressed, while disk compression provides for the automatic compression of all data that resides on the disk. To view a file-compressed file, you must extract, or decompress, the file first. Disk-compressed files are automatically extracted by the system as the data is viewed. The convenience of automatic compression and decompression comes at the price of CPU and system performance. With an XP system, this performance degradation may be negligible, but with a server, it can become quite costly. Microsoft strongly recommends against disk compression with Windows Server 2003.

FORMAT <DRIVELETTER or VOLUME> /FS:NTFS /C   Formats the *DRIVELETTER* or *VOLUME* and implements compression.

Unfortunately, there is no way to apply compression on a drive from the command line without reformatting the drive or losing data. In a situation where you are not formatting the drive anyway, you should apply compression through the drive properties in My Computer or Windows Explorer.

Encryption

As you learned earlier, encryption uses an algorithm to scramble data in such a manner that it cannot be viewed without the proper decryption algorithm. Encryption is used for security that, in conjunction with file permissions (discussed in Chapters 6 and 7), provides a high level of protection against hackers and intrusion.

Microsoft introduced the **Encrypting File System (EFS)** beginning with Windows 2000, and continues to include it in XP and Windows Server 2003. EFS works by encrypting a file and locking it with a file-specific key that can only be opened by the user's key. A key is the algorithm that is used to encrypt and decrypt the data. This means that an encrypted file can only be decrypted or viewed by the person who encrypted it in the first place. The beauty of EFS is that it is completely transparent to the user. Once a file is encrypted locally or on the network, other users are completely oblivious to the internal workings of the process. In actuality, the only time that a user or administrator needs to be concerned with the mechanics of encryption is when the encrypting user account is eliminated from the system.

If a user-encrypted file exists and the user who encrypted it is no longer with the company or the account has been changed, the file can only be decrypted by the **Recovery Agent**. A Recovery Agent is a special username and password that is defined when the system is installed and can be added or modified in the local or domain Group Policy. Only when the Recovery Agent user is logged on can an encrypted file can be recovered using the **CIPHER** command.

One additional note about encryption: A file can be encrypted on a local system, or it can be encrypted on a network server or other remote system. The file, however, is not encrypted when it is in transit between the two. This allows for a certain amount of risk, as this leaves the file data open to be viewed by a potential hacker.

CIPHER   Displays the encryption status of all files within the current directory.

CIPHER <*DIRECTORY*>*   Displays the encryption status of all files within *DIRECTORY*.

CIPHER /E /A <*FILENAME*>   Encrypts *FILENAME*.

CIPHER /E /S:<*DIRECTORY*>   Encrypts *DIRECTORY* and all of its contents. Any file subsequently added to this directory will be automatically encrypted. Files removed from this directory will be decrypted when they are saved elsewhere.

CIPHER /K   Creates a new key for the current user.

CIPHER /U /N   Updates the current user-encrypted files to the current key.

CIPHER /X:<FILENAME>   Backs up the EFS keys for the current user to *FILENAME*.

CIPHER /R:<FILENAME NO EXTENSION>   Restores the EFS keys for the current user from *FILENAME*.

Hands-on Project 5-8 teaches you how to create and encrypt a file and then log on as another user to view the results.

Hands-on Project 5-8

5

To encrypt a file:

1. Open a command window.

2. First, you need to create a plain text file. Type **edit hello.txt** and press **Enter**.

3. The Edit program opens with an empty document called hello.txt. Type **hello** and press **Enter**.

4. Save the hello.txt file by holding down the **Alt** key and pressing **F**. Release **Alt** and press **X**. Press **Enter** to confirm that the file should be saved.

5. To ensure that another user account has access to the file, you need to copy it to the root of the C drive. Type **copy hello.txt c:** and press **Enter**.

6. Navigate to the root by typing **cd** and pressing **Enter**.

7. Type **cipher /e /a hello.txt** and press **Enter**. This encrypts the file. Your screen should look like Figure 5-15.

Figure 5-15   Encrypting the hello.txt file

8. Next, you need to log off and then log on with another account that has appropriate permissions to the C drive. Click ▣ and then click the **Log Off** button ▣.

9. A confirmation dialog box appears. Click **Log Off** again.

10. Press **Ctrl+Alt+Delete** to begin. The logon dialog box appears. Log on to the system using the alternate account and password.

11. Open a command window.

12. Type **cd** and press **Enter** to navigate to hello.txt.

13. Attempt to view hello.txt by typing **type hello.txt** and press **Enter**. The system will respond with message indicating that access is denied.

14. Open Windows Explorer by clicking [Start], pointing to **All Programs**, pointing to **Accessories**, and then clicking **Windows Explorer**.

15. Click the plus sign to the left of **My Computer**, and then click **Local Disk (C:)**. In the right pane, scroll down to the entry for hello.txt. Notice that hello.txt is now green. This indicates that the file has been encrypted.

16. Close Windows Explorer.

17. Log off the system by clicking [Start], clicking [key], and then clicking **Log Off**.

CHAPTER SUMMARY

This chapter covered disk management methods from a command window. Disk and drive management is handled on the command line primarily through the **DISKPART** command and its variants. **DISKPART** commands provide capabilities for creating basic and dynamic disks, partitions, and volumes, including those involved with RAID and fault tolerance. General disk condition and viability can be automated using commands such as **CHKDSK** and **DEFRAG**, while **FSUTIL** is used to implement and manage disk quotas.

Both file and disk compression are supported with Windows Server 2003, allowing a user to compress individual files or all the contents of a drive. Although this may be valuable for a single-user system, it is not recommended for servers due to the additional CPU processing necessary to maintain disk compression. Encryption is a feature that was made available with Windows 2000 and continues with Server 2003. With encryption, you can encrypt files so that only you can view them.

COMMAND SUMMARY

Command	Function
CHKDSK	Checks a drive for physical errors.
CHKNTFS	Schedules automated CHKDSK on boot.
DEFRAG	Defragments a drive.
RECOVER	Recovers .chk files.
DISKPART|LIST DISK	Lists all disks on the server.
DISKPART|SELECT DISK	Selects a disk for subsequent commands.

Command	Function
DISKPART|CLEAN	Removes all partitions and volumes from the selected disk.
DISKPART|DELETE DISK	Deletes the selected disk from the server.
DISKPART|DETAIL DISK	Lists selected disk details.
DISKPART|ONLINE	Brings the selected disk online.
DISKPART|RESCAN	Updates the disk configuration.
DISKPART|CREATE PARTITION PRIMARY	Creates a primary partition on the selected disk.
DISKPART|CREATE PARTITION EXTENDED	Creates an extended partition on the selected disk.
DISKPART|CREATE PARTITION LOGICAL	Creates a logical drive on the selected partition.
DISKPART|LIST PARTITION	Lists all partitions on the server.
DISKPART|SELECT PARTITION	Selects a partition for subsequent commands.
DISKPART|DELETE PARTITION	Deletes a selected partition from the disk.
DISKPART|DETAIL PARTITION	Lists selected partition details.
DISKPART|ACTIVE	Mounts the selected partition.
DISKPART|INACTIVE	Dismounts the selected partition.
DISKPART|ASSIGN	Assigns a drive letter to the selected partition, logical drive, or volume.
DISKPART|LIST VOLUME	Lists all volumes on the server.
DISKPART|SELECT VOLUME	Selects a volume.
DISKPART|DELETE VOLUME	Deletes the selected volume.
DISKPART|DETAIL VOLUME	Lists details about the selected volume.
DISKPART|ASSIGN LETTER	Assigns the selected volume a drive letter.
DISKPART|CONVERT BASIC	Converts the selected dynamic disk to a basic disk.
DISKPART|CONVERT DYNAMIC	Converts the selected basic disk to a dynamic disk.
DISKPART|CREATE VOLUME SIMPLE	Creates a simple volume on the selected disk.
DISKPART|EXTEND DISK	Extends the simple volume on the selected disk or spans the simple volume across two disks.
DISKPART|ADD DISK	Creates a mirrored volume on the selected disk.
DISKPART|BREAK DISK	Breaks the mirrored volume, leaving both identical partitions intact.
DISKPART|CREATE VOLUME STRIPE	Creates a striped volume on the selected disk.
DISKPART|CREATE VOLUME RAID	Creates a RAID 5 volume.
DISKPART|REPAIR DISK	Restores data from a missing RAID 5 disk.
DISKPART|IMPORT	Imports a transplanted disk into a new server.
FORMAT	Formats the drive for FAT, FAT32, or NTFS.

5

Command	Function
LABEL	Labels a drive.
CONVERT	Converts a FAT or FAT32 format to NTFS.
FSUTIL DIRTY	Marks the drive as corrupt.
FSUTIL FSINFO	Obtains information about the file system or drive.
FSUTIL VOLUMEINFO	Displays volume information.
FSUTIL QUOTA	Configures and displays the disk quota.
FSUTIL VOLUME DISMOUNT	Dismounts a volume.
FSUTIL VOLUME DISKFREE	Displays the amount of free disk space on the disk.
COMPACT	Compresses files and folders; does not archive.
EXPAND	Decompresses distribution files.
CIPHER	Encrypts one or more files.

KEY TERMS

basic disk — A disk type that can contain primary or extended partitions.

boot drive — The disk and drive that contain the operating system.

compression — The reduction in file size resulting from the removal of redundant space in the file.

disk — A physical medium for storing data.

disk fault tolerance — The ability of a server to sustain a drive failure without having the entire server fail.

disk quota — A feature that allows restrictions to be placed on the amount of disk space used by one or more user accounts.

disk thrash — The constant use of the hard disk resulting from a fragmented drive.

distribution files — Files containing compressed data that are used to install an application.

drive — A volume, logical drive, or partition that has a drive letter.

drive compression — A feature that allows files and folders to consume less space on a drive.

duplexing — Identical to mirroring, only with a disk controller for each disk, providing controller fault tolerance in addition to disk fault tolerance.

dynamic disk — A disk type that can contain simple, extended, spanned, striped, mirrored, or RAID 5 volumes.

Encrypting File System (EFS) — The service that provides encryption within Windows Server 2003.

encryption — The process of enabling a user to exclusively view file and folder data. Encryption works by making the data unreadable without the user's specific credentials. Permissions do not modify the data. Instead, they grant and restrict file and folder access based on users' accounts.

extended partition — A type of partition that cannot contain an OS. There can only be one extended partition on a disk. There is no practical limit on the number of logical drives that can be created from an extended partition.

extended volume — A volume that occupies multiple locations on a single disk.

FAT (File Allocation Table) — A type of disk format that has little security, and has limitations on disk size, partition size, and filename conventions.

FAT32 — A type of disk format that has little security, but does not have the same limitations on disk size, partition size, and filename conventions that FAT does.

file compression — A feature that shrinks a file size.

format — The process of preparing a disk or drive to receive data.

fragmentation — The splitting of a single file across multiple sections of a drive.

logical drive — A drive that can be created on an extended partition. Not bootable.

mirrored volume — A volume that is replicated with an identical volume on another disk.

mirroring — A fault-tolerant disk storage method in which the contents of a disk or drive are constantly replicated to another disk or drive.

network share — A folder that has been configured for network access.

NTFS (New Technology File System) — A type of disk format that provides additional security and efficiency over FAT and FAT32.

partition — A portion or all of a basic disk; can either be primary or extended.

primary partition — A type of partition that is bootable, can have a drive letter assigned, and is formattable. A single disk can have up to three primary partitions and one extended partition or a total of four primary partitions on a disk.

Raid 1 — A technology that creates a synchronized copy of a volume or disk on another disk, enabling the system to sustain a single disk failure without loss of data or performance. Also called mirroring or duplexing.

Raid 5 — A technology that distributes data across three or more disks and maintains parity information, allowing the system to sustain a single disk failure without loss of data. Also called striping with parity.

Recovery Agent — A designated user account that allows a user to decrypt files encrypted by a different user.

simple volume — A volume that is not extended, spanned, striped, mirrored, or RAID 5.

spanned volume — A volume that occupies multiple locations on more than one disk.

striping with parity — A fault-tolerant disk storage method where data is spread across three or more disks, along with parity. This provides fault tolerance.

volume — The basic disk equivalent of a partition.

5

REVIEW QUESTIONS

1. Which command is used to scan a drive for physical errors?

   a. **SCANDISK**

   b. **DEFRAG**

   c. **SCANDRIVE**

   d. **CHKDSK**

2. What can you do if you need to run **CHKDSK** on your boot volume, but the system won't let you?

   a. Run **CHKDSK**, and schedule **CHKDSK** to run upon reboot.

   b. Run **SCANDISK**.

   c. Use **FSUTIL** to mark the disk as dirty.

   d. Reboot; **CHKDISK** will run automatically.

3. **CHKDSK** fixed some errors on the drive, and now you find that a document has become corrupted. What do you do?

   a. Rewrite the document.

   b. Run **CHKDSK** again.

   c. Run **RECOVER**.

   d. There is nothing you can do; the file is irretrievable.

4. **CHKDSK** automatically runs any time the boot drive is low on disk space. Most users, however, need extra time to read the screen before the countdown timer expires. What command can you use to give yourself time to read the screen?

   a. **CHKDSK C: /T:60**

   b. **DEFRAG C: /T:60**

   c. **SCANDISK C: PAUSE**

   d. **CHKNTFS C: /T:60**

5. To increase security, you have chosen to convert your disk from FAT format to NTFS. How can you ensure optimal efficiency?

   a. Use **CONVERT** with the **/X** option.

   b. Use **CONVERT** with the **/CVTAREA** option.

   c. Use **DISKPART CONVERT** with the **/CVTAREA** option.

   d. Use **CONVERT** with the **/NOSECURITY** option.

6. What's the difference between a disk and a drive?

   a. A disk contains drives; a drive contains partitions.

   b. A partition resides on a drive, a drive contains disks.

   c. A partition contains a drive; a disk contains a volume.

   d. A disk contains partitions; a drive has a letter.

7. Which **DISKPART** command can be used to show information about a particular volume? (Choose all that apply.)

   a. **DETAIL DISK**

   b. **LIST VOLUME**

   c. **DETAIL VOLUME**

   d. **LIST DISK**

8. You are upgrading Windows NT to Windows Server 2003. Windows NT currently has two mirrored drives and four drives configured with RAID 5. What do you need to do after the upgrade is completed to ensure that the mirrored and RAID 5 volumes are functioning appropriately?

   a. nothing

   b. Restore from tape.

   c. Re-enter all of the data.

   d. Reconfigure the mirror and RAID 5 drives.

9. You recently converted Disk 0 to a dynamic disk, and then decided that it is easier to administer basic disks. How do you convert it back?

   a. You can't convert a dynamic disk to a basic disk.

   b. Use the **DISKPART** command **CONVERT BASIC**.

   c. Back up the data, reinstall the disk, and restore the data.

   d. Use the **DISKPART** command **CONVERT DYNAMIC**.

10. Striping with parity is also known as:

    a. RAID 0

    b. RAID 1

    c. RAID 5

    d. RAID 10

11. Duplexing is also known as:

    a. RAID 0

    b. RAID 1

    c. RAID 5

    d. RAID 10

12. Which of the following volume types are not fault tolerant?

    a. simple

    b. extended

    c. spanned

    d. striped

    e. mirrored

    f. RAID 5

13. One of the disks in your RAID 5 volume has failed. What should you do after you replace it?

    a. Run the **DISKPART** command **REPAIR DISK**.

    b. Run the **DISKPART** command **RECOVER DISK**.

    c. Run the **DISKPART** command **BREAK DISK**.

    d. Restore from tape backup.

14. One of the disks in your RAID 0 volume has failed. What should you do after you replace it?

    a. Run the **DISKPART** command **REPAIR DISK**.

    b. Run the **DISKPART** command **RECOVER DISK**.

    c. Run the **DISKPART** command **BREAK DISK**.

    d. Restore from tape backup.

15. To prevent corruption, you need to dismount the D drive before running **CONVERT** on it. Which command do you use?

    a. the **DISKPART** command **CONVERT DYNAMIC**

    b. **CONVERT D: /X**

    c. the **DISKPART** command **OFFLINE**, then **CONVERT D:**

    d. the **DISKPART** command **INACTIVE**, then **CONVERT D:**

16. Which command is used to encrypt data?

    a. **EXPAND**

    b. **ENCRYPT**

    c. **PGP**

    d. **CIPHER**

17. The payroll specialist at your company was recently fired for embezzlement. You need to decrypt her files so that they can be used by the auditing firm. How do you do this?

    a. You don't. Encrypted files can only be read by the person who encrypted them.

    b. Log on as the Administrator and copy the files.

    c. Use the **CIPHER** command to decrypt the files.

    d. Log on as the Recovery Agent and use **CIPHER** to decrypt the files.

18. You need to enable disk compression on the C drive without losing the data. What command do you use?

    a. You can't compress a drive with a command.

    b. You can't compress the boot drive.

    c. **FORMAT C: /C**

    d. **COMPRESS C:/*.* /S**

19. A system file named oemdrivers.dll has become corrupt, and rather than reinstall the OS, you would like to retrieve the file from the original install.cab file. What command do you use?

a. `COMPACT /U INSTALL.CAB`

b. `EXPAND INSTALL.CAB -F:OEMDRIVERS.DLL C:\WINNT\SYSTEM32`

c. `EXPAND INSTALL.CAB C:\WINNT\SYSTEM32`

d. `COMPACT /U INSTALL.CAB OEMDRIVERS.DLL`

20. You need to enable disk quotas on your server's P drive and log an event every time a limit has been met. Which command(s) do you use? (Choose all that apply.)

a. `FSUTIL QUOTA QUERY`

b. `FSUTIL QUOTA ENFORCE`

c. `FSUTIL QUOTA TRACK`

d. `FSUTIL QUOTA ENABLE`

DISCOVERY EXERCISES

1. **DISKPART** can be automated within a batch file. Use the Help and Support Center Tool (on the Start menu) to find out how to do so, and then choose one of the Hands-on Projects from the chapter to perform the same task using batch.

2. Using commands, re-create the configuration shown in Figure 5-11.

3. Using **DISKPART**, create a spanned volume, and then extend it. Is it possible to use **DISKPART** to extend a mirrored volume?

4. Create a batch file that causes **CHKDSK** to run on the boot drive every time the system reboots. Place a 60-second timeout on the process.

USER ADMINISTRATION AND DATA SECURITY

After reading this chapter and completing the exercises, you will be able to:

♦ Create and delete user and group accounts

♦ Manage permissions for users

♦ Administer security and user authentication

Administration generally refers to the work that is involved in system upkeep and preventive maintenance tasks on a system. In the realm of computing, maintenance refers not only to actions required to keep the system running, but also to enhancements or configuration changes intended to improve the functionality of the computer or server. Once a Windows Server 2003 server is initially installed and configured—either by an administrator or by a configuration specialist—the majority of server administration tasks relate to the management of user needs and security. Both of these topics revolve around the protection of data from users who are not permitted to access it.

Management of data access seems like a simple idea, but when you consider potential complications dealing with who the user is (such as a manager) and where he or she may be located (such as across the hall or across the country), administration becomes more complex and time-consuming. You will learn about the details and implications of user location in Units 3 and 4 of this book, along with many aspects of data security. This chapter focuses mainly on local data, locally logged-in users, and basic security.

USER ACCOUNTS

Users can access the data contained on a server in one of three ways: through a logged-in user account, through a user group to which the user belongs, and through data permissions that the user can access. These three options apply to local and network server access.

A **user account** is what a user uses to log in to a server—either locally or remotely. The server relies on a user account, which includes permissions and other user specifications, to determine whether a specific user may access certain data and the level of access that he or she is granted. The level of data access is represented by **permissions**. Read and Full Control are examples of permissions. **User groups** are used as containers to group user accounts that have similar access needs. User groups primarily exist for administrative convenience, because permissions can be assigned to a user group, affecting all group members, instead of requiring the administrator to assign permissions user by user. Within this section, you will learn how to create and modify all three of these elements: users, groups, and permissions.

Creating and Deleting User Accounts

To be able to access programs, files, and other resources on a Windows Server 2003 server, each user must have a user account that acts as an identifying profile. User accounts that are created on a Server 2003 server or XP Professional system serve two purposes: They provide local logon and network access. This means that a user account can be configured to both log on to the server locally and access its data remotely over the network. The differences between the two configurations lie within local and group policies that can be configured to prohibit a specific user or user group from logging on locally.

Creating a user account on a stand-alone XP or Server 2003 system is accomplished using the **NET USER** command. The **NET USER** command can also be used to add users within a domain, as you will learn in Chapter 11.

NET USER   Lists the current user accounts stored on the server.

NET USER <*USERNAME*> /ADD   Adds the USERNAME account.

NET USER <*USERNAME*> <*PASSWORD*> /ADD   Adds the *USERNAME* account and a *PASSWORD* for the account.

Syntax **NET USER <*USERNAME*> <*PASSWORD*> /DELETE**   Deletes the *USERNAME* and *PASSWORD*.
NET USER <*USERNAME*> /DELETE   Deletes the *USERNAME*.

Generally, local user accounts are added to Windows XP or Server 2003 operating systems using the Computer Management GUI tool or, in the case of a domain controller, within Active Directory Users and Computers. You can access Computer Management by opening the Start menu, right-clicking My Computer, and selecting Manage. It can also be accessed from the Start menu's Administrative Tools, Computer Management option. Since Administrative Tools might be hidden, get into the habit of accessing Computer Management through My Computer to save time and effort during administration. From within Computer Management, user accounts are created by expanding the Local Users and Groups section under System Tools, selecting the Users folder, and then right-clicking an empty space in the right pane and selecting New User.

To properly confirm and troubleshoot the user and group commands that you will learn in this chapter, you should become familiar with Computer Management, which is the GUI tool for user and group administration. You will learn about Computer Management by completing Hands-on Project 6-1.

Hands-on Project 6-1

To create a new user account:

1. Click the **Start button** ![Start], right-click **My Computer**, and click **Manage** from the pop-up menu. The Computer Management window opens.

2. Double-click **Local Users and Groups** under System Tools.

3. Double-click the **Users** folder under Local Users and Groups.

4. Notice the users that are listed in the right pane of the window. Default users are Administrator and Guest, which is disabled.

5. Right-click anywhere in the right pane that is not occupied by a user account name, and select **New User**.

6. In the User name text box, type **test**. Click the **Create** button.

7. After you clicked Create in Step 6, the New User dialog box remained open; this allows multiple users to be added at the same time. Click **Close**.

You might have noticed that in the New User dialog box, there were options for enabling a user to change his or her own password and disabling the account. Windows Server 2003 requires only a username to create a new user account. When adding real accounts, you should always create a password for user accounts as an extra level of security against unauthorized or hacker intrusion. For this reason, group and local security policies can be created that require passwords and impose default account behavior (such as requiring the user to change the password when he or she next logs in). Password-controlled user requirements allow you to better secure the system.

The **NET USER** command is only used in scripts and batch files as an administrative time-saver during massive system rollouts or migrations in which dozens or even hundreds of user accounts need to be added quickly. This also provides extra error-prevention, as the command helps eliminate data-entry and typing mistakes that can occur by redundantly using the GUI utility.

Now that you are familiar with how to create a user account with Computer Management, you can learn to perform the same task much faster using a batch program. In Hands-on Project 6-2, you will use the **NET USER** command to create multiple user accounts.

Hands-on Project 6-2

To create multiple user accounts using a batch program:

1. Minimize the Computer Management window by clicking its **Minimize** button ![button].

2. Open a command window. Type **cd** and press **Enter** to move to the root of the drive.

3. Before going any further, check the user accounts that are already on the system. Type **net user** and press **Enter**.

   Notice the accounts that are on the system, including the one that you created in the previous project.

4. Type **edit useradd.bat** and press **Enter**.

5. Type the code shown in Figure 6-1.

Figure 6-1   Adding users with a batch file

6. Press and hold **Alt**. Press **f** to activate the File menu. Release the keys.

7. Press **x** to exit the program. The system prompts you to save the file. Press **Enter**.

8. Type **useradd.bat** and press **Enter**. Your screen should look like Figure 6-2.

```
C:\WINDOWS\system32\cmd.exe                                    _ □ X
Microsoft Windows [Version 5.2.3663]
(C) Copyright 1985-2001 Microsoft Corp.

C:\Documents and Settings\Administrator.MACHINE>cd\

C:\>edit useradd.bat

C:\>useradd

C:\>net user harry password /add
The command completed successfully.

C:\>net user ron password /add
The command completed successfully.

C:\>net user ginny password /add
The command completed successfully.

C:\>net user cedric password /add
The command completed successfully.

C:\>_
```

Figure 6-2   Running useradd.bat

9. Minimize the command window and maximize the Computer Management window.

10. Press **F5**, which refreshes the entries. Notice that all of the new accounts have been created.

In a secure lab environment, it is acceptable to create user accounts with generic passwords to minimize confusion. In an office environment, you would almost never create generic passwords as done in Hands-on Project 6-2 because the result is equivalent to no password at all. Many malevolent programs, such as Trojan horses and viruses automatically check for passwords such as "admin," "password," "administrator," and other obvious words. The only situation in which generic passwords might be acceptable would be if the accounts were created so that the user had to change the password the next time he or she logged on to the system. Unfortunately, there is no Windows Server 2003 command option that will force the user to change the password the next time he or she logs on.

Modifying Default Account Behaviors

The **NET ACCOUNTS** command can be used to modify the default behavior of every account that is created. Default behaviors are options that you can apply to all new accounts and include such characteristics as a minimum password length, maximum and minimum password age, and unique password limitation, which requires that all passwords be of mixed case and/or include symbols or numerals.

NET ACCOUNTS   Displays the default information that applies to all accounts.

NET ACCOUNTS /MINPWLEN:<NUMBER>   Sets the minimum number of characters in a logon password.

NET ACCOUNTS /MAXPWAGE:<DAYS>   Sets the longevity of a password before it expires and must be changed.

NET ACCOUNTS /MINPWAGE:<DAYS>   Sets the minimum interval of time between password changes.

NET ACCOUNTS /UNIQUEPW:<NUMBER>   Sets the number of passwords that the system accepts. This prevents users from simply changing an old password to the same password.

It is important to realize that changes made using the **NET ACCOUNTS** command apply only to accounts created after the command was used to change the defaults. Such changes are not applied to pre-existing accounts. Many companies' corporate security guidelines evolve over time. To implement changes that apply to account defaults, administrators need to first run the **NET ACCOUNTS** command, and then modify all existing accounts manually. Account settings can also be changed by modifying the local security policy of the server. In domain environments, modifications to group policies at the domain level can be used to change account settings.

The three most frequently used options for **NET ACCOUNTS** are **/MINPWLEN**, **/MAXPWAGE**, and **/UNIQUEPW**. The **/MINPWLEN** option effectively requires that users have passwords, and the **/MAXPWAGE** option sets them to expire on a regular basis. These two options, combined with **/UNIQUEPW**, which restricts how often a user can reuse a password, provide for a sound password security plan.

It is easy to become confused about the purpose of the **/MINPWAGE** option for the **NET ACCOUNTS** command. This option originated as a response by Microsoft to Trojan horse viruses, and particularly to **keylogger** programs. Keyloggers are programs that record every keystroke on the computer and dump the information into a file. A Trojan horse then retrieves the file and transmits it to the offending party either through e-mail or directly through network communications channels. A Trojan horse virus waits until a keylogger logs a password change, and then transmits the information to the offender. At that point, the hacker can gain entry to the system using the new password, and immediately change that password to prevent further access to the system. If the compromised password is for the Administrator account, and there are no other administrative-equivalent accounts on the system, the only solution becomes to reinstall the operating system—and format the disk in doing so. The **/MINPWAGE** option prevents users from changing their passwords within the timeframe that an administrator might deem as dangerous.

Modifying Existing User Accounts

You can both create and enhance a user account using a single command. Generally, it is better to separate the creation and enhancement processes into distinct commands, to cut down on confusion. From a scripting perspective, creating and modifying user accounts using separate commands is ideal because it allows you to separate account creation commands from account modification commands, providing for separate confirmation and troubleshooting. The User and Group utility also works in a two-step manner: First the account is created; then its properties are modified appropriately to the needs of the environment.

Once a user account has been created using **NET USER**, any of the following commands can be used to enhance the specific features of that account. These are the most frequently used account management commands.

NET USER <*USERNAME*> /EXPIRES: <*MM/DD/YYYY*> Sets the existing account to expire on the specified date.

NET USER <*USERNAME*> /PASSWORDCHG: *YES|NO* Allows the user to or prevents the user from changing his or her password.

NET USER <*USERNAME*> /PASSWORDREQ: *YES|NO* Changes the account either to require or not require a password.

Hands-on Project 6-3 teaches you how to modify user accounts with the Computer Management GUI.

Hands-on Project 6-3

To modify user accounts with Computer Management:

1. The Computer Management window should have the focus and should look like Figure 6-3 (your screen might show additional user accounts). Double-click the user account **test**.

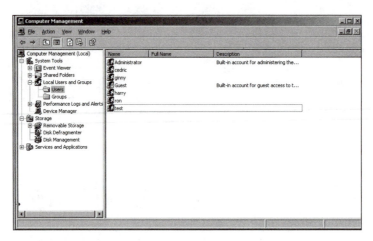

Figure 6-3   Newly added user accounts

2. Notice that the option for User must change password at next logon is selected. Click **OK**.

3. Double-click the user account **ron**.

4. Notice that the option for User must change password at next logon is *not* selected. This is the primary difference in default behavior between GUI and command-generated user accounts. Click **OK** again.

5. Double-click the user account **test**.

   Notice that there are several options available, including the ability to add information about the user. Most of the options are currently unavailable, but will become enabled once the User must change password at next logon option is unselected. You can learn about these options by clicking the Question button in the upper-right corner of the window and then clicking the option.

   Many other options are available within the User Account Properties tabs at the top of the dialog box. The most frequently used tabs are Member Of, Profile, Environment, and Remote control.

   The Member Of tab deals with user groups, which are covered in the next section. Items within Profile can be handled with the **NET USE** command. Items within the Environment and Remote control tabs have no command equivalents.

6. Click the **Cancel** button and minimize the Computer Management window.

The following three **NET USER** commands are equivalents to the Profile tab within the Computer Management GUI. Although profile information is usually used with domain-configured systems, they are also available locally and with peer-to-peer networks.

NET USER *<USERNAME>* **/HOMEDIR:***<HOMEDIRPATH>*   Sets the
home directory to the specified path.

NET USER *<USERNAME>* **/PROFILEPATH:***<PROFILEDIR>*   Configures
the stored profile location.

NET USER *<USERNAME>* **/SCRIPTPATH:***<SCRIPTDIR>*   Configures the
location of the logon script.

A user's **home directory** is a mapped drive that points to a network location where
the user can reliably store personal data. *<HOMEDIRPATH>* is the physical location
on the server of that home directory. If *<HOMEDIRPATH>* is defined, the drive letter
will automatically be assigned and mapped for that user when he or she logs on to the
server. *<HOMEDIRPATH>* can be in the form of a regular path such as `C:\USERS`, or
it can be in the form of a **Universal Naming Convention (UNC)**. A UNC format
allows you to assign a home directory that is located on another server or system on the
network. In a UNC path, the syntax would be `\\<SERVERNAME>\<SHARENAME>\`.
Examples of *<HOMEDIRPATH>* include `C:\USERS\%USERNAME%` and the UNC
`\\SERVERNAME\SHARENAME\%USERNAME%`. This UNC is a great example of using the
`%USERNAME%` variable to let the system fill in the username, reducing the possibility of
entering the wrong account name. A typical syntax for the **NET USER** command with
the `/HOMEDIR` option and the user homer might be: `net user homer/homedir:\`
`\server1\users\ %username%`.

Along with the `/HOMEDIR` option, networked Windows NT, 2000, and XP systems also
provide a feature called **roaming profiles**. A standard **profile** is a collection of information about a specific user's desktop settings, icons, resolution, background, Start menu,
and so on. By default, profiles are stored locally on the user's computer. To enable a user
to log in to multiple systems while maintaining the same icons and desktop settings, a
user's profile can be copied to a network location when the user logs off the system and
copied back to the computer when he or she logs back on to a system, no matter where
the system is, as long as the networked profile location is configured properly using the
`/PROFILEPATH` option.

Roaming profiles are generally reserved for domain environments where there is
centralized administration for account properties options such as `/HOMEDIR`,
`/PROFILEDIR`, and `/SCRIPTPATH`. If you need to implement roaming profiles in a nondomain environment, you will need to ensure that every user
account on every computer is configured identically with profiles enabled and
pointing to the same central location.

The `/SCRIPTPATH` option of the **NET USER** command simply enables the system to
refer to a central (usually networked) location to run a batch or script when a user logs

in to the system. Both the **/SCRIPTPATH** and **/PROFILEPATH** options should use UNC formats similar to this:

```
net user homer /scriptpath:\\server1\users\scripts
/profilepath:\\server1\users\profiles
```

Additionally, you should place appropriate permissions (using the **CACLS** command or through the folder's properties within Windows Explorer) in the target shares before implementing any of these profile commands, which allows these changes to be applied without errors. Commands that deal with sharing are covered in Chapter 7. Recall that shares are folders that have been configured for network access.

Hands-on Project 6-4 lets you modify the user accounts that you created previously. Now that accounts for users Harry, Ron, Ginny, and Cedric have been created, you should change the account properties to meet certain criteria. For this project, assume that your company has a security plan that requires all users to have a password, and that users can also change their passwords.

Hands-on Project 6-4

To modify user accounts using a batch program:

1. Minimize the Computer Management window, and maximize the command window.

2. At the command prompt, type **edit useradd.bat** and press **Enter**.

3. Navigate to the bottom of the batch file and press **Enter** twice to add a line, separating the new code section from the original code.

4. Type the code shown in Figure 6-4.

 The best way to type the code shown in Figure 6-4 is to type the first line of each section, copy it, paste it three times, and then change the names appropriately. Not only is this a time-saver, but it helps eliminate typing errors.

```
C:\WINDOWS\system32\cmd.exe - edit useradd.bat                          _ |□| x|
 File  Edit  Search  View  Options  Help
                              C:\useradd.bat
net user harry password /add
net user ron password /add
net user ginny password /add
net user cedric password /add

net user harry /passwordchg:yes
net user ron /passwordchg:yes
net user ginny /passwordchg:yes
net user cedric /passwordchg:yes

net user harry /passwordreq:yes
net user ron /passwordreq:yes
net user ginny /passwordreq:yes
net user cedric /passwordreq:yes



 F1=Help                                 | Line:14    Col:16
```

Figure 6-4   Allowing users to change their own passwords and requiring passwords

5. Save the file by pressing and holding **Alt** and pressing **f**. Release the keys. Press **x** to exit, and press **Enter** to confirm the save.

6. Type **useradd** and press **Enter**. You should see several messages indicating that the account already exists, and several others indicating that the changes were implemented successfully. Notice that when you attempt to add accounts that already exist, the system generates an error message.

7. Now, assume that your company requires that passwords are at least six characters long, have a maximum age of one month, that users are prevented from changing their own passwords within a day of a prior change, and that passwords may not be repeated over the course of one year. Type **edit useradd.bat** and press **Enter**.

8. Press **Enter** twice to create a new code section. Press the **up arrow** twice to place the cursor at the top of the document, and type **net accounts /minpwlen:6 /maxpwage:30 /minpwage:1 /uniquepw:12**.

9. Your screen should look like Figure 6-5. Save the file by pressing and holding **Alt** and pressing **f**. Release the keys. Press **x** to exit, and press **Enter** to confirm the save.

6

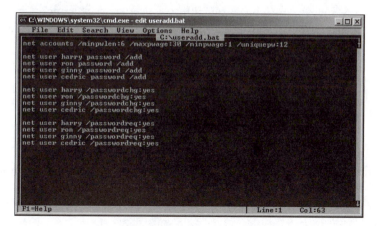

Figure 6-5   Changing default account properties

10. Minimize the command window and maximize the Computer Management window.

11. Click the **harry** user account. Press **Delete**, and then press **Enter**. Repeat this step for users Ron, Ginny, and Cedric.

12. Minimize the Computer Management window and maximize the command window.

13. At the command prompt, type **useradd** and press **Enter**. Having deleted the accounts in Step 11 allows you to run **USERADD** without creating duplicate

accounts. Scroll through the results and ensure that all commands have processed successfully.

14. Minimize the command window and maximize the Computer Management window. Press **F5** to refresh the contents. Notice that the accounts are present again.

15. Click the **Close** button to close the Computer Management window. In the command window, type **exit** and press **Enter** to close the window.

> The **NET USER** and **NET LOCALGROUP** commands can apply to both stand-alone servers and domain controllers. If the current system is a domain controller (DC), the changes will reflect in Active Directory, since local users are disabled on DCs. It is possible to perform these same commands on a workstation, applying them to a DC. In such environments, the **/DOMAIN** option must be added to the end of the command. Domain-related commands, including the **/DOMAIN** option, are covered in Chapters 10 through 12.

Changing a Password

Changing a user password is relatively simple to do from both the command window and the Computer Management window. Within Computer Management, you need to right-click the user account and select the Set Password option. From that point, the system prompts you for a new password. A password can be just as easily changed by using the **NET USER** command without the **/ADD** option.

NET USER <USERNAME> <PASSWORD>   Changes an existing user account's password.

In Hands-on Project 6-5, you will create a user account called henry with a password of newguy. You will then use the **NET USER** command to change the password to password.

Hands-on Project 6-5

To create the account and change the password:

1. Open a command window.

2. Type **net user henry newguy/add** and press **Enter** to create the account called henry with the password of newguy.

3. Type **net user henry password** and press **Enter** to change the password to password.

4. Type **exit** and press **Enter** to close the command window.

Disabling a User Account

You should never delete a user account once it has been established and used by a user. The reasoning behind this primarily lies with data retrieval and additional networked applications.

With regard to data retrieval, as mentioned in Chapter 4, encryption can become an annoyance if a user has left the company and you need to retrieve data owned by that user. If the user account has not been deleted, the easiest way to access the data is to change the user account password, log on as the user, and retrieve the data. With regard to networked applications, many applications utilize usernames and passwords as their methods of authentication. While this approach is found primarily in Active Directory domains, it can apply to peer-to-peer networks as well. The bottom line is that the relationship between user accounts and other applications involves data retrieval that is more system- and application-automated in nature instead of user-initiated. If an e-mail server application relies on Windows Server 2003 usernames and passwords for its authentication, eliminating the user account that the e-mail application references not only will prevent you from being able to access the e-mail, but usually will generate problems with the e-mail application. Because of these issues, it is highly recommended that well-established user accounts have their passwords changed, and the accounts be disabled rather than deleted. Disabling maintains the account's existence in the event that it is needed for data retrieval, but does not allow system or data access with that account name and password.

Disabling a user account from within Computer Management is similar to changing a password: You simply double-click the account and select the Account is disabled checkbox. Similarly, disabling an account in the command window requires the **NET USER** command.

NET USER <*USERNAME*> /ACTIVE:*NO*|*YES*   Disables an account.

In Hands-on Project 6-6, you will disable the account that you created in the previous project.

Hands-on Project 6-6

To disable an account:

1. Open a command window.

2. Type **net user henry /active:no** and press **Enter** to disable the account.

3. To ensure that the account is disabled, type **net user henry** and press **Enter**. The results should be similar to what is shown in Figure 6-6, where the Account active status is no.

4. Type **exit** and press **Enter** to close the command window.

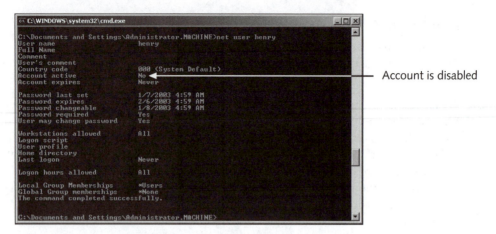

Account is disabled

Figure 6-6 Account properties for the henry account

Creating and Modifying User Groups

User groups simplify the task of configuring access for multiple users. User groups contain user accounts and exist to avoid the need to assign individual accounts specific access. Instead, similar user accounts can be assigned group membership, and access privileges can be assigned to the group. As a result, each member user account receives the proper data access without the administrator having to make the assignments individually or redundantly.

Creating and modifying user groups is similar to creating a user account, but it is actually much simpler because a group is a container for user accounts. The **NET LOCALGROUP** command is used for managing user groups. Once a group has been created, you must add users to it. User groups typically contain members with similar job functions or data access needs.

NET LOCALGROUP <*GROUPNAME*> /ADD   Adds the specified group.

NET LOCALGROUP <*GROUPNAME*> /DELETE   Deletes the specified group.

NET LOCALGROUP <*GROUPNAME*> <*USERNAME*> /ADD   Adds the specified user to the specified group.

NET LOCALGROUP <*GROUPNAME*> <*USERNAME*> /DELETE
Removes the specified user from the specified group.

In Hands-on Project 6-7, you will use the useradd.bat batch program to create a group called "engineers," assign new users to that group, and then check your work using the Computer Management GUI.

Hands-on Project 6-7

To assign group membership:

1. Open the Computer Management window, navigate to the Users folder, and click the **harry** account. Press **Delete**, and then press **Enter**. Repeat this step for users Ron, Ginny, and Cedric.

2. Minimize the Computer Management window and open a command window.

3. Type **cd** and press **Enter** to move to the root of the drive.

4. Type **edit useradd.bat** and press **Enter**.

5. Press the **down arrow** key several times until the cursor is at the bottom of the file, and press **Enter** twice to add a new section.

6. Type the code shown in Figure 6-7.

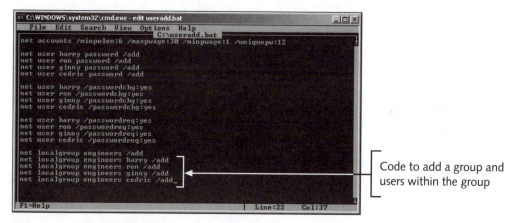

Figure 6-7 Creating a group and adding users

7. Save the file by pressing and holding **Alt** and pressing **f**. Release the keys. Press **x** to exit, and press **Enter** to confirm the save.

8. Type **useradd** and press **Enter**. The result should be successful messages.

9. Minimize the command window and maximize the Computer Management window.

10. Press **F5** to refresh the contents.

11. Click the **Groups** folder in the left pane. Notice that a new group called "engineers" has been added.

12. Click the **Users** folder in the left pane of the window. Double-click the **harry** account and select the **Member Of** tab. Your screen should look like Figure 6-8.

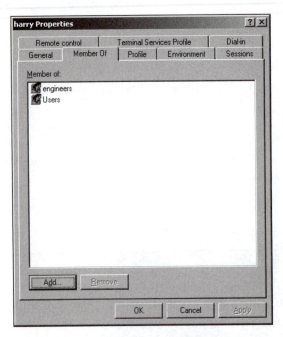

Figure 6-8   Updated user membership

13. Click the **Close** button ![X] to close the harry Properties dialog box.

14. Click the **Groups** folder in the left pane of the window.

15. Double-click the **engineers** group. Your screen should look like Figure 6-9.

16. Click ![X] to close the engineers Properties dialog box.

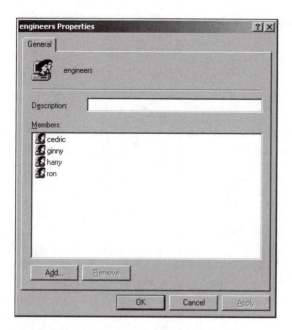

Figure 6-9   Updated group membership

PERMISSIONS

Every user on a system needs to access certain data on the system. Some users need to modify the data, while others need to simply look at it, and still others don't need to look at the data at all. Thus, varying levels of data access are needed.

To enable this kind of complex data access, files and folders that reside on an NTFS volume contain a list of users (either directly assigned or implied through group membership) called an **access control list (ACL)** and the access permissions each has to the particular file or folder. Folder permissions relate to the levels of access assigned to a user, as described below.

- **None (Deny)**—The user may not access the file. This permission overrides all others that may be implied or inherited. Represented by the letter N.

- **Read**—The user may read the file, but cannot change or write it. Represented by the letter R.

- **Write**—The user may create a new file, but cannot modify it. Represented by the letter W.

- **Change**—The user may change an existing file, but cannot create one. Represented by the letter C.

- **Full Control**—The user can do anything to a file, including assign permissions to another user and take ownership. Represented by the letter F.

Permissions for a user can be applied specifically to file, or they can be inherited from a parent directory of which the file is a member. It is possible to inherit one permission from a folder and have another permission explicitly applied to a given user within a specific file. More than one permission can also be assigned to a user through different group memberships. Typically, the most permissive permission supercedes all others, with the exception of None (Deny), which overrides everything else—inherited or specific.

By default, the Administrator account and members of the Administrators group can alter permissions for any file or folder on the system. This does not mean that these accounts will *always* have these privileges. By definition, Full Control is granted to these administrative accounts, and to the user accounts that created the data, but this does not mean that all accounts with Full Control permission to specific data can alter permissions. Only the creators of the data or other accounts have the status of **owner** over that data, which means they have the ability to change data permissions. This can lead to problems when administrators or owners inadvertently remove their own account or all others from the permissions list belonging to a particular piece of data, and remove their ownership privileges from the advanced permissions on the data. This effectively isolates the data and renders it inaccessible. The **CACLS** command is used by administrators to view and manage permissions. Windows Explorer can be used to do the same thing by right-clicking on a file or folder, selecting Properties, and clicking the Security tab, as shown in Figure 6-10.

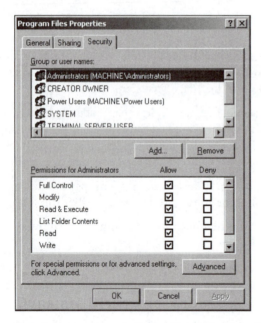

Figure 6-10   Permissions within Windows Explorer

CACLS <FILENAME>	Displays the current permissions for the file.
CACLS <FILENAME> /G <USERNAME>:R|W|C|F	Grants the user access to the folder or file with the specified permission (Read, Write, Change, or Full Control).
CACLS <FILENAME> /G <USERNAME>:R|W|C|F /T	Grants the user access to the folder, its contents, and all subfolders with the specified permission.
CACLS <FILENAME> /G <USERNAME>:R|W|C|F /E	Edits user access to include the specified permission.
CACLS <FILENAME> /R <USERNAME> /E	Revokes all access to the file.
CACLS <FILENAME> /P <USERNAME>: N|R|W|C|F	Replaces the existing folder or file permissions with the specified permission.
CACLS <FILENAME> /P <USERNAME>: N|R|W|C|F /T	Same as the previous option, but applies to all subfolders.
CACLS <FILENAME> /D <USERNAME>	Deletes from the file the entry for the specified user.

It is important to note here that the permissions described in the **CACLS** commands are **NTFS permissions**, which are permissions that are applied to files and folders on an NTFS-formatted disk. If the disk is not NTFS-formatted, these permissions are not available, because FAT and FAT32 do not support file-level security. As you will learn in Chapter 7, remote access through the network adds another level of security in the form of **share permissions**, which are similar to NTFS permissions, except that they only apply to network access. NTFS and share permissions effectively combine into a single permission for a given user where the most restrictive NTFS or share permission prevails.

As you will learn in Hands-on Project 6-8, NTFS permissions are usually altered by accessing the Security tab within the properties of the file or folder. In this project, you will create a folder and use the harry account to assign permissions.

Hands-on Project 6-8

To alter permissions using **CACLS**:

    1. Close the Computer Management window.

    2. Maximize the command window.

    3. Type **md test** and press **Enter**.

4. Minimize the command window and click the **Start** button . Click **Run**, type **explorer** on the Run line, and press **Enter**.

5. Maximize Windows Explorer, and then double-click **My Computer** in the left pane. This displays the drives attached to the system.

6. Click the **C drive**, which expands the list of folders located on that drive.

7. Scroll down, if necessary, and right-click the **test** folder (in either the left or right pane).

8. Click **Properties** on the pop-up menu. Click the **Security** tab. Notice the permissions that exist for this folder.

> **Tip**   If a Security tab is not displayed, then the drive is not NTFS-formatted. You will need to run the **CONVERT C: /FS:NTFS** command to complete this exercise.

9. Click **Cancel** to close the Properties window.

10. Minimize Windows Explorer and maximize the command window.

11. At the command prompt, type **cacls test /g harry:f** and press **Enter**.

12. The system prompts for confirmation. Press **y** and press **Enter**. Your screen should look like Figure 6-11.

Figure 6-11   Modifying permissions using **CACLS**

13. Type **cacls test** and press **Enter** to view the existing permissions for the test folder in the command window.

14. Minimize the command window and maximize the Windows Explorer window.

15. Right-click the **test** folder and click **Properties**. Click the **Security** tab, and notice that Harry now has full control (i.e., all permissions are selected).

16. Click **Cancel** to close the Properties window.

17. Minimize the Windows Explorer window and maximize the command window.

18. At the command prompt, type **cacls test /p harry:n** and press **Enter**.

19. The system prompts for confirmation. Press **y** and press **Enter**.

20. Repeat Step 13 to see the changes. Notice that Harry has been denied all permissions.

21. Minimize the Windows Explorer window and maximize the command window.

22. At the command prompt, type **cacls test /g engineers:f** and press **Enter**.

23. The system prompts for confirmation. Press **y** and press **Enter**.

24. Repeat Step 13 to see the changes again. Notice that Harry, despite membership within the Engineers group, still shows up with all permissions as denied.

25. Close all windows.

SECURITY AND AUTHENTICATION

System, server, and network security are major concerns for companies and computer users. Begin learning about security by learning about server-related security issues.

Stored Users and Passwords

Stored Users and Passwords is a utility within Control Panel that became available with Windows XP and Server 2003. It lets users avoid some of the username, password, and settings reconfiguration necessary with frequent access to multiple password-required Web sites and remote connections.

For example, if a user needs to access an FTP server with a specific username and password, he or she normally needs to either learn the FTP command language (covered in Chapter 7) or repeatedly enter the username and password for FTP connections within Internet Explorer. If the user needs to access different FTP servers using different usernames and passwords, he or she needs to modify the Internet Explorer settings each time a site is accessed.

Stored Users and Passwords lets you avoid some of this redundancy. With the functionality provided by Stored Users and Passwords, users can store usernames and passwords for remote sites that require usernames and passwords that are different than the system defaults on their computers and associate them with a specific network or Internet resource. Any time the user wants to access a specific server, the system automatically uses the stored username and password associated with that server to log in to the server and access data.

For the user, Stored Users and Passwords can come in handy. For the server, it can make data retrieval and automation faster. For example, system updates, program updates, or simple data often need to be retrieved on a regular basis and then shared on the network or used by the server. To access the data with Windows 2000 or NT, you would need to log on to the system with a username and password that allowed you to access the data appropriately, or you would need to modify the Internet Explorer settings. The same process can be handled automatically by Stored Users and Passwords in Windows Server 2003 without requiring a separate logon. This is an improvement in security, because you can't always be certain that the username and password that you are entering are encrypted.

Unencrypted usernames and passwords that cross the Internet are vulnerable to interception and theft. With Stored Users and Passwords, the system no longer assumes that the current logon account is identical to the remotely accessed account, eliminating the possibility that someone could grab an unencrypted username and password off the Internet and use them to infiltrate your local network or system.

The command equivalent of Stored Users and Passwords is **CMDKEY**. **CMDKEY** can be particularly valuable when configuring multiple systems for stored usernames and passwords, because the command can be run through a batch file automatically through several different startup methods, including a login script, the Startup folder, or a modification within the registry.

CMDKEY /LIST   Lists locally stored usernames and passwords.

CMDKEY /LIST:<COMPUTER or DOMAIN NAME>   Searches for the specified computer or domain within the current list of stored usernames and passwords.

CMDKEY /ADD:<COMPUTER or DOMAIN NAME> /USER: <COMPUTER or DOMAIN NAME>\<USERNAME> /PASS:<PASSWORD> Adds the remote resource (*COMPUTER* or *DOMAIN NAME*) to be accessed using the account (*COMPUTER* or *DOMAIN NAME\USERNAME*) with the specified password.

CMDKEY /ADD:<COMPUTER or DOMAIN NAME> /USER: <COMPUTER or DOMAIN NAME>\<USERNAME> /PASS   Same as above, with a blank password.

CMDKEY /ADD: <COMPUTER or DOMAIN NAME> /SMARTCARD Adds the remote resource and obtains the username and password from a smart card (a small device containing encrypted account and password information that is plugged into the system).

Using Elevated Privileges Without Logging Off

As an administrator, you will be called upon to fix problems and perform maintenance on users' computers. This is usually time-consuming because many administrative functions are not available on the standard user's system, and even when they are, users are prohibited from accessing the functions because of their login privileges. With Windows 2000 and XP, these limitations can be particularly annoying if you are dealing with user-specific profile information that cannot be fully accessed from any other account. The solution is the **RUNAS** command. **RUNAS** runs an application with the privileges of a certain username and password without requiring the user to log off and log back on. For example, an administrator can run a program on another user's system without having to log off and log back on as the administrator. Using **RUNAS** also prevents unauthorized access that may occur when the administrator logs on to the system and forgets to log back off.

The **RUNAS** command can also be used within batch files or on the command line to perform administrative tasks that would otherwise be disabled for a user. Such tasks include tape backup and program installation.

RUNAS /NOPROFILE /USER:<*USERNAME*> <*PROGRAM*>   Runs the specified program on behalf of the user without loading that user's profile. The password will be prompted as the program is run.

RUNAS /PROFILE /USER:<*USERNAME*> <*PROGRAM*>   Runs the specified program on behalf of the user and loads that user's profile. The password will be prompted as the program is run.

RUNAS /SAVECRED /USER:<*USERNAME*> <*PROGRAM*>   Runs the specified program on behalf of the user, prompts for a password, and saves the *USERNAME* and password locally. These credentials must be saved prior to automating other RUNAS command.

RUNAS /SMARTCARD <*PROGRAM*>   Runs the specified program using the username and password stored on the smart card.

Taking File Ownership

As you learned earlier in this chapter, every file on a system has an owner. The owner of the file is usually the person who created the file. To change the permissions on a file, you must be the file's owner or have the Full Control permission. If the owner of the file is unavailable, and file permissions must be changed, another person must take ownership of the file using the **TAKEOWN** command.

The ability to take ownership isn't granted to everyone; only members of the Administrators group or those given Administrative authority can successfully run the **TAKEOWN** command. If the current user is not a member of the Administrators group, he or she can still run the **TAKEOWN** command by using the account and password of someone who is.

TAKEOWN /F <*FILENAME*>   Takes ownership of the specified file.

TAKEOWN /S <*COMPUTERNAME*> /F <*FILENAME*>   Takes ownership of the *FILENAME* located on the network computer (*COMPUTERNAME*).

TAKEOWN /S <*COMPUTERNAME*> /U <*USERNAME*> /P <*PASSWORD*> /F <*FILENAME*>   Takes ownership of the file using the specified *USERNAME* and *PASSWORD*.

TAKEOWN comes in handy when a user leaves a company and his or her files need to be retrieved, but the user previously set permissions to deny access to other accounts.

CHAPTER SUMMARY

In this chapter, you learned some of the most frequently used commands for user and account management. The topic of security was also introduced. The **NET** command is frequently a part of creating and managing user accounts, specifically through the use of the **NET USERS** and **NET LOCALGROUP** commands. You also learned about how users access data based on a list of permissions called an ACL, increasing security by allowing users the minimum amount of access required to view or modify files and folders. Other topics in this chapter included Stored Users and Passwords, a utility that allows a user to enter multiple usernames and passwords to access remote Web and FTP sites. You also learned about using elevated privileges to run programs and commands as a different user account without logging in to the system as that user. Taking file ownership allows you to alter data permissions for files and folders that were not created by you.

COMMAND SUMMARY

Command	Function
NET USER	Lists the current user accounts on the system.
NET USER <USERNAME> <PASSWORD> /ADD	Creates a user account.
NET USER <USERNAME> <PASSWORD> /DELETE	Deletes a user account.
NET ACCOUNTS	Lists the current password policy on the system.
NET USER <USERNAME> <PASSWORD>	Changes an existing account's password.
NET USER <USERNAME> /ACTIVE:NO	Disables an account.
NET LOCALGROUP <GROUPNAME>	Creates and deletes local groups.
NET LOCALGROUP <GROUPNAME> <USERNAME>	Adds and removes user accounts from the local group.
CACLS <FILENAME>	Displays and modifies permissions for the file.
CMDKEY	Displays, creates, adds, and removes entries in the Stored Users and Passwords database.
RUNAS	Allows commands and programs to be run under a different user account without logging in to the system as that account.
TAKEOWN	Seizes ownership of a file or folder.
NET USER <USERNAME> <OPTIONS>	Modifies the properties of an existing user account.

KEY TERMS

access control list — A list of users that indicates the various permissions of each user.

home directory — A directory that is generated by the system and contains exclusive permissions for the user account.

keylogger — A type of Trojan horse virus program that records all key entries into a log.

NTFS permission — Security-level permission associated with all files and folders on an NTFS-formatted drive.

owner — The creator of an object, or someone who has seized ownership of an account to be able to change the permissions.

permission — Specific access privilege that is attached to data and associated with users. Permissions grant and deny specific levels of access to the data.

profile — Account-specific data containing system, icon, and desktop setting details.

roaming profile — A profile that is portable between multiple computers. Requires a common network storage location that can be accessed by all computers.

share permission — Network-only permission that is associated with network shares.

Universal Naming Convention (UNC) format — A standardized format for identifying the location of data on remote computers. The format is \\servername\sharename.

user account — A system account that consists of a username, password, and various properties and allows a user to log in to a computer and gain access to data.

user group — A collection of user accounts that is organized by similar access and permissions privileges. Permissions are assigned to the user group instead of to individual group members.

REVIEW QUESTIONS

1. Local user management occurs with which of the following tools or commands? (Choose all that apply.)

   a. User Manager for Domains

   b. **NET USER**

   c. Active Directory Users and Computers

   d. Computer Management

2. Which command is appropriate for adding the user Jeff to the system with the following properties: a password of ffej that expires on January 1, 2005, cannot be changed, and is required?

   a. `NET USER JEFF FFEJ /ADD`

   b. `NET USER JEFF FFEJ /EXPIRES:01/01/2005 /PASSWORDCHG:YES PASSWORDREQ:YES`

   c. `NET USER JEFF FFEJ /ADD /EXPIRES 01/01/2005 /PASSWORDCHG:NO /PASSWORDREQ:YES`

   d. `NET USER JEFF FFEJ /EXPIRES:01/01/2005 /PASSWORDCHG:NO /PASSWORDREQ:YES`

3. What command do you use to display the account properties for the account jeff?

   a. NET USER

   b. NET USER JEFF

   c. NET USER JEFF FFEJ

   d. NET USER JEFF /PROPERTIES

4. How do you refresh the contents of any window that contains lists of data?

   a. F3

   b. F2

   c. F5

   d. F8

5. What command do you use to display the current default account behaviors?

   a. **NET USER**

   b. **NET ACCOUNTS**

   c. **NET LOCALGROUP**

   d. **GROUP POLICIES**

6. You ran the **NET ACCOUNTS** command to implement some password policy restrictions. When you test it, you find that users can still change their passwords to contain fewer than four characters, and can change them within five days of previously changing their passwords. These restrictions are specifically what you used **NET ACCOUNTS** to change. What is the problem?

   a. You failed to apply the changes manually to all existing accounts.

   b. You did not use the correct options for **NET ACCOUNTS**.

   c. You cannot make these changes without modifying the local security policy on the system.

   d. **NET ACCOUNTS** does not implement password restrictions.

7. How do the Profile and Environment tabs within User Account Properties in Computer Management differ?

8. Jeff is a member of the Engineers group and the Managers group. He is also a director within the company, which gives him special privileges to specific accounting information regarding his division. Jeff needs to be able to read, modify, and create new files within the directory C:\Marketing. You check the permissions for that folder and find that members of the Managers group have Read and Write permissions. Engineers have the None (Deny) permission, and as a director, Jeff has been directly assigned the Full Control permission over that directory. What can Jeff do with the data in this directory?

   a. He can view it, but not change it.

   b. He can modify it, but not add new files.

c. He can add new files, but not change anything once it has been saved.

d. He can do nothing.

9. How do you display the permissions associated with a folder within Windows Explorer?

a. Right-click a folder, select Properties, and click the Security tab.

b. Double-click a folder, select Properties, and click the Security tab.

c. Right-click a folder, select Properties, and click the Sharing tab.

d. Double-click a folder, select Properties, and click the Sharing tab.

10. Which command is used to display the permissions associated with a folder named test?

a. **perms test**

b. **rights test**

c. **cacls test**

d. **cacls c:\test**

11. Which permissions cannot be modified using the **CACLS** command? (Choose all that apply.)

a. Read

b. Read and Execute

c. Write

d. Full Control

12. Who can change permissions?

a. the Administrator account

b. the owner of the account

c. members of the Power Users group

d. an account that has the Full Control permission assigned

13. You are an administrator sitting at a Windows XP system that is currently running under the user account Wendy. You need to change permissions to the C:\MODS directory for Wendy so that she can read, write, and modify the data in that directory. What is the best way to do this?

a. Use **TAKEOWN** to take ownership on Wendy's behalf and change the permissions.

b. Use **RUNAS** in conjunction with **CACLS** to change Wendy's permissions for the folder.

c. Use the Stored Users and Passwords command **CMDKEY** to retrieve your user-name and password.

d. Log off, log on as yourself, and change the permissions for the folder.

14. What command is used to remove an account?

   a. **NET USER /REMOVE**

   b. **NET USER /DELETE**

   c. **NET USER ACCOUNT /REMOVE**

   d. **NET USER ACCOUNT /DELETE**

15. Why should you disable an account rather than delete it?

16. What is the list of permissions that is attached to a file or folder called?

   a. access control list

   b. account capacity list

   c. administrative control list

   d. access capability list

17. Which option is used with the **NET USER** command to change an existing account's password?

   a. **/CHANGEPW**

   b. **PASSWORD:**

   c. **PW:**

   d. No option is used.

18. Which permission overrides all others?

   a. No Access

   b. None (Deny)

   c. Read Only

   d. Full Control

19. You need to create a batch program that will run **XCOPY** on specific data every night, regardless of the user accounts that are currently logged in. What is the best way to do this?

   a. Use **RUNAS** with **XCOPY** in the batch file, and schedule the batch program to run at the appropriate time.

   b. Use **XCOPY** in the batch file, and modify the **RUNAS** line of the registry to run it at the appropriate time.

   c. Use **RUNAS** in the batch file, and call the batch file using **XCOPY**.

   d. Modify the registry to run **XCOPY** at the appropriate time.

20. A home directory is _____.

   a. a directory containing information about the desktop, Start menu, and icons

   b. a directory containing information about installed programs

   c. a directory that is available as a mapped drive to all users

   d. a directory that is available as a mapped drive to a single user

DISCOVERY EXERCISES

1. Imagine that your classroom is a corporation. Create and document a username and password policy that provides the highest security for your environment. Make sure that users can only log in to the system during their designated working hours, and ensure that they can only log in to one or two assigned computers while maintaining the same profile and drive mappings. Make sure that passwords are at least eight characters in length and are highly secured. You will need to do additional research on some of the commands covered in this chapter. Once this rough security policy has been documented, create at least five new user accounts and implement these policies within those accounts using only commands. Check your work by logging in to the appropriate computers as the new accounts. Once you have successfully completed this task, delete the accounts and create new ones using the appropriate GUI tools.

2. Create folders for home directories and profiles on a server, and assign those folders as the home directories and profiles for each user created in Discovery Exercise 1.

3. Locate an FTP site on the Web that uses anonymous logins. One example is ftp.downloads.com. Insert this site into your list of stored users and passwords using the appropriate command, and test it to see if it works. Ask your instructor to provide you with the name of an FTP site that requires a specific username and password. Attempt to access that site with Internet Explorer before changing the stored usernames and passwords to include that site and its required username and password.

4. Assume that an employee of your fictitious corporation left the company and left some encrypted data on the server. Log in as this user and encrypt some data on the server. Experiment with various commands such as **RUNAS**, **CIPHER**, **TAKEOWN**, **NET USER /DELETE**, and **NET USER /ACTIVE:NO** to determine which methods you can use to access the data.

6

UNIT
3

NETWORKING

7

INTRODUCTION TO NETWORKING

> **After reading this chapter and completing the exercises, you will be able to:**
> - Understand how systems communicate
> - Understand basic networking protocols
> - Utilize commands to diagnose, configure, and troubleshoot networks using TCP/IP
> - Use commands to manage networks
> - Improve the security of networks

Much of the functionality of Windows Server 2003 depends on computers communicating with each other. Whether across the hall or around the world, networking, or connectivity between computers, is vital for a healthy computing environment. The primary physical requirements for establishing a network in a Windows Server 2003 environment are a **network interface card (NIC)** and the cabling media and equipment necessary to connect two or more computers. A NIC is a piece of hardware that provides a means for Windows Server 2003 to package data and place it on the network. In addition to the appropriate hardware and computers, the transfer of data relies on protocols.

OVERVIEW OF **TCP/IP**

Many **protocols** are used in the networking world. Protocols are rules for formatting, ordering, and error-checking data sent across a network. **Transmission Control Protocol/Internet Protocol (TCP/IP)** is a set of protocols that provides the basis for the operation of the Internet. TCP/IP comprises two primary protocols: the Transmission Control Protocol, which includes rules that a computer uses to establish and break connections, and the Internet Protocol, which determines the routing of data over the Internet. With the explosion of the Internet and the boost in enterprise-class network operating systems running TCP/IP, TCP/IP is considered the networking standard.

Because TCP/IP is considered the networking standard, you might wonder why there are other protocols running on networks. In the past, operating systems used proprietary protocols—for example, Novell NetWare incorporated its IPX/SPX protocol set. This integration allowed software vendors to maintain a presence in a company and make it difficult for companies to change operating systems. As network administrators realized the danger of staying with one vendor, they began using hybrid networks containing multiple protocols. This wasn't the best solution, because when multiple protocols run across multiple platforms on the same cabling, the result is a general increase in network traffic congestion.

Windows Server 2003 runs TCP/IP as its primary protocol, but there are technologies working behind the scenes, including **NetBEUI**, which is the protocol that transports **Network Basic Input Output System (NetBIOS)**. NetBIOS is an interface that lets computers communicate over a network. NetBEUI is used in computing environments in which servers are running operating systems other than Windows Server 2003. NetBEUI is a nonroutable network transport suited for small networks that consist of a single network segment with fewer than 50 computers. It is one of two network solutions for supporting NetBIOS. If you use Windows NT and many legacy software applications, NetBIOS is necessary.

TCP/IP is a **protocol suite**, or a collection of protocols, that contains multiple protocols working together. In addition to TCP and IP, the TCP/IP protocol suite contains FTP, HTTP, SNMP, Telnet, LDAP, ICMP, and other protocols that work behind the scenes on a computer. Later in this chapter, you will learn about the tasks each of the subprotocols accomplishes in the communication process.

In addition to TCP/IP, popular protocols or protocol suites in use in networked environments include IPX/SPX, AppleTalk, DECNet, and XNS. Detailed coverage of each of these protocols is beyond the scope of this text, but learning about these protocols puts you ahead of others in your field who only know about TCP/IP.

How Systems Communicate

For computers to communicate with one another over networks, they need to speak the same language. Protocols are like languages that computers use to communicate.

 A protocol is not the same thing as an operating system. Protocols such as TCP/IP are typically vendor neutral, meaning that they are not owned by a software company such as Microsoft or IBM. A protocol, once adapted, can run on many different types of wiring, networking equipment, and operating systems. In contrast, operating systems are typically proprietary and licensed from a software company.

Protocols allow networked computers, also called **hosts** or **nodes**, to send and receive data. To make this happen, part of the protocol's job is to identify hosts on a network. Hosts that are connected to the Internet and are responsible for determining the best way for packets to reach their destinations are known as **routers**. All major networking protocols, especially TCP/IP and IPX/SPX, use some sort of addressing scheme to identify hosts. A portion of the address identifies the network segment where the host exists, while the other portion of the address identifies the unique host. Figure 7-1 shows an example of an IP address and how it identifies the network and host.

7

Figure 7-1   Network and host portions of an IP address

Data that travels over a network is transmitted in **packets**. Packets are small pieces of files and e-mail messages that travel over networks and are reassembled into their original form upon reaching their destination.

When a user wants to send or receive information over a network (in other words, when one host needs to communicate with another host), the first host needs to know the address of the other host to establish a **session**. Sessions are like conversations between hosts; you can carry on more than one conversation at a time, but each conversation is separate from the other. During this session, the protocol makes sure that data is exchanged in a manner that is reliable or unreliable, depending on the preference of the application being used in the session. For example, a streaming audio application such as Windows Media Player doesn't rely on a protocol to make sure that the data is being sent reliably. Instead, it uses buffers to collect data and decide whether a resend is needed. Protocols also make sure that data is transferred in a way that allows the receiving host to translate it. Because you might have multiple sessions open between hosts, the protocol also keeps track of which data belongs to which session. For example, if you have Web browsers open to CNN.com and ESPN.com, the protocol makes sure that the data intended for the CNN browser window doesn't get sent to the one displaying the ESPN data.

Recall that a protocol helps hosts communicate with each other. To make sure that protocols follow standards, the International Organization for Standardization (ISO) developed the **Open Systems Interconnection (OSI)** model in 1977. The OSI model is a model of communication between two hosts over a network. Each layer of this model designates certain actions and information to be included in the communication and transmission of data. Figure 7-2 shows the OSI model and how the layers work together to ensure that data makes it from one host to another.

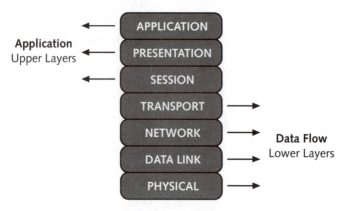

Figure 7-2   OSI model

TCP/IP preceded the OSI model. The TCP/IP layers don't match those of the OSI model. However, enough correlation exists that the OSI Reference Model layers can be used to describe the functions provided by the various protocols within their respective suites. Figure 7-3 compares the TCP/IP model and the OSI model.

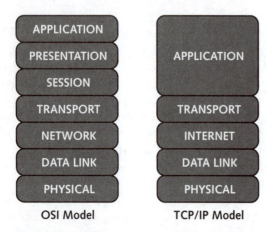

Figure 7-3   Comparison of OSI and TCP/IP

Protocols typically are developed in layers, or stacks, with elements operating at each layer of the OSI model.

IDENTIFYING HOSTS

A host can be one of several types of computers on a network. A server, such as a Windows Server 2003 system, can be a host. A host can also be a client that is connecting to the server to receive files. Finally, a computer workstation running an OS such as Windows XP, 2000, or 98 can also be a host.

A server "serves" up data, applications, and so on to clients. Clients are computers requesting a service and can include computers, printers, and routers. A **workstation** is the location at which the user is working. A workstation is almost always a client, unless it is in a peer-to-peer network. In a **peer-to-peer network**, the workstation can be a server and a client as all the computers are peers and contain data and services used by themselves and others.

7

In the Windows Server 2003 environment, you will deal mostly with servers and clients. Windows Server 2003 does not run on workstations, so the server and client aspects of networking are the focus of this chapter.

Recall that a protocol uses an addressing scheme to identify hosts on a network. These addresses are logical in nature, meaning that they can be assigned dynamically (through a DHCP server) or statically (entered manually at the computer). Addresses are assigned dynamically if you use a **Dynamic Host Configuration Protocol (DHCP)** server in your environment. DHCP is part of the TCP/IP protocol suite. It dynamically assigns IP addresses to hosts on a network segment. With DHCP, your computer receives an IP address automatically when it boots up. Typically this address will remain the same unless your computer is turned off for a prolonged length of time or moved to another part of the network.

If you are setting up the TCP/IP settings on a Windows Server 2003 system, you should use a static IP address. Your clients will need to know how to get to a specific address, so if the server's IP address keeps changing, problems will occur rather quickly when clients attempt to communicate with it. Along with this address, you will assign a **subnet mask**. A subnet mask is a binary number that indicates the portion of the IP address that identifies the network and the portion that identifies the host itself.

An administrator statically (manually) assigns a computer an address in the Internet Protocol properties of a network interface card. An example of the TCP/IP properties dialog box on a computer running Windows 2000 Professional is shown in Figure 7-4.

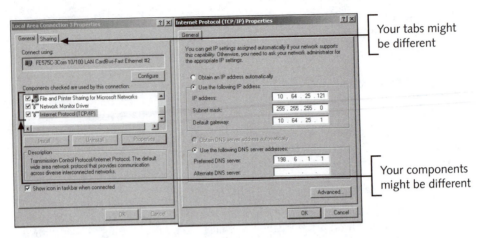

Figure 7-4   TCP/IP properties dialog box

Hands-on Project 7-1 teaches you how to set a static IP address on your Windows Server 2003 server. You also will learn how computers convert logical IP addresses to names such as *www.course.com* and FileServer1 using the Domain Name System (DNS). This type of conversion is referred to as *resolving*. DNS is examined in greater detail in Chapter 12.

Hands-on Project 7-1

To manually set your TCP/IP address settings:

1. Navigate to **My Network Places** and right-click it. Click **Properties**.

2. Right-click **Local Area Connection** and click **Properties**.

3. Scroll down the This connection uses the following items box and click **Internet Protocol (TCP/IP)** to select it. Click the **Properties** button.

4. Click the **Use the following IP address** radio button.

5. Click the field and type **10.1.1.5**.

6. Click the second field and type **255.255.0.0** for the subnet mask.

7. Click the third field and type the gateway (router used to get out of the network): **10.1.1.1**.

8. Click the **Use the following DNS server addresses** button. In the first field, type **10.1.1.2**. Your screen should look like Figure 7-5.

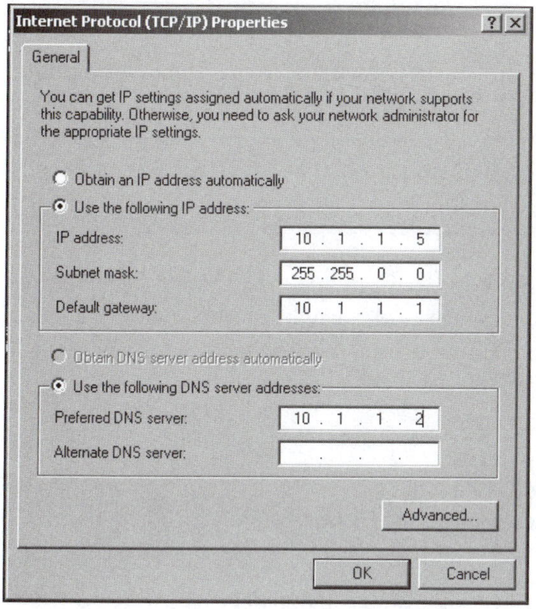

Figure 7-5 IP address settings

9. Click **Cancel** so that you don't lose any network connectivity. If instead you had clicked OK, the computer would have reset its IP address to 10.1.1.5 and would use this address when establishing communication over the network.

10. Click **Cancel** again to close the Local Area Connection Properties window.

Clients access a server using an IP address, which identifies the server on the network. Once the server is contacted by the client, the TCP/IP protocol suite begins the communication process and a session is established between the server and the client. Data is transferred between the two hosts. Information about connections between particular groups of routers, rules for handling heavy packet traffic and network congestion, and specifications on which connections to use first are maintained in routing tables. Once the client is finished accessing the server, the session is completed and disconnected. The server then waits until it is contacted again by another client. While it is important for servers to have a static IP address, it is likely that you will use DHCP to dynamically assign an IP address to clients.

MAINTAINING A NETWORK USING COMMANDS

When dealing with a networked environment, it is imperative that an administrator knows how to manage and maintain a network with the tools that are available. The networking commands fall into three basic categories: diagnostics, troubleshooting, and configuration.

Diagnostics

Diagnostic commands give you real-time information that can highlight issues before they arise. One such command is **NETSTAT**.

NETSTAT   Displays protocol statistics and current TCP/IP network connections. Only available if TCP/IP has been installed.

Hands-on Project 7-2 shows you how to find out what active connections are being made using IP. It also teaches you how to find out what routing table entries are on your server. You will need an Internet connection to complete this project.

Hands-on Project 7-2

To use **NETSTAT**:

1. Open an Internet browser window. Either Netscape Navigator or Microsoft Internet Explorer will work.

2. In the Location (Navigator) or Address (Internet Explorer) box, type **www.yahoo.com**.

3. Open a second browser window and type **www.msn.com**.

4. Open a command window. At the command line, type **netstat -n** and press **Enter**. You should see all your active connections showing the local address and port each is using.

5. Now you can learn what routing table entries exist on your server. Type **netstat -r** and press **Enter**. Notice that the loopback address of 127.0.0.1 is one of the entries listed.

6. Close Internet Explorer by clicking its **Close** button ✖, and then type **exit** and press **Enter** to close the command window.

NETDIAG is another diagnostic command. This command allows you to display statistics and run diagnostics on the NIC. Options for **NETDIAG** let you test for certain issues. This diagnostic tool is not available by default with Windows Server 2003; however, it can be downloaded from Microsoft's Web site at *www.microsoft.com/windows2000/techinfo/reskit/tools/existing/netdiag-o.asp*. You should install it to the system root drive (typically the C drive) on your server.

NETDIAG /TEST:SERVER   Displays statistics and runs diagnostics on the network card.

NETDIAG /TEST:SERVER /D:<DOMAIN>   Tests connectivity to a domain controller in a specific domain.

Windows Server 2003 also includes some GUI tools that can be used for network administration. Network Monitor is a GUI application that is used primarily on the network side of diagnostics in Windows Server 2003. This application is known as a **sniffer**. It examines packets by recording information that passes through a router from the data's source to its destination. All sniffer products run in one of two modes: standard or promiscuous. When the program is running in standard mode, only network traffic destined for the network interface is analyzed. When Network Monitor is running in promiscuous mode, it monitors all of the traffic that crosses the network.

Troubleshooting

Despite careful planning and optimism, it is inevitable that when you are connecting multiple computers and then adding servers to the mix, you will encounter problems. Several powerful commands included in the TCP/IP suite allow you to discover where things are going wrong. These include **PING**, **TRACERT**, and **PATHPING**.

PING <IPADDRESS>   Determines whether TCP/IP is working on the target computer *IPADDRESS*.

PING <IPADDRESS> /T   Issues PING commands continuously until stopped with a Ctrl+Z keystroke.

Issuing a **PING** command is referred to as "pinging."

When an attempt at connecting to a network resource fails, you typically start troubleshooting by first issuing a **PING** command to check on the computer you are trying to reach. Typing the IP address of the remote computer after the **PING** command gives you several types of responses, as shown in Table 7-1.

Table 7-1 **PING** responses

Ping Response	Response Meaning
Destination Unreachable	The destination was unreachable.
Request timed out	The destination was either too far away or the TTL (time to live) on the packets expired.
Reply from *IPADDRESS*:	The packets returned successfully.
Ping Statistics	Displays the number of packets that were sent and the number that were received back.

Sometimes it is useful to have the **PING** command continue executing automatically so that you can check for intermittent connectivity using the **/t** option. The host continues to send packets until you instruct it to stop (by typing Ctrl+Z). For example, a user complains that she is able to get to the file server, but when attempting to download or access a file, the file stops downloading halfway through. You issue a **PING** command with the **/t** option, and every 60 seconds the response is "Request timed out," which indicates a problem, rather than "Reply received from (*IP address*)," which indicates a successful connection. This problem eventually could be traced to a routing protocol overwhelming a router with a routing table update, and the router is unable to keep the connection open.

 Note that the **/t** option for the **PING** command is case sensitive; you must use a lowercase "t" in the syntax.

If the **PING** command fails to generate a response, the problem could be anywhere between the client and the server. If you are unable to Ping the server, you might Ping your default gateway next, followed by your local computer. To Ping your own computer, you use a special IP address: 127.0.0.1. This is known as the **loopback** address. It tests the TCP/IP functionality of your own network interface card.

Because the life of a data packet is not very long and networks today can be quite large and complex, you can also adjust the longevity, or time to live (TTL), of the packets using the **/i** option with the **PING** command.

 PING /i <*TTL*> <*IPADDRESS*>   Sets the time to live (TTL) in milliseconds on the packets.

If the **PING** command is successful on your local server or workstation and you are able to ping your default gateway successfully, you might need to use another of the TCP/IP troubleshooting commands, such as **TRACERT**.

 TRACERT <*IPADDRESS*>   Displays the name and IP address of every router that the packet travels across as it moves from the local computer to the remote host.

TRACERT shows the time it takes to complete each step, or hop, between routers. This information might indicate that one of the routers between you and the remote host is incorrectly configured or down. While **TRACERT** gives you the time between hops, another command, **PATHPING**, gives you even more information.

 PATHPING <*IPADDRESS*>   Displays the network statistics between each hop or router the packets cross.

PATHPING /H<*NUMBEROFHOPS*> <*IPADDRESS*>   Sets the maximum number of hops packets will take. The default is 30.

PATHPING is a route-tracing tool that combines features of the PING and TRACERT commands with additional information. The PATHPING command sends packets to each router on the way to a final destination over a period of time, and then computes results based on the packets returned from each hop. PATHPING shows the degree of packet loss at any given router or link, which helps you determine which routers or links might be causing network problems. You can also set the maximum number of hops that the packets will take as they cross the network. If you are trying to access a host across the Internet, this might be necessary.

> Don't type PATH PING (two words) instead of PATHPING as one word. The PATH command is used to show the current directories that are actively tracked and used by the operating system without requiring a full path. If you type PATH PING, you will reset the directories and replace them with the nonexistent PING directory!

7

These powerful commands allow you to troubleshoot connectivity problems you might encounter over the network. Hands-on Project 7-3 lets you practice with these commands.

Hands-on Project 7-3

To test connectivity to a remote host:

1. Open a command window.

2. Type **ping 127.0.0.1** and press **Enter** to test your network interface card's TCP/IP protocol stack. The results should look like Figure 7-6.

```
C:\WINNT\System32\cmd.exe                                          _ □ x

C:\>ping 127.0.0.1

Pinging 127.0.0.1 with 32 bytes of data:

Reply from 127.0.0.1: bytes=32 time<10ms TTL=128
Reply from 127.0.0.1: bytes=32 time<10ms TTL=128
Reply from 127.0.0.1: bytes=32 time<10ms TTL=128
Reply from 127.0.0.1: bytes=32 time<10ms TTL=128

Ping statistics for 127.0.0.1:
    Packets: Sent = 4, Received = 4, Lost = 0 (0% loss),
Approximate round trip times in milli-seconds:
    Minimum = 0ms, Maximum =  0ms, Average =  0ms

C:\>
```

Figure 7-6   Loopback PING results

3. Type **ping www.yahoo.com** and press **Enter**.

   Notice that your computer converts the hostname to an IP address and indicates that the PING command was successful.

4. To display information about the routers between your local host and the Web server you are contacting at Yahoo.com, type **tracert www.yahoo.com** and press **Enter**. Your screen should look similar to Figure 7-7.

```
C:\WINNT\System32\cmd.exe

C:\>tracert www.yahoo.com

Tracing route to www.yahoo.akadns.net [66.218.71.86]
over a maximum of 30 hops:

  1    10 ms    10 ms   <10 ms  10.128.0.1
  2    10 ms    10 ms    10 ms  ip68-2-7-1.ph.ph.cox.net [68.2.7.1]
  3   <10 ms    10 ms    10 ms  ip68-2-0-17.ph.ph.cox.net [68.2.0.17]
  4    10 ms   <10 ms    20 ms  ip68-2-0-9.ph.ph.cox.net [68.2.0.9]
  5    10 ms    10 ms    10 ms  chnddsrc02-gew0303.rd.ph.cox.net [68.2.14.13]
  6    10 ms    10 ms    10 ms  chndbbrc02-pos0101.rd.ph.cox.net [68.1.0.168]
  7    31 ms    20 ms    30 ms  dllsbbrc01-pos0102.rd.dl.cox.net [68.1.0.146]
  8    30 ms    30 ms    20 ms  dllsbbrc02-pos0100.rd.dl.cox.net [68.1.0.143]
  9    30 ms    30 ms    30 ms  unknown.Level3.net [209.246.136.33]
 10    30 ms    60 ms    30 ms  so-0-0-0.gar2.Dallas1.level3.net [64.159.3.186]

 11    30 ms    40 ms    40 ms  unknown.Level3.net [64.159.3.193]
 12    60 ms    51 ms    50 ms  so-3-0-0.mp2.SanJose1.Level3.net [64.159.1.130]

 13    50 ms    50 ms    50 ms  gige10-0.ipcolo3.SanJose1.Level3.net [64.159.2.4
1]
 14    50 ms    60 ms    50 ms  unknown.Level3.net [64.152.69.30]
 15    50 ms    50 ms    50 ms  w7.scd.yahoo.com [66.218.71.86]

Trace complete.

C:\>_
```

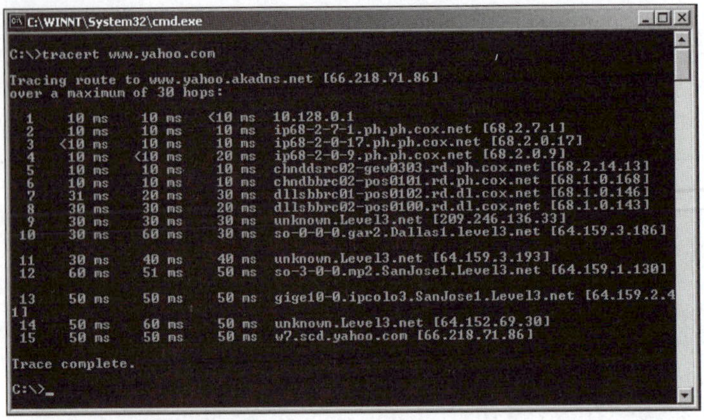

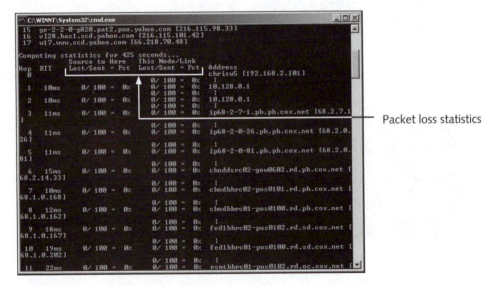

Figure 7-7 `TRACERT` results from Yahoo.com

5. Finally, discover how much packet loss there is between your local host and the server you are contacting at Yahoo.com. Type **pathping www.yahoo.com** and press **Enter**. The packet loss statistics are shown in Figure 7-8.

```
C:\WINNT\System32\cmd.exe
 15  ge-2-2-0-p820.pat2.pao.yahoo.com [216.115.98.33]
 16  v128.bas1.scd.yahoo.com [216.115.101.42]
 17  w17.www.scd.yahoo.com [66.218.70.48]

Computing statistics for 425 seconds...
            Source to Here   This Node/Link
Hop  RTT    Lost/Sent = Pct  Lost/Sent = Pct  Address
  0                                           chrisw5 [192.168.2.101]
                                0/ 100 =  0%   |
  1   10ms     0/ 100 =  0%     0/ 100 =  0%  10.128.0.1
                                0/ 100 =  0%   |
  2   10ms     0/ 100 =  0%     0/ 100 =  0%  10.128.0.1
                                0/ 100 =  0%   |
  3   11ms     0/ 100 =  0%     0/ 100 =  0%  ip68-2-7-1.ph.ph.cox.net [68.2.7.1
]
                                0/ 100 =  0%   |
  4   11ms     0/ 100 =  0%     0/ 100 =  0%  ip68-2-0-26.ph.ph.cox.net [68.2.0.
26]
                                0/ 100 =  0%   |
  5   11ms     0/ 100 =  0%     0/ 100 =  0%  ip68-2-0-81.ph.ph.cox.net [68.2.0.
81]
                                0/ 100 =  0%   |
  6   15ms     0/ 100 =  0%     0/ 100 =  0%  chnddsrc02-gew0602.rd.ph.cox.net [
68.2.14.33]
                                0/ 100 =  0%   |
  7   10ms     0/ 100 =  0%     0/ 100 =  0%  chndbbrc02-pos0101.rd.ph.cox.net [
68.1.0.168]
                                0/ 100 =  0%   |
  8   12ms     0/ 100 =  0%     0/ 100 =  0%  chndbbrc01-pos0100.rd.ph.cox.net [
68.1.0.162]
                                0/ 100 =  0%   |
  9   18ms     0/ 100 =  0%     0/ 100 =  0%  fedlbbrc02-pos0102.rd.sd.cox.net [
68.1.0.167]
                                0/ 100 =  0%   |
 10   19ms     0/ 100 =  0%     0/ 100 =  0%  fedlbbrc01-pos0100.rd.sd.cox.net [
68.1.0.202]
                                0/ 100 =  0%   |
 11   22ms     0/ 100 =  0%     0/ 100 =  0%  rsmtbbrc01-pos0102.rd.oc.cox.net [
```


Figure 7-8 Data packet statistics

6. Type **exit** and then press **Enter** to close the command window.

Configuration

Several command line utilities are specifically designed to configure network settings and information. While you will likely do the majority of your configuration using GUIs, these versions of the `IPCONFIG` command are quick and easy to master.

IPCONFIG   Displays the basic IP configuration information on your interfaces.

IPCONFIG /ALL   Displays all IP configuration information on each network interface card.

IPCONFIG /FLUSHDNS|DISPLAYDNS   Displays or flushes the contents of the DNS resolver cache.

IPCONFIG /RENEW{ADAPTER}   Renews the IP configuration on a particular network interface card (adapter).

IPCONFIG /RELEASE{ADAPTER}   Releases the IP configuration on a particular network interface card (adapter).

When dealing with clients, you will use **IPCONFIG** quite a bit. It quickly gives you the current IP configuration on all of your network interfaces. On a Windows Server 2003 system, you will likely have more than one network interface card, and this quick command gives you fast, reliable information about your IP address, subnet mask, and default gateway, if set. It also will tell you whether your network interface card is physically connected.

When you run **IPCONFIG** with the **/ALL** option, you will also see DNS, WINS, and additional naming information, as shown in Figure 7-9.

WINS, along with DNS, is covered in Chapter 12.

```
C:\WINNT\System32\cmd.exe                                              _ □ ×

C:\>ipconfig/all

Windows 2000 IP Configuration

        Host Name . . . . . . . . . . . . : chrisw4
        Primary DNS Suffix  . . . . . . . : geeks.com
        Node Type . . . . . . . . . . . . : Hybrid
        IP Routing Enabled. . . . . . . . : No
        WINS Proxy Enabled. . . . . . . . : No
        DNS Suffix Search List. . . . . . : geeks.com
                                            ph.cox.net

Ethernet adapter Local Area Connection 3:

        Connection-specific DNS Suffix  . : ph.cox.net
        Description . . . . . . . . . . . : PE575C-3Com 10/100 LAN CardBus-Fast
Ethernet #2
        Physical Address. . . . . . . . . : 00-00-86-5E-C1-49
        DHCP Enabled. . . . . . . . . . . : Yes
        Autoconfiguration Enabled . . . . : Yes
        IP Address. . . . . . . . . . . . : 68.3.112.121
        Subnet Mask . . . . . . . . . . . : 255.255.248.0
        Default Gateway . . . . . . . . . : 68.3.112.1
        DHCP Server . . . . . . . . . . . : 172.19.73.22
        DNS Servers . . . . . . . . . . . : 68.2.16.30
                                            68.1.208.30
        Lease Obtained. . . . . . . . . . : Sunday, October 13, 2002 12:34:29 AM

        Lease Expires . . . . . . . . . . : Monday, October 14, 2002 12:34:29 AM
```

Figure 7-9   Results of the **IPCONFIG/ALL** command

This is powerful information for an administrator. The **IPCONFIG** command is not only useful for showing current configuration information; you can also do basic configuration with this command using the **/RELEASE** or **/RENEW** options.

When using DHCP to assign IP addresses, it is sometimes necessary to flush or wipe out the IP configuration if the DHCP server mistakenly gives out the same IP address to more than one host. This can occur if a computer was unplugged from the network and was not plugged back in for a period of time. In that case, you would have more than one host with the same IP address. As mentioned earlier, the duplicate IP addresses will cause problems. Therefore, it is wise to use the **/RELEASE** option to test one or more interfaces, if necessary. The **/RENEW** option queries the nearest DHCP server for new IP configuration information. Again, you can do this on an interface-by-interface basis simply by identifying the particular network adapter after the command switch.

The **/FLUSHDNS** and **/DISPLAYDNS** options of the **IPCONFIG** command allow you to perform basic configuration of the DNS on your computer.

There will be times when you are unable to resolve a hostname correctly because of an improper entry. By flushing the DNS resolver cache, which is a small database of names and IP addresses stored on your computer, you force the computer to talk to the DNS server to resolve a hostname to an IP address. This clears out any outdated or poisoned entries. This feature is useful in the Windows Server 2003 or Windows 2000 environment because you don't have to deal with nonexistent hosts or IP addresses. Windows Server 2003 requires that your computer's hostname be registered in its DNS database. To make sure that your computer's hostname is properly registered, you can issue the **IPCONFIG /REGISTERDNS** command. This re-registers all DHCP names with the DNS server.

If you are having problems accessing hosts by their hostname, it might be necessary to reset your DNS resolver cache. If you can ping a host with its IP address, but not with its DNS hostname, try the technique in Hands-on Project 7-4 before troubleshooting your DNS server.

Hands-on Project 7-4

To reset your DNS resolver cache:

1. Open a command window.

2. Type **ipconfig /displaydns** and press **Enter**. You should see several entries that show hostnames and their corresponding IP addresses. Your screen should look like Figure 7-10.

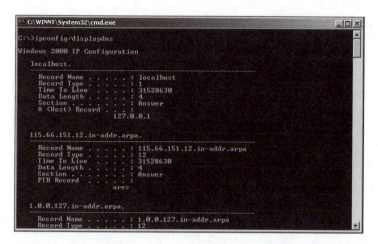

Figure 7-10   Results of the `IPCONFIG/DISPLAYDNS` command

3. If you had a bad entry, the computer would continually try to use the hostname's wrong IP address when resolving your request. Type **ipconfig /flushdns** and press **Enter** to delete all the cached entries.

4. Type **ipconfig /displaydns** and press **Enter**. Now you should see that only the local host entries are left. If you attempt to ping a remote host by its hostname, the computer will have to contact a DNS server to resolve the hostname to the IP address.

5. Type **exit** and press **Enter** to close the command window.

Another configuration command that is used frequently by network administrators is the **ROUTE** command. The **ROUTE** command manipulates routing tables and is available only if TCP/IP has been installed on the network. When you are dealing with static routes to servers or hosts, **ROUTE** can be very handy. Typically a computer will rely on routers on the network to handle any routing; however, there may be times when having a local static route in the computer's routing table is advantageous, as mentioned above. There are four commands that are used in combination with **ROUTE**.

ROUTE ADD <*DESTINATION*> <*GATEWAY*> METRIC   Adds a specified (metric) static route to the routing table through the identified gateway (router).

ROUTE PRINT   Displays a list of registered routes in the routing table.

ROUTE CHANGE   Modifies an existing route.

ROUTE DELETE   Deletes a static route from the routing table.

When used with the **ROUTE ADD** command, **/P** makes a route persistent every time the system is booted. By default, routes are not preserved when a system is restarted. Making a route persistent causes it to remain in the routing table even when the computer shuts off and turns back on. When used with the **ROUTE PRINT** command, **/P** displays the list of registered persistent routes.

By default, when adding a route, the address 255.255.255.255 is used for the subnet mask on the destination. You can change this by specifying a subnet mask for the destination using the **MASK** option. For example, if you wanted to place a static route to a particular network, you could use the following code:

```
ROUTE ADD 10.1.2.0 MASK 255.255.255.0 10.1.2.1 METRIC 3
```

ROUTE ADD *<DESTINATION>* MASK *<SUBNETMASK>*   Adds a specific subnet mask other than the default 255.255.255.255 to the destination.

You can also have the **ROUTE** command clear all of the gateway entries by using the **/F** switch. By doing so, the entries are cleared before the command is executed.

NETWORK MANAGEMENT

Now that you have a basic understanding of networking commands, you can learn about some more powerful commands that allow you to manage your network and files efficiently. Remember that TCP/IP is not the only protocol in use by Windows Server 2003. Recall that TCP/IP is a suite of protocols. One of the most powerful of these is File Transfer Protocol. The NetBIOS interface and Telnet terminal emulator also are important in network management.

FTP

File Transfer Protocol (FTP) is a TCP/IP protocol that allows you to manage files over networks. Using FTP, you can upload (send) and download (receive) files between FTP-compliant servers on your network, called FTP servers, and other remote computers through the Internet. For this to be accomplished, your computer and the remote site need to be running an FTP Server service. This service is included with the Web Services that are installed on the Windows Server 2003 server. You will learn more about services in Chapter 8. FTP functionality is also available in a command line environment comprising more than 50 commands.

Most companies have an FTP server that allows users to transfer large files between locations. This cuts down on the use of e-mail and avoids problems related to file attachments that exceed size limits.

You use a command to gain access to the FTP server, and from there you use other commands to store, download, or manage files. You begin with the **FTP** command.

C:_
Syntax

FTP *<SITENAME>*   Enters an FTP site.

Once you have accessed an FTP site, you typically are prompted for a username and password. Most public FTP sites and even some corporate FTP sites allow a username of *anonymous* with your e-mail address as a password. The e-mail address is used to track site usage. As you can guess, this is not a secure option for an FTP server. Anyone can enter a false e-mail address to fool the system. This anonymous account should not have access to trade secrets or other high-security items. Typically, such easily accessed FTP sites include advertising and white papers for a company, or a shareware program or free application. For more secure documents and applications, a username and password should be required to authenticate access.

Once you have entered your username and password, you will typically see a welcome message similar to the one shown in Figure 7-11.

7

Numbered messages

Figure 7-11   Typical welcome message in FTP

Notice that a number appears in front of the text generated by the command. These numbers represent different message types. For example, 220 would appear in front of the FTP server version, and 331 gives the anonymous access rule statement. After using FTP for a while, you will learn to recognize the numbers and what they represent.

Once you enter the FTP site by executing the **FTP** command, the command prompt changes to "ftp>," which indicates that you are in FTP command mode. Like the **DISKPART** command that you learned about in Chapter 5, FTP operates in its own environment. Once in FTP command mode, you can issue more than 50 FTP-specific commands. First, you would want to find out what files are available for downloading using the **FTP** command **DIR**.

C:_
Syntax

DIR   Shows a listing of files available in the root folder of the FTP server.

Within the FTP environment, you use many of the same commands you would use in the general command world. In fact, if necessary, you can use many of the same commands merely by preceding those commands at the FTP prompt with the exclamation point (!). This opens a command window and processes the command. However, many of the FTP commands are also available without the exclamation point. For example, if you want to change folders to another directory, you use the **CD** command.

Uploading Files

If you have users who need to transfer large files to your local servers, FTP is a great method to accomplish this task. It requires very low overhead on your server. Before you upload any files, you need to make sure that the FTP session is in the correct file transfer type. When transferring text, the **ASCII** method is used. This is also referred to as "text transfer" mode. If you are sending graphics, executable files, application documents, or zip files, you will need to use **Binary** mode. To find out what mode you are in, use the **TYPE** command from the FTP prompt.

TYPE   Displays which file transfer mode is in use: ASCII or Binary.

To change from one type to another, you simply type the file transfer mode you desire at the FTP prompt, like this:

```
ftp>ASCII
```

Once you have established the file transfer mode, you can begin to transfer files. To upload files to an FTP server, you can use the **PUT** command to store them on the server.

PUT *<FILENAME>*   Uploads a file to the current directory open on the FTP site.

While **PUT** works well when uploading a single file, it becomes very time-consuming if you have a large amount of files to transfer. That is why FTP allows you to place multiple files with a single command. By placing the letter M in front of the **PUT** command, you can upload as many files as you want.

MPUT *<FILENAMES>*   Uploads multiple files to the current directory open on the FTP site.

Downloading Files

File transfer is a two-way street with FTP. Downloading files is just as easy as uploading them. Once you have located the file or files you want to store, you use the **GET** command to retrieve them from the FTP server. An easy way to remember the difference between the **GET** and **PUT** commands is to think of a pantry shelf: I put the groceries on the shelf, but now I want to *get* them down.

GET *<FILENAME>*   Downloads a file from an FTP server.

As with the **MPUT** command, you can use the **MGET** command to download multiple files at the same time. While the files are downloading, you can perform other tasks.

You might be wondering how to determine when a file has been uploaded or downloaded. FTP lets you use hash marks to indicate the progress of a download or upload. For example, when downloading a file, you type the command **HASH** before you initiate the download. Once the download starts, FTP displays a hash mark in the command window (usually the # symbol) representing each block of data being transferred. Once the file is finished transferring, a "transfer complete" message appears. The results of the **HASH** command look similar to the output in Figures 7-12 and 7-13.

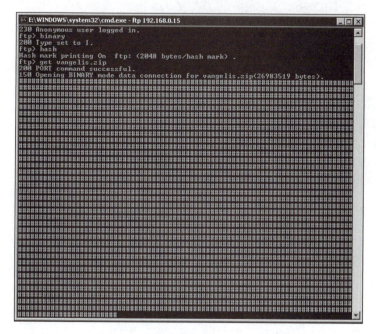

Figure 7-12   Starting an FTP download with hash marks

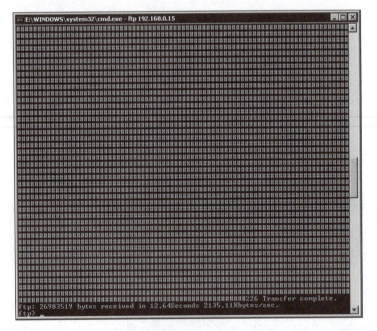

Figure 7-13   Completed FTP download

You might also be wondering where downloaded files go, or to what location they are downloaded. When performing the **GET** command in FTP, files are downloaded to whichever directory you are working in when starting the download. If you navigate to this directory, you will find the documents and applications you have downloaded from an FTP site.

The commands used most frequently in FTP are listed in Table 7-2.

Table 7-2   FTP commands

Subcommand	Function
!	Escapes from the FTP subsystem to the command shell.
?	Specifies the name of the command for which you want a description. If the command is not specified, **FTP** displays a list of all commands.
APPEND	Appends a local file to a file on the remote computer using the current file type setting.
ASCII/BINARY	Sets the file transfer type to ASCII, which is the default, or Binary.
BELL	Instructs a bell to ring after each file transfer command is completed. By default, the bell is off.
BYE	Ends the FTP session with the remote computer and exits FTP.
CLOSE	Ends the FTP session with the remote server and returns to the command prompt.

Table 7-2   FTP commands (continued)

Subcommand	Function
DEBUG	Turns debugging on or off. When debugging is on, each command sent to the remote computer is printed on screen, preceded by the string >. By default, debugging is off.
DELETE	Deletes files on remote computers.
GLOB	Turns filename globbing on or off. Globbing permits use of wildcard characters (* and ?) in local file or path names. By default, globbing is on.
LITERAL	Sends options to the remote FTP server exactly as the user types them. A single FTP reply code is expected in return.
LS	Displays an abbreviated list of a remote directory's files and subdirectories.
PROMPT	Turns prompting on or off. FTP prompts users during multiple file transfers to allow them to selectively retrieve or store files, while MGET and MPUT transfer all files if prompting is turned off. By default, prompting is on.
RECV	Copies a remote file to the local computer using the current file transfer type. RECV is identical to GET.
STATUS	Displays the current status of FTP connections and command toggles (for example, whether DEBUG is on or off).

In Hands-on Project 7-5, you access Course Technology's FTP site and download a file.

Hands-on Project 7-5

To download a file using FTP:

1. Open a command window.

2. Type **ftp** at the prompt and press **Enter**. Notice that the command prompt changes from "E:\>" to "ftp>."

3. Type **open ftp.course.com** and press **Enter**. You should see the welcome banner from Course Technology's FTP site, as shown in Figure 7-14.

Figure 7-14   Welcome banner from the Course Technology FTP site

4. The cursor should now be at the bottom of the command window. Type **anonymous** and press **Enter** to log in. For a password, type your e-mail address and press **Enter**.

5. Check to make sure that you are in ASCII transfer mode by typing **type** at the prompt and pressing **Enter**. You will see a message confirming that you are in ASCII mode.

6. Display a list of the available files by typing **dir** and pressing **Enter**.

The various areas of interest at Course Technology are listed here with detailed documentation available to the public. Figure 7-15 shows the listing of available files. Your results may differ.

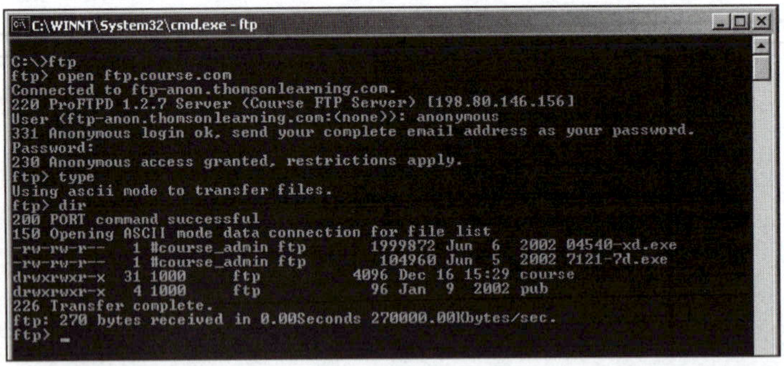

Figure 7-15 Files available for download from the Course Technology FTP server

7. At the prompt, type **bye** and press **Enter** to close your connection with Course Technology and end the FTP session. Type **exit** and press **Enter** to close the command window.

NetBIOS

NetBIOS is a high-level programming language interface. It was originally intended to be used with MS-DOS programs that network IBM PC-compatible microcomputers. To build LANs based on the networking hardware and software available for those computers, Microsoft and other vendors agreed on using NetBIOS as the standard interface to design their networking system components and programs. This interface uses names limited to 15 characters in length to identify each network resource. There is a 16th bit available that is used to identify the service that is running on that host. For example, you might have a computer that has a NetBIOS name of JOHNSMITHHOMEPC. The 15 characters identify the computer, but there would be an additional 16th bit identifying the different services such as FTP, TCP, and others.

NetBIOS names must be unique within a network. This is different from DNS, which is hierarchical in nature. In a NetBIOS environment, you cannot have two computers in your network named JOHNSMITH. In a DNS environment, you could have a JOHNSMITH.GEEKS.COM and a JOHNSMITH.SALES.GEEKS.COM. Both computers' names would be JOHNSMITH, but because they exist in different hierarchies, there is no redundancy. As you will learn later in this chapter, Active Directory in Windows Server 2003 uses the DNS convention. These names are dynamically registered when computers boot up, services start, or users log on. NetBIOS names can be registered as unique or as group names. Unique names have one address associated with a name. Group names have more than one address mapped to a name.

Prior to Windows 2000, all DOS-based and Windows-based operating systems required the NetBIOS naming interface to support network capabilities. Once Microsoft released Windows 2000, support for the NetBIOS naming interface was no longer required for networking computers. If you are running an entirely pure Windows 2000 or Windows Server 2003 network, you do not need NetBIOS. However, most networks still need to integrate legacy operating systems that require NetBIOS network names with computers running Windows 2000.

Because many legacy systems and some software applications still require the use of NetBIOS names, you will see support for NetBIOS in Windows Server 2003. NetBIOS is a LAN-based interface, so for information to cross from one network segment to another, you will need some help. NetBEUI, the protocol that was designed to use NetBIOS, is nonroutable. This means it can only stay in the local network segment and cannot be routed. This is different from TCP/IP, which can be routed and can cross network segments. This support is provided through NetBIOS over TCP/IP (NetBT) and can, if desired, be manually disabled. NetBIOS is not routable by default and needs help traversing networks. NetBIOS can reach beyond its local network by piggybacking on TCP/IP. NetBT allows piggybacking to happen. To start NetBIOS over TCP/IP, you use the **NET START** command, and to stop it you use the **NET STOP** command.

NET START TCP/IP NetBIOS HELPER   Starts the NetBT service.

NET STOP TCP/IP NetBIOS HELPER   Stops the NetBT service.

NBTSTAT   Displays protocol statistics and current TCP/IP connections using NetBT (NetBIOS over TCP/IP).

Several options are used with **NBTSTAT**. The most common are:

- **-N**: Lists local NetBIOS names. A status of "registered" indicates that the name is registered by broadcast (Bnode) or WINS (other node types). Node types indicate how the information is gained by the host.

- **-R**: Reloads the Lmhosts file after purging all names from the NetBIOS name cache. The Lmhosts file is a text file that contains manually entered NetBIOS-to-IP address name resolution entries.

- **-R**: Lists name resolution statistics for Windows networking name resolution. On a Windows 2000 computer configured to use WINS, this option returns the number of names resolved and registered by broadcast or WINS.

- **-RR**: Releases and refreshes NetBIOS names within the WINS Server database.

- **-A**: Lists the NetBIOS name table and corresponding IP addresses that are known by the host.

- **-c**: Lists NetBT's cache of remote machine names and their IP addresses.

Telnet

Telnet is a terminal emulation protocol for TCP/IP networks. The Telnet utility runs on your computer and connects your PC to a server on a network. You can enter commands through the Telnet program on your local computer and they are executed as if you were entering them directly on the remote server. This enables you to control the server and communicate with other servers on the network. To start a Telnet session, you must log in to a server by entering a valid username and password. Telnet is a common way to remotely control Web servers, routers, switches, and other networking equipment.

SECURITY

When network users access information over the network or over the Internet, security becomes increasingly important for network administrators. Hackers might attempt to gain entry to your networks and do damage or steal files. Two of the more powerful weapons against these attacks are NTFS and share permissions.

As you learned in Chapter 6, objects in a Windows Server 2003 environment have an access control list (ACL). ACLs describe the groups and individuals who have access to specific objects in Windows Server 2003. Typically, the individuals and security groups are defined in the Active Directory Users and Computers GUI. Many types of Windows 2000 and Windows Server 2003 objects have associated ACLs, including all Active Directory objects, local NTFS files and folders, the registry, and printers.

You can see the NTFS permissions for an object by right-clicking the object and selecting Properties, as shown in Figure 7-16. Select the Security tab to view the **Discretionary Access Control List (DACL)** on that object. If you don't see a Security tab, it is most likely because your hard drive is running as FAT32 instead of NTFS. A DACL is a list of access control entries that define what a user can do. Figure 7-17 shows that the currently logged-on user has Full Control permissions set on the D drive for the Authenticated Users group.

Typically the Authenticated Users group will have Read & Execute, List Folder Contents, and Read as default permissions.

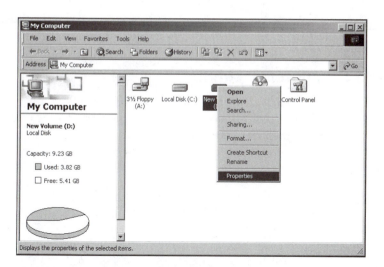

Figure 7-16   Properties of the D drive

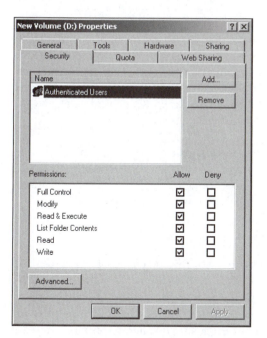

Figure 7-17   Security tab showing the DACL for the D drive

The Security tab shows the list of groups that have access to the selected object, plus a summary of the permissions assigned to each group. The Advanced button displays the group permissions in detail so that users can use more advanced features for granting permissions, such as defining access inheritance options. As a network administrator, you can use the **CACLS** command to gain greater and more specific control of these ACLs.

Next, you will learn about some of the settings you will be adjusting with this command, including user accounts, group accounts, and computer accounts.

User, Group, and Computer Accounts

As you learned in Chapter 6, each user on a network needs a user account that allows him or her to access files, folders, and other objects on the network. These accounts can be both local and domain based. If you have a local account, it is valid only on the local machine. Users with a domain user account can access files, folders, and other objects anywhere in the domain.

Adding permissions user by user for objects on the network is tedious. Part of Microsoft's Active Directory design and implementation uses groups to simplify administration. Groups act as containers for multiple user accounts that share common permissions. By placing users inside groups, you can more efficiently administrate users' access to network objects. For example, if you have 150 people on your sales staff and they all need access to a certain folder, you can place those 150 user accounts into a Sales group and grant permissions to the group rather than 150 individual accounts.

 You must plan your groups carefully, as some users might belong to multiple groups—which could affect permissions set on objects. Microsoft uses the following strategy when designing groups for access to data, applications, and so on: users go into global groups, global groups can go into other global groups, global groups go into local domain groups (or domain local), and you assign permissions for those local domain groups.

It might seem logical that only user accounts can be permitted or denied access to an object, but that is not true in your network. Many times, object access requires not only a valid user account, but also a valid computer account. ACLs accept computer accounts as well as user accounts.

More on the CACLS Command

Recall from Chapter 6 that the command you use to change permissions on an object in Windows Server 2003 is **CACLS**. **CACLS** can be used to modify the ACLs on files or directories. This ability is often useful for adding or deleting user or group permissions without modifying other existing permissions. **CACLS** can also be used to change permissions for groups with names containing a space: When specifying such a group, it is necessary to delimit the name of the group with double quotation marks (for example, "group name").

The **CACLS** command is very powerful and should be used only by experienced administrators. You can use the command to learn how group and user accounts are defined, and to see whether subfolders (directories) exist. Because inheritance does operate with NTFS permissions, inheritance status is important. Inheritance allows administrators to place permissions on parent objects that apply to a child object. For example, you might want to grant a contractor access to some sales data. You use the **CACLS** command to add her user account to the Sales folder's ACL with the Read/Write permission, which allows the contractor to read and revise every file within Sales. If Sales contains sub-folders that hold confidential data inside—say, if a Sales Finance folder exists within Sales—you have just granted the contractor access to this information as well.

You learned about the **N, R, C,** and **F** options for **CACLS** in Chapter 6. Other options for the **CACLS** command include:

- **/T:** Changes ACLs of specified files in the current directory and all subdirectories.

- **/E:** Edits ACLs instead of replacing them.

- **/C:** Continues changing ACLs, ignoring errors.

- **/G:<user|group> perm:** Grants specified user or group access permissions. Permissions can be **R** (Read), **C** (change or write), or **F** (full control).

- **/R <USERNAME>**—Revokes specified user's or group's access permissions.

- **/P:perm:** Replaces specified user's or group's access permissions. Permissions can be **N** (none), **R** (read), **C** (change or write), or **F** (full control).

- **/D:** Denies specified user access.

Using **CACLS**, you can perform multiple changes at the same time. For example, to change the ACLs of all files in the C:\Temp directory (but not its subdirectories), to add the Read permission for the Domain Users global group and the Users local group, and to remove any explicit permissions for the Everyone group, you would type the following at the command prompt:

```
cacls c:\temp\*.* /e /g "Domain Users":r Users:r /r Everyone
```

More on Permissions

As you learned in Chapter 6, Windows Server 2003 allows for share permissions and NTFS permissions. You can set up folders on your server to be shared using the Shared Folder snap-in in a Microsoft Management Console (MMC). Certain hidden shares are available by default with Server 2003. The C$, IPCSHARE$, and PRINT$ shares are just a few of the hidden shares. Only by typing them using the Universal Naming Convention (UNC) will the authorized user have access to these shares. For example:

```
\\JOHNSMITH\C$
```

You cannot change the permissions on default system shares.

 You can create other hidden shares by simply adding the $ symbol after the name of the folder. For example, the Sales folder can be hidden by adding a $ after it, making it Sales$.

One of the significant things to realize here is that even if you set share folder permissions, those permissions are worthless if someone accesses the folder locally. This is where NTFS permissions come into play.

NTFS File and Folder Permissions

Unlike share permissions, NTFS file and folder permissions are in effect when accessed locally and over the network. Folder permissions include Full Control, Modify, Read & Execute, List Folder Contents, Read, and Write. File permissions include Full Control, Modify, Read & Execute, Read, and Write.

It is also important to note what happens to file permissions when files and folders are copied or moved. The following guidelines apply when copying files or folders:

- When copying a file or folder *within the same NTFS partition*, the copy of the file or folder takes on the permissions of the destination.

- When copying a file or folder *between different NTFS partitions*, the copy takes on the permissions of the destination.

- When copying a file or folder to a *non-NTFS partition*, the file or folder loses all permissions.

When you move files or folders, the following rules apply:

- When moving a file or folder *within the same NTFS partition*, the file or folder retains its permissions.

- When moving a file or folder *between different NTFS partitions*, the file or folder takes on the permissions of the destination (because a move operation is actually a copy and delete).

- When moving a file or folder to a *non-NTFS partition*, the file or folder loses all permissions.

NTFS vs. Share Permissions

When both NTFS and share permissions exist on a folder, the permissions that are held in common by the folder or file apply to the user. For example, if you have Change and Read share permissions, but your only NTFS permission on that folder is Read, you will only have Read permission.

CHAPTER SUMMARY

In this chapter, you learned about how hosts (computers) communicate using protocols. The most popular of the protocols in use is TCP/IP. This suite of protocols is used in the Windows Server 2003 family. In addition to protocols, hosts require that some sort of naming convention be used. Primarily, hosts use the DNS naming convention. However, due to legacy software and applications, NetBIOS names are used as well.

When dealing with a networked environment, it is imperative that an administrator knows how to manage and maintain a network with the tools that are available. Networking commands fall into three basic categories: diagnostics, configuration, and troubleshooting.

1. Diagnostic commands give you real-time information that can be used to identify problems.

2. Configuration commands allow you to create settings in your networking protocols or on network adapters (interfaces).

3. Troubleshooting commands allow you to find issues that are causing problems on your network.

Not only can hosts communicate, but they can also exchange files with the use of the File Transfer Protocol (FTP), part of the TCP/IP suite. FTP allows a host to transfer or download files to a Windows Server 2003 system running FTP services. NetBIOS names are used by legacy applications and software. The protocol that transports NetBIOS is called NetBEUI. NetBEUI is not routable like TCP/IP, so it uses NetBEUI over TCP (NetBT) to route over network segments. Telnet is another popular application that is part of the TCP/IP protocol suite. It allows a user to remotely administrate a host as if the user was at the host.

Security is vital to any business, and Windows Server 2003 uses several methods to keep information safe and reliable. Discretionary Access Control Lists (DACLs) show which users or groups of users are allowed access to objects on your computers. Permissions through these DACLs can be assigned on files or folders with NTFS permissions as well as through Shared File and Folder permissions.

7

COMMAND SUMMARY

Command	Function
NETSTAT	Displays information in the routing table and current connections.
NETDIAG	Displays statistics and runs diagnostics on the network interface card.
PING	Tests TCP/IP connectivity.
TRACERT	Similar to PING but gives details of each router through which the packet passes.
PATHPING	Similar to TRACERT but gives even more detail.
PATHPING /H	Sets the maximum number of hops to search over.
IPCONFIG	Displays the IP address, subnet mask, and default gateway set on your interface.
IPCONFIG/ALL	Displays all relevant information about IP settings on a network interface card.
IPCONFIG/FLUSHDNS IPCONFIG/DISPLAYDNS	Deletes or displays DNS resolver cache entries.
IPCONFIG/RENEW	Renews the IP address lease from a DHCP server. Computers only "borrow" addresses from a DHCP server.

Command	Function
`IPCONFIG/RELEASE`	Releases the IP address lease from a DHCP server.
`ROUTE ADD`	Adds a route to a routing table.
`ROUTE PRINT`	Displays registered routes in the routing table.
`ROUTE CHANGE`	Modifies an existing route.
`ROUTE DELETE`	Deletes a static route from the routing table.
`FTP`	Opens the FTP prompt.
`FTP|DIR`	Lists all files in the current directory.
`FTP|TYPE`	Displays which download type is currently active (ASCII or binary).
`FTP|PUT<FILENAME>`	Places a file on the FTP server in the current directory.
`FTP|GET<FILENAME>`	Retrieves a file from the FTP server in the current directory.
`NET START TCP/ IP NetBIOS HELPER`	Starts the NetBT service.
`NET STOP TCP/ IP NetBIOS HELPER`	Stops the NetBT service.
`NBTSTAT`	Displays protocol statistics and current TCP/IP connections using NetBT.

KEY TERMS

ASCII — American Standard Code for Information Interchange. A file format where every numeral or character has an assigned ASCII code number.

Binary — A mathematical system that uses either a 1 or a 0 to designate whether a bit is on or off. Also used to describe the sending of applications or executable files in a file transfer process.

Discretionary Access Control List (DACL) — A list of access control entries that define who can do what to an object.

Dynamic Host Configuration Protocol (DHCP) — A protocol that is part of the TCP/IP protocol suite and dynamically assigns IP addresses to hosts on a network segment. Typically runs on a Windows Server 2003 system.

File Transfer Protocol (FTP) — A TCP/IP protocol that allows you to send and receive files over networks.

host — Computers or interfaces that exist on a network. Also called node.

loopback — An address set up on a local network interface card that allows you to test the TCP/IP setup. Typically this value is 127.0.0.1, but you can use any IP address in the 127 address range.

NetBEUI — The protocol that transports NetBIOS.

network interface card — A piece of hardware that provides a means for Windows Server 2003 to package data and place it on a network.

Network Basic Input Output System (NetBIOS) — The API that was developed by IBM to allow computers to communicate over a LAN.

node — *See* host.

Open Systems Interconnection (OSI) — A model of communication between two hosts over a network. Each layer of this model designates certain actions and information to be included in the communication and transmission of data.

packets — Small pieces of files and e-mail messages that travel over networks and are reassembled into their original form upon reaching their destination.

peer-to-peer network — A network in which all of the computers share files with each other. In this environment, accounts for each user must exist on every "peer" computer in the network.

protocol — A standard or set of rules that allows communication between computers. A method of communication shared by a source and destination. Typically protocols are developed in layers or "stacks" with elements operating at each layer.

protocol suite — Multiple applications and services operating within a protocol stack.

Router — A host that determines the best way for packets to reach their destinations.

session — A connection between two or more hosts over a network.

sniffer — An application that examines packets by recording information that passes through a router.

subnet mask — A 32-bit binary number that identifies the network and host portion of an IP address.

Transmission Control Protocol/Internet Protocol (TCP/IP) — A set of protocols that allows hosts to communicate with each other. It is used for communications over the Internet.

workstation — A computer that is not a server. Sometimes workstations do not have an operating system installed and rely on a server for the operating system.

7

REVIEW QUESTIONS

1. What task does an IP address perform?

   a. It identifies a computer.

   b. It identifies a user.

   c. It identifies a unique host on the network.

   d. It identifies the server.

2. What are the two methods of setting an IP address on your computer?

   a. static and dynamic

   b. static and manual

   c. static and random

   d. static and occasional

3. What device handles files and applications and typically utilizes a static IP address?

   a. workstation

   b. client

   c. host

   d. node

   e. server

4. Which command would you use to establish a static route to your routing table?

   a. **ROUTE ADD 10.20.30.40**

   b. **ROUTE ADD 10.20.30.40 255.255.255.0 10.20.30.1**

   c. **ROUTE ADD 10.20.30.40 MASK 255.255.255.0 10.20.30.1**

   d. **ROUTE ADD 10.20.30.40 MASK 255.255.255.0 DEST 10.20.30.1**

5. Which option ensures that a static route persists—even when you reboot your computer?

   a. **/BOOT**

   b. **/P**

   c. **/B**

   d. **/PERMANENT**

6. You are attempting to transfer a file from your server and you are not able to access it. Which IP address would you ping first?

   a. the server

   b. your default gateway

   c. another computer on your network segment

   d. the loopback address

7. Which option allows you to continually execute **PING** commands?

   a. **/C**

   b. **/P**

   c. **/R**

   d. **/E**

   e. **/t**

8. Which of the following are related to TCP/IP? (Choose all that apply.)

   a. TCP

   b. UDP

   c. ICMP

   d. GNS

   e. SAP

   f. IPX

9. Users sharing files on their computers is an example of which type of network?

   a. host-to-user

   b. peer-to-peer

   c. client/server

   d. shareware

10. FTP stands for:

    a. File Transmission Protocol

    b. Firewire Transmission Protocol

    c. File Transport Protocol

    d. File Transfer Protocol

11. Networks use the _____ Protocol as their primary means of communicating on the Internet.

    a. HyperText Transmission

    b. Secure Sockets Layer

    c. Internet

    d. Internetwork Exchange

    e. User Datagram

    f. HyperText Markup Language

12. If you wanted to remotely access another computer through a command prompt, which of these TCP/IP protocol suite components would you use?

    a. Telnet

    b. FTP

    c. TFTP

    d. SFTP

13. Which of the following protocols are not routable by default?

    a. IP

    b. NetBIOS

    c. DECNET

    d. AppleTalk

    e. IPX

14. The information that tells a computer whether to grant access to a file for someone is called a(n) _____.

    a. share

    b. NTFS

    c. ACL

    d. access

7

15. Microsoft recommends using which of the following guidelines for utilizing groups?

    a. Users, local domain, global, assign permissions at the local domain level

    b. Local domain, users, global, host machine

    c. Users, universal, global, host

    d. Users, global, local domain, assign permissions at local domain level

16. Bob, an accountant, needs to have access to a particular accounting/sales folder on the file server. He has NTFS permissions of Read on the folder and share permissions of Write/Change. Will this solution allow him to access the folder?

    a. yes

    b. no

17. Which command starts NetBIOS over TCP service?

    a. **NET START TCP/IP NetBIOS HELPER**

    b. **NET START SIMPLE TCP/IP**

    c. **NET START SERVER**

    d. **NET START TCP/IP NetBIOS**

    e. **NET START NetBIOS**

18. Which of these protocols is associated with Novell's NetWare network operating system?

    a. IPX/SPX

    b. DECNET

    c. AppleTalk

    d. NetBIOS

19. Which command is used to send packets and display the routers in between your computer and the destination you are trying to reach?

    a. **PING**

    b. **PATHPING**

    c. **PATH TRACE**

    d. **PING TRACE**

DISCOVERY EXERCISES

1. Enable the FTP services on your server and upload several pieces of documentation and a few small applications in the FTP site. You can find instructions on how to enable FTP on your Windows Server 2003 server in the help files. Then, attempt to access the site and download these files to another computer. Why are you able to download the text files, yet unable to download the applications? Try changing the type of transfer and see if you are able to download the applications. If you have Internet access, isolate the FTP server from a production environment and have a friend or associate attempt to access your FTP server.

2. Use the **IPCONFIG** command to determine your current IP address. Are you able to determine whether or not you are using a DHCP server for IP address assignment? If you are using DHCP, use **IPCONFIG** to renegotiate a new IP address. Did your IP address change?

3. From the command line, create a new user account named Joe User with the logon name juser. Use the **CACLS** command to assign juser Read-Only permission to the C:\Program Files directory. Attempt to access the Program Files directory from a remote computer.

4. Use the **TRACERT** command to see the path your packets are taking to *www.course.com*. Write down the routers that it passes through. Wait 10 minutes and then repeat the **TRACERT** command. Did the path change or remain the same? Wait 30 seconds and try it again. Did the path change or remain the same?

5. Talk with your network administrator and find out if you are running any software that requires NetBIOS. Make a list and do some research on the software companies' Web sites to see if they have a version that doesn't require the use of NetBIOS names. Send an e-mail to one of the companies asking if it plans on abandoning NetBIOS in the future and, if not, why.

7

8

NETWORKING A SERVER

After reading this chapter and completing the exercises, you will be able to:

♦ Work with services

♦ View and work with workstation elements

♦ View and work with network elements

♦ Use network resources

♦ Synchronize networked resources

Every feature that is provided by Windows Server 2003 over the network is provided through the use of specific programs called services. These services are used to broadcast and maintain network information, and also to allow computers to access the server over the network. In this chapter, you will learn how to recognize, configure, and manipulate the services that are essential for networking functionality.

SERVICES ESSENTIAL FOR NETWORKING

The primary physical requirements for network support in Windows Server 2003 are a network interface card (NIC) and the cabling media and equipment necessary to connect two or more computers. Recall that a NIC is a piece of hardware that provides a means for Windows Server 2003 to package data and place it on the network. As discussed in Chapter 7, networking support elements, such as drivers and protocols, must also be installed on the Windows Server 2003 system. Assuming that networking support exists, and that you are now familiar with GUI-based networking, you can begin to learn about how Microsoft networking works.

All Microsoft server-based functions such as networking are based on services. A **service** is a program that provides a basic task. Like people who provide services in the physical world—often in the background and unseen—Windows Server 2003 services maintain a background presence, providing the required tasks when necessary. Basic services available in Server 2003 are listed in Table 8-1. Additional services may appear on a server depending on installed applications and enhanced server functionality.

 These services are all listed as key terms at the end of this chapter.

Table 8-1   Windows Server 2003 services

Service	What it does
Alerter	Allows the system to send alerts to administrators. The users who receive these messages can be configured through the Manage Your Server wizard (within Administrative Tools).
Browser	Keeps a list of all computers on the network and delivers the list to programs that request it, such as Windows Explorer and My Network Places.
Clipbook	Allows you to cut and paste data to and from network-based files and folders.
DHCP Client	Enables you to automatically receive IP address configurations from a local or relayed DHCP server.
File Replication	Allows the server to perform coordination between domain controllers within the same domain to synchronize user accounts and login scripts.
Messenger	Allows the server to receive console messages from other systems on the network.
Netlogon	Handles user and computer account logon and authentication.
Plug and Play	Enables the system to automatically detect and install hardware.
Server	Enables file, folder, and printer sharing over the network. Allows systems on the network to access these resources.

Table 8-1 Windows Server 2003 services (continued)

Service	What it does
Spooler	Allows the server to maintain a memory pool for files that are sent to the printer. Printer memory is often too small to hold an entire file. To successfully print these files, the Spooler service must maintain a separate memory location for temporary storage, and then "feed" the printer the file(s) in chunks that the printer can handle.
Workstation	Allows the system to use resources on networked systems that are running the Server service.

The **SC** command, discussed in Chapter 4, and the **NET START** command can start and stop a service. You will learn about **NET START** next.

C:_
Syntax

NET START   Lists the services available.

NET START \<SERVICE\>   Starts the *SERVICE.*

NET STOP \<SERVICE\>   Stops the *SERVICE.*

NET PAUSE \<SERVICE\>   Pauses the SERVICE.

NET CONTINUE \<SERVICE\>   Restarts the *SERVICE* after it has been paused.

8

When you use either **SC** or any of the **NET** commands listed above to use a service, the standard command prompt disappears, the system displays a message indicating that it is attempting to stop or start the service, and once the processing of the command is complete, the command prompt returns. Depending on what other applications are installed on the system, other services may depend on the service for their own existence or status. For example, the Distributed File System (DFS) service and Computer Browser service depend on the Workstation service for their functionality. If any services are dependent on a service that is being altered, the system lists the affected service(s) and offers the option to stop those services as well. In Figure 8-1, you can see that the DFS and Computer Browser services are dependent on the Workstation service.

Figure 8-1   **NET STOP** Workstation dependencies

When stopping a service, you should write down all of the dependent services that are displayed, as shown in Figure 8-1. Once a service is stopped, all of its dependent services also are stopped. Unfortunately, when the original service is restarted, the dependent services are not automatically restarted by the system. Writing down the dependent services will help you to manually restart the dependents to ensure full working order. Any time you pause and restart the primary service, you will need to restart the services that depend on that primary service.

The Workstation Service

Once networking support is installed, the Workstation service is brought online automatically. The Workstation service allows the computer to access information and data located on other computers on the network. These computers can be servers or other workstations. Microsoft-networked computers can view information on other Microsoft-networked computers, regardless of the specific operating systems on either computer.

Occasionally, the Workstation service (or any service) needs to be paused or stopped. Any number of situations can arise that might require this action, but all of them occur for a similar reason: communications with another computer or the feature that the service provides needs to be discontinued immediately.

One way to stop a service is to shut down the computer. However, it is preferable to stop a particular service using various tools or commands instead of shutting down the computer. Discontinuing a service without shutting down the system allows the computer to continue performing other tasks.

The Workstation service can be stopped through the Start menu, Administrative Tools, Services (or Computer Management, Services) or through the **SC** or **NET STOP WORKSTATION** commands. The two GUI tools work well; however, they both offer additional features that are unnecessary when the goal is simply to stop the service. **NET STOP** works more quickly because it does not contain extra features. As is typically the case when troubleshooting a problem, it may be difficult to get GUI applications to function properly, so starting and stopping services from the command line is usually a faster, safer solution.

Similarly, the Workstation service can be restarted by using the **NET START WORKSTATION** command. If the service fails to start or stop, a message appears with some hint of what the problem is. At this point, you should check the Event Viewer for details.

In Hands-on Project 8-1, you will learn how to stop and restart the Workstation service. Although you can do this from the Services applet in Administrative Tools, often it is faster and more efficient to do so on the command line. When a server is running slowly or having problems, stopping a service from the command line may work when the GUI equivalent fails.

Hands-on Project 8-1

To stop and restart the Workstation service:

1. Open a command window.

2. Type **net stop workstation** and press **Enter**.

3. Your screen should look like Figure 8-1. Press **y** and press **Enter**.

4. After a few moments, all of the services should be stopped, and your screen should look like Figure 8-2.

```
C:\WINDOWS\system32\cmd.exe
Microsoft Windows [Version 5.2.3663]
(C) Copyright 1985-2001 Microsoft Corp.

C:\Documents and Settings\Administrator.MACHINE>net stop workstation
The following services are dependent on the Workstation service.
Stopping the Workstation service will also stop these services.

    Distributed File System
    Computer Browser

Do you want to continue this operation? (Y/N) [N]: y

The Distributed File System service was stopped successfully.

The Computer Browser service is stopping..
The Computer Browser service was stopped successfully.

The Workstation service is stopping.
The Workstation service was stopped successfully.

C:\Documents and Settings\Administrator.MACHINE>_
```

Figure 8-2   Stopping the Workstation service

5. To restart the Workstation service, type **net start workstation** and press **Enter**.

6. Notice that not all of the services that were stopped in Step 2 restarted. You will need to restart those as well to fully return your system to its normal status. Type **net start "distributed file system"** and press **Enter**. Be sure to type the quotation marks. This is necessary when entering names of services that contain spaces in the name so that the system understands which words belong to the service name and which words are options for the command.

Quotation marks are necessary for all commands where a single object, such as a filename, contains spaces.

7. Type **net start "computer browser"** and press **Enter**. The results should be similar to Figure 8-3.

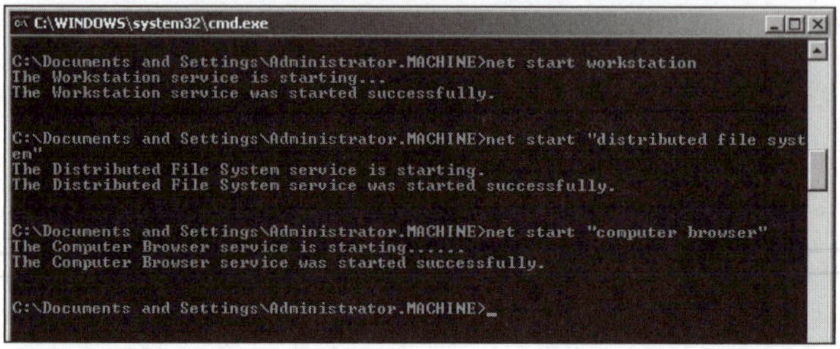

Figure 8-3   Restarting the Workstation service and its dependent services

8. Type **exit** and press **Enter** to close the command window.

Configuring the Workstation Service

Several features within the Workstation service can be configured using the **NET CONFIG** command. This command also can be used with the Server service, as you will learn later in this chapter.

NET CONFIG WORKSTATION /CHARCOUNT:<*BYTES*>   Lists bytes of data stored before that data is sent to the server.

NET CONFIG WORKSTATION /CHARTIME:<*MILLISECONDS*>
Displays the amount of time data is stored before that data is sent to the server.

NET CONFIG WORKSTATION /CHARWAIT:<*SECONDS*>   Specifies the amount of time to elapse before device timeout occurs and the device is no longer recognized by the network.

The **/CHARWAIT** option is used more often than the others. The idea behind **/CHARWAIT** is that a user attempts to connect to a specific computer that is listed within Windows Explorer, but it is either not on the network or responding slowly. The list of computers shown in Windows Explorer is not constantly updated, and sometimes it displays computers or resources that are not available. The **/CHARWAIT** option specifies the amount of time to elapse before the system determines that the networked computer is unavailable, and drops it from the Windows Explorer list. The default time is 3,600 seconds, which is equivalent to one hour.

The command for setting the **/CHARWAIT** time to 30 minutes would be:

```
NET CONFIG WORKSTATION /CHARWAIT:1800
```

The Server Service

The Server service enables other networked systems to access data on the current machine. By default, Windows Server 2003 runs the Server service. Windows XP and other workstation operating systems will not run the Server service until the File and Printer Sharing service is enabled. Once File and Printer Sharing is installed on the system, the system performs several tasks: the Server service automatically comes online, folders within Windows Explorer now include a Sharing tab, and other users can now access data on the server over the network.

Sometimes a situation will arise in which the system needs to stop acting as a server and sever all current network communications. This happens most often when administrators are installing software upgrades or performing backups. You might also need to stop connections on a Windows Server 2003 computer when network problems arise that may damage the system. Network problems can range from too much traffic to a malignant virus attack.

Stopping the Server service from the command line is accomplished by running the **NET STOP SERVER** command. The command causes the system to display any current connections to the server from the network, and prompts the user to continue the operation, after which any service dependencies are listed and the service stops.

Configuring the Server Service

While the usefulness of the **NET CONFIG WORKSTATION** command is up for debate, **NET CONFIG SERVER** is definitely useful. This is one of several commands that lacks a GUI counterpart. The options for **NET CONFIG SERVER** are as follows:

NET CONFIG SERVER /AUTODISCONNECT:<MINUTES>   The amount of idle connection time before the server terminates a given session.

NET CONFIG SERVER /HIDDEN:YES|NO   Removes the system name from server lists; it doesn't show up in My Network Places or as a listed computer within Explorer.

NET CONFIG SERVER /SRVCOMMENT: "<TEXT>"   Displays a text message or description with the computer name in My Network Places or Explorer.

By default, the **/AUTODISCONNECT** option is set at 15 minutes. This is generally enough time to ensure that the server machine isn't slowing down trying to track unresponsive connections while still allowing a reasonable amount of idle time to pass. The syntax for setting the **/AUTODISCONNECT** option to 30 minutes is as follows:

```
NET CONFIG SERVER /AUTODISCONNECT:30
```

The **/HIDDEN** option is particularly valuable for servers whose primary functionality relies on protocols and methods other than those involved with network browsing. For example, in a Web server or database system, administrators can still browse the server from other networked systems, but the server does not show up within My Network Places or Windows Explorer. This ensures that casual browsers or malevolent surfers are not able to readily detect and browse the contents of the server. The syntax for hiding the server is as follows:

```
NET CONFIG SERVER /HIDDEN:YES
```

In Hands-on Project 8-2, you will learn how to configure the server as hidden so that it will not appear on server lists within My Network Places or Windows Explorer.

Hands-on Project 8-2

To configure the server as hidden:

1. Open a command window.

2. Type **net config server** and press **Enter**. You should see that the hidden status is set to No.

3. Type **net config server /hidden:yes** and press **Enter**.

4. To confirm that the server is now hidden, type **net config server** and press **Enter**. The hidden status should now be set to Yes, as shown in Figure 8-4.

The server is now hidden

Figure 8-4   The hidden status of the server

5. Type **exit** and press **Enter** to close the window.

6. Open Windows Explorer. Click **My Network Places** in the left pane.

7. Press **F5** to update the networked systems. Notice that the server does not appear on the list.

The **/SRVCOMMENT** option lets you add a text description to any list in which the server might appear. This includes items displayed with the **NET CONFIG SERVER** and **NET VIEW** commands, as well as computers displayed within My Network Places or Windows Explorer.

Monitoring the Workstation and Server Services

To get a better idea of the specific tasks performed by the Workstation and Server services, you can use the **NET STATISTICS** command to view the current statistics of each service.

NET STATISTICS WORKSTATION   Displays the connectivity, networking, and session statistics for the Workstation service since the last time it was started.

NET STATISTICS SERVER   Displays session statistics, security violations, and device access information for the server since the last time the Server service was started.

The **NET STATISTICS** command can also act as a monitor, providing insight into networking problems, timeout problems, and security problems. There is no GUI equivalent for these commands, and their output, shown in Figures 8-5 and 8-6, is the only place to access these centralized statistics. Such information can indicate network-related problems.

8

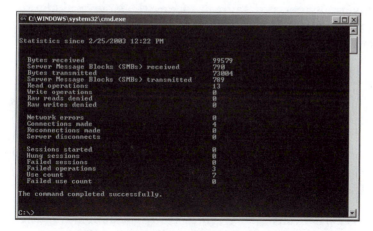

Figure 8-5   NET STATISTICS command for the Workstation service

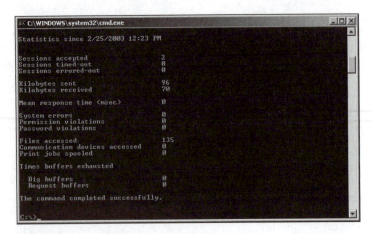

Figure 8-6 **NET STATISTICS** command for the Server service

VIEWING WORKSTATION COMPONENTS

All other **NET** commands associated with networking can be divided into the two categories relating to the service they deal with: Workstation or Server. If the associated service is stopped, down, or not functioning properly, the corresponding command will fail also.

The **NET SESSION** and **NET FILE** Commands

The **NET SESSION** command is related to the Server service. Say the server is running slowly, and you need to determine who is accessing data on the system from the network, or you need to run maintenance or shut down the system and determine who is currently connected to the computer through the LAN so that they can be notified of the pending downtime. You can determine active connections in both of these situations using Computer Management, Shared Folders or by using the **NET SESSION** command. Both methods are efficient; however, the Computer Management method displays how long the connection has existed and whether the connection is through the Guest account. While Computer Management may be preferable for displayed information, the **NET SESSION** command can provide more benefits in terms of speed and successful functionality.

NET SESSION   Displays all current connections to the server.

NET SESSION \\<*COMPUTERNAME*> /DELETE   Ends the connection between the server and the specified computer.

Figure 8-7 displays all active connections to the system. Severing a connection is a matter of typing **NET SESSION \\<*COMPUTERNAME*>/DELETE** where *COMPUTERNAME* is the computer listed on the screen. In the case of Figure 8-7, the command would read **NET SESSION \\BULLET /DELETE**.

Figure 8-7 `NET SESSION` connections

NET FILE is similar to the **NET SESSION** command in that it shows current activity on the server; however, instead of showing active connections, **NET FILE** lists open files. This can be particularly valuable if you need to determine which files on the network will not be backed up successfully, because **NET FILE** displays files that are currently locked. Locked files are files that are in use exclusively by a single user or computer and cannot be accessed by any other process.

NET FILE   Lists open files on the server.

NET FILE *<FILEID>*\CLOSE   Closes a file based on the file identification number listed with the NET FILE command.

More About Network Shares

Microsoft servers use network shares to make data available on the network. A network share consists of a folder within Windows Explorer or My Computer that has been flagged for sharing across the network, as shown in Figure 8-8. The banner is the name by which the share is known, which can be the folder name or another, more descriptive name.

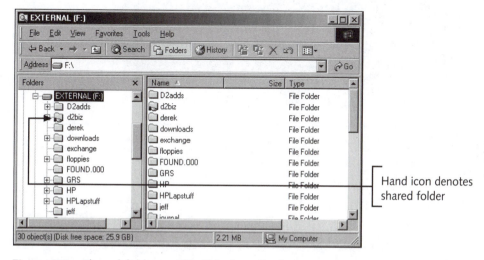

Hand icon denotes shared folder

Figure 8-8 Shared folders within Windows Explorer

As mentioned earlier, the Server service must be running on the server before you can share a folder and make it available for network access. By default, Windows Server 2003 is configured for file and folder sharing; Windows Server 2003 automatically installs and starts the Server service. Flagging a folder for sharing is relatively simple: you access the properties for the folder, select the Sharing tab, and select the Share This Folder radio button. There are other options available from this point, but these are associated with security: users, access, and permissions. Flagging a folder (enabling sharing) is not often done from the command line because it is easier to do from the GUI. However, creating and eliminating shares using commands can be handy when running scripts where data needs to be made available only for a short time.

By default, all hard drives and several folders are shared automatically once File and Print Sharing has been enabled. These default shares are called **administrative shares** and do not appear on any lists within My Network Places or Windows Explorer or using the **NET VIEW** command. Administrative shares are created by adding a dollar sign ($) to the end of the share name, and are accessed only when the specific share name ($ included) is entered on the address line of Windows Explorer or by using the **NET USE** command. Determining which shares are administrative shares can be done with the **NET SHARE** command, as shown in Figure 8-9. In this example, **NET SHARE C$** shows the properties for the administrative share labeled C$.

Figure 8-9 **NET SHARE** lists all shares and properties for a share

NET SHARE   Displays all active shares on the server.

NET SHARE *<SHARENAME>=<DRIVELETTER>:\<DIRECTORY>*
Creates a share and assigns it to the specified directory.

NET SHARE *<SHARENAME>$=<DRIVELETTER>:\<DIRECTORY>*
Creates a hidden administrative share and assigns it to the specified directory.

NET SHARE *<SHARENAME>* **/DELETE**   Deletes the specified share.

NET SHARE <SHARENAME> /USERS: <NUMBEROFCONCURRENTUSERS>   Configures the share for the specified maximum number of connections.

NET SHARE <SHARENAME> /USERS:UNLIMITED   Configures the share for unlimited concurrent connections.

NET SHARE <SHARENAME> /REMARK:<"DESCRIPTION">   Adds a description to the share. The description appears within My Network Places or Windows Explorer.

NET SHARE <SHARENAME> /CACHE:MANUAL|AUTOMATIC|NO Allows the share to be stored as part of a user's Offline Files and Folders configuration. A cache status of "Manual" means that changes to the offline content must be manually resynchronized with the share data. A cache status of "Automatic" means that changes to the offline content will be automatically resynchronized with the share data. A cache status of "No" disables the Offline Files and Folders configuration for this share.

By default, all hard disks on the server are shared as administrative shares. Creating a share is similar to creating a user account. To create a share on the D drive called "Userdata" based on the existing folder called Users, use the following command:

```
NET SHARE USERDATA=D:\USERS
```

You could also create the same share from the same folder, but add a comment to better describe the share's purpose and allow an unlimited number of users to access the resource. The following code creates the more complex share:

```
NET SHARE USERDATA=D:\USERS /UNLIMITED /REMARK:"D:\USERS
FOLDER"
```

A new feature of Windows Server 2003 is **share caching**. This feature, when coupled with Offline Files and Folders, determines whether a share that has been configured for offline storage is synchronized to a user's system automatically, manually, or not at all. This feature allows administrative control over what would otherwise be a user-defined function. The following example creates the share Userdata from the folder D:\USERS with a maximum of 15 concurrent users, adds a comment, and sets the share cache at automatic. The second example does the same with a pre-existing share called PROFILES.

```
NET SHARE USERDATA=D:\USERS /USERS:15 /REMARK:"Roaming
User Profiles" /CACHE:AUTOMATIC
```

```
NET SHARE PROFILES /USERS:15 /REMARK:"Roaming User
Profiles" /CACHE:AUTOMATIC
```

Offline Files and Folders is a Windows feature that allows users to access specific network data even when the network is down.

In Hands-on Project 8-3, you will learn how to create and share resources on your server. Later projects will access and utilize this share.

Hands-on Project 8-3

To experiment with shares:

1. Open a command window on the server.

2. Type **cd** and press **Enter** to navigate to the root directory of the C drive.

3. To create a share, a directory either must be created or must already exist. Type **md sharedata** to create the Sharedata directory and press **Enter**.

4. Future projects in this chapter require that you have at least one file inside the Sharedata directory. Type **cd sharedata** and press **Enter**, and then type **edit testshare.txt** and press **Enter**.

5. The Edit program opens. Type **I am learning how to be an awesome administrator** in the text editor window. Your screen should look like Figure 8-10.

Figure 8-10   Creating a text file that exists in the share

6. Save and close the file by pressing and holding **Alt** and pressing **f**. Release the keys. Hold down **Alt** and press **x** and then press **Enter** to save the file and exit the Edit program.

7. You should now be back at the command prompt. Type **cd** and press **Enter**.

8. To create a share called "userdata," type **net share userdata=c:\sharedata** and press **Enter**. If necessary, type the letter of the drive where you want to create the share, if it is not the C drive. You should see a confirmation message similar to the one shown in Figure 8-11.

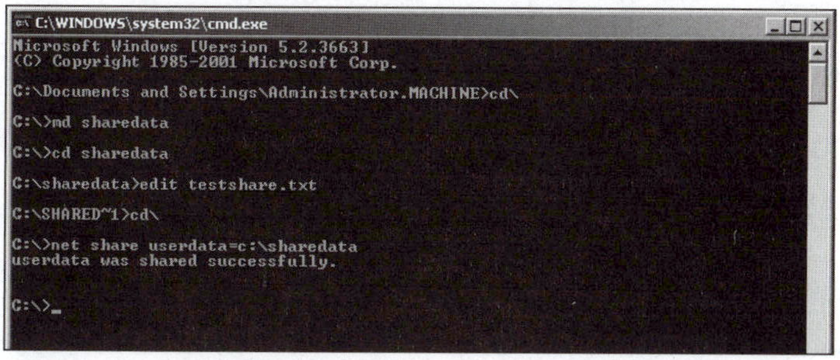

Figure 8-11   Sharing a directory

VIEWING NETWORK COMPONENTS

The existence of user accounts and shares allows network users to access data on a local computer. In this section, you will learn about the elements important to data access over a network.

Universal Naming Convention

The **Universal Naming Convention (UNC)** is a Microsoft naming standard that indicates the server name and share name that is used with commands or addresses.

UNC names can be used on the address line within Windows Explorer or My Network Neighborhood as a shortcut to data on a networked system, without spending time browsing the network. UNC names are also used frequently within networking commands to locate and map network data.

A UNC name can indicate the server, or it can be more detailed and specify a folder or resource that is located on a server. For example, the UNC name for the server "GOOGLIE" is simply \\GOOGLIE, while the UNC name for the "GLOP" share located on the GOOGLIE server is \\GOOGLIE\GLOP. Either UNC name can be used with commands on the command line and with GUI command equivalents.

Computers on the Network

Viewing active computers on the network is relatively simple, and is often done by administrators to test network connectivity. Using the Workstation service, the **NET VIEW** command queries the network for the **browse master** and retrieves a list of registered computers. The browse master is a system on the network that is responsible for maintaining a list of the computers on the network. This list is then given to any system that requests it from the browse master. If the browse master computer is not located on the network, the system that is running **NET VIEW** will become a browse master itself and take on the responsibilities of list maintenance. Browse master responsibilities can cause an otherwise healthy server to slow down, which might point to problems with networking on the server itself.

NET VIEW   Displays all computers on the network that are sharing resources.

NET VIEW /DOMAIN:<DOMAINNAME>   Displays all systems in the domain that are sharing resources. Not necessary if the current server is a domain controller or a member of a domain.

Many commands throughout this book provide features, such as speed, additional information, and enhanced functionality, that are unavailable with or unmatched by existing GUI counterparts. Unfortunately, the **NET VIEW** command is not one of them. Consider the following example:

An administrator is using a workstation on the LAN and needs to access a server that is located on the same LAN. One approach is to open My Network Places, locate the server name, and proceed from there. Another method is to do the same from Windows Explorer. Unfortunately, the server name may not be on the list, especially if the server has been marked as hidden. In this case, a third option would be to use the **NET VIEW** command to locate the server; however, if the server is not in My Network Places, it will not be in **NET VIEW** either. The solution: you need to know the name of the server you want to access. With that information in hand, here's how the administrator would access the server: open My Network Places and, on the address line, enter the server name preceded by two backslashes (\\). If the server exists anywhere on the network, My Network Places will display the available shares and the administrator can go from there. A seasoned administrator will often use this method before all others, just to save time.

Hands-on Project 8-4 will teach you how to use the **NET VIEW** command to confirm that the Userdata share was created (recall that you created it in the previous project).

Hands-on Project 8-4

To confirm that a share has been created:

1. Type **net view** followed by the UNC name of the server and press **Enter**. (You can determine the name of the server by clicking **Start**, right-clicking **My Computer**, and selecting **Properties**. The Computer Name tab displays the server name. The UNC for the server is two backslashes (\\) followed by the server name shown in My Computer, Properties.) In Figure 8-12, the command reads "net view \\machine".

2. All shares that are active on the server will be listed. This includes administrative shares, any pre-existing shares, and the Userdata share. Type **exit** and press **Enter**.

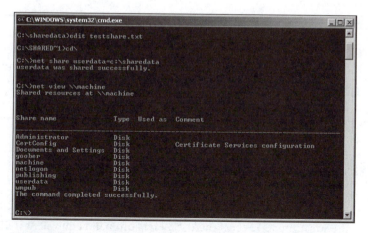

Figure 8-12   Using **NET VIEW** to view active shares

Again, **NET VIEW** by itself is not used very often because of its limited capabilities. However, the command does come in handy when testing network connectivity such as when booting to a floppy disk or CD.

Network Shares

Once you locate a computer on the network using the **NET VIEW** command, you can then use the command to determine what network shares are available to access. If a user needs to locate data on the network, he or she can browse the network using My Network Places or by simply using the **NET VIEW** command to locate a computer. Once the user finds a network computer to access, he or she can run **NET VIEW** followed by the computer name to display all of the shares that contain data on that computer. Figure 8-13 shows an example of using the **NET VIEW** command in this way.

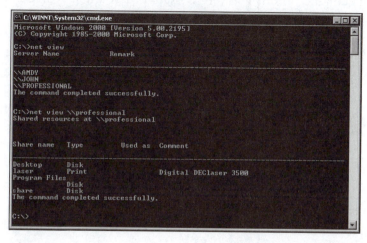

Figure 8-13   **NET VIEW** shows all computers on the network and all shares on the computer named \\professional

8

NET VIEW \\\\<COMPUTERNAME>   Displays all shares for the specified computer.

NET VIEW \\\\<COMPUTERNAME> /CACHE   Displays the cache status (the ability to enable the Offline Files and Folders feature) for all shares on the computer.

NET VIEW /NETWORK:NW \\\\<COMPUTERNAME>   Displays all accessible resources on the NetWare server.

USING NETWORK RESOURCES

Once a user has targeted the network data that he or she wishes to use, the next step is to access it. You can do this in Windows using the My Network Places or Windows Explorer GUIs to browse to the location and access the data. The command equivalent is **NET USE**, which you will learn about in the next section. This method of browsing to a network location is temporary and only applies to the current session; if the user closes the window and needs to access the same data at a later time, the entire browse process must be started again. In situations such as this, the connection can be maintained by assigning the network location to a virtual drive letter. This is called mapping a drive, and it enables a user to access the networked data by a drive letter in the same way that he or she would access local data on the C drive. Once a drive has been mapped to network data, the user references the drive letter instead of browsing to the networked computer. From the command line, the **NET USE** command is executed to establish both temporary and mapped connections to networked computers.

NET USE   Displays all mapped drives on the server.

The **NET USE** command on its own displays a list of all active outbound connections from the current computer to other servers. Be sure that you don't confuse **NET USE** with **NET SESSION**, which shows active inbound connections.

Mapping a Network Drive

Mapping a network drive lets you maintain specific network connections over time. Assume you are an administrator and need to scan some data located on Gene Halloway's computer. After determining that the computer name is GENE by using the **NET VIEW** command, you are unsure where the data is located on his system and figure that the best way to find it is to access his entire C drive. Establishing a connection to the C drive involves using the **NET USE** command to establish a connection and assign that connection to a drive letter.

NET USE <DRIVELETTER> \\\\<SERVERNAME>\\<SHARENAME>
Configures the system to assign the data located at \\\\<SERVERNAME>\\
<SHARENAME> to the specified DRIVELETTER.

**NET USE <DRIVELETTER> \\<SERVERNAME>\<SHARENAME>
/PERSISTENT:YES|NO**   Configures the system to assign the data located at
\\<SERVERNAME>\<SHARENAME> to the specified DRIVELETTER. The
/PERSISTENT:YES option allows the drive mapping to be permanent.

**NET USE <DRIVELETTER> \\<SERVERNAME>\<SHARENAME>
/USER:<USERNAME>**   Configures the system to assign the specified
DRIVELETTER to the appropriate server resources using the specified user account.
The system prompts the user for a password.

**NET USE <DRIVELETTER> \\<SERVERNAME>\<SHARENAME>
/USER:<USERNAME> /SAVECRED**   Configures the system to assign the drive
letter to the appropriate server resources using the specified user account, and to save
those credentials locally, so that (with the /PERSISTENT:YES|NO option) the user
is not required to enter a password every time the connection is established.

**NET USE <DRIVELETTER> \\<SERVERNAME>\<SHARENAME>
/DELETE**   Deletes the drive mapping.

**NET USE <DRIVELETTER> \\<SERVERNAME>\<SHARENAME>\
<SUBDIRECTORY>**   Assigns the specified DRIVELETTER to \\
<SERVERNAME>\<SHARENAME>\<SUBDIRECTORY>. Not available prior
to Windows 2000.

In the situation described above, you would use the following command to map the
G drive to the hidden C drive share on the GENE computer:

```
NET USE G: \\GENE\C$
```

At this point, you can move to the G prompt in a command window (using the command **G:**) and navigate anywhere on the drive. Now assume that you are currently logged
in to the network computer with a user account that does not exist on the GENE computer. In nondomain environments, networked computers use the current user account
and password when attempting to access a networked computer. If that account and password do not exist, access will be denied. If you were doing this within My Network
Places or Windows Explorer, the system would prompt for an administrator password.
From the command line, you would use the following command, which provides a user
account that is local to the remote computer. In this case, the LOUISE account resides
on the GENE computer, and the system will then prompt for a password for that account.

```
NET USE G: \\GENE\C$ /USER:LOUISE
```

After performing whatever tasks you need to accomplish, you should delete the drive
mapping for security reasons—having a persistent connection to someone's entire drive
can lead to security problems. When you are done using the G drive, you can delete the
mapping using the following code:

```
NET USE G: /DELETE
```

In Hands-on Project 8-5, you will learn how to use the share that was created and used in the previous projects. This project can be performed on the server or on another system running on the same LAN that has connectivity to the server.

Hands-on Project 8-5

To use a network share:

1. Open a command window.

2. Type **net use u: \\<servername>\userdata** and press **Enter** to map the drive to a drive named U. Be sure to replace "<servername>" with the name of your server. Refer to Figure 8-14, where the servername is "MACHINE."

3. To ensure that the drive mapping is in place, type **u:** and press **Enter**.

4. The prompt should show the U:> drive. Type **dir** and press **Enter**.

5. Notice that the testshare.txt file is located here. Now, close the window by typing **exit** and pressing **Enter**.

6. Reboot the server.

7. Open a command window, type **u:**, and press **Enter**. Notice that the drive mapping is persistent by default.

8. Type **exit** and press **Enter** to close the command window.

```
C:\WINDOWS\system32\cmd.exe                                    _ □ X
Microsoft Windows [Version 5.2.3663]
(C) Copyright 1985-2001 Microsoft Corp.

C:\Documents and Settings\Administrator.MACHINE>net use u: \\machine\userdata
The command completed successfully.

C:\Documents and Settings\Administrator.MACHINE>
```

Figure 8-14   Mapping the U drive to the Userdata share

SERVER TIME SYNCHRONIZATION

Since the days of DOS, setting the time on a Windows computer has been done using the **SET TIME** command or through the Date/Time applet within Control Panel. Windows 2000, XP, and Server 2003 all have the ability to synchronize their time to a local LAN server or a time server on the Web. When properly configured for all computers on the network, synchronization eliminates the possibility that a given server's time will differ from any other server's.

Administrators typically synchronize all workstations from a domain controller or designated server, and in turn, they set servers to synchronize with a time source on the Web, as shown in Figure 8-15. You can locate various time servers on the Web by executing a

Web search with the keywords "time server." **NET TIME** is used to synchronize all network computers with a particular server and synchronize that server with a Web time server. There is no GUI equivalent for this command.

NET TIME \\<*SERVERNAME*>   Displays the current time of the server.

NET TIME \\<*SERVERNAME*> /SET   Configures the current system to synchronize its time with that of the server.

NET TIME /SETSNTP:<*SERVERIPADDRESS*>   Configures the server to synchronize its time with an external Web time server.

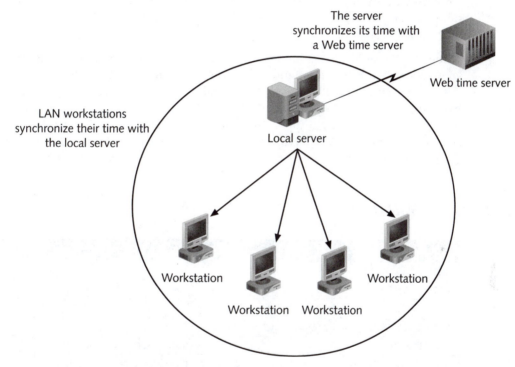

Figure 8-15   Synchronizing time on a network

The first example below synchronizes the time of the GENE computer with the domain controller MACHINE:

```
NET TIME /DOMAIN:MACHINE
```

The following code, run from the MACHINE server, synchronizes MACHINE's time with a Web time server; in this case, it is the time on the ntp2.usno.navy.mil site:

```
NET TIME /SETSNTP:NTP2.USNO.NAVY.MIL
```

The following command, run on the GENE computer, checks and resynchronizes the GENE computer's time with another computer on the network:

```
NET TIME \\GENE /SET
```

CHAPTER SUMMARY

This chapter focused on the variations of the **NET** command that are used to handle networking configuration. The **NET** command handles a variety of tasks for both servers and workstations. From a networking perspective, the Workstation and Server services are configured using the **NET CONFIG** command, while all services can be started, stopped, paused, and continued using the **NET START**, **NET STOP**, **NET PAUSE**, and **NET CONTINUE** commands.

Using the **NET** series of commands, you can determine and eliminate active inbound connections and files that are in use. You can also configure shared folders on one computer and establish connections to those folders from a different computer on the network using **NET SHARE** and **NET USE**. **NET USE** is also used to create persistent network connections by mapping network drives. Overall network timing can also be assured by using the **NET TIME** command to synchronize all workstation times with a server, and also to synchronize that server time to a time server on the Web.

COMMAND SUMMARY

Command	Description
NET START	Starts a service.
NET STOP	Stops a service.
NET PAUSE	Pauses a service.
NET CONTINUE	Restarts a paused service.
NET CONFIG	Displays and configures Server and Workstation service properties.
NET STATISTICS	Displays network I/O status and performance.
NET SESSION	Displays all connections on the server.
NET FILE	Displays all open networked files residing on the server. Can close specific files.
NET SHARE	Displays and configures network shares.
NET VIEW	Displays all systems on the network that have shared resources.
NET USE	Opens a connection and maps a drive letter to a share.
NET TIME	Configures local time clock synchronization.

KEY TERMS

administrative share — A hidden share that contains a dollar symbol ($) after its name. The share itself does not appear when using Explorer or **NET VIEW.**

Alerter service — Enables administrative alerts over the network.

browse master — A central computer that is responsible for maintaining the authoritative list of computers and shares on the network.

Browser service — Maintains a list of computers on the network.

Clipbook service — Enables copy and paste functions with network data.

DHCP Client service — Enables a client machine to automatically receive TCP/IP configuration information from the nearest DHCP server.

File Replication service — Allows coordination between domain controllers.

Messenger service — Enables a client machine to receive alerts and console messages.

Netlogon service — Handles system logon and authentication.

Plug and Play service — Enables the system to automatically detect and install hardware.

Server service — Enables a computer, workstation, or server to share resources over a network.

service — A background application that performs specific automated tasks.

share caching — A server feature that enables different levels of Offline File and Folder storage for network clients.

Spooler service — Coordinates and feeds print jobs to a printer.

Universal Naming Convention (UNC) — A computer and share naming method consisting of the server name and the share name: \\servername\sharename.

Workstation service — Allows a system to access data on a remote server.

REVIEW QUESTIONS

1. What service(s) make(s) up the core of networking? (Choose all that apply.)

   a. Alerter

   b. Workstation

   c. Netlogon

   d. Server

2. What service is responsible for authentication and logon?

   a. Server

   b. Workstation

   c. Netlogon

   d. Messenger

3. What command(s) can be used to start a service? (Choose all that apply.)

   a. **SC CONTINUE**

   b. **NET START**

   c. **SC START**

   d. **NET CONTINUE**

4. You need to run an **XCOPY** command to back up several files on the server. What can you do to make the process easier, and better ensure its success? (Choose all that apply.)

   a. Stop the Workstation service.

   b. Stop the Server service.

   c. Run **NET SESSION**.

   d. Run **NET FILE**.

5. You need to temporarily share some files located in the C:\Sensitive directory on the server to make a file transfer. Due to the sensitive nature of these files, you want to ensure that the share isn't available after you've made the transfer. What is the correct syntax for the proper commands?

   a. Run `net use c:\sensitive /persistent:no` and then `net use c:\sensitive /delete` after the task has completed.

   b. Run `net share temp c:\sensitive /persistent:no` and then `net share temp /delete` after the task has completed.

   c. Run `net share temp=c:\sensitive` and then `net share temp /delete` after the task has completed.

   d. Run `net share temp=c:\sensitive /persistent:no` and then `net share temp /delete` after the task has completed.

6. Which command can you use to disable the Offline Files and Folders feature for a shared folder?

   a. `net share <sharename> /cache:manual`

   b. `net share <sharename> /cache:no`

   c. `net share <sharename> /cache:automatic`

   d. Uninstall the program from the client computers.

7. You need to access a folder called Blueprints located in the Engineers share on the server CORPY. How can you do this using the fewest commands?

   a. `net use \\engineers\c$`

   b. `net use \\corpy\engineers\blueprints`

   c. `net use \\engineers\blueprints\corpy`

   d. `net use \\corpy\blueprints\engineers`

8. One of your users is unable to configure a specific share for Offline Files and Folders on her system. What command can you use to determine if that share is configured for such usage?

   a. `net share <sharename>`

   b. `net view \\<servername>`

   c. `net share sharename /cache:automatic`

   d. `net view \\<servername> /cache`

9. What command can you use to establish a network connection to a server?

   a. `net view \\<servername>`

   b. `net share \\<servername>\<sharename>`

   c. `net use \\<servername>\<sharename>`

   d. `net use lpt1: \\<servername>\<sharename>`

10. You administer a workgroup of 15 computers. What command do you use to synchronize all of the systems to the workgroup server?

    a. `net time \\<servername>`

    b. `net time \\<servername> /set`

    c. `net time /domain:<servername> /set`

    d. `net time /setsntp:<servername> /set`

11. You need to configure your server to receive time updates from a global time server on the Web. What command do you use?

    a. `net time \\<servername>`

    b. `net time \\<servername> /set`

    c. `net time /domain:<servername> /set`

    d. `net time /setsntp:<servername> /set`

12. You need to prevent users from accessing the network while you perform some maintenance. You don't want to stop any dependent services. What command do you use?

    a. `net start server`

    b. `net stop server`

    c. `net pause server`

    d. `net continue server`

13. Users are having problems accessing data on the server. It persistently gives a message indicating that their usernames or passwords are incorrect. You check the Microsoft Web site and determine that some files dealing with the Netlogon service have become corrupted. How can you replace those files?

a. Stop the Netlogon service and use the **INUSE** command to replace the files.

b. Reboot the server.

c. Use the **INUSE** command and replace the files.

d. Stop and restart the Netlogon service.

14. What is the difference between the Workstation service and the Server service?

a. The Server service allows networked computers to access the local server, while the Workstation service allows the local computer to access a networked server.

b. The Workstation service allows networked computers access to the local server, while the Server service allows the local computer access to a networked server.

c. The Server service only exists on Windows Server 2003 servers and not on clients such as Windows XP.

d. The Workstation service only exists on clients such as Windows XP and not on servers.

15. Due to cabling restrictions, your network runs very slowly, and running **NET STATISTICS SERVER** indicates a high number of session timeouts. What command can you use to help solve the problem?

a. `net statistics /timeout:3000`

b. `net statistics server /timeout:3000`

c. `net config server /autodisconnect:15`

d. `net config server /autodisconnect:30`

DISCOVERY EXERCISES

1. Create a share and configure it for only two concurrent connections. Then, using the **NET USE** command, map a drive to the share and open a file. Do this again for another computer on the network, and try it with a third. Does it work? What messages do you receive? Reconfigure the share for unlimited concurrent connections, and try connecting with as many computers as are available. Are there any limits on the numbers of connections? If a Windows XP system is available, try this exercise with that system acting as a server. Are there any limitations on the number of concurrent connections with Windows XP?

2. Create a logon script that maps all users to at least two shares on the server. Then assign the login script to a user account and test it to see if it works. Make sure that the users can read, write, and create data on the mapped drives.

3. Create a folder on the server and share it as a hidden administrative share (using the $ after the share name will create the share as a hidden share). Can regular user accounts access data in this hidden share? Can members of the Power Users group? Can Administrators? Change the permissions on the folder to Everyone|Full Control. Which of these groups can access and change the data after these permissions have changed?

4. Use the **NET** **/?** command to display a complete list of the **NET** commands available. Using this help method, document the category for which each command is used (networking, server administration, domain administration, user administration, or remote administration).

5. Create a script that synchronizes all workstations to the server and implement this script as a part of the logon process for each workstation. Create another script that synchronizes the server to a Web time server running SNTP (Simple Network Time Protocol) and cause that script to execute at midnight every evening.

8

MANIPULATING NETWORK RESOURCES

After reading this chapter and completing the exercises, you will be able to:

♦ Use Remote Desktop and Remote Assistance GUIs to administer systems remotely

♦ Run programs remotely

♦ Gather system information about remote computers

♦ Change system information and data on remote computers

♦ Administer network printers

Managing and administering network resources are time-consuming and often chaotic tasks, especially in large environments with multiple operating systems. As a network administrator, you can expect to handle all day-to-day administrative tasks associated with servers, as well as those that come from desktops on the network. Because most servers are stored in a closet or in some out-of-the-way place, and because users' desktop computers can be located anywhere within a building, campus, city, or the country, network administration can become not only time-consuming, but also very expensive. Remote administration tools that are available with Windows Server 2003 can be used to administer both servers and workstations. These tools, when coupled with specific remotely tuned commands, batch programs, and scripts, eliminate the need to personally visit each system that needs maintenance in all but the most complex of scenarios.

Remote administration is the process of administering a server without physically being in front of the computer. Situations where this is a benefit include administering from home, administering an enterprise server in a different city, and enhancing a server's secure environment by administering it from your desk. There are many ways to remotely administer a computer or system on the network. Many of the commands that you have learned about in previous chapters of this book can be run over a network. In addition to these commands, Windows Server 2003 provides utilities and tools specifically designed for remote administration. In this chapter, you will learn about ways to remotely administer network resources. Keep in mind that you should always be able to change data that resides on the server through mapped drives (which you learned about in Chapter 8) and standard file modification methods. You already know how to modify server data and files; now you will learn how to administer a server remotely by viewing system information and configuration.

GUI Tools for Network Administration

Windows Server 2003 and XP provide two new tools for remote administration: Remote Assistance and Remote Desktop. Several commands are associated with these GUI utilities, and because both of these programs are new with Windows Server 2003 and XP, you must understand how to use and configure Remote Assistance and Remote Desktop to fully master remote administration.

Remote Assistance was introduced with Windows XP and is more a remote desktop administration or technical support tool than a means of managing a network. In XP and Server 2003 computers where a user can allow an administrator to establish a live connection with his or her networked computer, Remote Assistance lets an administrator take remote control over the user's current console session, which is the interface screen that the user sees on his or her monitor.

Remote Desktop, known in previous Windows versions as Terminal Server Administration mode, is similar to Remote Assistance in that it provides remote administration, but it is different in that it does not require a user to be logged on to the host computer. Instead, the server provides a remote console environment. In a remote console environment, the user logs on to the remote computer and views a desktop interface and program just as if he or she were working at the server.

Remote Desktop is the preferred method of remote administration within a LAN environment. The best way to distinguish between Remote Assistance and Remote Desktop is to drop the "remote" from their names and just consider the differences between "assistance" and "desktop."

Remote Assistance

Remote Assistance is similar to programs such as Symantec pcAnywhere, in which an assistant user taps into the computer of a currently logged-on client user and takes control of the keyboard and mouse remotely. The local user can see everything that's being done by the remote user on the local computer. The local user can accept or reject the initial connection and can sever an active connection at any time. The general idea of Remote Assistance is shown in Figure 9-1.

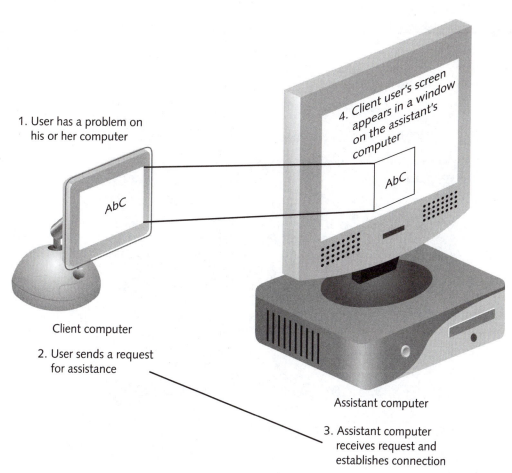

1. User has a problem on
   his or her computer

4. Client user's screen
   appears in a window
   on the assistant's
   computer

AbC

AbC

Client computer

2. User sends a request
   for assistance

Assistant computer

3. Assistant computer
   receives request and
   establishes connection

Figure 9-1   A client computer receives help from an assistant computer

Connection Matters

As mentioned earlier, Remote Assistance is more of a technical support tool than a remote administration tool because it requires an actively logged-on user on the remote computer, which makes it better suited for situations where a user needs help solving a technical problem on the computer. It is automatically enabled with XP and disabled with Server 2003. Some administrators may consider these default settings a drawback, but you should consider it a feature for the time being. In general networking contexts, the client is always the system that receives services, functions, or data—usually from a server. The server provides services, functions, and data to a client. With Remote Assistance, the local computer is the Windows XP system, and the server (assistant) is either another remote Windows XP system or a Server 2003 system.

Remote Assistance is relatively easy to configure. On the remote machine, the Remote option first needs to be enabled through Control Panel, System, Remote. After it has been enabled, you need to create an assistance invitation from within the Help and Support Center, as shown in Figure 9-2.

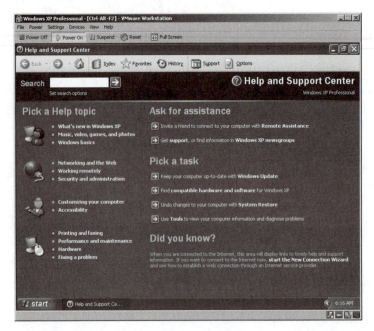

Figure 9-2   The Help and Support Center

Creating a Remote Assistance invitation is straightforward. The user (on the destination XP system) is prompted to send an invitation to a remote user in one of three ways: by MSN messenger (both users must have current connections to MSN), by e-mail, or through an invitation file that gets delivered by some other means. The invitation consists of a username, password, and time of expiration. Once the assistant computer receives the invitation, the assistant user is prompted to enter a password and the connection is initiated. Once the XP client has been contacted, the client user is prompted to accept the connection and, once that happens, a control panel is presented, as shown in Figure 9-3.

During the entire connection process, the assistant system manipulates the client XP system from a window (shown in Figure 9-4) that also displays a chat history and has the ability to send and receive messages from the XP system.

Once the connection has been accepted and established, the assistant can take control of the system (with the XP client's permission) and perform diagnostics, administrative functions, or other tasks. Integrated with Remote Assistance is the ability to send files directly between the connected systems and to conduct a voice conversation. Although the sound quality of the conversation depends on the bandwidth available between the connections, this feature is a great tool for remote training as well as for conducting technical assistance.

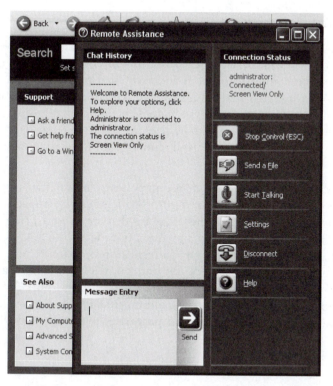

Figure 9-3   Remote Assistance control panel

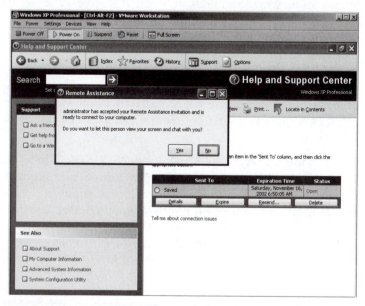

Figure 9-4   Remote Assistance session

Remote Assistance Security

Remote Assistance has a few security features that users can implement to provide assurance that unauthorized users cannot access the host computer. Even though the client can accept or reject remote connections, grant and terminate remote control, and stop any action that a remote assistant is performing with a Remote Assistance connection, this doesn't necessarily mean that the system is secure. The reasons that businesses implement mandatory profiles and restrictive group policies are the same reasons that Remote Assistance provides security: to limit, restrict, and eliminate unnecessary tampering with users' computers.

Security features of Remote Assistance include group policies, firewall management, and user account property configuration. Local and group policies can be implemented that prevent an XP client from requesting assistance. Systems that are behind a firewall might have connection problems when connecting to users outside of the LAN or on the Internet. This is often intentionally configured as a security precaution to eliminate certain kinds of communications between the LAN and the Web. The administrator can configure the firewall or router to allow communications through port 3389, which allows Remote Assistance communications to pass unhindered. Finally, administrators can configure remote control within a user's account properties to enable or disable his or her ability to become an assistant.

Remote Desktop

Remote Desktop is the Windows Server 2003 equivalent of Windows 2000's Terminal Server remote administration, which is a GUI utility used to access a server remotely as if the administrator were standing in front of the system. Remote Desktop generates a new remote **console**, complete with user login and desktop settings, a Start menu, icons, and a user profile. A console is the environment that is created when a user locally logs on to a Windows system. Remote Desktop generates a remote console for a remote user as if he or she were physically logging on to the server itself. System settings that are changed from within Remote Desktop are applied directly to the server; this includes a system shutdown. A system shutdown does not require that a user be actively logged on, nor does it require user consent.

Remote Desktop works for both Server 2003 and Windows XP. The Windows 2000 version of remote administration is available only with Advanced Server, requires Terminal Services installation, and requires a client installation before it can work. In comparison, the new feature is completely integrated with both Windows Server 2003 and XP and is capable of being client or server. Older versions of Windows can access a Windows 2003 or XP server as a remote desktop by using the Terminal Services Client installation program that is available on the Server and XP installation CD.

Configuring the Server for Remote Desktop

From the server perspective, Remote Desktop is configured through Control Panel, System, Remote on the same screen as Remote Assistance. As an advanced option, an administrator can restrict Remote Desktop to work only on specific user accounts. By default, only members of the Administrators group have the access privileges to use Remote Desktop as a client. To enable other users to use Remote Desktop, you must add their account to the built-in group Remote Desktop Users.

Configuring the Client for Remote Desktop

From a client perspective, remote desktop sessions are initialized through the Start menu, All Programs, Accessories, Communications, Remote Desktop Connection. A window prompts the user to enter a computer name or IP address, which should be that of the remote server. Once that information is entered, the normal desktop is replaced by a server session that initializes as if the user were physically working at the server. By default, the Remote Desktop session is full screen, as shown in Figure 9-5. Notice the posted bar at the top: This is important because this bar is your only conduit to the original host system. Everything you type after launching a Remote Desktop session appears on the server rather than on your local computer. Without this bar at the top (which can be removed by clicking the pushpin on the left end of the bar), the only way you can get back to your local system is either by logging off the remote session (which terminates the session) or by pressing Ctrl+Alt+Del. The bar lets you minimize the session and run it in a window for easier access to your own desktop.

Access bar

Figure 9-5   Remote Desktop session

Windows Server 2003 can run multiple Remote Desktop sessions concurrently, although it is dangerous to run more than one because of demands on server overhead and performance. Also, Remote Desktop sessions that have been aborted from the client maintain an open connection on the server, which diminishes performance and prevents users from running subsequent remote sessions. Windows XP, although it now supports Remote Desktop, can only support one session at a time. This means that if a Remote Desktop session is initiated on an XP host, the currently logged-on user will be locked out of the system. If he or she subsequently logs on again, the Remote Desktop session will be terminated.

Older versions of Windows can use Remote Desktop with a Windows Server 2003 or XP system as long as the appropriate Terminal Services Client is installed on the operating system. The client is available on the server (XP or Server 2003) within the \system32\ clients\tsclient directory.

Configuring a Remote Desktop Web Interface

Remote Desktop can be configured to connect remote systems through the Internet using Internet Explorer or another Web browser. This means that a user can access a remote desktop session through a specific site on his or her Web browser. By enabling this type of Web access, you avoid program installation on the client systems (those accessing the server). Enabling a Web client for Remote Desktop can also help with remote administration where the client is offsite or located outside of the LAN. What's more, the Web interface doesn't require a client installation and is not restricted to certain operating systems, which in many ways makes it preferable to the standard GUI for Remote Desktop.

Configuration of Remote Desktop over the Web begins with the Control Panel's Add or Remove Programs applet. Even without the Internet Information Server (IIS) Web server software that comes installed with Windows Server 2003, you can enable the Remote Desktop Web components and the system will install only the IIS components necessary for running Remote Desktop. In other words, you will be installing a scaled-down version of IIS with the inherent security issues that come with it. On the bright side, this configuration only serves Remote Desktop sessions.

In Hands-on Project 9-1, you will learn how to configure Windows XP or Windows Server 2003 for Remote Desktop administration over the Web.

Hands-on Project 9-1

In this project, you need to have two systems on the network. Ideally, they should be one Server 2003 and one XP system, but the instructions still apply for two Server 2003 systems or two XP systems.

To set up Remote Desktop:

On the server:

1. Click the **Start** button ▄Start, point to **Control Panel**, and click **Add or Remove Programs**.

2. On the left side of the window, click the **Add/Remove Windows Components** button.

3. Click **Application Server** and then click **Details**.

4. Click **Internet Information Services (IIS)** and then click **Details**.

5. Click the **World Wide Web Service** and then click **Details**.

6. Click the **Remote Desktop Web Connection** option to insert a check in the checkbox and then click **OK**, as shown in Figure 9-6.

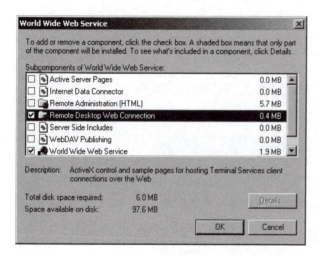

Figure 9-6   Remote Desktop Web connection

7. Click **OK** twice, and then click **Next**.

The system will configure the additional components, which might require the Windows Server 2003 installation disk, depending on your current system settings. If necessary, insert the installation disk and click the **Finish** button to complete the configuration. Close the Add/Remove programs window by clicking its Close box ⊠ .

On a networked client machine:

8. Open Internet Explorer (on any system running Windows 9x, Me, XP, 2000, or Server 2003) and in the Address box, type **http://<computername>/tsweb**.

Be sure to replace *<computername>* with the name of your computer.

 You might receive a request to install and run the Remote Desktop ActiveX control. Click Yes to continue.

9. The system will prompt for a server with which to connect and a window size. Type your server name or IP address in the blank and click the **Connect** button.

You also have the option of sending the credentials of the currently logged-on user, which will, if correct, bypass the login screen for you.

Your screen should look like Figure 9-7, which displays the desktop for the remote system as if you were logged on locally at the computer.

At this point, the Manage Your Server dialog box might open. You can either close the window to continue, or you can check the Don't display this page at logon checkbox and then close the window.

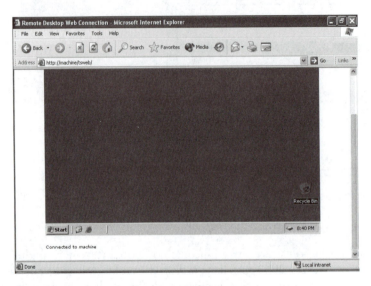

Figure 9-7   Remote Desktop Web session

Active Remote Desktop Connections on the Server

While the purpose of Remote Desktop is to enable remote administration, Remote Desktop has one major problem: When a remote user makes system-related changes within Remote Desktop, those changes are applied to the server itself. This means, for example, that running the Start menu, Shut Down option from within Remote Desktop causes the server to shut down (or reboot). Hands-on Project 9-2 teaches you how to work around this situation.

Hands-on Project 9-2

To safely log off and reboot from Remote Desktop:

1. On the client machine, click the **Start menu** within the Internet Explorer window. Click either **Shut Down** or **Log Off** (depending on the client OS and policy settings).

2. Press **1** to select the logoff option and press **Enter**. The Remote Desktop Connection window appears within Internet Explorer.

3. On the address line, type the server name or IP address and then press **Connect**.

4. Log on using the Administrator account or another account provided by your instructor.

5. Click the **Start menu** within Internet Explorer, and click the **Shut Down** button.

6. In the drop-down menu, click the **Restart** option and press **Enter**.

   Notice that the Remote Desktop Connection window appears within Internet Explorer, and that the server is now preparing to shut down.

7. Once the server is restarted, log on as usual.

One of the most frequent problems that occurs with Remote Desktop happens when the remote user inadvertently reboots the server by literally shutting down the Remote Desktop session. This problem is solved by logging out instead of shutting down the system or simply closing the Remote Desktop window. You should not shut down the system from within Remote Desktop unless you want to shut down the server itself. Additionally, you should not close the Remote Desktop window because that will lead to an orphaned session, as you will see in the next hands-on project. An **orphaned session** is one in which the user is no longer connected but the server's system resources are still reserved as if the user were connected. Orphaned sessions consume system resources and put a load on the server that causes it to slow down and eventually stop.

Regardless of the precautions you take, orphaned sessions will occur, and you will need to know how to detect and deal with them. You will also need to work with several other functions associated with Remote Desktop. Since Terminal Services may not be installed on the server, the command line is often your only recourse for Remote Desktop administration.

Using Commands with Remote Desktop

Now that you understand how Remote Desktop functions, you need to understand how to administer Remote Desktop sessions. Every time a Remote Desktop connection is established, a console session is initialized on the server that provides the desktop—the remote computer. Just as with any other session (established through network or local logon), you have the ability to view and terminate these sessions. The following commands will help you complete these tasks:

QUERY SESSION   Displays all current sessions on the server. These include console sessions where the user is logged on locally and Remote Desktop sessions.

CHANGE LOGON /DISABLE   Disables logons for all types of network connections, including network logons and Remote Desktop logons.

CHANGE LOGON /ENABLE   Enables server logon for all sessions.

LOGOFF <*SESSIONNAME*>   Forcefully logs a session off the system based on the *SESSIONNAME* entered.

LOGOFF <*SESSIONID*>   Forcefully logs a session off the system based on the *SESSIONID* number entered.

In Hands-on Project 9-1, you learned how to configure the server to enable Remote Desktop sessions and you initiated a session on a client computer. In Hands-on Project 9-3, you will learn how to administer these Remote Desktop sessions from the command line.

Hands-on Project 9-3

To administer Remote Desktop sessions:

On the server:

1. On the server system, open a command window.

2. Type **query session** and press **Enter**.

    The results should be similar to Figure 9-8. The command displays the locally logged-on user as the "console" session. Following that are two sessions that begin with RDP in the leftmost column, indicating Remote Desktop sessions. The second of these is the active session that is being used on the client machine.

On the client:

3. Walk to the client machine and click the **Close** button ☒ to close the Remote Desktop window.

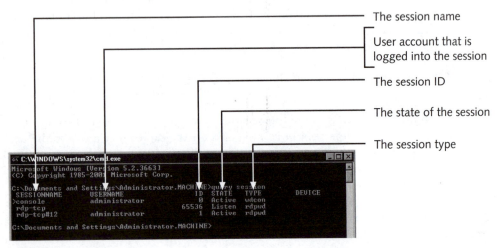

Figure 9-8   The QUERY SESSION command

On the server:

4. Walk back to the server, type **query session**, and press **Enter**. Your screen should look like Figure 9-9. Notice that the session that was previously active is now labeled as "Disc", which indicates that the session was unexpectedly disconnected. This is an orphaned session.

Figure 9-9   An orphaned session

5. To safely eliminate the orphaned session, type **logoff** followed by the session ID that is shown in the ID column. Press **Enter**. In Figure 9-9, the example shows the session ID of 1.

6. Type **query session** and press **Enter** to list the current sessions. Notice that the orphaned session no longer appears.

7. Type **change logon /disable** and press **Enter** to disable all network and Remote Desktop logons.

On the client:

8. On the client machine, repeat Steps 8 and 9 from Hands-on Project 9-1 and attempt to re-establish a Remote Desktop connection to the server. Notice that logon has been disabled.

9. On the server system, type **change logon /enable** and press **Enter**.

10. On the client machine, repeat Steps 8 and 9 from Hands-on Project 9-1 and attempt to re-establish a Remote Desktop connection to the server.

In addition to the basic remote administration commands, Windows Server 2003 provides commands to allow an administrator to terminate network and Remote Desktop sessions. Sometimes, when an orphaned Remote Desktop session is actively processing data or has open files, the **LOGOFF** command is unable to eliminate the session. In such situations, you use the **RESET SESSION** command. If **RESET SESSION** fails, you will need to use the **TSDISCON** command. It's important to note that **TSDISCON** will forcefully disconnect the session, but the session then shows a status of disconnected (in other words, you have created an orphaned session), after which you will need to use the **LOGOFF** command to completely clear it from the system.

RESET SESSION <*SESSIONID*>   Forcefully closes all applications and logs off a session.

TSDISCON <*SESSIONID*>   Forcefully disconnects a session; the session is orphaned.

RUNNING PROGRAMS REMOTELY

In addition to Remote Desktop, there are several ways to perform administrative tasks on other systems on the network. These methods include using login scripts, batch files, and the registry to run programs. These alternative administration tools are especially applicable in heterogeneous networks running multiple versions of Windows, because most of the commands listed in this chapter can be run on older versions of Windows, as you will learn later in this chapter.

There are several ways to run programs remotely on networked computers. One way is to create a batch file that runs a program and place it within the Start menu, Programs, Startup folder of the remote system. Another way is to place the same batch program name and path within the remote computer's registry in the HkeyLocalMachine | Software | Microsoft | Windows | CurrentVersion | Run key. A third potential solution is to add the file path to whatever program you need to run to a server's login script so that the program will run whenever a user logs on to the system. All three of these solutions are frequently used, but each is somewhat tricky because without additional logic within the login script or batch file, the program(s) will run repeatedly every time the user logs on to the system or starts the computer. In the case of the login script, you also have an additional quandary in determining which users should run the program. The logon problem can be resolved through batch logic as well.

The best way to run programs remotely on networked computers involves the **AT** command. **RSH** and **REXEC** commands also can be used for remote execution, but these programs are intended to work with UNIX and minicomputer systems and not Windows systems.

AT \\<*COMPUTERNAME*> <*TIMEOFDAY*> <*COMMAND*>   Schedules the *COMMAND* to occur on the networked computer at the specified time.

AT \\<*COMPUTERNAME*> <*TIMEOFDAY*> /EVERY:*M* | *T* | *W* | *TH* | *F* | *S* | *SU* <*COMMAND*>   Schedules the *COMMAND* to run at the specified time every day on the indicated day.

AT \\<*COMPUTERNAME*> <*TIMEOFDAY*> /EVERY:<*DAYOFMONTH*> <*COMMAND*>   Schedules the *COMMAND* to run at the specified time every month on the specified date (1, 2...31).

AT \\<*COMPUTERNAME*> <*TIMEOFDAY*> /INTERACTIVE <*COMMAND*>   Schedules the *COMMAND* to run at the specified time, allowing the command to interact with the currently logged-on user.

Hands-on Project 9-4 teaches you how to use the **AT** command to run a batch file on a remote system. You will also learn how **AT** behaves and how batch programs behave when using it.

Hands-on Project 9-4

In this project, you will need to have two networked systems, preferably a Windows Server 2003 and an XP system.

To use **AT** on a remote computer:

From the client machine:

1. Open a command window.

2. Type **cd** and press **Enter** to navigate to the root of the C drive.

3. Type **edit atbat.bat** and press **Enter**. This opens the Edit program with a new file called atbat.bat.

4. Type **echo hithere** and press **Enter**.

5. Save the atbat.bat file by pressing and holding **Alt** and pressing **f**. Release the keys. Press **x** and press **Enter** to save the file.

6. You should now be at the command prompt. Test the functionality of atbat.bat by typing **atbat** and pressing **Enter**. Your screen should look like Figure 9-10.

Figure 9-10   Running atbat.bat locally

7. Type **exit** and press **Enter** to close the command window.

From the server machine:

8. Open a command window.

9. Type **cd** and press **Enter**.

Many of the commands in this chapter require that the currently logged-on user be a member of the Administrators group on the client machine. If your client computer is a member of the same domain as the server, any member of the Administrators group on the server machine will automatically be added to the client computer's Administrators group. If your system is part of a workgroup, this may become more of a challenge. Instead, you can establish an active connection through My Network Places to the client computer. After this is done, you can proceed.

10. Run atbat.bat on the client system by typing **at \\<*computername*> <*time+2 minutes*> <am/pm> c:\atbat.bat** and pressing **Enter** (replace <*computername*> with your system's name and add two minutes to the current time. Remember that the angle brackets <> that surround the system name and time should not be typed.) The results should be similar to Figure 9-11, which shows that the job has been successfully added to the scheduler.

Figure 9-11   Scheduling atbat.bat to run on a networked system

On the client machine:

11. Minimize any open windows. Click the **Start** button ![Start], point to **All Programs**, point to **Accessories**, point to **System Tools**, and then click **Scheduled Tasks**. Notice that a new task is shown in the window.

12. Click the Schedule Task window's **Minimize** button ![Minimize] and wait for the batch program to run.

13. At the scheduled program execution time, you will notice that nothing happens on the screen. Click the Schedule Task window again and look for the task that appeared in Step 11.

If the task does not appear on the list, then it successfully ran. Tasks that are scheduled to run through the **AT** command run in the background and are not seen by the user.

REMOTE SYSTEM INFORMATION

As a system administrator, you are responsible for the hardware that comprises your computers as well as the software that resides on those systems. Gathering information about systems on the network is a tedious job because without thought and careful planning, gathering this information will require that you personally visit, open, and inspect each computer that is under your care. Third-party utilities and programs are available that can essentially take an inventory of all networked systems and provide information about system components in report form. Unfortunately, these applications can be expensive. Instead, administrators can use commands from the server to gather information about networked systems' components and performance and redirecting the output to a file, often in various file formats that can be imported into Microsoft Word, Excel, Access, or even SQL Server.

Variations of the **SYSTEMINFO**, **DRIVERQUERY**, and **FREEDISK** commands provide system data for networked computers. Recall that you first learned about these commands in Chapter 4.

SYSTEMINFO /S <COMPUTERNAME> /U <USERNAME> /P <PASSWORD> Displays system information such as CPU speed and BIOS version for the specified remote computer.

SYSTEMINFO /S <COMPUTERNAME> /U <USERNAME> /P <PASSWORD> /FO TABLE|LIST|CSV /NH Displays system information for the remote computer and outputs it in either table, list, or comma delimited format.

DRIVERQUERY /S <COMPUTERNAME> /U <USERNAME> /P <PASSWORD> Displays a list of the installed device drivers for the specified remote computer.

DRIVERQUERY /S <COMPUTERNAME> /FO TABLE|LIST|CSV /NH Displays the current drivers in either table, list, or comma delimited format with no header information.

DRIVERQUERY /S <COMPUTERNAME> /SI Displays information about signed drivers.

FREEDISK /S <COMPUTERNAME> /U <USERNAME> /P <PASSWORD> /D <DRIVELETTER> Displays the available hard disk space for the specified hard drive on the specified remote computer.

Most hardware information can be gathered through the **SYSTEMINFO** and **DRIVERQUERY** commands. Using the **/FO** (file output) option for each of these commands enables you to gather system information, import it into a database program such as Access or SQL, and then filter, sort, or manipulate the information. You can use the manipulated data to compile a complete hardware profile for all systems on the network.

You can also gather information about programs on remote systems and their performance using the **REG QUERY** and **TASKLIST** commands from the server. You can compile a complete list of installed programs by first scanning the contents of a system's Program Files directory. Then, you can use **REG QUERY** to look at the programs installed in the registry. A list of installed programs can be found by looking at the list of programs from Control Panel's Add or Remove Programs applet. This list is located in the HKLM|Software|Microsoft|Windows|CurrentVersion|Uninstall registry key.

HKLM is an abbreviation for HKeyLocalMachine.

REG QUERY \\<*COMPUTERNAME*>\<*KEYNAME*>   Displays the remote computer's registry entries for *KEYNAME* and first-level subkeys for the specified key or hive.

REG QUERY \\<*COMPUTERNAME*>\<*KEYNAME*> /S   Displays the remote computer's registry entries for *KEYNAME* and subkeys for the specified key or hive, including the entire subtree structure.

REG QUERY \\<*COMPUTERNAME*>\<*KEYNAME*> /V <*ENTRY*>   Displays the remote computer's specified subkey entry data that is located in *KEYNAME*.

TASKLIST /S <*COMPUTERNAME*> /U <*USERNAME*> /P <*PASSWORD*>   Displays all the processes currently running on the remote computer. /U and /P are used to authenticate against the remote computer to ensure that the user is a member of the remote computer's Administrators group.

TASKLIST /S <*COMPUTERNAME*> /U <*USERNAME*> /P <*PASSWORD*>/FO *TABLE*|*LIST*|*CSV* /NH   Displays all the processes in the specified output format of table, list, or comma delimited for the remote computer using the specified username and password. Used primarily with redirection to a file.

EVENTQUERY /S <*COMPUTERNAME*> /U <*USERNAME*> /P <*PASSWORD*>   Displays all events in the event logs for the specified remote computer using the specified username and password.

EVENTQUERY /S <*COMPUTERNAME*> /U <*USERNAME*> /P <*PASSWORD*>/FO *TABLE*|*LIST*|*CSV* /NH   Displays all events in the event logs for the specified remote computer in the specified output format of table, list, or comma delimited for the remote computer using the specified username and password. Used primarily with redirection to a file.

EVENTQUERY /S <*COMPUTERNAME*> /U <*USERNAME*> /P <*PASSWORD*> /FI "TYPE EQ *ERROR*|*WARNING*|*INFORMATION*"   Displays all events in the event logs.

In Hands-on Project 9-5, you will learn how to obtain a software inventory from a networked system using the **REG QUERY** command.

Hands-on Project 9-5

To use **REG QUERY** to produce a software inventory:

1. On the server, open a command window.

2. Type **reg query \\<*computername*>\hklm\software\Microsoft\windows\currentversion\uninstall** and press **Enter**. Replace <*computername*> with the name of the remote computer and do not type the angle brackets (<>)

that surround the name. This displays the programs that are listed in Add/Remove Programs.

Your screen should look like Figure 9-12 (your list of installed programs will vary).

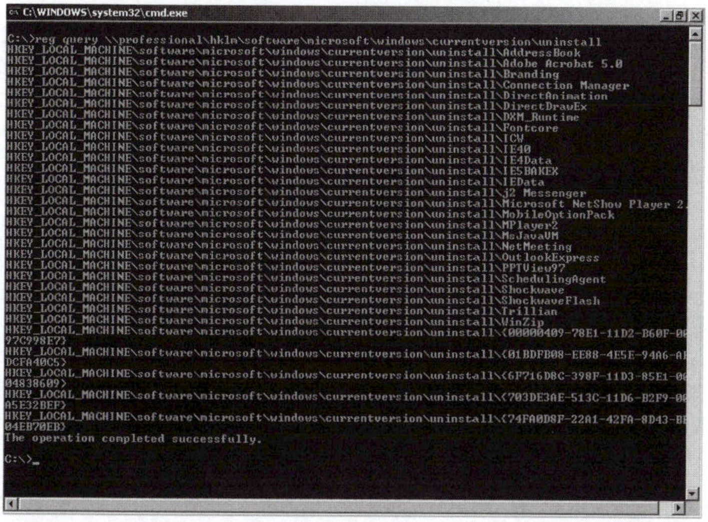

Figure 9-12   Running **REG QUERY** on a networked computer

3. Close the command window by typing **exit** and pressing **Enter**.

While Windows Server 2003 can perform certain tasks when the system or a service fails, these tasks add processing and overhead demands on the server, which might worsen the overall problem. Instead, you can use the **EVENTQUERY** command to eliminate much of the additional processing by directing the processing to a different system. Additionally, **EVENTQUERY** reports on system and service failures, along with other event types.

Ideally, you should regularly query all of your servers for errors. To perform this query, you can create a batch file containing the **EVENTQUERY** command for a single server or multiple servers using the **/FI** option for **TYPE EQ ERROR** and schedule it (using the **AT** command) to run as often as you feel necessary. This, along with output redirection to a file, enables you to proactively gather information that can both alert you to potential problems and help you resolve critical issues by looking at the past behavior of the system(s).

Changing Configurations on Remote Computers

Although being able to gather data about networked systems can be useful for inventory and troubleshooting purposes, changing software, settings, and other data on networked systems can be more valuable as a timesaver. Imagine that you were responsible for desktop administration on 100 systems and you needed to reconfigure system settings on all of them in preparation for a new software deployment. Windows Server 2003 can deploy and install applications to Windows 2000, XP, and Server 2003 clients within a domain, but there is no easy way to change system components without visiting each system individually and changing them through the GUI. With the help of the Windows Management Interface (WMI) service that comes with Windows 2000, XP, and Server 2003, an administrator can change settings on multiple networked systems without leaving his or her own desk.

The WMI service that allows for remote system changes comes with Windows NT SP4 and above, and is also available for download from Microsoft (search for WMICORE.EXE) for Windows 95 and 98 systems. With WMI installed and running on these systems, you should be able to run the commands in this section on any Windows system on your network.

Many of the local administration commands covered in Chapter 6 also have options for remote execution. Included among these are the **PAGEFILECONFIG** command, which can be used to display the page file configuration, and the **BOOTCFG** command, which is used to view and modify the boot sequence and environment.

PAGEFILECONFIG /QUERY /S <COMPUTERNAME> /U <USERNAME> /P <PASSWORD>   Displays the page file configuration on the specified remote computer using the specified administrative username and password.

PAGEFILECONFIG /QUERY /S <COMPUTERNAME> /U <USERNAME> /P <PASSWORD>/FO TABLE|LIST|CSV   Displays the page file configuration in the specified output format for the remote computer using the specified administrative username and password. This is ideal for documentation purposes when used with redirection.

BOOTCFG /QUERY /S <COMPUTERNAME> /U <USERNAME> /P <PASSWORD>   Displays the boot.ini configuration for the specified remote computer using the specified administrative username and password.

BOOTCFG /DEFAULT /ID <OSID> /S <COMPUTERNAME> /U <USERNAME> /P <PASSWORD>   On a multi-OS system, sets the default operating system (the line number for the OS displayed using the /QUERY option) with which the remote system boots. The specified username and password are authenticated on the remote computer.

BOOTCFG /TIMEOUT <TIMEINSECONDS> /S <COMPUTERNAME> /U <USERNAME> /P <PASSWORD>   On a multi-OS system, sets the amount of time the remote system waits before automatically selecting the default OS. The specified username and password are authenticated on the remote computer.

SETX /S <COMPUTERNAME> /U <USERNAME> /P <PASSWORD> <VARIABLENAME> <VARIABLEVALUE>   Creates the variable *VARIABLENAME* on the remote computer and assigns it the value of *VARIABLEVALUE*. The specified username and password are authenticated on the remote computer.

Occasionally during troubleshooting and problem resolution, it becomes necessary to start and stop services, or end processes and tasks. You can use the **SC** command to remotely stop and start system activities when performing system upgrades remotely or before performing specific tasks, such as a system tape backup.

C:_
Syntax

SC \\<COMPUTERNAME> QUERY   Displays a list of all the services on the specified remote computer.

SC \\<COMPUTERNAME> GETKEYNAME <DISPLAYNAME>   Returns the formal service keyname for the specified display name.

SC \\<COMPUTERNAME> QUERY <KEYNAME>   Displays the services associated with the specified *KEYNAME*.

SC \\<COMPUTERNAME> ENUMDEPEND <KEYNAME>   Displays the services that depend on the specified *KEYNAME*.

TASKKILL /S <COMPUTERNAME> /U <USERNAME> /P <PASSWORD> /IM <PROCESSNAME>   Stops the specified process on the remote computer.

TASKKILL /S <COMPUTERNAME> /U <USERNAME> /P <PASSWORD> /FI "STATUS EQ|NE RUNNING|NOT RESPONDING" Stops a process that matches the criteria (equal/not equal) of Running or Not Responding.

TASKKILL /S <COMPUTERNAME> /U <USERNAME> /P <PASSWORD> /FI "SERVICES EQ|NE <KEYNAME>"   Stops all tasks on the remote computer associated with the specified service.

TASKKILL /S <COMPUTERNAME> /U <USERNAME> /P <PASSWORD> /FI "WINDOWTITLE EQ|NE <WINDOWNAME>"   Stops all processes associated with the specified application window on the remote computer.

EVENTCREATE /S <COMPUTERNAME> /U <USERNAME> /P <PASSWORD> /L APPLICATION /SO <ADMIN or APPLICATION NAME> /T ERROR|WARNING|INFORMATION /ID <EVENT ID> /D <DESCRIPTION>   Creates an application event for the event viewer on the specified remote computer with *ADMIN* or *APPLICATION NAME* as the title; an event type of *ERROR*, *WARNING*, or *INFORMATION*; the listed *EVENT ID*; and the *DESCRIPTION*. *EVENT ID* can be any number, and *DESCRIPTION* should be a word or phrase that adequately describes the event.

9

In Hands-on Project 9-6, you will use the **PAGEFILECONFIG**, **BOOTCFG**, and **SC** commands to determine what and how a system is running on the network. You will then place these commands in a batch file and redirect the output to a single data inventory file for this system.

Hands-on Project 9-6

To perform the steps in this project, you will need to have two networked systems: one remote system, preferably running Windows XP, to gather information about, and another one, ideally a Windows Server 2003 system, to run the commands. You also need to be logged on to the local system as an Administrator and have an identical account and password on the remote system.

To gather and inventory system data for a networked system:

On the server:

1. Open a command window.

2. Type **pagefileconfig /query /s *<computername>*** and press **Enter** (make sure to replace *<computername>* with the name of your remote system). Your output should include the page file configuration settings similar to what is shown in Figure 9-13.

You might see a dialog box that indicates that the script should be run using cscript.exe. If this happens, type **cscript //h:cscript //s**, as shown in the dialog box, and press **Enter**. Once you complete this step, rerun Step 2.

```
C:\WINDOWS\system32\cmd.exe
Microsoft Windows [Version 5.2.3663]
(C) Copyright 1985-2001 Microsoft Corp.

C:\Documents and Settings\Administrator.MACHINE>pagefileconfig /query /s profess
ional
Microsoft (R) Windows Script Host Version 5.6
Copyright (C) Microsoft Corporation 1996-2001. All rights reserved.


Host Name:          PROFESSIONAL
Drive/Volume:       C:
Volume Label:       N/A
Location\File Name: C:\pagefile.sys
Initial Size:       768 MB
Maximum Size:       1536 MB
Current Size:       768 MB
Total Free Space:   5971 MB


Host Name:                              PROFESSIONAL
Total (All Drives): Minimum Size:       2 MB
Total (All Drives): Recommended Size:   765 MB
Total (All Drives): Currently Allocated: 768 MB


C:\Documents and Settings\Administrator.MACHINE>_
```

Figure 9-13   Using PAGEFILECONFIG /QUERY /S

3. Type **bootcfg /query /s *<computername>*** and press **Enter** (replace *<computername>* with the name of your remote system). The results should display a boot configuration similar to what is shown in Figure 9-14.

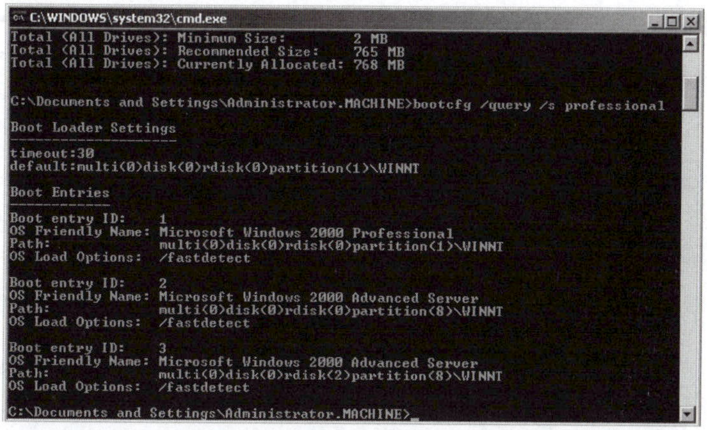

Figure 9-14 Using BOOTCFG /QUERY /S to display remote computer boot settings

4. Type **sc \\<*computername*> query** and press **Enter** (replace <*computername*> with the name of your remote system). The results should look like Figure 9-15.

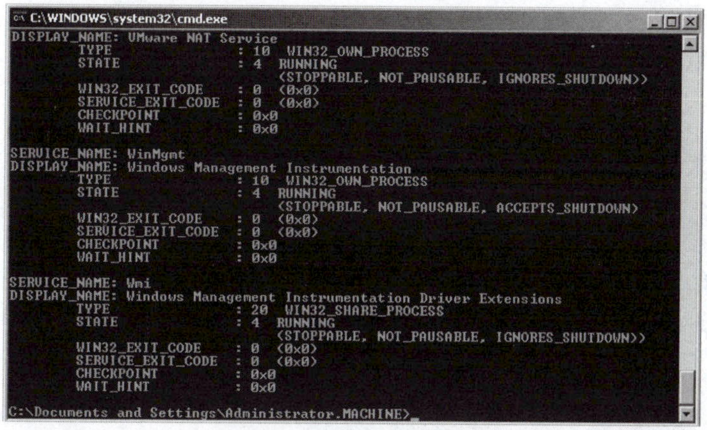

Figure 9-15 Using SC \\ *COMPUTERNAME* QUERY to display the services that are running on a remote computer

5. Type **cd** and press **Enter** to navigate to the root of the drive.

6. Type **edit swinv.bat** and press **Enter**. This launches the Edit program and opens a new file named swinv.bat.

7. Modify swinv.bat as shown in Figure 9-16. Be sure to replace each instance of professional with <*computername*> where <*computername*> is the remote computer. Swinv.bat runs all three of the previous commands and redirects the output to a file.

Remember that redirection can be tricky: To append data or output to an existing file, you can use >>. If the file should be created first, use the > symbol.

Figure 9-16   The swinv.bat file

8. Save the file by pressing and holding **Alt** and pressing **f**. Release the keys. Press **x** and then press **Enter**.

9. Run swinv.bat by typing **swinv** and pressing **Enter**. This may take a few minutes.

10. As each command runs on the remote computer, the command appears on the local computer screen. Once the commands finish running and the command prompt reappears, type **type inv.txt | more** and press **Enter**.

The first page of the results should look like Figure 9-17, which shows the output from **PAGEFILECONFIG**, **BOOTCFG**, and **SC** all in the file inv.txt.

Figure 9-17   The inv.txt inventory file

11. Press the spacebar several times to page through the entire document.

12. Press and hold **Ctrl** and press **c** to stop the **TYPE** display. Release the keys.

13. Type **exit** and press **Enter** to close the command window.

One of the final commands covered in this chapter is the **SHUTDOWN** command, which shuts down or restarts a system on the network. This command is not frequently used because it is so powerful. However, **SHUTDOWN** is helpful for running system updates or automating scheduled system shutdowns.

Windows Server 2003 is considerably more stable than its predecessors, but this does not guarantee that applications running on Server 2003 are equally stable. Many programs and services that run on Server 2003 have system issues and memory leaks that might be acceptable as long as the program functions appropriately, despite the cost in server performance. One of the ways you can reduce problems of this nature is to reboot the system regularly; this removes orphaned processes and allocated memory.

SHUTDOWN /I   Executes the Remote Shutdown dialog box on the local computer. From within the GUI, you can specify one or more computers to shut down or restart, along with reason codes for the reboot.

To properly use the **SHUTDOWN** command, the logged-on user on the server must be a member of the client (destination) computer's Administrators group. Even if the same account name and password exist on both computers, you must add the server (source) computer's account to the client computer's Administrators group.

Gathering Remote Network Data

Many networking commands were covered in Chapters 7 and 8; however, there are a few that are specifically geared toward gathering information about a system's network settings. The first is **GETMAC**, which is a command that displays the **MAC address** of the target system. A MAC address is a unique number that identifies the computer and is programmed into the network interface card by the manufacturer. Several protocols and newer technologies use MAC addresses as a method of computer identification that is singular and unique. Computers worldwide can have the same system names and even the same TCP/IP addresses (thanks to routing technologies), but no two computers have the same MAC address. From a practical standpoint, you probably will never directly deal with a system's MAC address. However, the MAC address does display all protocols (as shown in Figure 9-18) currently running on a system, which can become valuable when you are remotely troubleshooting specific network issues.

Figure 9-18   Using the GETMAC command to retrieve a list of protocols running on a remote system

GETMAC /S <COMPUTERNAME> Displays the MAC address and all associated protocols for the specified networked computer.

Another network-related command is **NET TIME**, which you learned about in Chapter 8. **NET TIME** enables you to retrieve the current system time for any computer on the network, as shown in Figure 9-19. This is a convenient feature that you can use to determine whether network time synchronization is functioning properly, or if a particular system's CPU battery is failing.

```
C:\WINDOWS\system32\cmd.exe

C:\Documents and Settings\Administrator.MACHINE>net time \\corpx
Current time at \\corpx is 11/14/2002 5:54 AM

The command completed successfully.

C:\Documents and Settings\Administrator.MACHINE>_
```

Figure 9-19 Retrieving the system time from a networked system

NET TIME \\<COMPUTERNAME> Displays a networked system's time.

NETWORK PRINTING

Printing is usually considered a "personal" computing experience because printers require installation of a printer device driver on the local computer—even when the printer is accessed over the network. Network printing is often a requirement due to the prohibitive cost and space required to place a printer on every user's desk. As a result, a printer can be configured for a specific server and then shared with the network population in the same way that files and folders are shared. Network printer administration is sometimes an annoying task because there are a few additional features, such as print queue management.

Installation of a networked printer is similar to a standard printer installation; the only additional task relates to sharing the printer among multiple users. Sharing a network printer is relatively easy to manage because the process is almost identical to sharing a folder, permissions included. Unlike sharing a folder, whose data is often stored locally, printers can be connected to a given server in one of three ways: directly through the parallel port, directly to the network through a NIC installed on the printer, or through a connection to a print service device that in turn connects either to the server itself or to the network. For these nonlocal connections to be recognized by the server, all you need to do is install the printer driver appropriately on the server and follow the instructions provided by the manufacturer for printer installation. Client installation requires that the same printer driver be installed on the client, appropriate to the OS, with initial configuration indicating that the printer is on the network rather than connected locally.

Beyond installation, sharing, and permissions, printer administration lies primarily within the realm of fixing corrupted printer drivers, either on the server or on a user's desktop. This usually involves a trip to the desktop computer to remove and reinstall the driver.

You may be called upon to fix **print jobs** that are having problems. A print job is a specific document that has been transmitted to the printer. Since a printer can only print one job at a time, a line of print jobs often forms in a memory location called a **print queue**, which resides on the server.

As an administrator, you can also expect to be called on to pause or stop print jobs that are graphics-intensive or that have so many pages that the print job may not complete for some time. This request usually arises when a person sends a large document to print, and then other people attempt to print, and the later print jobs end up waiting in the queue. You can also be expected to cancel print jobs that were inappropriately transmitted (such as when a user calls you and says, "Oops! I didn't mean to print that!") or when a print job has become corrupted within the queue and the printer ends up printing dozens of pages of gibberish. All of these tasks can be accomplished using the `NET PRINT`, `PRNJOBS`, and `PRNQCTL` commands.

NET PRINT \\\<*COMPUTERNAME*>\\<*PRINTERNAME*>   Lists all print jobs being routed to the printer that is attached to *COMPUTERNAME*.

NET PRINT \\\<*COMPUTERNAME*> <*JOBNUMBER*> /HOLD   Pauses the print job on the printer that is attached to *COMPUTERNAME*. *JOBNUMBER* is determined by the results of running NET PRINT.

NET PRINT \\\<*COMPUTERNAME*> <*JOBNUMBER*> /RELEASE
Resumes the print job.

NET PRINT \\\<*COMPUTERNAME*> <*JOBNUMBER*> /DELETE   Deletes the print job.

PRNJOBS –L –S <*COMPUTERNAME*> –U <*USERNAME*> –W <*PASSWORD*>   Lists all print jobs on the printer attached to *COMPUTERNAME*, using the *USERNAME* account and *PASSWORD*.

PRNQCTL –X –S <*COMPUTERNAME*> –U <*USERNAME*> –W <*PASSWORD*> –P <*PRINTERNAME*>   Deletes all print jobs from the printer queue for the printer attached to *COMPUTERNAME*, using the *USERNAME* account and *PASSWORD*.

CHAPTER SUMMARY

In this chapter, you learned about remote administration technologies that come with Windows Server 2003. These include Remote Desktop, which is used to administer servers remotely by emulating a logon session and desktop as if the user were logged onto the server locally, and Remote Assistance, which is used to aid an existing user session's console, settings, and desktop by taking control of the screen, keyboard, and mouse remotely. You also learned how many of the commands discussed in previous chapters, such as **PAGEFILECONFIG** and **BOOTCFG**, can be used to gather page file configuration and boot configuration information about networked systems. Many commands can also be used to change the configuration of a remote server by modifying the running services, creating environmental variables, and even synchronizing the system time with another computer using the **SC**, **SETX**, and **NET TIME** commands. Because the printer is often the most-used peripheral on the network, you also learned how to administer a printer remotely.

COMMAND SUMMARY

Command	Description
QUERY SESSION	Displays all current and active sessions on the server.
CHANGE LOGON /DISABLE	Disables logons.
CHANGE LOGON /ENABLE	Enables logons.
LOGOFF	Forces a logoff of a session name or session ID.
RESET SESSION	Disconnects a Remote Desktop session.
TSDISCON	Disconnects a Remote Desktop session; session is orphaned.
AT	Schedules programs to run on a remote system.
SYSTEMINFO	Displays system hardware and configuration information.
DRIVERQUERY	Displays all loaded drivers.
FREEDISK	Displays free space on the disk drive.
REG QUERY	Displays registry key information.
TASKLIST	Displays running tasks and processes.
EVENTQUERY	Displays event logs.
PAGEFILECONFIG	Displays and modifies the pagefile configuration.
BOOTCFG	Displays and modifies the boot.ini file.
SETX	Creates a variable.
SC	Lists and administers services.
TASKKILL	Terminates a task, program, or process.
EVENTCREATE	Creates an event.
SHUTDOWN	Shuts down or restarts the system.

Command	Description
GETMAC	Retrieves the MAC address on the system and all associated protocols.
NET PRINT	Lists, pauses, and resumes print jobs.
PRNJOBS	Administers print jobs.
PRNQCTL	Administers a print queue.

KEY TERMS

console — A locally logged-on session that includes login and desktop settings, a Start menu, icons, and a user profile.

MAC address — A unique identifying address on the NIC.

orphaned session — A task or session that continues even when the parent process has stopped.

print job — A document that has been transmitted to the printer for printing.

print queue — A memory or disk location that contains all print jobs waiting to be printed.

Remote Assistance — A remote control application that allows someone to connect to an active user console and take control of the system.

Remote Desktop — A remote administration application that allows a user to connect to a server and log on as if he or she were physically at the server.

REVIEW QUESTIONS

1. Which of the following is controlled by the logged-on user?

   a. Remote Assistance

   b. **TSDISCON**

   c. Remote Desktop

   d. Shutdown

2. How is Remote Desktop enabled?

   a. Control Panel, System

   b. Computer Management, Remote

   c. Control Panel, System, Remote

   d. Computer Management, Connections

3. Which utility is not used to shut down a system?

    a. Remote Assistance

    b. Remote Desktop

    c. **TASKKILL**

    d. Shutdown

4. How can you safely configure a user for Remote Desktop?

    a. Add the user account to the Administrators group.

    b. Add the user account to the Remote Desktop group.

    c. You can't; users are configured by default.

    d. Add the user account within Remote Desktop administration.

5. Which command will not terminate a Remote Desktop session?

    a. **LOGOFF**

    b. **RESET SESSION**

    c. **CHANGE LOGON DISABLE**

    d. **TSDISCON**

6. Which command creates an orphaned session?

    a. **LOGOFF**

    b. **RESET SESSION**

    c. **CHANGE LOGON DISABLE**

    d. **TSDISCON**

7. Which of the following instructions completely describes how to automatically start a program on a remote computer?

    a. autoexec.bat, startup folder, registry key: HKLM\ software\ Microsoft\ Windows\ CurrentVersion\ Run \create a service **AT**

    b. startup folder, registry key: HKLM\ software\ Microsoft\ Windows\ CurrentVersion \login script **AT**

    c. autoexec.nt, startup folder, registry key: HKLM\ software\ Microsoft\ Windows\ CurrentVersion \login script **AT**

    d. startup folder, registry key: HKLM\ software\ Microsoft\ Windows\ CurrentVersion\ run \login script \create a service **AT**

8. Which command displays a list of installed hardware?

    a. **SYSTEMINFO**

    b. **DRIVERQUERY**

    c. **FREEDISK**

    d. **REG QUERY**

9. If you need to import system information into a database, which command is the best way to do this?

   a. `SYSTEMINFO /FO CSV`

   b. `DRIVERQUERY /FO CSV`

   c. `SYSTEMINFO /FO CSV>SYSTEMINFO.TXT`

   d. `DRIVERYQUERY /FO CSV<SYSTEMINFO.TXT`

10. How do you obtain a list of installed programs on a system?

    a. `dir *.*`

    b. `dir .\program files`

    c. `reg query \\<computername>\software\microsoft\windows\`
       `currentversion\run`

    d. `reg query \\<computername>\software\microsoft\windows\`
       `currentversion\uninstall`

11. Which command is used to determine the programs that are running on a system?

    a. `TASKLIST, EVENTQUERY, SC, BOOTCFG`

    b. `TASKLIST, EVENTQUERY`

    c. `TASKLIST, SC`

    d. `TASKLIST, BOOTCFG`

12. How do you set a variable on a networked system? (Choose all that apply.)

    a. `SET`

    b. `AT SET`

    c. `SETX`

    d. `REMOTESET`

13. You need to upgrade your server, but before you do that, you need to disable all network connections to the system. How do you do this? (Choose all that apply.)

    a. `LOGON DISABLE`

    b. `LOGON ENABLE`

    c. `LOGOFF`

    d. `SC`

14. A print queue is _____.

    a. a print job

    b. a list of print jobs

    c. the location of a print job

    d. the location of a list of print jobs

15. Which command is used to delete a single print job?

    a. **PRINT**

    b. **PRNQCTL**

    c. **PRNJOBS**

    d. **NET PRINT**

16. Which command is used to list print jobs on a printer? (Choose all that apply.)

    a. **PRINT**

    b. **PRNQCTL**

    c. **PRNJOBS**

    d. **NET PRINT**

17. Which command is used to delete all print jobs from a printer?

    a. **PRINT**

    b. **PRNQCTL**

    c. **PRNJOBS**

    d. **NET PRINT**

18. Which command is used to display and modify the startup environment for a server?

    a. autoexec.bat

    b. **BOOTCFG**

    c. **CHANGE LOGON**

    d. **AT**

19. Which command is used to set the time on a remote system?

    a. **SET TIME**

    b. **NET TIME**

    c. **SETX TIME**

    d. **NETX TIME**

20. Which command displays the protocols running on a server?

    a. **GETMAC**

    b. **PROTOLIST**

    c. **NET**

    d. **NETBT**

DISCOVERY EXERCISES

1. You need to have all users run notepad.exe when they logon to the network. Create a batch file that does this, and test it by placing it in the proper registry key. If the file runs successfully, remove it from the registry key, and test it by placing the batch file in the startup folder. As an additional challenge, place the batch file into the networked users' startup folders through their networked profiles.

2. Modify the Notepad batch file that you created in Discovery Exercise 1 to run only once. You can do this by creating a file within the batch program. (This file can contain anything, as its purpose is only to indicate that Notepad has been run once. This type of file is commonly called a flag file.) Have this subprogram check for the flag file's existence prior to running notepad.exe. Test the modified batch file using the methods you used in Discovery Exercise 1. Be sure to delete the flag file between each test to ensure that the batch program will proceed with the registry change only when the flag file is not present. In a network environment, you can use this method to deploy program upgrades and system patches.

3. Create and modify a login script to run notepad.exe. Ensure that it works by logging in using a nonadministrative user account. Now, choose a specific user, and modify the login script to only run notepad.exe for that user. Once you have tested this appropriately, make the run-once changes that you made in Discovery Exercise 2 to the login script and test it again.

4. Use the **EVENT QUERY** command with the **/FI** option to query a networked system for events whose type is Error and write the output to a file. Use this command in a batch file so you can run it on multiple systems once a day (using the **AT** command). Create another batch program that will gather these output reports into a single source for you to view each day.

5. Using the **SYSTEMINFO** and **DRIVERQUERY** commands, create a batch file that retrieves hardware information for every system on your network and outputs it to a file.

6. Combine the batch file created in Discovery Exercise 3 with the swinv.bat file that you created in Hands-on Project 9-6. Replace all computer names in the commands with batch parameters, and send the output to a file whose name is the computer name. The goal is to run the batch program with a parameter of the computer name, and result in an output report that includes the computer name and all of its appropriate inventory information. Add commands to the batch file to start each file with "Inventory report for" followed by the computer name. Separate the output from each command with a line of asterisks to make it easier to read.

9

UNIT 4

DOMAIN ADMINISTRATION

10

ACTIVE DIRECTORY: THE WINDOWS SERVER 2003 DOMAIN

After reading this chapter and completing the exercises, you will be able to:

♦ Understand the standard protocols and logical and physical structure of Active Directory

♦ Install Active Directory

♦ Describe the roles of users and groups

♦ Use commands to configure and administer Active Directory

A **directory service** is typically a network service used to store information about network resources such as users, computers, files, folders, and printers. The information stored within a directory service includes the resource name, a list of users who can access that resource, and the level of security assigned to a particular resource. Directory services provide a consistent way of naming, describing, locating, accessing, managing, and securing information about network resources.

UNDERSTANDING ACTIVE DIRECTORY

Microsoft **Active Directory** is the directory service provided with Windows Server 2003. Active Directory simplifies network resource utilization by making the physical location and transport protocol mechanisms of a resource transparent to the user. For example, users do not need to know the print server name to find and use a printer on the network in an Active Directory environment. Active Directory simplifies administration by centralizing management. For example, system configuration information, user profiles, and applications are all stored within Active Directory. Administrators can use Active Directory to manage desktops, network services, and applications from a central location using a standard interface.

Standard Protocols for Active Directory

Microsoft Active Directory supports many Internet standard protocols and application programming interfaces (APIs). With Active Directory, an entire network looks and behaves consistently across multiple protocols and APIs. Because Microsoft Active Directory supports these various technologies, a network can have a single namespace (domain name) managed by a single directory. Microsoft Active Directory is like one-stop shopping for information. Want to know which printers are on the third floor? Ask Active Directory. Want to know someone's e-mail address? Look in Active Directory. Want to know who someone's manager is? Query Active Directory. Before the introduction of Active Directory (which first became available with Windows 2000), you would have had to look up those answers in several different sources. To find a printer, you would have had to ask the Windows NT print server. To look up someone's e-mail address or manager, you might have had to query a mainframe. Now, all that information is stored in a single location.

Active Directory supports many technologies. For example, in Chapter 7, you learned that computers require an IP address to participate in a TCP/IP network such as the Internet or a corporate local area network (LAN). Administrators can use the Dynamic Host Configuration Protocol (DHCP), which is supported by Active Directory, to automatically assign IP addresses to host computers on the network. Active Directory supports the Dynamic Domain Naming Service (DDNS), an upgraded version of DNS, for hostname management, registration, and address resolution. The integration of DDNS with Active Directory allows organizations to achieve an organization-wide naming scheme that is compatible with the Internet. In Chapter 11, you will learn about the Lightweight Directory Access Protocol (LDAP), a key protocol supported by Active Directory for performing directory searches and updates. LDAP increases the interoperability between Microsoft Active Directory and other non-Microsoft applications and directory services.

Active Directory supports a wide range of security mechanisms, including **X.509 version 3** certificates and **Kerberos version 5**, for authentication. Kerberos version 5 and X.509 certificates allow companies to implement a security model that can be deployed both internally and over the Internet. In brief, Kerberos version 5 authentication mechanisms use tickets for network resource access. These tickets store encrypted data, including an encrypted password, that confirms the user's identity to the requested service. You will learn more about this technology in the next chapter.

Active Directory's Logical and Physical Structure

Active Directory is made up of two structures. The logical structure includes domains, organizational units (OUs), forests, and trees, while the physical structure comprises special servers called domain controllers and sites. This structure is illustrated in Figure 10-1.

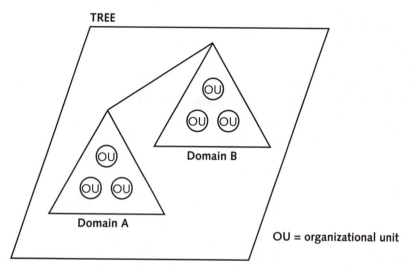

Figure 10-1   The logical structure of Active Directory

Domains

At the core of Active Directory lie domains. Recall that domains are logical groupings of computers as defined by the network administrator. Computers in a domain share security policies and may maintain a relationship with computers in other domains. A domain is essentially an administrative security. As you learned in Chapter 1, certain Windows Server 2003 systems are called domain controllers. Active Directory is housed on these servers. Active Directory uses a **multi-master replication model**, in which a copy of the directory exists on each domain controller. This is a major benefit because it makes Active Directory inherently fault-tolerant, which means that if one domain controller crashes, the directory isn't lost and is available to users on other domain controllers in the environment. Because of the tight integration of DDNS—the method of name resolution on the Internet, and Active Directory—administrators can name their domains after their company's Internet domain or they can make up an internal name. For example, let's say you work for the ABC Company and it has registered abccomp.com as its Web site name. You could use that same name when you create your corporate Active Directory domain. You could have also named the domain abccomp.internal to specify internal use only, making your private network resources more secure.

For security reasons, many companies maintain two domain names. Usually a company's .com address is available to the public, whereas the .internal or .corp domain is only accessible within the company's network.

To simplify the concept, think of Active Directory as your local yellow pages phone book. Everyone in your neighborhood has a complete copy. No one in your neighborhood has a part of the yellow pages. For instance, you don't have the A–F's while the people across the street have the G–L's, and the people next door have the M–R's, and so on. If you misplace your yellow pages, you can simply go to a neighbor's house to perform your query.

Organizational Units

Within an organization are users, groups of users, printers, contacts, and more. Active Directory allows for the storage of these types of objects in special containers called **organizational units (OUs)**. An OU is a container object that allows you to store other objects such as users, groups, and printers. An OU can even contain other OUs.

Here's another way to think about domains and OUs: Say that you are in charge of lunch for three of your coworkers. One coworker likes peanut butter and jelly with the crust cut off, grapes, and carrot sticks for lunch every day. Another coworker likes bologna and cheese, chips, and celery sticks for lunch every day. The final coworker always wants a turkey sandwich with bacon, a few cookies, and some sliced green bell pepper for lunch. Every day you could prepare these meals by throwing the items all together in one huge cooler. Distributing the lunches could get confusing and meals might get mixed up between your coworkers. To resolve this issue, you buy some brown paper lunch bags. Those brown paper lunch bags act as individual domains. Remember that domains are a security boundary. Do you just throw the lunch into each bag? Of course not. You organize your domains, or, in this case, your lunch bags. You grab some Tupperware (which represents the OUs), and place each food item in its own Tupperware. Finally, you place the appropriate food item within each coworker's bag.

In a business setting, network administrators might design OUs around departments. For example, within ABC Company there are the marketing, sales, research, and technical support departments. The network designer might make an OU for each different department.

Trees, Forests, and Trusts

Like trees in nature, which have a standard root, trunk, branch, and leaf structure, domains in Active Directory are organized in hierarchal structures. These structures are called **domain trees**. In each domain tree, there is one distinct root with several branches, known as subdomains. You are probably familiar with several root, or top-level, domains. For example, .com, .edu, .org, and .gov are all examples of top-level domains on the Web. Examples of Web subdomains are microsoft.com, sun.com, java.com, netscape.com, asu.edu, and nih.gov. Microsoft has domains beneath the microsoft.com domain. For example, msdn.microsoft.com, technet.microsoft.com, and support.microsoft.com are all subdomains. Therefore, when you add a domain to an existing tree, the new domain is a child domain of the parent domain. The child domain's name is a combination of the parent domain along with the child name. For example, if you add a child domain called visualbasic to the msdn.microsoft.com parent domain, the newly created domain would be called visualbasic.msdn.microsoft.com. See Figure 10-2.

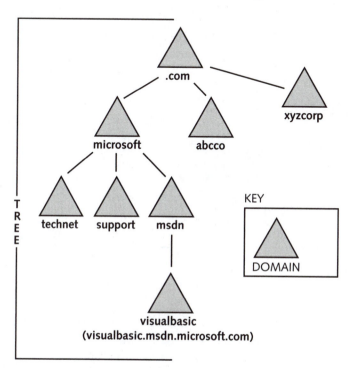

Figure 10-2   The domain tree structure

What if microsoft.com wanted to do business with abcco.com, which is a completely different domain? The two companies could implement what's known as a **forest**. A forest is a group of trees with different namespaces that share some common aspects of Active Directory. Another very important distinction is that trees in a forest share a two-way transitive **trust**. A trust between domains is a relationship such that users in one domain can be authenticated by domain controllers in another domain. A two-way transitive trust relationship between domains gives domain users the ability to use resources in the other domain and vice versa. Trust relationships are important when you want to give users the ability to use resources in other domains. In this example, you want users in the microsoft.com domain and users in the abcco.com domain to share resources. Figure 10-3 shows the two-way transitive trust relationship that exists between the microsoft.com domain and the abcco.com domain. The parallelogram enclosing the two domains indicates that the microsoft.com domain and the abcco.com domain are in the same forest. Notice that the xyzcorp.com domain is not participating in the forest.

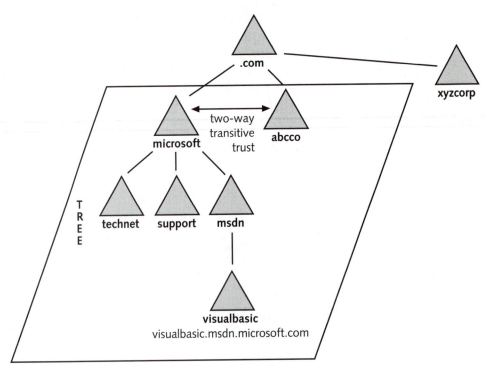

Figure 10-3 Trees, forests, and trusts

Schema

The rules governing Active Directory are contained within its **schema**, which is the set of object definitions indicating what can be stored in Active Directory. An installation of Active Directory can have one and only one schema, which resides on a special domain controller called the schema master. The schema stores object definitions for computers, users, printers, and other objects. When a change is made to the schema, those changes are replicated to every domain controller in the forest. The schema is extensible. That means software developers can create their own custom objects and add those to the schema. Microsoft Exchange 2000 Server is an example of a product that modifies the Active Directory schema.

Sites and Domain Controllers

Sites and domain controllers make up the physical components of Active Directory. Sites are IP subnets connected by a reliable high-speed link, such as a T1 connection. Sites and domain controllers handle such issues as where and how often Active Directory replication occurs, as well as managing logon traffic. Sites optimize replication traffic, or the communication between domains, and enable users to connect to domain controllers. Sites and domains are completely separate. For example, you might have many domains within one site or one domain spanning multiple sites. Domains may have one or more domain controllers depending on the need. Figure 10-4 represents the ABC Company's domain and site structure. ABC Company has three domains: the Marketing domain, the Sales domain, and the IT domain. Each domain is indicated by a triangle. ABC Company is geographically located in two cities: Phoenix (Site A) and Chicago (Site B). Notice that each domain spans geography. For example, the Marketing domain (in black) has two domain controllers in Phoenix, Site A, and two domain controllers in Chicago, Site B.

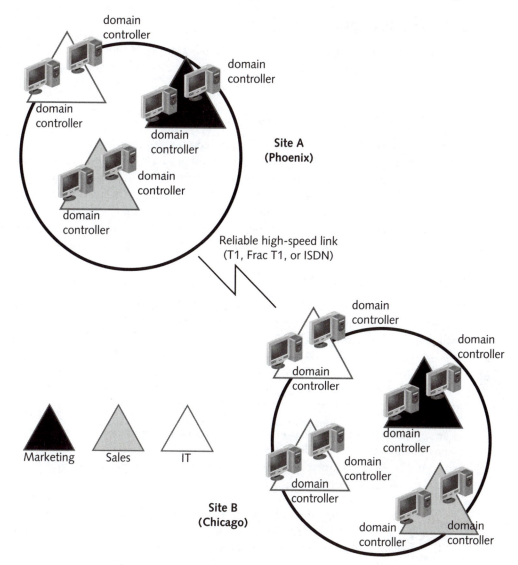

Figure 10-4   Sites and domain controllers

Within an Active Directory environment are special domain controllers called **Global Catalog servers**. Global Catalog servers manage queries to the **Global Catalog**. The Global Catalog is the subset of data in Active Directory to which users have access. The

Global Catalog performs two important functions. First, the Global Catalog aids in the logon process, and second, the Global Catalog allows users to query Active Directory for information, such as an e-mail address, throughout the entire forest. Global Catalog servers cache and process queries to the Global Catalog.

INSTALLING ACTIVE DIRECTORY

Active Directory is not part of the default installation for Windows Server 2003. Installing Active Directory requires specific physical requirements and the use of specific commands, as you will learn in the following sections.

Preinstallation Requirements

Both your server and network must meet certain requirements before you can install Microsoft Active Directory. To install Microsoft Active Directory, you will need a computer running either Microsoft Windows Server 2003, Microsoft Windows Enterprise Server 2003, or Microsoft Windows Datacenter Server 2003. You will need at least a 1 GB, NTFS-formatted partition to store Active Directory. Your network must be running TCP/IP and have a DDNS server that supports the SRV (service) resource record type. It is recommended that you also have a DDNS server that supports dynamic updates.

The DCPROMO Command

To install Active Directory, use the command **DCPROMO** from the command line or from the Start menu's Run line. **DCPROMO** starts the Active Directory Installation Wizard. You will learn the specific steps for Active Directory installation in Hands-on Project 10-1.

DCPROMO   Starts the Active Directory Installation Wizard, which is used to install or uninstall Active Directory.

The Active Directory Installation Wizard allows you to create a new forest with a new root domain. You can also use the wizard to add additional domain controllers to an existing domain. The Active Directory Installation Wizard is also used to add child domains or add a new tree to an existing forest.

You must have the appropriate permission to run the Active Directory Installation Wizard. The wizard will ask you for the username, password, and domain of an account with the proper credentials.

Hands-on Project 10-1 leads you through the process of installing Active Directory in Microsoft Windows Server 2003.

Hands-on Project 10-1

To install Active Directory:

1. Open a command window. To initiate the Active Directory Installation Wizard, type **dcpromo.exe** and press **Enter**.

2. On the Welcome to Active Directory Installation Wizard page, click **Next**. You might see a dialog box titled Operating System compatibility. If necessary, click **Next** to continue the installation.

3. Verify that the default setting of creating a new domain controller for a new domain is selected and click **Next**.

4. On the Create New Domain page, verify that the default setting of Domain in a new forest is selected and click **Next**.

5. To name the new domain, type **ct.net** for the full DNS name and click **Next**.

If DNS is not currently installed, you will need to select the "No, just install and configure DNS on this computer" option.

10

6. Note that the entry field is populated with the default CT domain name for the backward-compatible NetBIOS name on the NetBIOS Domain Name page. Click **Next**.

7. Accept the default directories for database and log folders and click **Next**.

8. Accept the default directory for the shared system volume and click **Next**.

9. On the Active Directory Installion Wizard DNS registration diagnostics page, click **Next** to accept the default configuration to install and configure the DNS server on this computer.

10. Click the **option button** that sets permissions to be compatible with Windows 2000 or Windows Server 2003 and click **Next**.

11. Type **password** as the restore mode password and click **Next**. This password is vital if you need to restore this server to its original role as a member server rather than a domain controller.

12. Review the summary and click **Next** to install Active Directory. If necessary, insert the Windows Server 2003 disk as prompted and click **OK**.

13. When the wizard is done, click **Finish** and then click **Restart Now** to restart Windows Server 2003.

The Active Directory Installation Wizard is an amazing program. What you are waiting for while you are watching the little pencil writing to the directory icon (see Figure 10-5) is for the Active Directory Installation Wizard to validate all the parameters you specified during the installation process.

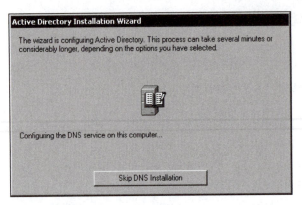

Figure 10-5   Waiting for the Active Directory Installation Wizard to finish

The wizard is performing such actions as validating whether this is the first server in the domain and determining whether a domain controller already exists. In fact, the **DCPROMO** command starts the validation process long before you even see the wizard's welcome window. Before popping up the welcome window, the wizard has verified that you are a member of the Local Administrators group, confirmed that the computer is indeed running Microsoft Windows Server 2003, and determined whether Active Directory has been previously installed. The installation wizard also checks to make sure that the NetBIOS name and server name are unique within your domain. The wizard verifies that TCP/IP has been installed and configured correctly. DDNS and NetBIOS domain names are verified. Finally, the wizard verifies the user credentials and makes sure the directories specified are located on an NTFS partition with the appropriate hard disk space.

Verifying Active Directory Installation

After you install Active Directory, or any service for that matter, you should check to make sure that the installation process finished properly. There are several ways to verify that Active Directory was installed properly on your servers. A good first step is to make sure that the Active Directory database and log files have been installed in their proper location. The project instructed you to accept the default database and log file locations of C:\Windows\NTDS. See Figure 10-6.

Within this directory, you will find the ntds.dit file. The ntds.dit file contains all of the data stored in Active Directory. You will also see the edb.log file and both res1.log and res2.log files in the NTDS directory; these files are log files. These log files contain a record of all the changes made to Active Directory and then commit them to Active Directory permanently when the files become full. The log files are used to restore Active Directory from a crash.

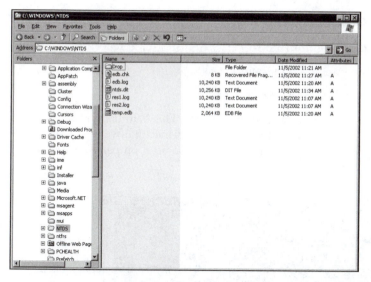

Figure 10-6 Verifying the contents of the C:\Windows\NTDS directory

Another way to verify that Active Directory was installed is to make sure that the SRVrecords have been properly registered in DDNS. You can do this by using the DNS snap-in on the Administrative Tools menu or use the **NSLOOKUP** command.

NSLOOKUP Queries a DNS server.

If when using the DDNS snap-in you see the _msdcs, _sites, _tcp, and _udp folders within your domain, as shown in Figure 10-7, then you know that the SRV resource records were registered correctly.

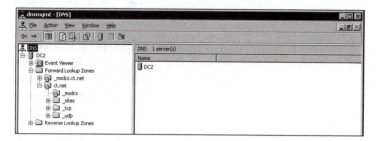

Figure 10-7 Using the DNS snap-in to verify SRV resource record registration

Hands-on Project 10-2 teaches you how to use the **NSLOOKUP** command to verify SRV resource record validation.

10

Hands-on Project 10-2:

To use the **NSLOOKUP** command to verify SRV resource record registration:

1. Open a command window.

2. Type **nslookup** and press **Enter**.

3. Type **ls –t SRV ct.net** and press **Enter**. This command instructs **NSLOOKUP** to perform a DDNS zone transfer as if your machine were a DDNS server. The resource records will be listed if they have been properly created, as shown in Figure 10-8.

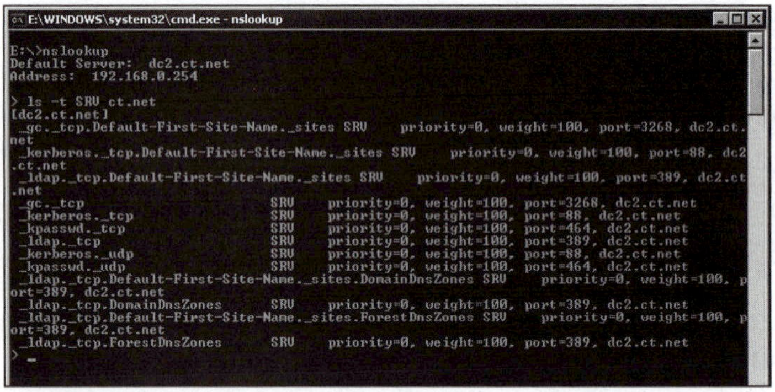

Figure 10-8   Verifying SRV resource record registration

4. Type **exit** and press **Enter** to close the command window.

> If you have not previously created a DDNS reverse lookup zone, which allows for reverse name resolution, the **NSLOOKUP** command will generate errors. These errors are actually time-out errors, which occur because **NSLOOKUP** is generating a reverse lookup zone to determine the hostname of the DDNS server based on the IP address. A possible solution is to issue the **SERVER** subcommand and specify the DDNS server's name. The first step would be to enter the **NSLOOKUP** interactive mode by simply typing "nslookup" at the command prompt. To change your default server, enter the **SERVER** subcommand by typing "server" followed by the IP address of the desired DDNS server and pressing the Enter key.

After you have verified that the SRV resource records have been registered, verify the sysvol. The sysvol share contains Windows Server 2003 software distribution files, scripts, and ADM templates as well as the Group Policy template. To verify the sysvol, you first check to make sure that the folder structure was created and then check to make sure the proper folders were shared. Hands-on Project 10-3 leads you through the necessary steps in verifying the sysvol and using the **NET SHARE** command to verify that the appropriate shares have been completed. Recall that you first learned about the **NET SHARE** command in Chapter 8.

Hands-on Project 10-3

To verify the sysvol and use the **NET SHARE** command to verify shares:

1. Click the **Start** button ![Start], and then click **Run** and type **%systemroot%\sysvol** in the Open box.

2. Click **OK**. You should see the contents of the C:\Windows\sysvol folder. The folder should contain the domain, staging, staging areas, and sysvol subfolders, as shown in Figure 10-9.

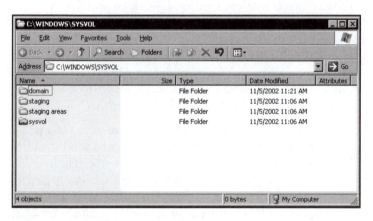

Figure 10-9 Verifying the sysvol

3. Open a command window. To verify that the Netlogon and sysvol shares are included in the list of shares returned by the **NET SHARE** command, type **Net share** and press **Enter**.

4. Type **exit** and press **Enter** to close the command window. Click the **Close** button ![X] to close the Windows\sysvol window.

Dealing with Active Directory Installation Problems

It is possible to encounter problems while installing Active Directory. While installing Active Directory, for example, you might encounter an "Access Denied" error. Remember, to install Active Directory on the first domain controller, you must be a part of the Local Administrators group. If you are adding a new domain controller to an existing domain, you might have supplied the wrong credentials to the Active Directory Installation Wizard. Another common problem deals with DDNS and NetBIOS name uniqueness. When creating a domain, you must be sure that the name isn't already being used. A simple quick fix to resolving this error is to simply give your domain a new name. As you learned earlier,

Active Directory and DDNS are tightly integrated. You must have a DDNS server on the network that supports the SRV resource record. If while installing Active Directory your potential domain controller can't successfully make contact with a DDNS server, you will encounter DDNS-related errors. Finally, recall that Active Directory requires at least 1 GB of hard disk space. You will definitely run into problems if your server doesn't have sufficient hard disk resources to install Active Directory. These are some typical installation errors. Be aware that you might encounter other potential errors not discussed here.

ACTIVE DIRECTORY DOMAIN ADMINISTRATION

Simply put, Active Directory stores objects. For the most part, Active Directory objects are an abstraction of the objects that exist in most work environments. You have users, printers, shared folders, and an address book in your office. Microsoft Active Directory needs some way of mimicking those real-world objects inside the server. Active Directory has user objects that represent humans, printer objects that represent printers, folders that represent physical folders, and contacts that represent an address book. Active Directory is extensible, which means that as software vendors come out with new software, the software makers could store their objects in Active Directory, as well.

As discussed earlier, organizational units allow you to organize your objects. Say you have 125 users in your company. The marketing department might have 30 members, the sales department might have 50 members, the accounting department might have 20 members, and IT might have 25 members in their group. You could use OUs to organize your users by department. In this example, creating OUs for marketing, sales, accounting, and IT makes the most sense. Because OUs help administrators to manage and organize the objects in Active Directory, there are tools to assist in these tasks. You will learn about these tools in the next section.

Managing Active Directory

The two ways of managing Active Directory are by using the GUI and by using command line tools. You can use both methods to create and manage Active Directory objects such as users, groups, or computers.

Active Directory Command Line Tools

Windows Server 2003 comes with Active Directory service tools that can help you perform common administrative tasks on the server.

DSADD   Uses options to add objects such as users (**DSADD USER**), computers (**DSADD COMPUTER**), contacts (**DSADD CONTACT**), groups (**DSADD GROUP**), and OUs (**DSADD OU**) to Active Directory.

DSMOD   Modifies users, computers, servers, contacts, OUs, or groups.

DSRM	Removes objects from Active Directory.
DSMOVE	Renames or moves an object.
DSQUERY	Queries Active Directory for a list of objects using specified search criteria.
DSGET	Shows attributes of a specified object.
NTDSUTIL	Performs Active Directory database maintenance and allows an administrator to perform such tasks as database compacting.

The most common GUI tool for daily administration of Active Directory is Active Directory Users and Computers, shown in Figure 10-10. Active Directory Users and Computers is actually a snap-in in a Microsoft Management Console (MMC). MMCs provide a centralized tool for Windows Server 2003 administration. MMCs may be customized to contain several snap-ins easing Windows Server 2003 administration. Figure 10-10 shows an open MMC containing the following snap-ins: Active Directory Users and Computers, Computer Management, Device Manager, DHCP, and DDNS. Using this MMC, an administrator can perform common tasks such as resetting a user's password, updating a driver, creating a DHCP scope providing a range of IP address for computers configured to receive their IP address automatically, and adding a host to the DDNS database.

10

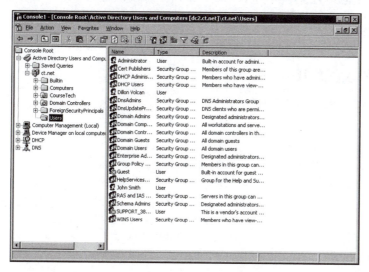

Figure 10-10 Active Directory Users and Computers

Not all Windows Server 2003 systems will have the Active Directory administration tools. You must be on a domain controller or a machine with the administration tools installed to use Active Directory Users and Computers.

Managing Users

Administrative tasks for Active Directory in the Windows Server 2003 environment can be broken down into a few main tasks. The first main task of administration is user management. User management includes such functions as creating accounts for new users, resetting passwords, disabling or enabling user accounts, and deleting users from Active Directory. You can use the **DSADD** command and its options to perform user management tasks such as adding new users or resetting passwords.

Some of the common options used with **DSADD USER** include:

- **–PWD**—Sets the user's new password.
- **–MAIL**—Sets the user's e-mail address.
- **–MOBILE**—Sets the user's cell phone number.
- **–MUSTCHPWD** *YES|NO*—Determines whether a user must change his or her password at next logon.
- **–CANCHPWD** *YES|NO*—Specifies whether a user can change his or her password.
- **–DISABLED** *YES|NO*—Specifies whether a user can log on to the network.

Hands-on Project 10-4 teaches you how to use commands to perform several common user-related administrative tasks that modify Active Directory.

Hands-on Project 10-4

To manage users in Active Directory:

1. Open a command window.

2. Type **dsadd user "CN=John Smith,CN=Users,DC=ct,DC=net"** and press **Enter** to add a new user. Because there is a space between John and Smith, quotation marks must surround this command.

3. Click the **Start** button [Start]. Click **All Programs**, click **Administrative Tools**, and then click **Active Directory Users and Computers**. You should see the John Smith user account in the Active Directory Users and Computers window. Figure 10-11 shows the new user within Active Directory Users and Computers.

4. Return to the command window. Type **dsadd user "CN=Jane Doe, CN=Users,DC=ct,DC=net" -pwd HaveFun** to create a new user with a password of HaveFun.

5. Refresh the Active Directory Users and Computers window by clicking **Action** and then clicking **Refresh**. In the Active Directory Users and Computers window, you should see that Jane Doe has been added to the Users folder. See Figure 10-12.

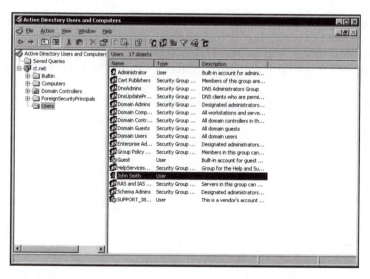

Figure 10-11 Verifying the John Smith user account

To refresh Active Directory Users and Computers at any time, click the Action menu and then click Refresh.

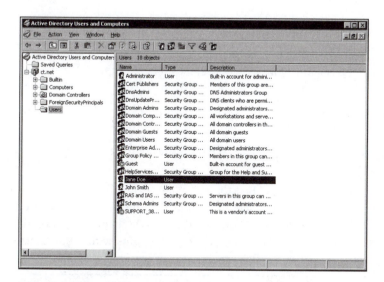

Figure 10-12 Verifying the Jane Doe user account

You cannot add multiple users simultaneously with Active Directory Users and Computers. Later in this chapter you will learn how to perform multiple operations using bulk change commands.

6. Type **dsmod user "CN=Jane Doe,CN=Users,DC=ct,DC=net" -disabled yes** to disable Jane Doe's account for logon. Your screen should look like Figure 10-13, which shows Jane Doe's account in Active Directory Users and Computers; the x in the red circle indicates that the account is disabled.

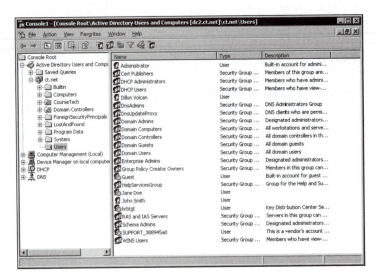

Figure 10-13 Disabled account

7. Type **dsrm "CN=Jane Doe,CN=Users,DC=ct,DC=net"** to delete Jane Doe's account.

8. At the "Are you sure you wish to delete CN=Jane Doe,CN=Users,DC=ct, DC=net (Y/N)? prompt," type **Y** and press **Enter** to complete the step.

9. Click the **Close** button ![X] on the Active Directory Users and Computers window to close the tool.

10. At the command prompt, type **exit** and press **Enter** to close the command window.

In addition to the **DSADD** command, the **NET USER** command can be used to create domain user accounts by including the **/DOMAIN** option at the end of the command. Recall that you first learned about the **NET USER** command in Chapter 6. Due to backward compatibility, **NET USER** always places the new user accounts within the Users folder OU in Active Directory.

NET USER /DOMAIN   Displays all users within the domain.

NET USER <USERNAME> <PASSWORD> /ADD /DOMAIN   Adds the *USERNAME* with the *PASSWORD* to the domain.

NET USER <USERNAME> <PASSWORD> /DOMAIN   Changes the password for *USERNAME* to *PASSWORD* within the domain.

NET USER <*USERNAME*> /DELETE /DOMAIN   Removes the *USER-NAME* account from the domain.

Setting User Account Properties   Using the **NET** command, you also can change the default account behaviors for user accounts. Within a domain, this is usually done using Group Policy, which is a feature with which you can apply restrictions and security features to computer and user accounts belonging to specific organizational units. Large numbers of group policies can become complex to manage and administer, and you should remember that there are other factors, such as the results of running the **NET ACCOUNTS** command, which can have an impact on the effective results of group policy changes dealing with account security.

NET ACCOUNTS /DOMAIN   Displays the default account behaviors for the current domain.

NET ACCOUNTS /MINPWLEN:<*NUMBEROFCHARACTERS*> /DOMAIN Requires that all new accounts have a minimum password length of *NUMBEROFCHARACTERS*.

NET ACCOUNTS /MAXPWAGE:<*NUMBEROFCHARACTERS*> /DOMAIN Requires that passwords for all new accounts expire every *NUMBEROFCHARACTERS* days.

NET ACCOUNTS /MINPWAGE:<*NUMBEROFCHARACTERS*> /DOMAIN Requires that passwords for all new accounts be changed again *NUMBEROFCHARACTERS* days after the password is changed.

NET ACCOUNTS /UNIQUEPW:<*NUMBEROFPWSREMEMBERED*> /DOMAIN   Remembers the number of account passwords for the domain and will not allow a user to enter a new password that is a repeat.

Group Management

The second main administrative task of Active Directory is group management. Group management involves creating new groups, adding users to groups, and deleting groups. Another common task of group and user administration involves determining to which group or groups a user belongs.

There are three different types of groups within Active Directory: domain local, global, and universal groups. The functional differences between these three occur only in multiple-domain environments and multiple-forest situations.

A domain local group is a group whose membership and access privileges are not shared between domains. A global group is just the opposite: With the appropriate domain trusts in place, global group membership is accessed across domains within the same forest to allow resource access to occur between domains—without re-creating user accounts. The top part of Figure 10-14 shows that without global groups, duplicate user accounts would need to be created in each domain, compounding the administrative nightmare resulting from changes to user passwords, because each domain would require the same password. Realistically, such a setup would not work anyway because each user account contains a unique **security identifier (SID)**, which is a unique code that is assigned to all resource objects within a domain. The bottom part of Figure 10-14 illustrates how global and local groups allow resource access between trusted domains.

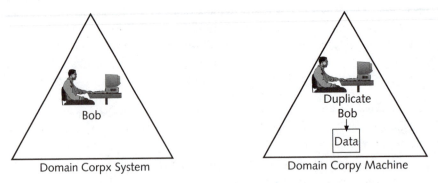

Domain Corpx System

Domain Corpy Machine

From within Corpx System, Bob would have to log in to Corpy Machine using a duplicate account to access the data located within Corpy Machine. The security structure of Server 2003 does not allow this.

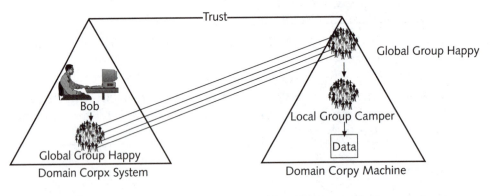

Instead, Bob becomes a member of the global group called Happy.

Since the Happy group in Corpx System is global, Corpy Machine can view its membership. The members of the global group called Happy are added into the Local Group Camper, which has access to the data.

Figure 10-14   Global groups, trusts, and resource access across domains

Universal groups accomplish the same purpose as a global group, but have the ability to cross forest boundaries. The mechanics of universal groups are more complex than those of global groups because each forest has its own Active Directory database, and inter-forest resource access (outside of services such as FTP or IIS) is possible. It is possible to have a **mixed domain**, which means that a domain can contain domain controllers running NT, 2000, or Server 2003. Because universal groups function only with Server 2003 or Windows 2000, each domain using universal groups must be a **native domain**, meaning that all domain controllers are running Server 2003 or Windows 2000. Native and mixed domains are illustrated in Figure 10-15.

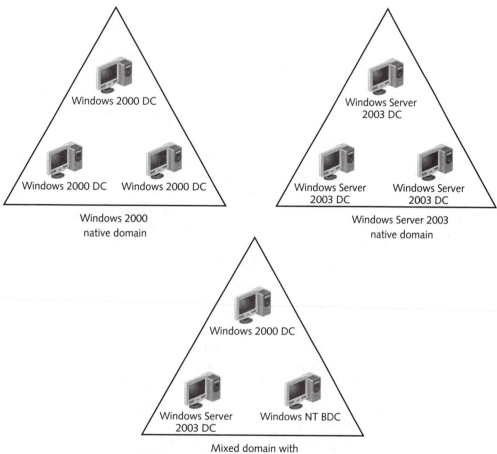

Windows 2000 DC

Windows 2000 DC   Windows 2000 DC

Windows 2000
native domain

Windows Server
2003 DC

Windows Server   Windows Server
2003 DC   2003 DC

Windows Server 2003
native domain

Windows 2000 DC

Windows Server   Windows NT BDC
2003 DC

Mixed domain with
Windows Server 2000, Server 2003, and NT

Figure 10-15   Native and mixed domains

Hands-on Project 10-5 teaches you how to create groups and add members to a newly created group. You will also learn how to determine the group or groups to which a user belongs.

Hands-on Project 10-5:

To manage groups:

1. Open a command window.

2. Type **dsadd group CN=sales,CN=Users,DC=ct,DC=net** and press **Enter** to create a new group called sales.

3. Type **dsmod group CN=sales,CN=Users,DC=ct,DC=net -addmbr "CN=John Smith,CN=Users,DC=ct,DC=net"** and press **Enter** to add John Smith (from the previous project) to the sales group.

4. Type **dsget user "CN=John Smith,CN=Users,DC=ct,DC=net" -memberof** to verify that John Smith is a member of the sales group.

5. Type **dsrm CN=sales,CN=Users,DC=ct,DC=net** and press **Enter** to delete the sales group.

6. At the "Are you sure you wish to delete CN=sales,CN=Users,DC=ct, DC=net (Y/N)?" prompt, press **Y** and press **Enter** to complete the project.

7. Type **exit** and press **Enter** to close the command window.

The **NET** command can also be used to add objects to a domain, but it is limited in its abilities because of its backward compatibility with Windows NT and 2000. Despite this limitation, it remains remarkably useful because of this same backward compatibility. **NET GROUP** can be executed on any Windows 9x, Me, NT, 2000, XP, or Server 2003 system, while **DSADD** is restricted to Windows 2000 and Server 2003 environments. When running **NET GROUP** on any of these platforms, you can add domain local or global groups to the domain, or you can add local user groups if you are running Windows NT, 2000, XP, or Server 2003.

NET GROUP <*GROUPNAME*> /ADD /DOMAIN   Creates a domain global group called *GROUPNAME*.

NET GROUP <*GROUPNAME*> /DELETE /DOMAIN   Deletes the domain global group *GROUPNAME*.

NET GROUP does not have the ability to place a group in a specific location within Active Directory, as **DSADD** does. All groups are placed in the Users folder within Active Directory Users and Computers, as shown in Figure 10-16, for a group called testgroup that was created using the **NET GROUP /ADD** command.

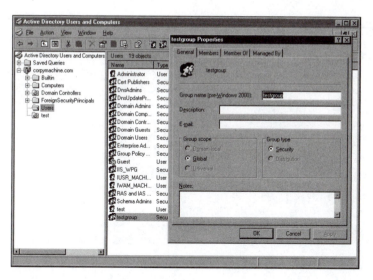

Figure 10-16   The testgroup group created using **NET GROUP /ADD**

NET LOCALGROUP <*GROUPNAME*> /ADD /DOMAIN   Creates a
domain local group called *GROUPNAME*.

NET LOCALGROUP <*GROUPNAME*> /DELETE /DOMAIN   Deletes the
domain local group called *GROUPNAME*.

10

NET LOCALGROUP /ADD is another command used to manage groups. It differs from **NET GROUP /ADD** only in the type of group that is generated, which is a domain local group. Like **NET GROUP**, **NETLOCAL GROUP** cannot place a group in a specific location in Active Directory. Figure 10-17 shows the properties of a local group created using the **NET LOCALGROUP /ADD** command.

Be aware that if you are running **NET GROUP** or **NET LOCALGROUP** on a domain controller, it is not necessary to use the **/DOMAIN** option because the system only deals with Active Directory from the domain controller. This ensures that local physical access to the domain controller is completely integrated with the security that the domain controller houses.

You should also know that the system you use to run these **NET** commands must be a member of the same domain that you are administering, and you must be logged in to that domain. It is possible to get around this particular limitation by using the **RUNAS** command in conjunction with the **NET** command, but you will need to have an appropriate user account and password to ensure success.

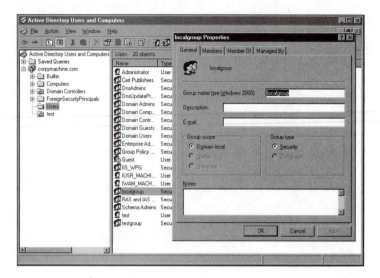

Figure 10-17   The localgroup group created using **NET LOCALGROUP /ADD**

Creating Organizational Units

A third major task for Active Directory administrators is managing organizational units. Recall that OUs give administrators the ability to organize domain users, printers, and contacts in smaller, more manageable units. Managing OUs involves creating and deleting OUs as needed.

In Hands-on Project 10-6, you will use commands to create and search for an OU. At the end of this project, you will delete the newly created OU.

Hands-on Project 10-6

To add and delete an OU:

1. Open a command window.

2. Type **dsadd ou OU=CourseTech,DC=ct,DC=net** and press **Enter** to create an OU called CourseTech. See Figure 10-18.

Figure 10-18   Creating the CourseTech OU

3. Click the **Start** button ![Start], point to **All Programs**, and then click **Administrative Tools**. From Administrative Tools, click **Active Directory Users and Computers** and confirm that the OU was added to Active Directory. See Figure 10-19.

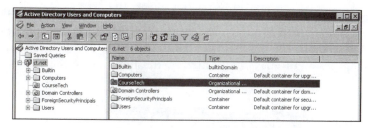

Figure 10-19   Verifying the CourseTech OU

4. Switch back to the command window. Type **dsquery ou DC=ct,DC=net**
   and press **Enter** to search Active Directory for all OUs in the ct.net domain
   created earlier.

5. Type **dsrm OU=CourseTech,DC=ct,DC=net** and press **Enter** to delete the
   CourseTech OU.

6. At the "Are you sure you wish to delete OU=CourseTech,DC=ct,DC=net
   (Y/N)?" prompt, press **Y** and press **Enter** to complete the project.

7. To close Active Directory Users and Computers, click its **Close** button ☒ .

8. Type **exit** and press **Enter** to close the command window.

Domain Membership

Every domain consists of at least one domain controller. Ideally, a domain also contains
several computers that rely on the protective security of the domain for security and
resource access. For these computers to take advantage of domain membership, they
must become members of the domain. The **DSADD** command can be used for this, as can
the **NET COMPUTER** command.

NET COMPUTER \\\<COMPUTERNAME> /ADD   Adds the computer to
the domain database.

NET COMPUTER \\\<COMPUTERNAME> /DEL   Removes the computer
from the domain database.

Making Bulk Changes

The directory service commands are useful when dealing with one or two users.
However, it would be extremely inefficient and difficult to use those commands if you
were adding or deleting hundreds of users. **CSVDE** and **LDIFDE** allow administrators to
make bulk changes, or changes to hundreds of Active Directory objects, in one action.

CSVDE   Imports and exports Active Directory data from a comma-separated file.

LDIFDE   General Active Directory utility tool that allows for bulk changes.

The **CSVDE** command performs import and export data operations on Active Directory using a comma-separated data source file with a .csv extension. As you learned in Chapter 2, the .csv (comma-separated value) format is made up of lines of data, with each value separated by a comma. The header, or the first line in the file, defines the data. See Figure 10-20.

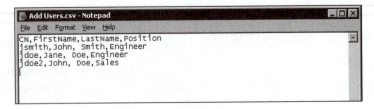

Figure 10-20   The Add Users.csv file

CSVDE can be used in Visual Basic scripts as well as in batch files. A good example of a bulk insert into Active Directory would be to use Microsoft Excel to create a spreadsheet of users, save the file as a .csv file, and use **CSVDE** to import the data into Active Directory.

Hands-on Project 10-7 teaches you how to perform a simple data export of your domain using **CSVDE**.

Hands-on Project 10-7

Using **CSVDE** to perform a basic Active Directory data export:

1. Open a command window. If necessary, type **cd** and press **Enter** to move to the root of the drive.

2. Type **csvde -f myDomain.csv** and press **Enter** to perform a simple domain export.

3. Click the **Start** button ![Start], and then click **Run**. Type **Notepad c:\myDomain.csv** on the Run line, and then click **OK** to examine the contents of the myDomain.csv export file.

4. Type **exit** and press **Enter** to close the command window.

5. Click the **Close** button ![X] on the Notepad window to close Notepad.

Another tool that can be used to perform bulk data operations on Active Directory is **LDIFDE**, which can be used on computers running Windows Server 2003 and Windows XP Professional. In general, **LDIFDE** is used for creating, modifying, or deleting objects within a directory such as Active Directory. **LDIFDE** can also be used to extend the schema, export Active Directory user and group information, and populate Active Directory with data from other directory sources. When creating import files to use with **LDIFDE**, you must define the type of change being made using a changeType command.

The following code shows how to use an **LDIFDE** import file format with the add value. Table 10-2 lists changeType values for **LDIFDE** and their descriptions.

```
DN: CN=SampleUser,DC=DomainName
changetype: add
CN: SampleUser
description: DescriptionOfFile
objectClass: User
sAMAccountName: SampleUser
```

Table 10-2   **LDIFDE** changeType values

Value	Description
add	Import file contains new content.
modify	Import file data will modify existing data.
delete	Content in the import file has been deleted.

Naming in Active Directory

Microsoft Active Directory can store millions of objects. That means if you work for an organization that has 100,000 employees, 25,000 printers, and 502,932 shares, Active Directory is the right tool to help you manage all those items.

 Active Directory is a great improvement over the Windows NT Directory Services (NTDS) feature. The Windows NT directory had a size limitation of 40 MB. That limited you to about 25,000 users, groups, and computers. With Active Directory, Microsoft has made tremendous improvements over NTDS.

To use network resources, users and applications must be able to identify the name of the resource they are trying to use. The naming convention that a directory service uses affects how resources will be identified. All objects within Active Directory have a **distinguished name**. An object's distinguished name identifies the domain in which it is located, in addition to the complete path by which the object is reached. In the previous projects, you created a domain called ct.net. You also created the John Smith user name. John Smith's distinguished name would be `CN=John Smith,CN=Users,DC=ct,DC=net`. In a distinguished name, CN is an abbreviation for common name and DC is an abbreviation for domain component. Therefore, John Smith is a user object in the Users container in the ct.net domain. Distinguished names are guaranteed to be unique. You cannot create two objects with the same name in the same container. For example, let's say you have two John Smiths at your company and both work in the marketing department. You cannot place them both in the Marketing OU. In this example you might have to create the user account object name John Smith1 or John Smith2 to accommodate this situation.

ACCESSING DOMAIN RESOURCES

To use networked or domain resources, you must first determine what resources are available on the network. As you learned in Chapter 8, the **NET VIEW** command is used to view all computers on the network. In many ways, this simple command will be suitable for your needs; however, many larger companies have multiple domains residing on the same network together. As a general rule, access to domain data requires a domain user account, so you can save time while searching the network for data if you first determine to which domain it belongs.

NET VIEW /DOMAIN   Lists all domains that are available on the network.

NET VIEW /DOMAIN:<DOMAINNAME>   Displays all the computer accounts belonging to *DOMAINNAME*.

NET VIEW \\<COMPUTERNAME>   Displays all network shares on *COMPUTERNAME*, provided the host computer and *COMPUTERNAME* are in the same domain.

NET VIEW \\<COMPUTERNAME> /DOMAIN:<DOMAINNAME>
Displays all network shares on *COMPUTERNAME*.

In Hands-on Project 10-8, you will use **NET VIEW** to view all domains on the network, view all computers belonging to that domain, and then display a list of all available resources on one of the systems.

Hands-on Project 10-8

To use **NET VIEW** to determine network shares:

1. Open a command window.

2. Type **net view /domain** and press **Enter**. This displays a list of all domains on the network. Choose one of the entries, and make a note of it.

3. Type **net view /domain:<*domainname*>** where *domainname* is the domain you noted in Step 2. Press **Enter**. This displays a list of all the computers belonging to that domain. Choose one of the computer entries, and make a note of it.

4. Type **net view \\<*computername*> /domain:<*domainname*>** where *computername* is the computer you noted in Step 3 and *domainname* is the domain you noted in Step 2. Press **Enter**. The results will be a list of all network shares and resources available for use on that computer. Figure 10-21 displays the results for a domain containing one computer.

5. Make a note of one of the listed shares whose type is labeled as disk. You will use this information in the next project. Different types of shares are available. As shown in Figure 10-21, a printer whose name is "dex" and whose type is "Print" is attached to \\professional.

Figure 10-21   Using **NET VIEW** to view a computer's resources

6. Type **exit** and press **Enter** to close the command window.

As you may have already guessed, viewing network resources that belong to a system in the domain you are currently logged into does not require the **/DOMAIN:<*DOMAINNAME*>** option because it is automatically assumed. Accessing network shares within a domain is similarly assumed, provided two separate assumptions are made: First, your computer is a member of the same domain; and second, you wish to access the data using the same user credentials (username and password) with which you are logged on. This means that if your system is a member of the domain, and you wish to access data located on another system that is located in the same domain, you can use the **NET USE** command without the **\USER** option, as shown below. The system will automatically assume that since you haven't used this option, the domain is your current one, and the username and password are those of the currently logged-on user. Both domain and credentials will be forwarded to the target computer for authentication.

Just because a share is displayed in the **NET VIEW** list doesn't necessarily mean that you can access that data. Resource access is similar to a trip to the library. If the network is running, you should always be able to step into the library to view the resources (books, in this case) that it contains. Borrowing and reading a book requires a library card, which equates to appropriate permissions on the target computer.

NET USE \\<*COMPUTERNAME*>\<*SHARENAME*>   Establishes a connection to the share.

NET USE \\<*COMPUTERNAME*>\<*SHARENAME*> /USER: <*DOMAINNAME*>\<*USERACCOUNT*>   Establishes a connection to the specified share using *DOMAINNAME* and *USERACCOUNT*.

NET USE <*DRIVELETTER*>: \\\\<*COMPUTERNAME*>\\ <*SHARENAME*> /USER:<*DOMAINNAME*>\\<*USERACCOUNT*>
Establishes a connection to the share using *DOMAINNAME* and *USERACCOUNT* and assigns that connection to a drive letter.

It is possible that the currently logged-on user does not have the appropriate permissions to access the data indicated by *SHARENAME*. In this case, the command returns a message indicating that access has been denied. This will happen in one of two situations: The share permission Read has been denied for the user account, or the NTFS permission for List Folder Contents has been denied for the user account. Normally there are good reasons for access denial, but in cases where a one-time exception must be made, such as for a manager or temporary worker, the **/USER** option should be used. This allows access to the data without forcing you or someone else to log on to the computer.

Permissions can become tricky, so a quick review here is helpful. Remember that combining NTFS and share permissions yields the most restrictive results. In this situation, a user may have established a connection based on a share permission of Read and an NTFS permission for List Folder Contents. It is only later when the user attempts to open, save, or modify data in that share that access is denied. Imagine a situation where you are called to map a drive on a user's computer to a particular server share. This is easily done, but if the user's permissions are not appropriate and a user is unable to gain the correct access to the data, you will be called again to solve the problem. It is a good idea to confirm access permissions before using **NET USE** to connect to network resources.

In Hands-on Project 10-9, you will practice using the **NET USE** command to access a network share on a domain.

Hands-on Project 10-9

To establish a connection to a system using alternate credentials:

1. Open a command window.

2. Using the computer name, share name, and domain name from Hands-on Project 10-8, type **net use t: \\\\<*computername*>\\<*sharename*> /user:<*domainname*>\\accountname** and press **Enter**. The system will attempt to establish a connection to the share.

3. If you receive a message indicating that the username or password is invalid, don't worry. All this means is that the system checked the account name against the current password and found that they did not match. The system will prompt for the password that corresponds to the account name. Type the appropriate password and press **Enter**. The system indicates that the command completed successfully, as shown in Figure 10-22.

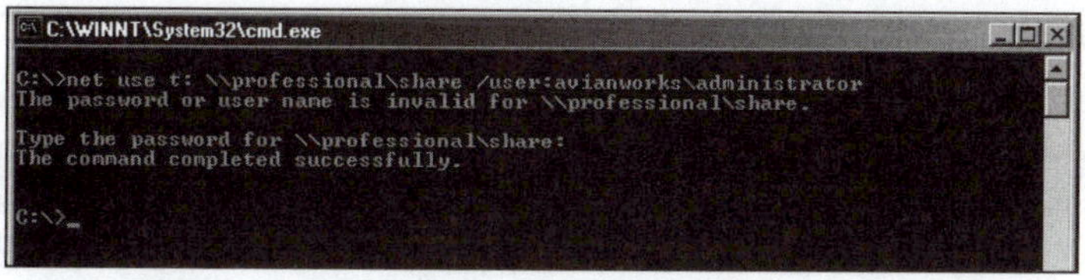

Figure 10-22 Using **NET USE** in a domain

4. There are two ways to confirm that the connection is valid. Type **net use** and press **Enter**. A list of connections is displayed, including the one that was just established.

5. Now try the second confirmation method. Type **dir t:** and press **Enter**. This is a more direct method to test that the connection has been established.

6. Type **exit** and press **Enter** to close the command window.

CHAPTER SUMMARY

This chapter introduced you to directory services, particularly Microsoft Active Directory. Directory services such as Microsoft Active Directory store information about network resources. Network users use Active Directory to locate network resources such as files and printers. Active Directory is a key component of the Microsoft Windows Server 2003 operating system. Active Directory is made up of two components, the logical structure and the physical structure. The logical structure of Active Directory is made up of domains, organizational units (OUs), trees, and forests. The physical structure of Active Directory is made up of special servers called domain controllers and sites. To install Active Directory, use the **DCPROMO** command. The **DCPROMO** command initiates the Active Directory Installation Wizard.

This chapter also covered Active Directory administration and the necessary administration commands. Administration can be broken up into several categories. User management deals with creating and deleting users and resetting passwords. Group management involves creating groups, adding users to groups, and determining group membership. Managing OUs deals with creating and deleting OUs as well as adding objects such as users, computers, or groups to those OUs. Finally, you will search Active Directory. Common searches are conducted to find users, contacts, groups, computers, and OUs, or you may even define your own custom search.

10

COMMAND SUMMARY

Command	Function
DCPROMO	Starts the Active Directory Installation Wizard.
NSLOOKUP	Used to query and diagnose a DDNS server.
DSADD	Adds computers, contacts, groups, OUs, or users to Active Directory.
DSMOD	Modify existing Active Directory objects such as users, groups, or computers.
DSRM	Deletes an object from Active Directory.
DSMOVE	Renames or moves an object.
DSQUERY	Queries Active Directory for a list of objects using specified search criteria.
DSGET	Displays the selected properties of computers, contacts, groups, OUs, or users.
NTDSUTIL	Performs Active Directory database maintenance and allows an administrator to perform such tasks as database compacting.
NET USER	Displays, adds, and removes users within the domain database.
NET ACCOUNTS	Displays behaviors for domains.
NET GROUP	Manages global groups in domains.
NET LOCALGROUP	Manages local groups in domains.
NET COMPUTER	Adds and removes computers to and from the domain database.
CSVDE	Imports and exports data to and from Active Directory using a comma-separated formatted file as a data source.
LDIFDE	A general Active Directory utility tool that allows for bulk changes.
NET VIEW	Displays all network or domain resources available.
NET USE	Establishes a connection to a network or domain resource.

KEY TERMS

Active Directory — The directory service for Microsoft Windows Server 2003.

directory service — A network service used to store information. Directory services typically store information about network resources, security, and network configuration.

distinguished name — The unique name of an object in Active Directory.

domain tree — A relationship between multiple branches and a single root. Trees are commonly used to describe the relationship between child domains and their parent domain.

forest — One or more domains sharing a common schema, configuration, and Global Catalog. Domains in a forest are linked with a two-way transitive trust.

Global Catalog — A subset of Active Directory used by clients and applications to query and locate objects in a forest. The Global Catalog is maintained on one or more domain controllers in the forest.

Global Catalog server — Windows Server 2003 domain controller maintaining the Global Catalog.

Kerberos version 5 — The default authentication mechanism used by Windows Server 2003 to validate a user's credentials.

mixed domain — A domain that contains non-Windows Server 2003 domain controllers.

multi-master replication model — A model for distributing Active Directory data between all domain controllers. Other methods for distributing data include the distributed method where only parts of the data are replicated, or the single-master replication model as used in Microsoft Windows NT.

native domain — A domain that exclusively contains Windows 2000 or Server 2003 domain controllers.

organizational unit (OU) — An Active Directory container object used to store such items as users, computers, and groups within Active Directory.

schema — The set of object definitions indicating what can be stored in Active Directory.

security identifier (SID) — A unique code that is assigned to each resource object within a domain.

site — One or more reliably connected IP subnets. Sites form a replication boundary and help make up the physical structure of Active Directory.

trust — A logical connection between domains allowing one domain to authenticate users from another domain. Trust relationships allow users to securely share resources between domains.

X.509 version 3 — A security certificate that contains information about the user as well as the user's public key.

10

REVIEW QUESTIONS

1. The command used to query and diagnose DDNS servers is _____.

    a. **NSQUERY**

    b. **NSDIAGNOSE**

    c. **NSLOOKUP**

    d. **DDNSLOOKUP**

2. The recommended partition type for Active Directory is _____.

    a. NTFS

    b. FAT

    c. FAT32

    d. HPFS (high-performance file system)

3. The two structures that make up Active Directory are _____ and _____.

   a. intelligent

   b. physical

   c. design

   d. logical

4. Organizational units (OUs) are an example of _____.

   a. Active Directory logical structure

   b. Active Directory physical structure

   c. folders

   d. groups

5. Domains in a forest have _____.

   a. a one-way nontransitive trust

   b. a two-way transitive trust

   c. a one-way transitive trust

   d. a two-way nontransitive trust

6. The Active Directory schema stores definitions for which of the following objects?

   a. group objects

   b. user objects

   c. computer objects

   d. contact objects

7. Active Directory is stored on which type of server?

   a. primary domain controller

   b. Global Catalog server

   c. domain controller

   d. authentication server

8. Which command uses the data from a comma-separated formatted file as a data source for importing information into Active Directory?

   a. **CSVDE**

   b. **DSADD**

   c. **CSVADD**

   d. **BULK INSERT**

9. John Smith's user account object resides in the Marketing OU within the abc.internal domain. Which of the following would be John Smith's distinguished name?

   a. "CN=John Smith,CN=MARKETING,DC=abc,DC=internal"

   b. "CN=John Smith,CN=USERS,DC=abc,DC=internal"

   c. "CN=John Smith,CN=MARKETING,DC=abc,DC=com"

   d. "CN=John Smith,OU=MARKETING,DC=abc,DC=internal"

10. The command to install Active Directory and initiate the Active Directory Installation Wizard is _____.

    a. **PROMO**

    b. **DCPROMO**

    c. **ADSINSTALL**

    d. **CREATE DIR**

11. What is the minimum amount of hard disk space required to install Active Directory?

    a. 500 MB

    b. 100 MB

    c. 1 GB

    d. 1.5 GB

12. An example of the Active Directory's logical structure includes _____.

    a. OUs

    b. sites

    c. domains

    d. domain controllers

13. To install Active Directory, you must have a DDNS server that supports which of the following record types?

    a. SOA

    b. CNAME

    c. SRV

    d. MX

14. The Active Directory services command used to move or rename an object is

    _____.

    a. **DSRM**

    b. **DSMOVE**

    c. **DSREN**

    d. **DSMOD**

10

15. Which option would you use to change a user's password with the **DSADD** command?

    a. **-pass**

    b. **-sec**

    c. **-pword**

    d. **-pwd**

16. Using the **NSLOOKUP** command, what subcommand do you use to verify whether a domain has successfully been registered with a DDNS server?

    a. `dir -1 ADS ct.net`

    b. `ls -1 ADS ct.net`

    c. `ls -t SRV ct.net`

    d. `domain lookup ct.net`

17. Where is the local copy of Active Directory stored?

    a. the ntds.dit file

    b. the DDNS database

    c. the registry

    d. the ntds.dat file

18. Which **DSADD USER** option would you supply to add a user's cell phone number to Active Directory?

    a. **-cell**

    b. **-altph**

    c. **-mobile**

    d. **-cellph**

19. To search Active Directory for an OU, you use the _____ command.

    a. **LDAPLOOKUP**

    b. **ADSEARCH**

    c. **DSLOOKUP**

    d. **DSQUERY**

20. The main GUI tool used in daily user administration in an Active Directory domain is called _____.

    a. Active Directory Users and Computers

    b. User Manager for Active Directory Domains

    c. **CONFIGUSERS**

    d. User Manager

DISCOVERY EXERCISES

1. ABC Corp. is based in Chicago with regional offices in New York, Seattle, Phoenix, San Diego, and London. ABC Corp. has employees in its sales, marketing, finance, accounting, and IT departments. Design an OU structure suitable for ABC Corp.

2. Timberland Paper Corp., based in Dallas, is an international company. Timberland has offices in North America, South America, Europe, and Japan. Timberland's North American outfit has offices in Dallas, Los Angeles, Cincinnati, and Portland. Timberland's South American operations include offices in Caracas and Buenos Aires. Timberland's European offices are located in London, and Timberland's Japan office is located in Osaka. Each of Timberland's offices includes members from the marketing, sales, accounting, shipping, and IT departments. Design Timberland's Active Directory using domains, sites, and OUs.

3. Using commands, create six users and three groups. Assign two users to each group. Use command line tools to reset User 1's password to HaveANiceDay. Write a batch file performing the same task.

4. Your company has decided to merge the accounts payable team and the accounts receivable team into one team called finance. Use the command line to create the AP OU, AR OU, and Finance OU. Create three users in each OU using commands. Do a bulk export of the AP and AR OUs, and save the information in a .csv file. Modify the .csv file to reflect the new team merger and perform a bulk insert of those users into the Finance OU.

10

11

SECURING ACTIVE DIRECTORY

> **After reading this chapter and completing the exercises, you will be able to:**
> ♦ Understand Lightweight Directory Access Protocol (LDAP) and how it can be used to manage Active Directory
> ♦ Secure objects and object access in Active Directory
> ♦ Understand Kerberos version 5 authentication
> ♦ Use commands within Active Directory
> ♦ Repair and configure domain controllers with **DCDIAG**

In Chapter 10 you learned about Microsoft's Active Directory and how this directory is the logical, central repository of objects in a network. In Active Directory, objects such as users, groups, computers, printers, and files can be accessed from one central directory, unlike in the old days of Windows NT 4.0, which required SAM databases. Security Account Manager (SAM) databases were not very scalable or redundant, unlike Active Directory, which is both highly scalable and redundant. One of the great accomplishments of Microsoft was to make Active Directory compliant with industry standards. For example, Active Directory is based on the X.500 directory structure, which is similar to Novell's Network Directory Services (NDS). Active Directory uses the X.500 standard as its hierarchical base, which allows administrators to use standards-based protocols, such as Lightweight Directory Access Protocol, to help manage and configure objects within the Active Directory database. You will learn about this protocol in the next section.

Lightweight Directory Access Protocol

The X.500 directory specifications were defined by the **Open Systems Interconnection** (**OSI**) in 1988. OSI is a standards body that defines network communications protocols and the mechanisms for transporting those messages. The **X.500** standard defines how to electronically store information about users in an organization and how to make that information available globally in a directory service. Entries in an X.500 directory are arranged hierarchically in a structure referred to as the **directory information tree (DIT)**. All entries are uniquely identified by a distinguished name (DN). Recall that you learned about distinguished names in Chapter 10. **Directory Access Protocol (DAP)** is the primary communications protocol used to query an X.500 directory.

Lightweight Directory Access Protocol (LDAP) is the main protocol used to access Active Directory. It is rooted in the original X.500 DAP and has become the standard protocol for working with X.500 directories. LDAP allows users and applications to locate information such as a user's e-mail address from either corporate or public directories. LDAP has major improvements over DAP when it comes to communicating over the Internet. LDAP runs over TCP/IP and provides security options, such as placing access limitations on DNs. LDAP version 3 is part of Windows Server 2003.

For an X.500 client to query the directory, a session with the directory server must first be established. To establish a session with the directory server, a **bind operation**, including some form of **authentication**, must occur. A bind operation is an association between two or more programming objects or value items for some scope of time and place, while authentication is the process of determining whether someone or something is, in fact, who or what it is declared to be. Once the session has been established, the client can then run a search to query, read, modify, add, or abandon directory operations based on specific search criteria.

LDAP Searches

When performing LDAP searches in Active Directory, there are two primary methods that Windows Server 2003 administrators use. The first method uses the GUI administration tools provided with Server 2003. The primary LDAP tool used to perform GUI LDAP searches is the Active Directory Users and Computers GUI, which you first learned about in Chapter 10.

With Active Directory Users and Computers, you can search for users, groups, and contacts. You can even specify advanced search options. The advanced search options of Active Directory Users and Computers allows you to specify search criteria. For example, you could search for users who live in a specified city by specifying "city" as a search criteria.

DSQUERY is a command line LDAP querying tool. The **DSQUERY** command finds any object in Active Directory according to a specified search criteria using LDAP. **DSQUERY** uses the search criteria as input and returns a list of objects matching the search. The data returned from a **DSQUERY** operation can be directed as input into **DSGET**, **DSMOD**, **DSMOVE**, or **DSRM** commands, which are the other directory services commands available in Windows Server 2003. Recall that you first learned about these commands in Chapter 10.

DSQUERY COMPUTER   Searches for computers in the directory.

DSQUERY CONTACT   Searches contacts in the directory.

DSQUERY SUBNET   Searches subnets in the directory.

DSQUERY GROUP   Searches groups in the directory.

DSQUERY OU   Searches organizational units in the directory.

DSQUERY SITE   Searches sites in the directory.

DSQUERY SERVER   Searches domain controllers in the directory.

DSQUERY USER   Searches users in the directory.

DSQUERY *   Searches for any object in the directory by using a generic LDAP query.

If you need help using the command, you can type **DSQUERY /?** at the command line to review the online help. Figure 11-1 shows the help available for **DSQUERY**.

11

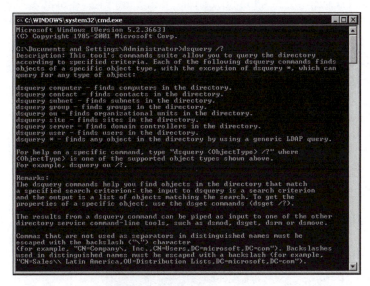

Figure 11-1   DSQUERY online help

In Hands-on Project 11-1, you will create a domain user account using Active Directory Users and Computers. You will provide various data about the users to be used as LDAP search criteria for upcoming projects. To perform this project, you will need access to a Windows Server 2003 domain controller and be able to use the Active Directory Users and Computers administration tool.

Hands-on Project 11-1

To create user accounts with Active Directory Users and Computers:

1. Click **Start**, click **All Programs**, click **Administrative Tools**, and then click **Active Directory Users and Computers**. See Figure 11-2.

2. Click the **Users** folder to begin the user creation process. Right-click the **Users** folder, click **New**, and then click **User** from the submenu.

3. In the First name field, type **Dillon**, and in the Last name field, type **Volcan**. In the User logon name field, type **dvolcan**, and then click **Next**. In the Password and confirm Password fields, type **L84WORK**, and then click **Next**. Read the summary and click **Finish**.

4. Now you add more information to your newly created account. Right-click the **Dillon Volcan** account in Active Directory Users and Computers and click **Properties**. In the Office field, type **Main**. In the Telephone number field, type **(877) 555-1212** to set Dillon's telephone number. In the E-mail field, type **dvolcan@ct.net**, and set his Web page by typing **http://www.ct.net/dvolcan** in the Web page field.

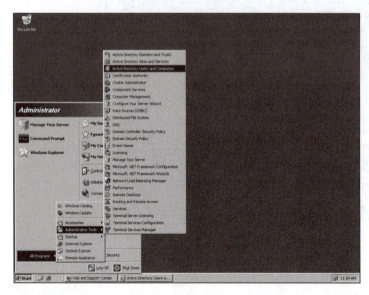

Figure 11-2   Opening Active Directory Users and Computers

5. Click the **Address** tab and type **Phoenix** for the city.

6. Click the **Organization** tab. In the Title field, type **Engineer** to set Dillon's title. Click **OK**.

7. Close the Active Directory Users and Computers window by clicking **File** to open the File menu and then clicking **Exit**.

You have now created a user account with all the necessary data associated with it. You will use this account in future projects in this chapter.

In Hands-on Project 11-2, you will search for a domain user account using Active Directory Users and Computers.

Hands-on Project 11-2

To perform an LDAP search with Active Directory Users and Computers:

1. Click **Start**, click **Control Panel**, click **Administrative Tools**, and click **Active Directory Users and Computers**.

2. Click **Action** to open the Action menu, and then click **Find** to open the Find Users, Contacts, and Groups window, as shown in Figure 11-3.

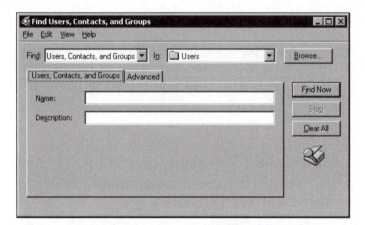

11

Figure 11-3   The Find Users, Contacts, and Groups dialog box

3. In the Name field, type **Dillon** and press **Find Now**. You will see Dillon Volcan in the search results. Double-click Dillon's name in **Search results** to view more information about Dillon. The additional information is shown in Figure 11-4. Click **OK** to close the Properties box.

4. Close the Find box and then close the Active Directory Users and Computers window by clicking **File** to open the File menu and then clicking **Exit**.

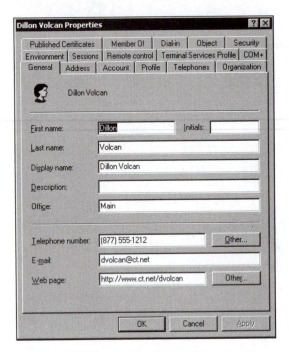

Figure 11-4 Search results

Now that you have completed a basic search, you will learn how to use the Active Directory Users and Groups tool's more advanced features. In Hands-on Project 11-3, you will search for a domain user account with Active Directory Users and Computers using advanced search criteria for your LDAP query.

Hands-on Project 11-3

To perform an advanced LDAP search with Active Directory Users and Computers:

1. Click **Start**, click **All Programs**, click **Administrative Tools**, and then click **Active Directory Users and Computers**.

2. Click **Action** to open the Action menu, and then click **Find** to open the Find Users, Contacts, and Groups window.

3. Click the **Advanced** tab to access the area in which you can enter advanced search criteria.

4. Click **Field** to open the Field menu. From the Field menu, click **User**, and then click **Office Location**, as shown in Figure 11-5.

5. Leave the default setting of Starts with as the condition, type **Main** in the Value field, and then click **Add**.

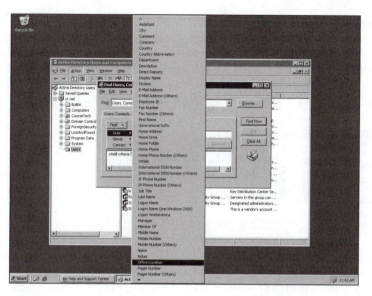

Figure 11-5   Specifying Office Location as a search criterion

6. Click **Find Now** to run the LDAP query. You should see Dillon Volcan appear in your search results.

7. Close the Find box and then close the Active Directory Users and Computers window by clicking **File** to open the File menu and then clicking **Exit**.

In Hands-on Project 11-4, you will search for a domain user account using the **DSQUERY** command. You also specify advanced search criteria.

Hands-on Project 11-4

To perform LDAP searches using **DSQUERY**:

1. Open a command window.

2. Type **dsquery user domainroot –name *volcan** and press **Enter** to display the distinguished names of all users in the current domain whose names end with "Volcan." Be sure to include a space before the hyphen and before the asterisk. The results of the command are shown in Figure 11-6.

Figure 11-6   Results of the **DSQUERY** command

3. Recall that in Hands-on Project 11-1, a phone number of (877) 555-1212 was specified for Dillon Volcan's user account. At the command prompt, type **dsquery * domainroot –filter (telephoneNumber=*877*)** and press **Enter** to perform an LDAP query for all users who have 877 in their phone number. Figure 11-7 shows an example of running the **DSQUERY** command with a filter.

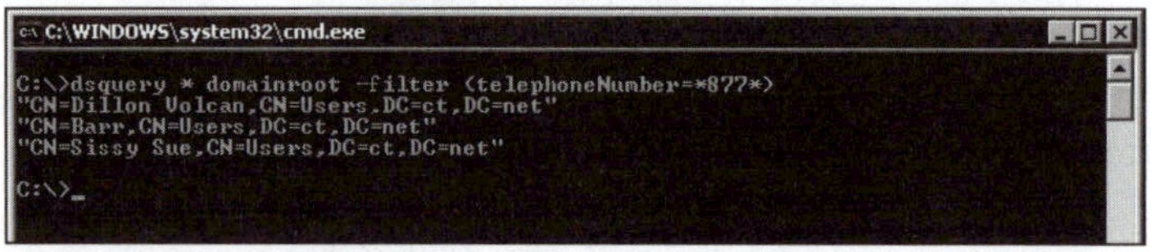

Figure 11-7   Running the **DSQUERY** command with a filter

4. Recall that in Hands-on Project 11-1, a title of Engineer was specified for Dillon Volcan's user account. At the command prompt, type **dsquery * domainroot –filter (title=Engineer)** and press **Enter** to perform an LDAP query for all users who have the title of Engineer.

5. Close the command window by typing **exit** and pressing **Enter**.

You have now used both GUI and command tools to perform LDAP searches of Active Directory. You can review Chapter 10 of this book to learn about more ways to utilize the LDAP features of Active Directory.

ACTIVE DIRECTORY SECURITY

Storing all network data and objects in one logical, central repository can be helpful when dealing with data replication and access. However, ease of access for authorized users also tends to simplify access for unauthorized users. When monitoring security-based Web sites such as SANS Institute and McAfee, you will find new viruses, Trojan horses, and denial of service (DoS) attacks added by the day, if not hour. There are many people on the Internet who are quite willing to break into your network. Some are doing it simply for the challenge, while others are planning malicious attacks.

Now that you have your information in Active Directory, you need to think about the steps you can take to defend your information/objects from attack. Defensive options include physical and logical methods and command line tools. Active Directory-related questions need to be addressed. These include:

- How do you allow authorized users access?

- How do you prevent unauthorized users from accessing confidential and sensitive data?

There are basically three methods to address these questions:

- **Authentication**: Kerberos version 5 allows you to ensure the authenticity of the user accessing the network.

- **Object access**: As you learned earlier, objects are contained in a logical central repository called Active Directory. You can control access to these objects through access control lists (ACLs).

- **Group policies**: Active Directory allows you to use policies to grant users and computers access to resources and areas of the network, and even allows you to distribute and control software access.

Several command line utilities are available to aid you in these tasks. First, you will take a look at object access, followed by an in-depth look at the primary security command **SECEDIT**. After object access, you will learn about Kerberos authentication. Finally, you will learn about group policies and their command line utility, **GPUPDATE**, later in the chapter.

Before learning about these three topics, it is a good idea to get an idea of what tools are available when it comes to security for Windows Server 2003. You can configure and analyze security settings for computers in the following areas:

- Account policies
- Local policies
- Event logs
- Restricted groups
- System services
- Registry
- File systems
- Wireless networks (IEEE 802.11)
- Public key policies
- Software restriction policies
- IP security policies on Active Directory

Because Active Directory is the database of users, computers, and other objects in Windows Server 2003, it is imperative that you secure this vital resource. When using the Active Directory GUI, you will encounter two Microsoft Management Consoles (MMCs): Security Templates and Security Configuration and Analysis.

11

Security Templates

Security Templates is a stand-alone MMC snap-in that enables the creation of a text-based template file that can contain just a few security settings, or it can contain settings that are in force for every security area in your Server 2003 environment. Once you have created these template files, you can apply the template using the Security Configuration and Analysis tool.

 It is important to note that when you apply the new template, it will merge with existing security settings. It is wise to test these settings and to document any changes you plan on making.

There are several predefined security templates included with Windows Server 2003. You can simply apply these security templates or make changes as necessary with the Security Templates tool. Later in this chapter, Hands-on Project 11-5 teaches you how to work with these templates. Table 11-1 describes the templates and their attributes. Templates with similar functions are grouped in the same cell.

When applying these templates, remember that they will merge with existing security policies that are in effect. When applying templates, typically you start with the defaults and apply each of the templates in Table 11-1 incrementally to ensure that you do not miss any of the settings as the templates are applied.

Table 11-1   Predefined security templates for Windows Server 2003

Template	Settings
Setup Security.inf and DC Security.inf	The setup security template is the default security setting when installing Windows Server 2003. When you promote your server to a domain controller, the DC Security template sets up the default settings necessary for a domain controller.
Compatws.inf	Used to prevent users from having to be a member of the Power Users group. May have compatibility problems when used with older applications if permissions are too restrictive. This template relaxes the restrictions typically placed on user accounts. Not considered very secure.
Securews.inf and SecureDC.inf	Increases security by removing all members in the Power Users group on Windows 2000 Professional and Windows XP machines. Adds more security for the domain controller in the areas of account policy, auditing, and registry keys.
Hisecws.inf and HisecDC.inf	Used on computers running in Windows 2000 native mode or Windows Server 2003 domain functionality native mode. Requires digital signatures on all communications as well as encryption. Essentially locks the computers down so that only Windows 2000, XP, and Server 2003 systems can communicate.
Rootsec.inf	Resets the default permissions for the system root folder.

Security Configuration and Analysis

Like any savvy defense strategist, it is a good idea to run simulations and scenarios to prepare for actual interactions. You will want to know what is going to happen when you apply a security template to large groups of computers. You can perform this strategic testing using the Security Configuration and Analysis GUI. Whether utilizing the Security Configuration and Analysis tool or the **SECEDIT** command, you should use these tools to forecast what will happen when applying a template you have designed or one of the samples provided by Microsoft.

When running security forecasts, the Security Configuration and Analysis tool analyzes the security configuration of the local computer and compares it to the template you intend to apply. You accomplish this by importing the template (.inf file) and storing it in a database file (.sdb file). The existing settings, which are contained in the .sdb file, are compared to the new template and the results tell you how your scenario will come out. The results appear in the configuration tree as either a red X, which indicates a discrepancy, or a green checkmark, which indicates a consistency. Settings without a mark by them are not configured in the database. At this point you can either remove the discrepancies by changing the settings in the database to match the current computer settings, or you can import another template file. Another option is to export the current database settings to a template file. Export is one of the options available in the Security Configuration and Analysis GUI and the **SECEDIT** command. You can then change any settings necessary to gain the results you are looking for. It is a good idea to perform a second analysis at that point.

 Perform any analysis or configuration tasks during off-peak usage hours. These tasks can disrupt your workload.

As you will learn in the next section, the **SECEDIT** command not only performs the same tasks as the Security Configuration and Analysis tool, but also has unique abilities not found with the GUI version.

The SECEDIT Command

One of the most powerful tools in your arsenal against attacks on your network is the **SECEDIT** command. This command allows you to perform configuration and analysis for multiple computers.

Just like its GUI counterpart, Security Configuration and Analysis, **SECEDIT** enables you to perform security configuration and analysis in conjunction with other administrative tools, such as Microsoft Systems Management Server or the Task Scheduler. However, the command gives you more flexibility in applying and analyzing security templates than its GUI counterpart.

SECEDIT /ANALYZE   Analyzes the security settings on a computer by comparing them against the baseline settings in a database.

SECEDIT /CONFIGURE   Configures local computer security settings by applying the settings stored in a database.

SECEDIT /EXPORT   Exports the security settings that are stored in the database file.

SECEDIT /IMPORT   Imports a security template into a database so that the settings specified in the template can be applied to a system or analyzed against that system.

SECEDIT /VALIDATE   Validates the syntax of a security template to be imported into a database for analysis or application to a computer.

SECEDIT /GENERATEROLLBACK   Generates a rollback template with respect to a particular security template. When you apply the security template, you'll have the option of creating a template that can be used to set the settings back to the way they were before the template was applied.

Begin by learning about **SECEDIT /ANALYZE**. Similar to the Security and Configuration Analysis GUI, you will need to select a database file to be used for the analysis, a security template to import into the database prior to performing the analysis, and a file in which to log the status of the configuration process. If the log file isn't specified, the data will be logged in the scesrv.log file located in your local %windir%\security\logs directory. For example, if you wanted to analyze the effects of the Hisecws.inf template against your current configuration, you would use the following command:

```
secedit /analyze /db c:/windows/security/database/hisecdc.sdb
   /cfg c:/windows/security/templates/hisecdc.inf /log hisecurity.log
```

This command would compare the Hisecws template to your current settings. The results of the comparison are placed in the Hisecurity.log file. This information allows you to see how your current setting compares to the template you wish to apply.

To accomplish this comparison, you need to create a database file (.sdb) in the appropriate directory. This can be accomplished by creating a file called Hisecdc.sdb in the c:/windows/security/database/ folder. You can accomplish this in the Security Configuration and Analysis GUI or by creating it in a text editor such as Notepad as a blank file with the name of Hisecdc.sdb.

The security templates are listed in Table 11-1 earlier in the chapter.

When you issue the **SECEDIT** command, you will need to specify the directory where the .inf files are located. The templates are located in the %systemroot%\security\templates folder.

Using the **SECEDIT /CONFIGURE** command, you can apply a security template to your computer or domain controller. The syntax is almost identical to the **/ANALYZE** version of the **SECEDIT** command, but you do have a few different options. One of the major differences is the **/OVERWRITE** option, which specifies that the database should be emptied prior to importing the .inf file. If this option is not specified, the settings in the security template will be accumulated into the database. If you already have some settings in the database, the template being imported will override those in your database.

For example, if you want to implement the SecureDC.inf template on a domain controller while logging the results, you would type the following:

```
secedit /configure /db c:/windows/security/database/
  securedc.sdb /cfg c:/windows/security/templates/
  securedc.inf /overwrite /log securedc.log
```

This command would also overwrite any settings accumulated in the Securedc.sdb database file. Again, you will create the .sdb file before you run this command. Hands-on Project 11-5 demonstrates how this command could work and also shows the GUI for the Security Configuration and Analysis MMC.

11

Hands-on Project 11-5

To analyze a security template using the **SECEDIT** command:

1. First create a custom MMC by clicking the **Start** button [Start], clicking **Run**, and typing **mmc** on the Run line. Press **Enter**.

2. Click **File** and **Add/Remove Snap-in** to open the Add/Remove Snap-in dialog box. Click the **Add** button to bring up a list of available snap-ins. Click the **Security Configuration and Analysis** tool and then click **Add**. Click **Close** and then click **OK** to close the Add/Remove Snap-in dialog box.

3. Right-click the **Security Configuration and Analysis** node in the left pane of the MMC.

4. Select **Open Database** from the menu, type **securetest**, and then click **Open**. You should see the Import Template window, as shown in Figure 11-8.

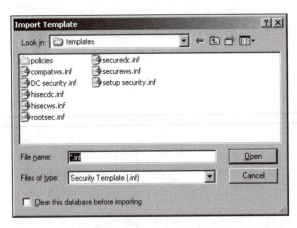

Figure 11-8   The Import Template dialog box

5. Click **securedc.inf** and then click **Open**.

6. In the left pane, right-click the **Security and Configuration Analysis** node and click the **Analyze Computer Now** option.

7. Type the path to the database file you created earlier or browse to the file (it should be already populated in the text box) and click **OK**.

8. Expand the **Security Configuration and Analysis** node in the left pane, if necessary.

9. Click the **+** sign next to Account Policies. Click **Password Policy** and view the results, which appear in the right pane. They should be similar to the results shown in Figure 11-9.

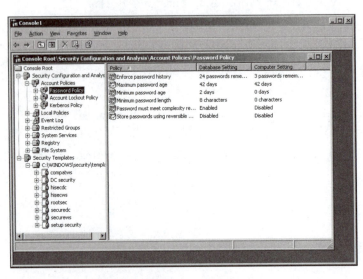

Figure 11-9   Template analysis results for Password Policy

10. Click the window's **Close** button ![X]. When prompted to save the information, click **Yes**. The Save As dialog box opens. Save Console1.msc in the default location.

11. Open a command window. At the prompt, type **cd my documents\ security\database** and press **Enter**.

12. Type **secedit /analyze /db securetest.sdb /cfg c:\windows\security\ templates\securedc.inf** and press **Enter**. You should see a "Task Complete" message after the analysis completes.

13. Now you need to view the log that was created. Type **exit** and press **Enter** to close the command prompt. Press ![Start] and then click **My Computer**. Double-click **C:**, then double-click the **Windows** folder, double-click the **Security** folder, and then double-click the **Logs** folder.

14. Double-click the **scesrv.log** file. If necessary, select Notepad to open the file. Your results should look similar to Figure 11-10.

15. Close all windows.

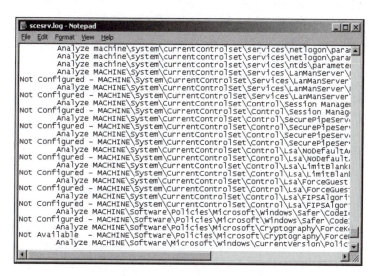

Figure 11-10   Log results of **SECEDIT** template analysis

The **/AREAS** option is unique to the **SECEDIT** command. This option allows you to configure or export specific aspects of security settings. This option is used only with the **SECEDIT /CONFIGURE** and **SECEDIT /EXPORT** commands. The security areas that you can configure are shown in Table 11-2.

Table 11-2   Security areas

Security area name	Description
securitypolicy	Manages local policy and domain policy for the system, including account policies, audit policies, etc.
group_mgmt	Restricts group settings for any groups specified in the security template.
user_rights	Controls user logon rights and granting of rights.
regkeys	Manages security on local registry keys.
filestore	Manages security on local file storage.
services	Manages security for all defined services.

For example, the command:

```
secedit /configure /db c:/windows/security/database/
  sharisecure.sdb /areas USER_RIGHTS FILESTORE
  /log c:\windows\security\logs
  \sharisecure.log
```

configures the user logon rights and local file storage security instead of all the possible areas.

One of the most important things to consider when working with Active Directory is the objects that it stores. These objects are at the core of the operating system and network in the Windows Server 2003 environment. Begin by learning how you can secure these objects.

Object Access

Active Directory permissions provide security for resources by enabling an administrator to control which administrators or users can gain access to individual objects or object attributes. These permissions can also define the type of access allowed. You can use permissions to assign administrative privileges for an organizational unit (OU) or an entire hierarchy of OUs.

Another use of permissions is to allow a specific user or group to have administrative privileges on a single object. For example, you might want to allow a junior administrator permission to change passwords on user accounts in a particular organizational unit.

How are these tasks accomplished? Each object in Active Directory has a list of user permissions called the Discretionary Access Control List (DACL), which you first learned about in Chapter 7. The DACL tells Active Directory who can access the object and what they can do with the object. For example, say Susan in Accounting needs to be able to access a printer on the third floor that prints in color because she is in charge of printing out the color graphs for the sales manager. The color printer is an object in the Active Directory, and as such would have a DACL entry that would allow Susan to print on the color printer. Meanwhile, Robert in Sales would like to print out a picture of his new sailboat on the color printer. Active Directory would check the DACL to see if

Robert has permission to print on that printer. If he isn't allowed to print personal color pictures on that printer, it is most likely that Robert's user account does not have an entry and thus it is denied.

To view the permissions for an Active Directory object, you must enable the advanced features on the View menu in the Active Directory Users and Computers MMC. Hands-on Project 11-6 teaches you how to view permissions.

Hands-on Project 11-6

To complete this project, you need access to a domain controller in your network or testing environment. To view permissions on Active Directory objects:

1. Click **Start**, click **All Programs**, click **Administrative Tools**, and click **Active Directory Users and Computers**.

2. Click **View** to open the View drop-down menu, and then click **Advanced Features**. This will allow you to see the Security tab in the properties of the Active Directory object.

3. In the left pane of the Active Directory Users and Computers window, right-click **ct.net**, click **New**, and then click **Organizational Unit**. Type **SalesWest** for the OU's name and click **OK**.

4. In the left pane of the Active Directory Users and Computers window, right-click the OU **SalesWest**. Click **Properties**.

5. Click the **Security** tab to view the DACL for the OU you created in Step 3. The window should look similar to Figure 11-11. Close the Properties window.

6. Click the **Close** button **X** to close Active Directory Users and Computers.

You have successfully turned on the Security tab and viewed the DACL of an Active Directory object.

11

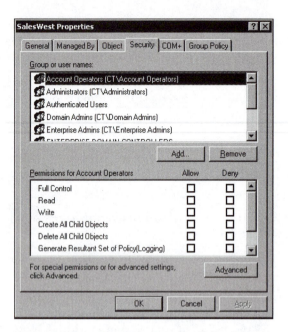

Figure 11-11   The Security tab of the SalesWest OU

You can use the Active Directory Users and Computers tool to manipulate permissions, but sometimes you might need to do this from a command line. This is where the **CACLS** command becomes very useful. You first learned about **CACLS** in Chapter 6. Below are additional options for the **CACLS** command.

CACLS <*FILENAME*> /T   Changes DACLs of specified files in the current directory and all subdirectories.

CACLS <*FILENAME*> /E   Edits a DACL instead of replacing it.

CACLS <*FILENAME*> /C   Continues to change DACLs, ignoring any errors encountered during the process.

When using the **CACLS** command, you have several options for changing permissions for users. As you learned in Chapter 6, the syntax for changing permissions is **CACLS <FILENAME> /G <USERNAME>:R|W|C|F** (for Read, Write, Change, or Full Control permissions). The results of changing user permissions using the **CACLS** command can look strange. Table 11-3 shows sample results of permission changes, along with the meanings of the results. The **access control entry (ACE)** information shown in the table is an entry in a DACL that specifies a permission for a particular group or user. There are typically many ACEs in every DACL.

Table 11-3 CACLS results defined

Command result	Means that ACE applies to:
OI	The current folder and its files.
CI	The current folder and its subfolders.
IO	The ACE does not apply to the current file/directory.
No message	The current folder only.
(IO)(CI)	The current folder, subfolders, and files.
(OI)(CI)(IO)	Subfolders and files only.
(CI)(IO)	Subfolders only.
(OI)(IO)	Files only.

In the **CACLS** permission for changing syntax, *USERNAME* can refer to an individual user's account name or a group (either local or global). If a username or group name includes spaces, it must be surrounded with quotation marks, for example, "Authenticated Users." If no options are specified, **CACLS** will display the ACLs for the file(s). When using a batch file, the **CACLS** command does not provide a **/Y** option to automatically answer Y at the Y/N prompt. However, you can insert the Y character into the **CACLS** command using **ECHO** with the following syntax:

```
ECHO Y| CACLS /G <USERNAME>:<PERMISSION>
```

To edit a file, you must have the Change ACL permission (or be the file's owner), and to use the **CACLS** command and change an ACL requires Full Control permission. File ownership permission always overrides all ACLs, because you always have full control over files that you create. If **CACLS** is used without the **/E** option, all existing rights on the file are replaced and any attempt to use the **/E** option to change a user or permission that already exists causes an error. For the **CACLS** command to work without errors, use **/E /R** to remove ACL rights for the user, then use **/E** to add the desired rights. The **/T** option will only affect subfolders below the current directory.

The following code example shows how to add new file permissions to a group of users:

```
CACLS testfile.txt /E /G "Power Users":F
```

If you grant Read permission to the Power Users group using the following code, the group members still have Full Control permission:

```
CACLS testfile.txt /E /G "Power Users":R
```

The following command replaces the first ACL granted and allows the Power Users group to have only Read access:

```
CACLS testfile.txt /E /P "Power Users":R
```

11

As you learned in Chapter 6, objects have owners. The person who creates an object automatically becomes the owner of that object. The owner controls the permissions granted for an object, and controls to whom permissions are granted. The one exception to the ownership rule is a member of the Administrators group. As an administrator, you can take ownership of an object and define permissions for the object—regardless of the permissions granted by the object's owner. The interesting thing about granting permission is that as an owner, you are granting permission for someone else to take ownership of that object. You cannot simply assign ownership; the new permission (and inherent ownership) must be acknowledged by the person taking ownership.

If you need to transfer ownership to another user, you simply add that user to the object's DACL with the Modify Owner permission. The person taking ownership would then need to go to the Properties dialog box for an object in Active Directory and select his or her user account. Ownership would then pass to that person.

Hands-on Project 11-7 teaches you how to take ownership of an object as an administrator.

Hands-on Project 11-7

To take ownership of an object:

1. Log on to your domain controller as an administrator.

2. Click the **Start** button ![Start], click **All Programs**, click **Administrative Tools**, and then click **Active Directory Users and Computers**.

3. Right-click **ct.net** and click **New>Organizational Unit**. In the Name field, type **Marketing** and click **OK**. Repeat this step to create another OU with the name Sales.

4. Right-click the **Users** container and click **New>User**. Fill in the name fields with the information shown in Figure 11-12. Click **Next**. Type a password. Click **Next**. Click **Finish**.

5. In the Users container, locate and right-click the **Greg Kwan** account. Select **Add to a group**. This will open the Select Group dialog box. In the window, type **Administrators** and click the **Check Names** button.

6. Click **OK**. In the Active Directory dialog box, click **OK** to validate that the Add to Group operation was successfully completed.

7. Click the **Marketing** OU to select it.

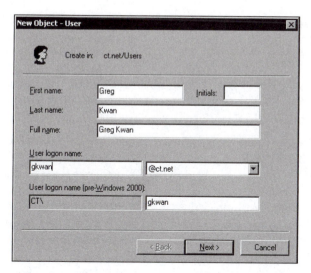

Figure 11-12   New user information

8. Right-click the **Marketing** OU and then click **Properties**.

9. In the Properties dialog box for the Marketing OU, click **Advanced** on the Security tab.

10. Add the Greg Kwan user account to the DACL for the Marketing OU by clicking **Add**, then click **Advanced** in the Select User, Computer, or Group dialog box. In the Name Starts with text box, type **G** and click **Find Now**. Highlight Greg's user account in the list of users and click **OK** twice. Grant Modify Owner permission to Greg's account by placing a check mark in the Allow column for the Modify Owner permission. Click **OK** three times and then click the **Close** button ✕ to close the Active Directory Users and Computers window.

11. Log off the domain controller.

12. Log back into the domain controller as Greg Kwan instead of the Administrator account. Click **Start**, click **All Programs**, click **Administrative Tools**, and then click **Active Directory Users and Computers**.

13. Right-click the **Marketing** OU and click **Properties**.

14. In the Properties dialog box for the Marketing OU, click **Advanced** on the Security tab. If necessary, enable Advanced Features in the View menu of Active Directory Users and Computers.

15. Click the **Owner** tab, and then click the **Greg Kwan** user account.

16. Click **OK**, and then click **OK** again to take ownership.

17. The Greg Kwan account has successfully taken ownership of the Marketing OU. Click ✕ to close Active Directory Users and Computers.

Additional Security Tools

Some of the Windows Server 2003 security tools are included as additional support tools on the Server 2003 installation CD. These additional tools are typically used only by qualified network administrators. To access this advanced functionality, you can install additional tools from the Suptools.msi file from the Windows Server 2003 CD. Two of these tools are the **ACLDIAG** command and the **GPUPDATE** command, which you learn about in this section.

The **ACLDIAG** command can be used for help in accessing objects in Active Directory. **ACLDIAG** is a command that helps you diagnose and troubleshoot problems that you might experience with permissions on objects in Active Directory. It reads security attributes from access control lists (ACLs) and reproduces the information in either straight text or tab-delimited format. You can upload the tab-delimited format output generated by **ACLDIAG** into a text file to search for particular permissions, users, or groups. You can also upload the output into a spreadsheet or database for reporting. You can also use this command to provide simple cleanup of unnecessary ACL entries. In the syntax below, *OBJECTDN* indicates a distinguished name for a valid Active Directory object.

ACLDIAG <*OBJECTDN*> /CHKDELEG   Checks to determine whether the security on the object includes any of the delegation templates currently in use by the Delegation of Control wizard in the Active Directory Users and Computers snap-in. Standard delegations are typically the settings applied when transferring ownership.

ACLDIAG <*OBJECTDN*> /FIXDELEG   Fixes any delegations that have been applied to the object by the Delegation of Control wizard.

ACLDIAG <*OBJECTDN*> /GETEFFECTIVE:<*USERNAME GROUP*>
Prints permissions of the specified *USERNAME* or *GROUP* in a readable format.

ACLDIAG <*OBJECTDN*> /SCHEMA   Checks to determine whether the security on the object includes schema defaults.

ACLDIAG <*OBJECTDN*> /SKIP   Does not display the security description.

ACLDIAG <*OBJECTDN*> /TDO   Writes tab-delimited output instead of readable format. This is useful when loading the output into databases or spreadsheets.

ACLDIAG compares the ACL on a directory services object to the permissions that are defined in the default settings for the schema. It can also check or fix the standard delegations that were performed using templates from the Delegation of Control wizard within Active Directory Users and Computers. Another handy feature of the command is its ability to grant effective permissions to a specific user or group, or to all users and groups that show up in the ACL.

ACLDIAG displays only the permissions of objects that the user has the right to view. You will want to use this tool as an Administrator so that you have the broadest possible permissions. Because Group Policy objects are virtual objects without distinguished names, this tool cannot be used on them.

The GPUPDATE Command and Group Policies

GPUPDATE is another security command for Windows Server 2003. **GPUPDATE** refreshes local and Active Directory Group Policy settings, including the security settings.

GPUPDATE /TARGET: <COMPUTERNAME|USERNAME>   Processes only the computer or current user settings. Typically both the user and computer settings are processed.

GPUPDATE/FORCE   Ignores all optimization and reapplies all settings.

GPUPDATE/WAIT: <TIMEINSECONDS>   Specifies the number of seconds that policy processing waits to finish.

GPUPDATE/LOGOFF   Logs the user off after the refresh has completed. This forces any background policies that only refresh when a user logs on.

GPUPDATE/BOOT   Forces the computer to restart after refreshing the policies. This ensures that any policies that only refresh at startup run.

Group Policy settings affect security by forcing changes to go into effect when you use either a command or a GUI to change any security settings. This enforcement is valuable when making sure that domain controller replication is secure and updated.

Another security method is user authentication. Next, you learn how Kerberos provides user authentication.

11

Kerberos and Authentication

When people began to use electronic methods of accessing information, user identity came into question—in other words, how do I know you are who you say you are? Computers must somehow be able to authenticate a user's identity. As you learned in Chapter 10, Kerberos version 5 is an authentication method used in the Windows Server 2003 family. Kerberos protects networks from "spoofing" and "man in the middle" attacks. Spoofing is a hacker's method of pretending to be someone by imitating his or her IP address. Man-in-the-middle attacks involve a computer that intercepts a transmission, modifies the content, and then sends it to the intended destination.

Kerberos (sometimes spelled Cerberus) was the three-headed dog that guarded the gates of Hades. It was his job to keep the dead in and the living out.

Kerberos is a network authentication system for use on physically insecure networks. Kerberos is based on the **key distribution model**, which is a security model that distributes keys or tickets to authenticate objects. It allows entities communicating over networks to prove their identity to each other while preventing eavesdropping or replay attacks. It also provides for data stream integrity (detection of modification) and secrecy (preventing unauthorized reading) using cryptographic systems such as the Data Encryption Standard (DES).

Kerberos works by providing users with a ticket, usually a few hundred bytes in size, that they use to identify themselves to Active Directory and domain controllers. Along with the tickets, users require a secret cryptographic key for secure communication with other users. These tickets can then be embedded in virtually any network protocol, allowing the processes implementing that protocol to be sure about the identity of the users or computers involved.

Kerberos is primarily used in application-level protocols such as Telnet or FTP to provide security for both users and hosts. An industry standard, Kerberos was developed at Massachusetts Institute of Technology (MIT) and is recognized by the ISO.

It is important to realize that Kerberos, on its own, is used only to authenticate a user's identity. Kerberos provides for mutual authentication and secures communication between principals on an open network by manufacturing secret keys for requestors and providing a mechanism for these secret keys to be safely propagated through the network. Kerberos does not provide for authorization or user accounting, although applications can use their secret keys to perform those functions securely.

ANALYZING ACTIVE DIRECTORY WITH THE DCDIAG COMMAND

DCDIAG analyzes the general condition of domain controllers in a forest or enterprise and reports any problems to assist in troubleshooting. One important feature of **DCDIAG** is a tool that generates reports. Administrators use these reports to help diagnose how DCs are functioning.

DCDIAG conducts certain types of tests on a domain. A testing framework selects which domain controllers to test according to the scope defined by the administrator. **DCDIAG** can test a range of systems—from a single server to every domain controller on the entire network.

The **DCDIAG** command syntax contains references to the tests it can perform. Table 11-4 lists the **DCDIAG** tests that can be run on a domain controller, along with brief descriptions of what they can accomplish.

Table 11-4   DCDIAG tests

Test	Description
Connectivity	Tests whether domain controllers are DNS registered, can be pinged, and can have other computers connect to it either through LDAP or RPC (Remote Procedure Call).
Replication	Checks for timely replication and any replication errors between domain controllers.
Topology	Confirms that the Knowledge Consistency Checker (KCC) has generated a fully connected topology for all domain controllers. The KCC service makes sure that all domain controllers can replicate to each other.
CutoffServers	Checks for servers that are not receiving replications because their partners are down.
NetLogons	Confirms that the appropriate logon privileges exist to allow replication to proceed.
Advertising	Checks to determine whether each domain controller is advertising itself in the roles it should be capable of. This test fails if the Netlogon service has stopped or failed to start.
KnowsOfRoleHolders	Checks to determine whether the DC can contact the servers that hold the five FSMO (Flexible Single Master Operations) roles. These roles decide many things, such as which domain controller holds the PDC Emulator, Relative ID (RID) Master, and Schema Master roles.
FSMOCheck	Checks that the DC can contact a Key Distribution Center (KDC), a Time Server, a Preferred Time Server, a Primary Domain Controller (PDC) emulator, and a Global Catalog server. It does not test any of the servers for FSMO roles.
RidManager	Checks whether the RID Master is accessible and determines whether it contains the information necessary to hand out the RIDs.
MachineAccount	Checks to determine whether the machine (computer) account has been properly registered in Active Directory and the services are advertised.
Services	Checks to determine whether appropriate domain controller services are running.
OutboundSecureChannels	Tests connectivity between the DC and other DCs outside the network. Confirms that secure channels exist from all of the domain controllers in the domain to the domains specified by /testdomain. The **/NOSITERESTRICTION** option prevents the test from being limited to the domain controllers in the site.
ObjectsReplicated	Checks that machine account objects have replicated. Use `/objectdn:dn` with `/n:nc` to specify an additional object to check.
FrsSysvol	Checks that the file replication system (FRS) Sysvol is ready.
Kccevent	Confirms that the KCC is running without errors.
Systemlog	Confirms that the system is running without errors.

11

Table 11-4   DCDIAG tests (continued)

Test	Description
DCPromo	Tests the existing DNS infrastructure for promotion to domain controller. If the infrastructure is sufficient, the computer can be promoted to a domain controller in a domain specified in /DnsDomain:Active_Directory_Domain_DNS_Name. Reports whether modifications to the existing DNS infrastructure are required. Required argument: /DnsDomain:Active_Directory_Domain_DNS_Name One of the following options is required: /NewForest /NewTree /ChildDomain /ReplicaDC If NewTree is specified, then the ForestRoot argument is required: /ForestRoot:Forest_Root_Domain_DNS_Name
RegisterInDNS	Tests whether the DC can register the domain controller locator DNS records. These records must be present in DNS in order for other computers to locate this domain controller for the Active_Directory_Domain_DNS_Name domain. Reports whether modifications to the existing DNS infrastructure are required. Required option: /DnsDomain:Active_Directory_Domain_DNS_Name
VerifyReplicas	Verifies that all application directory partitions are fully established on all replica servers.
CheckSDRefDom	Verifies that all application directory partitions have appropriate security descriptor reference domains.

(Source: www.technet.com)

The **DCDIAG** command syntax is explained next.

DCDIAG /S:<DOMAINCONTROLLER>   Specifies *DOMAINCONTROLLER* as the home server. This option is required.

DCDIAG /S:<DOMAINCONTROLLER> /N:<NAMINGCONTEXT>   Uses *NAMINGCONTEXT* as the naming format to test. Domains may be specified in NetBIOS, DNS, or distinguished name format.

DCDIAG /S:<DOMAINCONTROLLER> /U:DOMAIN|USERNAME /P:<*|PASSWORD|"">   Uses *DOMAIN* or *USERNAME* credentials for binding, with *PASSWORD* as the password. Use "" for an empty or null password, or use * to prompt for the password.

DCDIAG /S:<DOMAINCONTROLLER> /A   Tests all the servers on the site.

DCDIAG /S:<DOMAINCONTROLLER> /E   Tests all the servers in the entire network. Overrides the /A option.

DCDIAG /S:<*DOMAINCONTROLLER*> /Q   Tests in quiet mode, which prints only error messages.

DCDIAG /S:<*DOMAINCONTROLLER*> /V   Tests in verbose mode, which prints extended information.

DCDIAG /S:<*DOMAINCONTROLLER*> /D   Tests in debug mode, which prints configuration information for the entire network and displays verbose output information. Can be useful to discover detailed information about a domain controller.

DCDIAG /S:<*DOMAINCONTROLLER*>/   Ignores superfluous error messages.

DCDIAG /S:<*DOMAINCONTROLLER*> /FIX   Only affects the MachineAccount test. It causes the test to fix the service principal names (SPNs) on the DC's Machine Account object.

DCDIAG /S:<*DOMAINCONTROLLER*> /F:<*LOGFILE*>   Redirects all output to *LOGFILE*. The /F option operates independently of /FERR (below).

DCDIAG /S:<*DOMAINCONTROLLER*> /FERR:<*ERRLOG*>   Redirects fatal error output to *ERRLOG*, a separate file.

DCDIAG /S:<*DOMAINCONTROLLER*> /C   Tests in comprehensive mode. Runs all tests except DCPromo and RegisterInDNS, including nondefault tests. Can be used with the /SKIP option to skip specified tests.

DCDIAG /S:<*DOMAINCONTROLLER*> /C /SKIP:<*TEST*>   Skips the specified *TEST*. Must be used with /C. The only test that cannot be skipped is Connectivity.

DCDIAG /S:<*DOMAINCONTROLLER*> /TEST:<*TEST*>   Runs the specified *TEST* and the nonskippable Connectivity test. Should not be run in the same command with /SKIP.

11

Figures 11-13 through 11-16 show what the output would look like if you issued a **DCDIAG** command on a domain controller named dc2 on the CT.net domain using the following code:

```
C:\Program Files\Support Tools>dcdiag /s:dc2.ct.net
/u:ct.net\administrator /p:password
```

```
Domain Controller Diagnosis

Performing initial setup:
   Done gathering initial info.

Doing initial required tests

   Testing server: Default-First-Site-Name\DC2
      Starting test: Connectivity
         ......................... DC2 passed test Connectivity
```

Figure 11-13   Initial test results

```
Doing primary tests

  Testing server: Default-First-Site-Name\DC2
      Starting test: Replications
          ......................... DC2 passed test Replications
      Starting test: NCSecDesc
          ......................... DC2 passed test NCSecDesc
      Starting test: NetLogons
          ......................... DC2 passed test NetLogons
      Starting test: Advertising
          ......................... DC2 passed test Advertising
      Starting test: KnowsOfRoleHolders
          ......................... DC2 passed test KnowsOfRoleHolders
      Starting test: RidManager
          ......................... DC2 passed test RidManager
      Starting test: MachineAccount
          ..................... DC2 passed test MachineAccount
      Starting test: Services
          ......................... DC2 passed test Services
      Starting test: ObjectsReplicated
          ......................... DC2 passed test ObjectsReplicated
      Starting test: frssysvol
          ......................... DC2 passed test frssysvol
      Starting test: kccevent
          ......................... DC2 passed test kccevent
      Starting test: systemlog
          ......................... DC2 passed test systemlog
      Starting test: VerifyReferences
          ......................... DC2 passed test VerifyReferences
```

Figure 11-14 Primary test results

```
  Running partition tests on : DomainDnsZones
      Starting test: CrossRefValidation
          ......................... DomainDnsZones passed test CrossRefValidation

      Starting test: CheckSDRefDom
          ......................... DomainDnsZones passed test CheckSDRefDom

  Running partition tests on : ForestDnsZones
      Starting test: CrossRefValidation
          ......................... ForestDnsZones passed test CrossRefValidation

      Starting test: CheckSDRefDom
          ......................... ForestDnsZones passed test CheckSDRefDom

  Running partition tests on : Schema
      Starting test: CrossRefValidation
          ......................... Schema passed test CrossRefValidation
      Starting test: CheckSDRefDom
          ......................... Schema passed test CheckSDRefDom

  Running partition tests on : Configuration
      Starting test: CrossRefValidation
          ......................... Configuration passed test CrossRefValidation
      Starting test: CheckSDRefDom
          ......................... Configuration passed test CheckSDRefDom

  Running partition tests on : ct
      Starting test: CrossRefValidation
          ......................... ct passed test CrossRefValidation
      Starting test: CheckSDRefDom
          ......................... ct passed test CheckSDRefDom
```

Figure 11-15 Partition test results

```
Running enterprise tests on : ct.net
    Starting test: Intersite
        ........................ ct.net passed test Intersite
    Starting test: FsmoCheck
        ........................ ct.net passed test FsmoCheck
```

Figure 11-16   Enterprise test results

As the figures indicate, the tests are conducted one after another and the results are displayed on the screen. You can have **DCDIAG** place these results into a database file that you can access later, using the data for analysis and appropriate configuration changes.

This chapter scratches the surface of **DCDIAG** command's power. If you cannot get into the GUI of the MMC and need to know why domain controllers are acting up, you will definitely want to use this tool.

CHAPTER SUMMARY

In this chapter you learned about Lightweight Directory Access Protocol (LDAP) and how it can be used to manage an Active Directory database. Because there are many objects located in Active Directory, it becomes imperative to secure objects and object access with DACLs. As a user, you need to prove to Active Directory that you are who you say you are, thus the need for authentication. Kerberos version 5 authentication allows very secure identity in your Windows Server 2003 environment.

Windows Server 2003 makes it easy to apply security settings using security templates with prebuilt settings. You can use the Security Configuration and Analysis MMC or the **SECEDIT** command to analyze the effects of these templates on your environment and configure the templates to be used. If you need to analyze domain controllers to ensure proper operation, the **DCDIAG** command is a very powerful tool to accomplish this task.

11

COMMAND SUMMARY

Command	Function
DSQUERY	Finds any object in a directory based on specified search criteria.
SECEDIT	Allows an administrator to analyze and configure security policy settings.
ACLDIAG	Troubleshoots and diagnoses problems with permissions on objects.
GPUPDATE	Updates group policies instantly in order to implement the policies.
DCDIAG	Analyzes the condition of domain controllers in a network.

KEY TERMS

access control entry (ACE) — An entry in a DACL that specifies a permission for a particular group or user. There are typically many ACEs in every DACL.

authentication — The process of determining whether someone or something is, in fact, who or what it is declared to be.

bind operation — An association between two or more programming objects or value items for some scope of time and place. In the realm of LDAP, a bind operation makes an association between a query and the object you are requesting.

Directory Access Protocol (DAP) — A protocol for querying and updating a directory database. Used in X.500 implementations. It was replaced by LDAP.

directory information tree (DIT) — Hierarchy on which Active Directory is based.

key distribution model — A security model that operates by giving out keys or tickets to authenticate objects.

Lightweight Directory Access Protocol (LDAP) — The main protocol used to access Active Directory; it is based on X.500's DAP.

Open Systems Interconnection (OSI) — A standards body that defines network communications protocols and the mechanisms for transporting those messages.

X.500 — A standard way to develop an electronic directory of people in an organization so that it can be part of a global directory available to anyone in the world with Internet access. Such a directory is sometimes called a global White Pages directory.

REVIEW QUESTIONS

1. What command is used to determine domain controller information?

   a. **POWERCFG**

   b. **DCDIAG**

   c. **SYSTEMINFO**

   d. **PAGEFILECONFIG**

2. Which command can be used to configure and analyze security templates?

   a. **SYSTEMINFO**

   b. **DIR**

   c. **SECEDIT**

   d. **VER**

3. X.500 defines _____.

   a. an e-mail address format

   b. a relational database directory

   c. a distributed directory

   d. a hierarchal directory

4. Which authentication mechanism is used by Windows Server 2003?

   a. NTLM

   b. NTFS

   c. Kerberos

   d. PPP

5. Which command(s) search sites in Active Directory? (Choose all that apply.)

   a. **DSQUERY SITE**

   b. **DSQUERY SITES**

   c. **DSQUERY SERVER**

   d. **DSQUERY SITE /:LOOKUP**

6. Which command is used to perform a security analysis of your system? (Choose all that apply.)

   a. **DCDIAG /SECURE**

   b. **ANALYZE /SECEDIT**

   c. **SECEDIT /ANALYZE**

   d. **ANALYZE /TYPE: SECURITYANALYSIS**

7. Which command(s) determine whether a user has been assigned or denied access to a directory object? (Choose all that apply.)

   a. **DSQUERY /ACL**

   b. **SECEDIT /ACL**

   c. **ACLDIAG**

   d. **DACL**

8. What is the primary communications protocol used to query an X.500 directory?

   a. DAP

   b. Kerberos

   c. TCP/IP

   d. LDAP

9. Additional commands are found in the Support\Tools directory on the Windows Server 2003 CD. What is the name of the file that installs the additional support tools?

   a. Suptools.msi

   b. Setup.exe

   c. SupportTools.exe

   d. SupportTools.MSI

11

10. X.500 provides a standard to develop _____.

    a. a schema

    b. an authentication model

    c. an electronic directory of objects

    d. high-speed Internet access

11. Which command searches Active Directory for all the accountants in your company?

    a. `dsquery domainroot -search("accountant")`

    b. `dsquery * domainroot -filter(title=accountant)`

    c. `dsquery * -filter (title=accountant)`

    d. `dsquery search (title=accountant)`

12. All entries in an X.500 directory are uniquely identified by their _____.

    a. DNS

    b. UPN

    c. UNC

    d. DN

13. Which tool(s) can you use to query Active Directory?

    a. Active Directory Users and Groups

    b. Dsquery.exe

    c. Search.exe

    d. User Manager for Domains

14. Which predefined security template would you use to relax security permissions for users?

    a. DC Security.inf

    b. Secure*.inf

    c. hisec*.inf

    d. Compatws.inf

15. Which version of LDAP comes with Windows Server 2003?

    a. version 3

    b. version 2

    c. version 3 annex C

    d. version 3 annex D

16. Which command(s) displays or modifies DACL?

    a. **DACLS**

    b. **CACLS**

    c. **NTFSEDIT**

    d. **SECURE**

17. Microsoft Active Directory is based on which directory format?

    a. X.409

    b. X.400

    c. X.500

    d. X.509

18. What is the method used in validating users?

    a. authentication

    b. accounting

    c. answer keys

    d. ID checks

19. Which command analyzes the condition of a domain controller in a forest or enterprise and reports any problems?

    a. **DCDIAG**

    b. **DOMDIAG**

    c. **DCPROMO**

    d. **DCQUERY**

20. The security templates for the **SECEDIT** command are located in _____.

    a. Active Directory

    b. the Support Tools CD

    c. System Root\security\templates

    d. NDS

DISCOVERY EXERCISES

1. Research information about MIT's implementation of Kerberos version 5 and how you can authenticate to a UNIX domain or MIT Realm from Windows Server 2003. Write down how your work would increase or decrease by using Kerberos in this environment.

2. Explore the contents of the Support\Tools directory of the Windows Server 2003 CD-ROM. What other files besides Suptools.msi exist within that directory? What is gbunicnv.exe used for?

3. Explore the contents of your ProgramFiles\SupportTools directory. What does the **XCACLS** command do? How is **XCACLS** different from **CACLS**? Open a Web browser and navigate to www.altusnet.com/lti/455web/cacls.htm.

4. Use the **SECEDIT** command to configure your Windows Server 2003 with a custom security template. Create this custom template in the Security Templates MMC (this is another option that can be added in a custom MMC). Once you have created the custom template by changing settings in one of the built-in templates, run the **SECEDIT** command with the **/CONFIGURE** option, as shown in this chapter. Run an analysis after the configuration is complete to ensure that all settings have been made.

12

NAME RESOLUTION USING DNS, WINS, AND DHCP

After reading this chapter and completing the exercises, you will be able to:

♦ Understand name resolution in a Windows Server 2003 environment

♦ Utilize commands to diagnose, configure, and troubleshoot DNS, WINS, and DHCP

♦ Understand the differences between Fully Qualified Domain Names and NetBIOS names

♦ Utilize the **NETSH** command environment to perform WINS and DHCP maintenance over WAN links

M any network administrators are baffled by the complexities of name resolution, which is the correlation between computer identities (names) and various network addressing methods. This chapter provides an overview of how name resolution works in the networking world. As mentioned in Chapter 7, protocols allow communication between hosts, which might lead you to wonder how you identify a host. You can assign it a logical address, such as an IP address, but it would quickly become difficult to remember every IP address in your network.

To make naming easier to manage, you can assign names to hosts. For example, you can search for a computer named Tanya Gray, which is the name that you used to identify employee Tanya Gray's workstation when you set up her system. You know that Tanya's workstation has an IP address, so you need to "resolve," or match, the name to the number. This correlation is what name resolution is all about. Besides the need for name resolution, we also need to assign IP addresses to workstations and servers. If you do this automatically, you will need to use the Dynamic Host Configuration Protocol (DHCP). DHCP is covered later in this chapter.

In the world of Windows Server 2003, you can use the Domain Name System (DNS) or Windows Internet Name Service (WINS) to resolve easily remembered names to IP addresses. You will first learn about the more powerful of the two, DNS.

NAME RESOLUTION FOR A NETWORK

As you learned earlier in this book, DNS is a Windows Server 2003 service consisting of a distributed database that puts administration authority in the hands of local administrators while allowing users network-wide access to data. Information on DNS servers (a computer running the DNS service) is propagated to other DNS servers through data replication mechanisms. Clients access data on DNS servers (they query DNS servers) using the client-server architecture. **Name servers** make up the server portion of the client-server architecture, while **resolvers** comprise the client portion. Figure 12-1 shows these components.

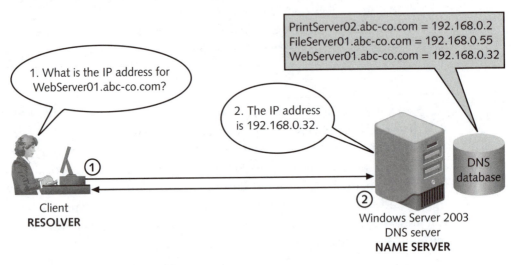

Figure 12-1   How DNS works

A DNS database is structured in a hierarchy similar to that of the Windows NTFS file system, which is shown in Figure 12-2.

Windows NTFS file system

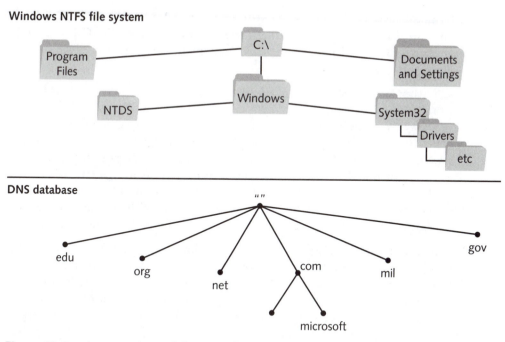

DNS database

Figure 12-2   A comparison of the DNS database and the Windows NTFS file system

A DNS database structure, like a file system structure, resembles an upside-down tree with the **root node** at the top and **child nodes** branching from the root. Child nodes act as root nodes for subtrees. Subtrees represent partitions in the DNS database, and are the equivalent of a directory or folder in the Windows file system. And just like the Windows file system, DNS folders can contain subfolders, also called subdomains. Just as folders on a hard drive must have a unique namespace (absolute pathname), a domain's name must be unique as well. Figure 12-3 shows an example of a file directory.

File directory

Figure 12-3   Directory example

12

Notice that a July02 directory exists in Figure 12-3. If a user attempted to add a second directory named July02 using the **MKDIR** command, Windows Server 2003 would generate an error. In the same sense, a domain can contain only one microsoft.com domain name.

The pathname or namespace character used in Windows Server 2003 is the backslash (\). Consider a folder named etc, which is a subdirectory of the drivers directory, which is a subdirectory of the System32 directory, which is a subdirectory of the Windows directory, which is a subdirectory of the root (C). The unique path to the etc directory would be c:\Windows\System32\drivers\etc. In DNS, the unique path or namespace is denoted with a dot (.) notation. For example, the governor of Arizona has a server called www, which is a subdomain of the governor domain, which is a subdomain of the state domain, which is a subdomain of the az domain, which is a subdomain of the us domain; therefore, to access the host, www, you would use the absolute path of www.governor.state.az.us.

When using this naming structure in a Windows Server 2003 environment, a computer will have a hostname similar to the naming structure previously discussed. The name given to objects in a Windows Server 2003 environment is a Fully Qualified Domain Name (FQDN). Like the Web domain names with which you may be familiar, a FQDN is hierarchical in nature. For example, you might have the phoenix.corp.abc-co.com domain. A file server called FileServer01 within this domain would have the FQDN of FileServer01.phoenix.corp.abc-co.com.

DNS administration and management is not centralized. Most DNS administration occurs at the domain level. For example, the **InterNIC**, the organization that registers public domain names, manages the com (.com) domain but appoints Microsoft the authority to manage the microsoft.com subdomain.

Hosts (computers) on a network have hostnames and domain names. The domain name refers to the host's IP address as well as other information. Figure 12-4 shows that a file server in ABC Corporation's Phoenix office has a domain name of FileServer01.phoenix.corp.abc-co.com and an IP address of 192.168.0.15.

DNS and Windows Server 2003

Having DNS running on a Windows Server 2003 network makes life easier for administrators and their users. DNS resolves FQDNs to IP addresses, meaning that users can find resources on a network by using a simple name such as PrintServer02 rather than an IP address such as 192.168.0.12. DNS is also required if you plan on installing and running Active Directory. DNS is required to find domain controllers. Domain controllers list all the resources on a network and authenticate users to use those resources.

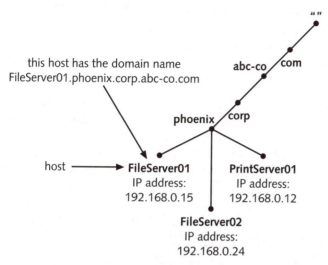

Figure 12-4   Host information

Microsoft has included new features into the Windows Server 2003 DNS service, including **conditional forwarders**. Conditional forwarders are settings that allow a DNS administrator to configure his or her server to forward a DNS query (a request to resolve a name to an IP address) with a specific domain name, such as abc-co.com, to a specified DNS server.

Microsoft has also improved the security mechanisms of DNS, allowing for more control in security administration. Windows Server 2003 DNS servers now perform **round-robin rotation** by default. Round-robin rotation is a method used to distribute a workload between multiple hosts.

Zoning for DNS

As mentioned earlier, the DNS database is distributed. This means that there is not one huge DNS server, but rather hundreds of DNS servers that collectively make up DNS. A storage database for a single DNS domain name is called a **zone**. For example, abc-co.com would be in its own zone. A subdomain of abc-co.com called west could be added to the abc-co.com zone, or it could be created in its own zone. If you wanted west.abc-co.com to be managed by the same administrator who manages abc-co.com, you would leave it in the abc-co.com zone. If you would rather have another administrator, perhaps one on the West Coast, manage west.abc-co.com, you need to create a separate zone. To create a new zone, you can use the Create New Zone wizard in the DNS Microsoft Management Console (MMC).

DNS has three types of zones: forward lookup zones, reverse lookup zones, and Active Directory integrated zones. **Forward lookup zones** resolve hostnames to IP addresses, while **reverse lookup zones** resolve IP addresses to hostnames. **Active Directory**

12

integrated zones allow zone information to be replicated along with Active Directory. Zones are a major component of Microsoft DNS. If a DNS server that hosts a zone fails, clients will be unable to have their DNS queries resolved for that zone; a copy of the zone file actually exists on that server. DNS administrators can replicate zone information onto other DNS servers, making the DNS infrastructure fault tolerant.

DNS zones require two servers, called primary and secondary DNS zone servers. Windows Server 2003 servers can be either the primary or secondary DNS zone server. The primary server hosts the master copy (read/write) of zone data for a particular zone, while a secondary server hosts a copy (read only) of zone data for a particular zone. Primary and secondary DNS servers perform zone transfers to synchronize zone data. Windows Server 2003 supports full zone transfers and incremental zone transfers. A full zone transfer replicates the entire database. Replicating the entire database is useful when adding an additional secondary server. Incremental zone transfers replicate the only changes to data within a zone, which is more efficient.

In Windows Server 2003, the DNS service and Active Directory have been tightly integrated. Using the Active Directory integrated zone allows DNS administrators to store the information in their zones in Active Directory and take advantage of an already-established replication topology. Recall that Active Directory uses a multi-master replication model. Unlike the single-master replication model used between primary and secondary DNS servers, which has a potential single point of failure, there is no single point of failure in Active Directory because all directory information is maintained on all domain controllers (DCs). Directory-integrated zones scale better than primary zones because each additional Windows Server 2003 DC server automatically receives zone information and participates in zone replication and synchronization.

Fine-Tuning Your DNS Installation

You create a DNS server by installing the DNS service on a computer running Windows Server 2003. You should configure a static IP address on any machine running the DNS service. Microsoft also suggests that you configure the domain name on the computer on which you are installing the DNS service. To configure the name, click the Change button within the Computer Name section of the My Computer properties. To install the DNS service, you must be a member of the local Administrators group, or if your server belongs to a domain, you must be a member of the Domain Admins group.

Hands-on Project 12-1 teaches you how to create zones within DNS.

Hands-on Project 12-1

To create a DNS zone:

1. Click the **Start** button [Start], click **Control Panel**, click **Administrative Tools,** and then click **DNS** to launch the DNS Management MMC.

2. Expand your server by clicking the **plus sign** next to it. For example, in Figure 12-5, the server's name is DC2.

3. Expand the Forward Lookup Zones node in the left pane by clicking the **plus sign** next to it. Your DNS administration tool should look similar to Figure 12-5.

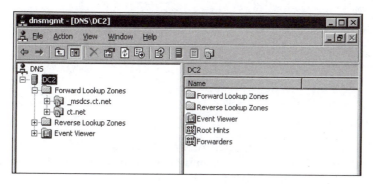

Figure 12-5   DNS Management MMC

4. Right-click the **Forward Lookup Zones** node and click **New Zone** to open the New Zone wizard. Press **Next** to continue.

You can create three types of zones with Windows Server 2003. Creating a primary zone on this server would create a read/write zone on the server. Creating a secondary zone would create a read-only zone to provide fault tolerance and load distribution. Creating a stub zone would create a zone on the server that contains that minimal DNS records without authoritative rights. The default setting for zone creations would create any one of those zones; however, their contents would be stored in Active Directory.

5. Keep the default settings as they are set (the default options for zone creation are to create a primary zone stored in Active Directory). Click **Next**.

6. In the Active Directory Zone Replication Scope dialog box, keep the default option to replicate to all domain controllers in the Active Directory domain ct.net and click **Next**.

7. In the Zone Name field, type **abc-co.com** for the zone name and click **Next**.

8. Keep the default option in the Dynamic Update dialog window to only allow secure updates and press **Next**.

9. Complete the New Zone wizard by clicking **Finish**. You will see the new zone in the DNS Management MMC. Your screen should look like Figure 12-6.

12

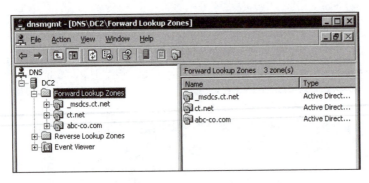

Figure 12-6   The newly created abc-co.com zone

DNS Administration

Microsoft has two main methods for administering Windows Server 2003 DNS servers. The primary method for DNS server administration is the DNS Management MMC, which you learned about in Hands-on Project 12-1.

Microsoft also provides a new command line tool for Windows Server 2003, **DNSCMD**, which is part of the Windows Support tools. **DNSCMD** allows you to script batch files, automate management, and update existing DNS server configurations. You can also use it to perform setup and configuration of new DNS servers on a network. Options for the **DNSCMD** command are varied, providing a wide range of features.

DNSCMD   Manages DNS server configuration.

DNSCMD <*ZONENAME*> /INFO   Gets server information.

DNSCMD <*ZONENAME*> /CONFIG   Resets server or zone configuration.

DNSCMD <*ZONENAME*> /ENUMZONES   Enumerates zones.

DNSCMD <*ZONENAME*> /STATISTICS   Queries/clears server statistics.

DNSCMD <*ZONENAME*> /CLEARCACHE   Clears the DNS server cache.

DNSCMD <*ZONENAME*> /WRITEBACKFILES   Writes back all zone or root-hint datafiles.

DNSCMD <*ZONENAME*> /STARTSCAVENGING   Initiates server scavenging.

DNSCMD <*ZONENAME*> /RESETLISTENADDRESSES   Sets server IP addresses to serve DNS requests.

DNSCMD <*ZONENAME*> /RESETFORWARDERS   Sets DNS servers to forward recursive queries.

DNSCMD <*ZONENAME*> /ZONEINFO   Views zone information.

DNSCMD <*ZONENAME*> /ZONEADD   Creates a new zone on a DNS server.

DNSCMD <*ZONENAME*> /ZONEDELETE   Deletes a zone from a DNS server.

DNSCMD <*ZONENAME*> /ZONEPAUSE   Pauses a zone.

DNSCMD <*ZONENAME*> /ZONERESUME   Resumes a zone.

DNSCMD <*ZONENAME*> /ZONERELOAD   Reloads a zone from its database (file or directory service).

DNSCMD <*ZONENAME*> /ZONEWRITEBACK   Writes back a zone to a file.

DNSCMD <*ZONENAME*> /ZONEREFRESH   Forces a refresh of a secondary zone from a master.

DNSCMD <*ZONENAME*> /ZONEUPDATEFROMDS   Updates a directory service integrated zone by data from a directory service.

DNSCMD <*ZONENAME*> /ZONEPRINT   Displays all records in a zone.

DNSCMD <*ZONENAME*> /ZONERESETTYPE   Changes the zone type.

DNSCMD <*ZONENAME*> /ZONERESETSECONDARIES   Resets secondary/notify information for a zone.

DNSCMD <*ZONENAME*> /ZONERESETSCAVENGESERVERS   Resets scavenging servers for a zone.

DNSCMD <*ZONENAME*> /ZONERESETMASTERS   Resets a secondary zone's master servers.

DNSCMD <*ZONENAME*> /ZONEEXPORT   Exports a zone to a file.

DNSCMD <*ZONENAME*> /ZONECHANGEDIRECTORYPARTITION Moves a zone to another directory partition.

DNSCMD <*ZONENAME*> /ENUMRECORDS   Enumerates records at each name.

DNSCMD /RECORDADD <*RECORDNAME*>   Creates a record in a zone or RootHints.

DNSCMD /RECORDDELETE <*RECORDNAME*>   Deletes a record from a zone, RootHints, or cache.

DNSCMD /NODEDELETE   Deletes all records at a name.

DNSCMD /AGEALLRECORDS   Forces aging on a node(s) in a zone.

DNSCMD /ENUMDIRECTORYPARTITIONS   Enumerates directory partitions.

DNSCMD /DIRECTORYPARTITIONINFO   Gets information on a directory partition.

DNSCMD /CREATEDIRECTORYPARTITION   Creates a directory partition.

DNSCMD /DELETEDIRECTORYPARTITION   Deletes a directory partition.

12

DNSCMD /ENLISTDIRECTORYPARTITION   Adds a DNS server to a partition replication scope.

DNSCMD /UNENLISTDIRECTORYPARTITION   Removes a DNS server from a replication scope.

DNSCMD /CREATEBUILTINDIRECTORYPARTITIONS   Creates built-in partitions.

In Hands-on Project 12-2, you will use **DNSCMD** to obtain server information about a DNS server. You must perform this project on a Windows Server 2003 domain controller running the DNS service.

Hands-on Project 12-2

To gather server information using **DNSCMD**:

1. Open a command window.

2. Type **dnscmd /info** and press **Enter**. Your results will be similar to Figure 12-7.

```
C:\WINDOWS\system32\cmd.exe

C:\>dnscmd /info
Query result:
Server info
        server name              = dc2.ct.net
        version                  = 0E4F0205 (5.2 build 3663)
        DS container             = cn=MicrosoftDNS,cn=System,DC=ct,DC=net
        forest name              = ct.net
        domain name              = ct.net
        builtin domain partition = DomainDnsZones.ct.net
        builtin forest partition = ForestDnsZones.ct.net
        last scavenge cycle      = not since restart (0)
Configuration:
        dwLogLevel               = 00000000
        dwDebugLevel             = 00000000
        dwRpcProtocol            = FFFFFFFF
        dwNameCheckFlag          = 00000002
        cAddressAnswerLimit      = 0
        dwRecursionRetry         = 3
        dwRecursionTimeout       = 15
        dwDsPollingInterval      = 180
Configuration Flags:
        fBootMethod              = 3
        fAdminConfigured         = 1
        fAllowUpdate             = 1
        fDsAvailable             = 1
        fAutoReverseZones        = 0
        fAutoCacheUpdate         = 0
        fSlave                   = 0
        fNoRecursion             = 1
        fRoundRobin              = 0
        fStrictFileParsing       = 0
        fLooseWildcarding        = 1
        fBindSecondaries         = 0
        fWriteAuthorityNs        = 1
        fLocalNetPriority        = 1
Aging Configuration:
        ScavengingInterval       = 0
        DefaultAgingState        = 0
        DefaultRefreshInterval   = 168
        DefaultNoRefreshInterval = 168
ServerAddresses:
Addr Count = 1
                Addr[0] => 192.168.0.254
```

Figure 12-7   DNSCMD /INFO results

3. Use the output from your results to determine the name of the DNS server, the domain name, and the IP address(es) of the configured forwarder(s).

4. Type **exit** and press **Enter** to close the command window.

In Hands-on Project 12-3, you will use **DNSCMD** to obtain zone information concerning the ct.net zone.

Hands-on Project 12-3

To gather zone information using **DNSCMD**:

1. Open a command window.

2. Type **dnscmd /zoneprint ct.net** and press **Enter**. Your results will be similar to Figure 12-8.

Figure 12-8 Gathering zone information

3. Use the output from your results to determine the name of the zone, the FQDN of the DNS server, and the IP address of the DNS server.

4. Type **exit** and press **Enter** to close the command window.

Once you have created a zone, you will need to add records such as host, start of authority, and so on, to that zone. You will do this in Hands-on Project 12-4. You can use **DNSCMD** to add a record to the ct.net zone and then use **DNSCMD** to reload the ct.net zone, verifying that the new record was successfully added to the ct.net zone.

Hands-on Project 12-4

To add a record using **DNSCMD**:

1. Open a command window.

2. Type **dnscmd /recordadd /?** and press **Enter**. Your screen should look like Figure 12-9.

```
C:\WINDOWS\system32\cmd.exe

C:\>dnscmd /recordadd /?
Usage: DnsCmd <ServerName> /RecordAdd <Zone> <NodeName> [/Aging] [/OpenAcl]
                          [<Ttl>] <RRType> <RRData>

   <RRType>              <RRData>
    A                    <IPAddress>
    NS,CNAME,MB,MD       <HostName!DomainName>
    PTR,MF,MG,MR         <HostName!DomainName>
    MX,RT,AFSDB          <Preference> <ServerName>
    SRV                  <Priority> <Weight> <Port> <HostName>
    SOA                  <PrimaryServer> <AdminEmail> <SerialN>
                         <Refresh> <Retry> <Expire> <MinTTL>
    AAAA                 <Ipv6Address>
    TXT                  <String> [<String>]
    X25,HINFO,ISDN       <String> [<String>]
    MINFO,RP             <MailboxName> <ErrMailboxName>
    WKS                  <Protocol> <IPAddress> <Service> [<Service>]..]
    KEY                  <Flags> <KeyProtocol> <CryptoAlgorithm> <Base64Data>
    SIG                  <TypeCovered> <CryptoAlgorithm> <LabelCount>
                         <OriginalTTL> <SigExpiration> <SigInception>
                         <KeyTag> <Signer's Name> <Base64Data>
    NXT                  <NextName> <Type> [<Type>...]
    WINS                 <MapFlag> <LookupTimeout>
                         <CacheTimeout> <IPAddress> [<IPAddress>]
    WINSR                <MapFlag> <LookupTimeout>
                         <CacheTimeout> <RstDomainName>
   <Zone>             -- <ZoneName> | /RootHints
   <ZoneName>         -- FQDN of a zone
   <NodeName>         -- name of node for which a record will be added
                         - FQDN of a node  (name with a '.' at the end) OR
                         - node name relative to the ZoneName            OR
                         - "@" for zone root node                        OR
                         - service name for SRV only (e.g. _ftp._tcp)
   <Ttl>             -- TTL for the RR  (Default: TTL defined in SOA)
   <HostName>        -- FQDN of a host
   <IPAddress>       -- e.g. 255.255.255.255
   <ipv6Address>     -- e.g. 1:2:3:4:5:6:7:8
   <Protocol>        -- UDP | TCP
   <Service>         -- e.g. domain, sntp
   <TypeCovered>     -- type of the RRset signed by this SIG
   <CryptoAlgorithm> -- 1=RSA/MD5, 2=Diffie-Hellman, 3=DSA
   <SigExpiration>   -- yyyymmddhhmmss - GMT
   <SigInception>    -- yyyymmddhhmmss - GMT
   <KeyTag>          -- used to discriminate between multiple SIGs
   <Signer's Name>   -- domain name of signer
   <KeyProtocol>     -- 1=TLS, 2=email, 3=DNSSEC, 4=IPSEC
```

Figure 12-9 DNSCMD /RECORDADD /? results

3. To add a new host (a record) with the same IP address as your server, type **dnscmd dc2.ct.net /recordadd ct.net test A 192.168.0.254** and press **Enter**.

4. To reload your zone, type **dnscmd /zonereload ct.net** and press **Enter**.

5. Next, use the **DNSCMD** command to query the zone and verify that your newly created host has been added to your zone. Type **dnscmd /zoneprint ct.net** and press **Enter**. Your results will be similar to what you see in Figure 12-10.

```
;
; Zone:    ct.net
; Server:  dc2.ct.net
; Time:    Thu Dec 26 13:23:27 2002 UTC
;
@ [Aging:3522498] 600 A 192.168.0.254
                 [Aging:3523717] 3600 NS        dc2.ct.net.
                 [Aging:3522498] 3600 SOA       dc2.ct.net. hostmaster. 49 900 6
00 86400 3600
_msdcs 3600 NS   dc2.
_gc._tcp.Default-First-Site-Name._sites [Aging:3522498] 600 SRV 0 100 3268 dc2.c
t.net.
_kerberos._tcp.Default-First-Site-Name._sites [Aging:3522498] 600 SRV   0 100 88
 dc2.ct.net.
_ldap._tcp.Default-First-Site-Name._sites [Aging:3522498] 600 SRV       0 100 38
9 dc2.ct.net.
_gc._tcp [Aging:3522498] 600 SRV        0 100 3268 dc2.ct.net.
_kerberos._tcp [Aging:3522498] 600 SRV  0 100 88 dc2.ct.net.
_kpasswd._tcp [Aging:3522498] 600 SRV   0 100 464 dc2.ct.net.
_ldap._tcp [Aging:3522498] 600 SRV      0 100 389 dc2.ct.net.
_kerberos._udp [Aging:3522498] 600 SRV  0 100 88 dc2.ct.net.
_kpasswd._udp [Aging:3522498] 600 SRV   0 100 464 dc2.ct.net.
dc2 [Aging:3523714] 3600 A      192.168.0.254
DomainDnsZones [Aging:3522499] 600 A    192.168.0.254
_ldap._tcp.Default-First-Site-Name._sites.DomainDnsZones [Aging:3522499] 600 SRV
        0 100 389 dc2.ct.net.
_ldap._tcp.DomainDnsZones [Aging:3522499] 600 SRV       0 100 389 dc2.ct.net.
ForestDnsZones [Aging:3522499] 600 A    192.168.0.254
_ldap._tcp.Default-First-Site-Name._sites.ForestDnsZones [Aging:3522499] 600 SRV
        0 100 389 dc2.ct.net.
_ldap._tcp.ForestDnsZones [Aging:3522499] 600 SRV       0 100 389 dc2.ct.net.
test 3600 A     192.168.0.254
;
; Finished zone: 48 nodes and 21 records in 0 seconds
;
```

Figure 12-10 Verifying the new zone

6. Close all open windows to finish the project.

Troubleshooting DNS

DNS servers play a critical role in today's networks. They perform name resolution for end users and provide name resolution for software applications such as an ASP Server 2003 Web application. As a DNS administrator, it is imperative that you spend time troubleshooting, maintaining, and optimizing DNS servers.

Troubleshooting DNS issues can take many forms, including troubleshooting the client, troubleshooting the server, troubleshooting dynamic updates, and troubleshooting zones. There are several tools to help you maintain your DNS servers. The main command that you will use for such tasks is **NSLOOKUP**, which was introduced in Chapter 10.

The **NSLOOKUP** command is very powerful and has two modes of operation: interactive mode and non-interactive mode. For quick operations requiring single bits of data, you use non-interactive mode. Interactive mode is used for multiple **NSLOOKUP** operations.

To enter **NSLOOKUP** interactive mode, type "nslookup" and press Enter, as shown in Figure 12-11. To quit **NSLOOKUP** interactive mode and return to the command prompt, type "exit" and press Enter.

Figure 12-11   NSLOOKUP interactive mode

You can interrupt commands issued in **NSLOOKUP** interactive mode by typing the Ctrl+C key combination. Finally, you must use the backslash escape character (\) when specifying a computer name in **NSLOOKUP** interactive mode; otherwise, the name will be interpreted as an **NSLOOKUP** subcommand.

The **NSLOOKUP** command has many subcommands, which follow.

EXIT   Quits **NSLOOKUP** and returns you to the command prompt.

FINGER   Connects you to the Finger service of the current computer, allowing you to specify a username to look up.

HELP   Lists a brief summary of **NSLOOKUP** subcommands.

LS   Lists information for a DNS domain.

LS –T *<DOMAIN>*   Specifies a query type.

LS –A *<DOMAIN>*   Lists aliases.

LS –D *<DOMAIN>*   Lists all records for a domain.

LSERVER   Changes the default server.

ROOT   Makes the server for the root domain namespace the default server.

SERVER   Specifies a different server to use.

SET   Changes the configuration settings of the **NSLOOKUP** command and alters the operation of lookups. Various **SET** versions are available for specific settings.

VIEW   Sorts and lists the output of the **LS** subcommand.

For example, to test for basic DNS server functionality, you can type `nslookup <serveripaddress>` at the command prompt, as shown in Figure 12-12.

One issue that you might face when dealing with DNS is whether Windows Server 2003 DCs have been added to the DNS database. In Hands-on Project 12-5, you use the **NSLOOKUP** command to verify that a Windows Server 2003 DC has been added to the DNS database.

Figure 12-12   Using **NSLOOKUP** to verify minimal DNS server functionality

Hands-on Project 12-5

To troubleshoot Windows Server 2003 DNS registration:

1. Open a command window.

2. Type **nslookup** and press **Enter** to enter **NSLOOKUP** interactive mode.

3. Type **set q=** (don't type a space between the q and the =) and press **Enter**.

4. Type **_ldap._tcp.dc._msdcs.ct.net** to enter the LDAP record name. Your results should show the server name, the IP address, and the LDAP record name.

5. Type **exit** and press **Enter** to quit the **NSLOOKUP** command. Type **exit** again and press **Enter** to close the command window.

THE NETSH COMMAND ENVIRONMENT

Later in this chapter, you will learn about a legacy method of name resolution called WINS (Windows Internet Name Service). You will also work with DHCP (Dynamic Host Configuration Protocol), which is a method of assigning IP addresses to your computers. Before mastering those topics, you first need to know about the **NETSH** command environment.

As you move into the legacy name resolution of WINS and the address assignment capabilities of DHCP, you will see that the majority of commands and capabilities for these two tools exist within the **NETSH** command utility. **NETSH** is a command line and scripting utility for Windows Server 2003 networking components for local or remote computers. The **NETSH** utility can also save a configuration script in a text file for archival purposes or for configuring other servers. Just like with **NSLOOKUP**, **NETSH** is a command environment, or shell, that runs at the Windows Server 2003 command prompt.

The **NETSH** utility can support multiple Windows Server 2003 components through the addition of **NETSH** helper **dynamic link libraries (DLLs)**. A DLL is a collection of small programs, any of which can be called when needed by a larger program. A **NETSH** helper DLL extends **NETSH** functionality by providing additional commands to monitor or configure a specific Windows Server 2003 networking component. Each **NETSH** helper DLL provides a **context**, which is a group of commands for a specific networking component. Within each context, subcontexts can exist. Command line options for the **NETSH** command are listed below.

NETSH -A   Specifies that an alias file is used. An alias file allows you to create alias (shortcut) commands instead of using the **NETSH** command.

NETSH -C   Specifies the context of the command that corresponds to an installed helper DLL.

NETSH –F <*SCRIPTFILE*>   Specifies that all of the **NETSH** commands in *SCRIPTFILE* are run.

NETSH –R <*REMOTECOMPUTER*>   Specifies that the **NETSH** commands are run on a remote computer specified by either its name or IP address.

Like the **DISKPART** command that you learned about in Chapter 5, **NETSH** operates in its own environment. A **NETSH** context is identified by a string that is appended to a command. Commands entered in a specific context are passed to an associated helper. The contexts available depend on the Windows Server 2003 components installed. For example, typing "WINS" at the **NETSH** prompt switches to the WINS context. Likewise, typing "DHCP" at the **NETSH** prompt switches to the DHCP context.

In Hands-on Project 12-6, you will open the **NETSH** utility and change context from WINS to DHCP. Make sure these services are running on your Windows Server 2003 system before beginning the project.

Hands-on Project 12-6

To change context in the **NETSH** utility:

1. Open a command window.

2. Type **netsh –c wins** and press **Enter**.

3. Notice that the prompt has changed to "netsh wins>." Now change contexts by typing **dhcp** at the prompt and pressing **Enter**. Notice that the prompt changes to "netsh dhcp>." You have successfully switched from the WINS context to the DHCP context in **NETSH**. From here, you can type "list" and see what commands are available to you from this prompt.

4. Type **exit** to quit the **NETSH** command. Then type **exit** again and press **Enter** to close the command prompt.

When managing WINS and DHCP servers in wide area networks (WANs), you can use commands in interactive mode at the **NETSH** command prompt to better manage servers across slow-speed network links. When managing a large number of DHCP and WINS servers, commands can be used in batch mode to help script and automate recurring administrative tasks that need to be performed for all servers.

WINS NAME RESOLUTION

In Chapter 7, you learned about the use of NetBIOS names in networks. Recall that NetBIOS started as a high-level programming language interface for MS-DOS programs used to network IBM PC-compatible microcomputers introduced during the late 1980s. To build LANs based on the networking hardware and software available for those computers, Microsoft and other vendors standardized on using the NetBIOS interface to design their networking system components and programs. This interface uses names that are limited to 15 characters in length to identify each network resource. A 16th byte is used to identify the service that is running on that host. For example, you might have a computer that has a NetBIOS name of JOHNSMITHHOMEPC. The 15 characters identify the computer, and an additional 16th byte identifies the host's different services, such as SMTPTCP, workstation, or server.

Prior to Windows 2000, all MS-DOS and Windows-based operating systems required the NetBIOS naming interface to support network capabilities. Once Microsoft released Windows 2000, support for the NetBIOS naming interface was no longer required for networking computers. If you are running an entirely pure Windows 2000 or Server 2003 network, you will not need NetBIOS. However, most networks still need to integrate legacy operating systems and applications that require NetBIOS network names with computers running Windows 2000.

Because many of the legacy systems and some software applications still require the use of NetBIOS names, you will see support for NetBIOS in Windows Server 2003. NetBIOS is a LAN-based interface, so to cross networks to other networks, you will need some help. This support is provided through NetBIOS over TCP/IP (NetBT) and can, if desired, be manually disabled.

As a network administrator, you need to know how to perform name resolution for these NetBIOS names. This name resolution can be handled with WINS. In a WINS system, all names are registered with a WINS server—a Windows Server 2003 system running WINS. The names are stored in a database on the WINS server, which answers requests for name-to-IP-address resolution based on the entries in this database.

The WINS Naming Resolution Process

WINS is a dynamic service, meaning that the hosts will attempt to register their NetBIOS names if allowed to. Name registration consists of a WINS client requesting the use of a NetBIOS name on the network. The NetBIOS name will be the computer name assigned when Windows Server 2003 was installed. The request may be for a unique (exclusive) or a group (shared) name. NetBIOS applications can also register one or more names. There can be one or more WINS servers in a network depending on the number of clients in that network.

To understand the way WINS assigns names, assume that you are on a computer named HOST_A and you are powering on the computer. The computer will attempt to register its name (HOST_A) with the WINS server. If the name does not exist in the database, the WINS server accepts it as a new registration and the following process occurs:

- The name for HOST_A is entered with a new version of the HOST_A name, or version ID, given a time stamp, and marked with the owner identity of the WINS server.

- A positive registration response is sent back to HOST_A with a time to live (TTL) value equal to the time stamp recorded for the name at the WINS server.

This process is illustrated in Figure 12-13.

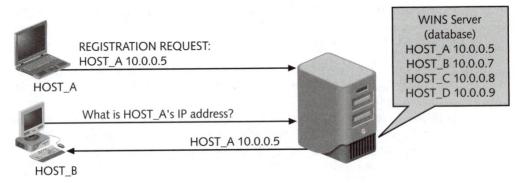

Figure 12-13   WINS registration and name resolution

If the HOST_A name is already entered in the database with the same IP address as that being requested, the action taken by the WINS server depends on the state and owner-ship of the existing name. If the entry is marked as active and the WINS server owns the entry, the server updates the time stamp for the record and returns a positive response back to the client, which indicates that the name is registered.

If the entry is marked as being either released or "tombstoned" (available), or if another WINS server owns the entry, the registration is treated as a new registration. Time stamp, version ID, and ownership are all updated and a positive response is returned, inform-ing the computer that its name is successfully registered.

This is the positive scenario. What if another computer has attempted to register the NetBIOS name already?

WINS Name Resolution with Existing Names

In the case where the NetBIOS name exists in the WINS database but is associated with an IP address other than that being requested, the WINS server is expected to avoid duplicate names. If the database entry is in the released or tombstone state, the WINS server is free to assign the existing name to the new host that is requesting it.

If, however, the entry is in the active state, the host holding the name is challenged to determine if it still exists on the network. If it does still exist, the WINS server could perform a challenge of the name, enquiring whether the name is in use by another host. The WINS server can send a wait for acknowledgment (WACK) response to the requesting host (HOST_A), stating that the host should wait a bit while the WINS server checks on the name.

The WINS server then attempts to contact the computer that already claims to be HOST_A. If the computer exists, it sends a positive response back to the WINS server, letting the computer requesting the HOST_A name know that it was unable to register HOST_A because it already exists on the network. See Figure 12-14.

If a positive response is not received back from the first challenge query made by the WINS server, the server will try twice more. After three attempts with no response, the WINS server will let the requesting computer know that it was successful in registering the HOST_A name to its IP address in the WINS database.

Configuring WINS Servers

Because the WINS database can become quite important, you will likely want to use more than one WINS server in your network. The service can run on any Windows Server 2003 system, but be careful that the machine on which you place this database is secure and not overworked already. It will definitely be utilized when acting as a WINS server.

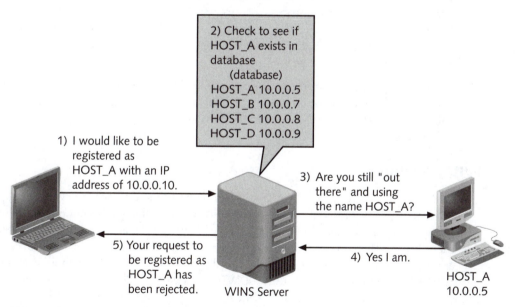

Figure 12-14   WINS name resolution conflict

If you have more than one WINS server, you will need replication to take place in order for the databases to remain current. Later in this chapter, you will learn how this is accomplished.

Each name has an entry in the WINS database. The name is owned by the WINS server it registered with and exists as a replica on all other WINS servers. Each entry has a state associated with it—the entry can be in the active, released, or tombstone state. Entries are also assigned a version ID number. This number is used in the replication process.

WINS also allows the registration of static names. This enables the administrator to register names for servers running operating systems that are not capable of dynamic name registration, such as older forms of Windows and some forms of UNIX. WINS distinguishes between dynamic and static entries. Static names are treated differently than dynamic names. Unlike dynamic mappings, which can age and be automatically removed from WINS over time, static mappings can remain in WINS indefinitely unless administrative action is taken. You can also place a static name-to-IP-address resolution on your computer using the **LMHOST** file located in the %systemroot%\ system32\drivers\ ETC folder. The LMHOST file is checked before a computer checks a WINS server for name resolution.

Maintaining WINS

Several things need to occur in your network for WINS to operate effectively. One of these is the registration process that you learned about in the previous section. It is also vital that the replication process occur between WINS servers. You can configure a WINS server to automatically configure other WINS server computers as its replication partners. With this automatic partner configuration, other WINS servers are discovered when they join the network and are added as replication partners.

Automatic replication configuration is possible because each WINS server announces its presence on the network through periodic multi-casts. Multi-cast announcements are sent as **Internet Group Membership Protocol (IGMP)** messages for the multi-cast group address of 224.0.1.24. This multi-cast address is reserved for WINS servers.

WINS Partners

In WINS replication, there are two types of partners: push partners and pull partners. You can also combine the two to form a third type called push/pull partners. Push partners wait until a certain number of changes have been made to the WINS database and then "push" that replication out to their partners. Pull partners wait until a certain amount of time has passed and then "pull" the information from their partners with a request to replicate. By default, all Windows Server 2003 WINS servers are set as push/pull partners. This means WINS servers engage in both push and pull replication. If you want to change a WINS server's partner type, you can do so using the WINS MMC or variations of the **NETSH** command.

NETSH –C WINS   Enters the WINS context of the **NETSH** utility.

Once you have typed **NETSH WINS** and pressed Enter to launch the NETSH WINS context, you can use specific commands available within the context.

SET AUTOPARTNERCONFIG   Sets the automatic replication partner configuration for the server.

SET PULLPARTNERCONFIG   Sets the configuration parameters for the specified pull partner.

SET PUSHPARTNERCONFIG   Sets the configuration parameters for the specified push partner.

SET PULLPARAM   Sets the default pull parameters for the server.

SET PUSHPARAM   Sets the default push parameters for the server.

Planning WINS Server Replication Configuration

The frequency of WINS database replication between WINS servers is a major planning issue. The WINS server database should be replicated frequently enough to prevent the downtime of a single WINS server from affecting the reliability of the mapping information in other WINS servers. However, the time interval between replications should not be so small that it interferes with network throughput.

Network topology can influence your decision on replication frequency. For example, if your network has multiple hubs connected by relatively slow WAN links, you can configure WINS database replications between WINS servers on the slow links to occur less frequently than replication on the LAN or on fast WAN links. This reduces traffic across the slow link and reduces contention between replication traffic and WINS client name queries.

On occasion, you might have to initiate replication manually. There are several WINS commands that you can issue within the **NETSH** shell.

INIT PULL   Initiates and sends a pull trigger to another WINS server.

INIT PULLRANGE   Initiates and pulls a range of records from another WINS server.

INIT PUSH   Initiates and sends a push trigger to another WINS server.

INIT REPLICATE   Initiates replication of the database with replication partners.

INIT SCAVENGE   Initiates scavenging of the WINS database for the server.

The scavenging feature digs out old and outdated information and ensures that this information is not perpetuated throughout the network when replication occurs. When you scavenge the database, you remove old and released entries that were registered at another WINS server.

12

Another feature in a Windows Server 2003 WINS server is the ability to tombstone records. Tombstoning marks the selected records locally as extinct and immediately releases them from active use by the local WINS server. The tombstoned records remain present in the server database so that they can be replicated to other servers in the network. The tombstoned records notify the other WINS servers that the records should be eliminated.

The replication process continues as the tombstoned records are replicated to all of the other partner WINS servers. When a specified amount of time has elapsed (the verification interval), the records are automatically removed from each database.

Hands-on Project 12-7 teaches you how to begin the scavenging process, erasing any old or outdated WINS records from the database.

Hands-on Project 12-7

To initiate a database scavenge:

1. Install WINS on your Windows Server 2003 system by clicking the **Start** button **Start**, then clicking **Control Panel**. Click **Add or Remove Programs**.

2. Click **Add/Remove Windows Components** (on the left side of the Add or Remove Programs window). In a moment, the screen will list the available options. Scroll down to **Networking Services**. Click **Networking Services**, but *do not* click the checkbox. If you clear the checkbox, you will uninstall all your networking services. Click the **Details** button.

3. Select the **Windows Internet Name Service (WINS)** option by clicking the checkbox next to it. Then click **OK**.

4. Click **Next** to begin installing the WINS service on your Windows Server 2003. Be sure to have your Windows Server 2003 CD available; you will need it to complete the WINS installation.

5. You should configure the advanced TCP/IP settings so your server is a WINS client itself (registers itself in the WINS database). To do this, right-click **My Network Places**, and then click **Properties**. In Network Connections, right-click **Local Area Connection** and then click **Properties**.

6. Click **Internet Protocol (TCP/IP)**, and then click **Properties**. In the dialog box, click **Advanced**, and then click the **WINS** tab. Click **Add**.

7. In the TCP/IP WINS Server dialog box, type the IP address of your computer, and then click **Add**. Click **OK** to close the dialog box.

8. Click **OK** to close the Internet Protocol (TCP/IP) Properties dialog box. Then click **OK** again to close the Local Area Network Properties dialog box.

9. Open a command window.

10. Enter the WINS context of the **NETSH** utility by typing **netsh –c wins** and pressing **Enter**.

11. You should see the command prompt change to "netsh wins>." Type **?** and press **Enter** at the netsh wins> prompt to see all the available WINS commands.

12. Change to your server context by typing **server** and pressing **Enter**. Your command prompt should now be "netsh wins server>."

13. Type **?** and press **Enter** at the netsh wins server> prompt to see all the available WINS commands.

14. Notice that one of these commands is **INIT**. Type **init scavenge** and press **Enter** at the prompt. This will initiate the scavenging feature on your WINS database.

15. Close all of the command windows.

USING DHCP TO MANAGE CONNECTIVITY

The Dynamic Host Configuration Protocol (DHCP) is an Internet protocol for automating the configuration of computers that use TCP/IP. DHCP can be used to automatically assign IP addresses, deliver TCP/IP stack configuration parameters such as the subnet mask and default router, and provide other configuration information such as the addresses for the DNS server, the WINS server, and printer, time, and news servers. DHCP is an industry standard—it is not used only in Microsoft Windows networks. However, it is used purely in IP addressed networks.

DHCP allows a Windows Server 2003 administrator to drastically reduce the time and effort of maintaining connectivity in an IP addressed network. Instead of having to statically assign by hand each and every IP address in a network (after about 30 addresses this would become an administrative nightmare), DHCP handles the IP addressing task. It allows you to assign not only an address, but in Windows Server 2003's DHCP service, you can assign DNS, WINS, and time servers to a client. Using dynamic DNS, DHCP can also update the DNS servers with IP address information on behalf of a client. It is a powerful service and, if configured correctly, will enable smooth connectivity for end users.

How DHCP Works

Computers acting as DHCP clients and servers use two different processes to communicate. Clients obtain an address configuration from servers in a leasing process, the steps of which vary depending on whether the client is starting up or renewing its lease for an IP address. The process begins when a client computer first starts and attempts to join a network. The renewal process occurs after a client has a lease, but needs to renew that lease with the server. An IP address lease is similar to getting a driver's license. If you meet certain requirements, you are given a license to operate on the highways with your vehicle, but you periodically need to reregister, or contact the Motor Vehicle Department, so that it can reissue your license. An IP address is like a license to operate on the information superhighway.

The first time a DHCP-enabled computer starts up, it recognizes that it needs an IP address to communicate across the network. You enable DHCP on a client computer by telling it in the TCP/IP properties to "Obtain an IP address Automatically." Because it has been told to use DHCP to gain that information, the computer sends over the network a broadcast called a DHCPDISCOVER, which is an attempt to talk to a DHCP server. When a DHCP server hears this message, it responds to the client with a DHCPOFFER packet that contains an IP address for the client. There could be more than one DHCP server on the network, so the client takes the first IP address that arrives and responds to that DHCP server with a DHCPREQUEST message with a formal acceptance of the IP address. The server then acknowledges the client with a DHCPACK message. The client now has an IP address and is able to communicate on the network. Figure 12-15 illustrates the leasing process.

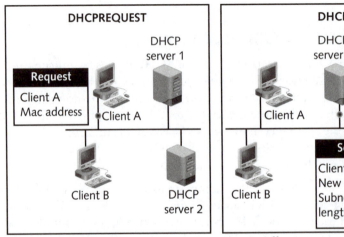

Step 1: Discover   Step 2: Offer

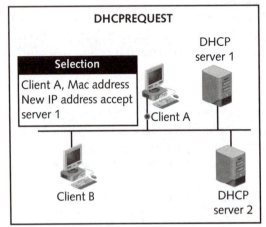
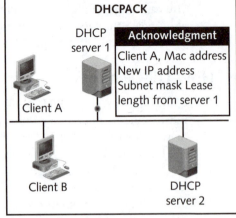

Step 3: Request   Step 4: Acknowledge

Figure 12-15   The DHCP address lease process

A great way to remember the lease process is to use the acronym DORA, which stands for **D**iscover, **O**ffer, **R**equest, **A**cknowledge.

When a computer shuts down and then starts up on the same network segment within a short period of time, it will typically receive the same IP address it had prior to shutting down. Turning off your computer and restarting it starts the initial process of DHCP. But what if a computer stays on (which is typically recommended these days) and the DHCP lease period is eight days? The lease renewal process begins halfway through the client lease period. In the case of an eight-day lease, the client attempts to renew the lease for four days. The client and server will skip the DHCPDISCOVER and DHCPOFFER packets, and instead the client sends the DHCPREQUEST message to the DHCP server that originally granted the lease. If the DHCP server is reachable, and the IP address has not been removed from the address pool, the server will reply with a DHCPACK message telling the client to renew the lease for another eight days.

Setting Up DHCP

For DHCP to run on a network, the network must have a Windows family server (NT, 2000, 2003) with the DHCP service loaded and started. You will also need to set up a pool of addresses to assign to clients. To set up this pool of addresses, you will need to use the DHCP MMC. This pool of addresses belongs to a **scope**. A scope is the full consecutive range of possible IP addresses for a network. Scopes typically define a single physical subnet on a network to which DHCP services are offered. Scopes also provide the primary way for the server to manage distribution and assignment of IP addresses and any related configuration parameters to clients on the network.

You will also need to set up an **exclusion range**, which is a range of IP addresses that are excluded from a scope. These IP addresses are statically assigned to Web, DNS, WINS, and other servers that do not use DHCP to gain an IP address. After you define the scope and apply the exclusion ranges, the remaining addresses are used to make up the address pool from which clients running DHCP draw their leases. You can also set up a reservation for a particular device to gain an IP address. Just like an airplane reservation guarantees you a certain seat on the plane, the DHCP reservation guarantees a network resource, such as a printer, the same IP address every time it turns on.

Recall that you can assign not only an IP address and subnet mask with a DHCP server, but also other options. These options are called option types. Option types allow you to assign things such as default gateways, WINS servers, and DNS servers to networked computers. What makes DHCP even more powerful is the ability to assign options classes. These options classes allow a server to further manage the option types by providing class-specific option types to clients for their configuration. For example, you could set up a Sales class and a Marketing class. Computers within these classes would have specific option types based on which class they belong to.

12

Maintaining DHCP

Like WINS, DHCP uses the **NETSH** command environment to provide access to advanced commands used for configuring and maintaining DHCP servers. Typically, administrators use the DHCP GUI console to start and stop the DHCP service or configure scopes. However, the **NETSH** command environment can be used on remote computers with less overhead.

Like the **DISKPART** command that you learned about in Chapter 5, DHCP operates in its own environment. The DHCP environment exists within the **NETSH** command shell. The **NETSH –C DHCP** command opens a **NETSH** shell with the DHCP environment running. Within the DHCP environment, the prompt appears as "netsh dhcp>." The following commands are available within the DHCP environment.

ADD SERVER   Adds a DHCP server to the DHCP console.

DELETE SERVER   Deletes a DHCP server from the DHCP console.

SHOW SERVER   Displays all DHCP servers currently added under the DHCP console.

SERVER <*SERVERNAME|IPADDRESS*>   Shifts the current DHCP context to the server specified by name or IP address.

In Hands-on Project 12-8, you learn how to use the **NETSH** command environment to access a DHCP server. To complete the project, you will need to be logged in and have access and permission to a Windows Server 2003 server running the DHCP service.

Hands-on Project 12-8

To use **NETSH** to connect to a DHCP server:

1. Install DHCP on a Windows Server 2003 system by clicking the **Start** button ![Start], then clicking **Control Panel**. Click **Add or Remove Programs**.

2. Click **Add/Remove Windows Components** (on the left side of the Add or Remove Programs window). In a moment, the screen will list the available options. Scroll down to **Networking Services**. Click **Networking Services**, but *do not* click the checkbox. If you clear the checkbox, you will uninstall all your networking services. Click the **Details** button.

3. Select the **Dynamic Host Configuration Protocol (DHCP)** option by checking the box next to it. Then click **OK**.

4. Click **Next** to begin installing the DHCP service on the Windows Server 2003 system.

5. Once the service has been installed, close all dialog boxes. Click **Finish** once the service installation is complete.

6. Open a command window.

7. At the command prompt, type **netsh** and press **Enter**. The prompt changes to "netsh>."

8. At the netsh> prompt, type **dhcp** and press **Enter**. The prompt changes to "netsh dhcp>." At the netsh dhcp> prompt, type the name or IP address of the DHCP server you are attempting to reach, for example, netsh dhcp>server \\tgray1 and press **Enter**. The prompt will change as shown in Figure 12-16. Your screen will reflect the name of your server.

```
C:\WINDOWS\system32\cmd.exe - netsh
C:\>netsh
netsh>dhcp
netsh dhcp>server \\dc2
netsh dhcp server>_
```

Figure 12-16   **NETSH** results

9. You have successfully connected to a DHCP server with the **NETSH** command shell. Close all command windows when you have finished.

Once you are at the DHCP server that you wish to configure or maintain, you can issue the DHCP server commands that follow. All the commands are issued from the netsh dhcp server> prompt.

12

ADD CLASS <*CLASS*>   Adds a class to the currently specified DHCP server.

ADD MSCOPE   Adds a multi-cast scope to the currently specified DHCP server.

ADD OPTIONDEF <*OPTIONDEFINITION*>   Adds a new option type definition.

ADD SCOPE <*SCOPE*>   Adds a new scope to the current DHCP server.

DELETE CLASS <*CLASS*>   Deletes a class.

DELETE MSCOPE <*MULTISCOPE*>   Deletes a multi-cast scope from the current DHCP server.

DELETE OPTIONDEF   Deletes a defined option type definition from the current DHCP server.

DELETE SCOPE <*SCOPE*>   Deletes a scope from the current DHCP server.

DELETE SUPERSCOPE <*SUPERSCOPE*>   Deletes a new superscope from the current DHCP server. A superscope is two or more scopes combined to create a larger scope of addresses.

INITIATE AUTH   Initiates authorization of the currently specified DHCP server in Active Directory.

SCOPE <*SCOPEIPADDRESS*>   Switches to the scope subcontext and enables those commands on the specified IP network address.

MSCOPE<*MULTISCOPE*>   Switches the command context to the DHCP multicast scope specified by the name, for example, 239.239.240.0

SET DATABASEBACKUPINTERVAL <*INTERVAL*>   Sets the backup interval for the database information contained in DHCP.

SET DATABASEPATHBACKUP <*PATHOFDATABASE*>   Sets the database backup path to be used to save the database information when the backup interval occurs.

SET DETECTCONFLICTRETRY <*NUMBEROFRETRIES*>   Sets the number of conflict detection attempts made by the DHCP server.

SET DNSCONFIG   Sets the Dynamic DNS update configuration for the DHCP server.

SET OPTIONVALUE <*OPTIONVALUE*>   Sets a server option value, which will be applied for all scopes defined on that DHCP server.

SET USERCLASS <*USERCLASS*>   Sets the user class name for use in subsequent command operations.

SHOW ALL   Displays all information for the current DHCP server.

SHOW CLASS   Displays all class information for the current DHCP server.

SHOW DNSCONFIG   Displays the Dynamic DNS configuration information for the current DHCP server.

SHOW MIBINFO   Displays the Management Information Base (MIB) information for the current DHCP server.

SHOW SCOPE   Displays all the current information about scopes for the current DHCP server.

SHOW SERVERSTATUS   Displays status information for the current DHCP server.

As you learned earlier, you must have scopes defined and activated on a DHCP server in order for addresses to be assigned to clients. Included in the scope definition are any IP address ranges and exclusions as well as any reservations. To access the DHCP scope commands, you type **scope [*ipaddress or subnet address*]** at the dhcp server> prompt. The prompt then changes to "dhcp server scope>." The subcommands that follow can be executed from the dhcp server scope> prompt.

ADD EXCLUDERANGE   Adds a range of excluded addresses to the current scope.

ADD IPRANGE   Adds a range of IP addresses to the current scope.

ADD RESERVEDIP   Reserves an IP address for use by a specified MAC address.

DELETE EXCLUDERANGE   Deletes an exclusion range of previously excluded IP addresses.

DELETE IPRANGE   Deletes a range of IP addresses from the current scope.

DELETE OPTIONVALUE   Removes or clears an assigned scope option value.

DELETE RESERVEDIP   Deletes a reservation for an IP address.

INITIATE RECONCILE   Checks and reconciles the current scope.

SET NAME   Sets the name of the current scope.

SET OPTIONVALUE   Sets an option value for the current scope.

SET SCOPE   Sets the scope to be used in subsequent operations. Typically used in a batch file.

SET STATE *ACTIVE|INACTIVE*   Sets/resets the state of a current scope to either active or inactive.

SET SUPERSCOPE   Sets the superscope to be used in subsequent operations. Typically used in a batch file.

SHOW CLIENTS   Displays all available version 4 clients for the scope.

SHOW CLIENTSV5   Displays all available version 5 clients for the scope.

SHOW EXCLUDERANGE   Displays all currently excluded ranges of IP addresses.

SHOW IPRANGE   Displays all available address ranges for the scope.

SHOW OPTIONVALUE   Displays all option values.

SHOW RESERVEDIP   Displays all currently reserved IP addresses.

SHOW SCOPE   Displays all information about the current scope.

SHOW STATE   Displays the state of the current scope as to whether it is active or inactive.

12

Chapter Summary

This chapter covers the basics of name resolution in a Windows Server 2003 environment. It includes basic configuration and troubleshooting of DNS, which is the name resolution service used by Active Directory. You also learned about WINS, a legacy name resolution service that allows NetBIOS names to be resolved to IP addresses. To assign those IP addresses automatically, you can use DHCP.

COMMAND SUMMARY

Command	Function
DNSCMD	Used to set up and configure new DNS servers on a network.
NSLOOKUP	Used to verify resource records and troubleshoot DNS issues.
NETSH - CWINS	Subcommand of NETSH used to start the WINS context of the NETSH command program.
NETSH WINS> INIT SCAVENGE	Used to initiate the scavenge feature on the specified WINS server.
NETSH - CDHCP	Starts the DHCP context of the NETSH command program.
NETSH DHCP> SERVER	Contacts a DHCP server by name or IP address.
NETSH DHCP SERVER> SCOPE	Used to configure a specific scope on a specified DHCP server.

KEY TERMS

Active Directory integrated zone — A type of DNS zone that stores its zone information inside Active Directory.

child node — A node in the DNS structure beneath a parent node; a subdomain.

conditional forwarder — A new feature of the Microsoft DNS service incorporated into Windows Server 2003. This features allows a DNS server to forward DNS queries according to specified domain names.

context — A grouping of commands for a specific network component.

dynamic link library (DLL) — A collection of small programs, any of which can be called when needed by a larger program that is running on the computer. The small program that lets the larger program communicate with a specific device such as a printer or scanner is often packaged as a DLL program.

exclusion range — A range of IP addresses that are excluded from a scope. They are typically used for Web servers and other computers that need to have an IP address that is set statically.

forward lookup zone — Resolves a hostname to an IP address.

Internet Group Management Protocol (IGMP) — An Internet protocol that provides a way for a computer to report its multi-cast group membership to adjacent routers.

InterNIC — An organization licensed to the Internet Corporation for Assigned Names and Numbers, it registers public domain names.

LMHOST file — A text file located in the %systemroot%\ system32\drivers\etc folder that contains static records of IP address to NetBIOS names to IP address resolution. Replaced by WINS. Similar to a HOSTS file.

name server — The "server" component in the client-server architecture of a DNS system.

resolver — The "client" component in the client-server architecture of a DNS system. Clients send DNS query requests to name servers.

reverse lookup zone — Resolves an IP address to a hostname.

root node — The topmost node in the DNS hierarchy, it is represented by a period (.) or "".

round-robin rotation — A method of load distribution used by DNS servers.

scope — The full consecutive range of possible IP addresses for a network. Typically a subnet or logical network segment.

zone — A storage database for a single DNS domain name.

REVIEW QUESTIONS

1. Which command issued in **NSLOOKUP** interactive mode returns you to the command prompt?

   a. **QUIT**

   b. **RETURN**

   c. **EXIT**

   d. **END**

2. To obtain more information on adding records to the DNS database using the **DNSCMD** command, what would you type?

   a. **dnscmd /recordadd /?**

   b. **dnscmd help /recordadd**

   c. **dnscmd /addrecord /?**

   d. **dnscmd help /addrecord**

3. To install DNS on a Windows Server 2003 system, you must be a member of which of the following group(s)? (Choose all that apply.)

   a. Power Users

   b. Server Administrator

   c. Domain Admins

   d. Administrators local

4. DNS uses which of the following replication models?

   a. single-master replication model

   b. multi-master replication model

   c. distributed-replication model

   d. depends on the DNS zone type being used

12

5. To get a printout of zone information, which command would you issue?

   a. **dnscmd /list**

   b. **dnscmd /zoneprint**

   c. **dnscmd /printzoneinfo**

   d. **dnscmd /printzone**

6. Forward Lookup Zones perform which type of name resolution?

   a. resolve hostname(s) to IP address(es)

   b. resolve NetBIOS names to IP addresses

   c. resolve a host's IP address to a hostname

   d. resolve a host's IP address to a NetBIOS name

7. Name the **NSLOOKUP** command mode(s). (Choose all that apply.)

   a. mixed mode

   b. interactive mode

   c. native mode

   d. non-interactive mode

8. Which type of DNS zone stores its zone information in Active Directory?

   a. stub zone

   b. standard primary

   c. Active Directory integrated

   d. standard secondary

9. DNS servers use _____ to distribute work among multiple hosts.

   a. a round-robin query

   b. the Network Load Balance Service

   c. directory-integrated zones

   d. the **dnscmd /workdistrib** command

10. A storage database for a single DNS domain is called a _____.

   a. database partition

   b. zone

   c. subdomain

   d. DNS area

11. WINS handles name resolution for what type of names?

    a. NetBIOS

    b. hosts

    c. A records

    d. MX records

12. WINS stands for _____.

    a. Windows Internal Naming System

    b. Windows Internal Naming Service

    c. Windows Internet Name Service

    d. Windows Integrity Nameresolution Service

13. You can have push, pull, and push/pull replication partners in WINS.

    a. True

    b. False

14. Extinct records that will be replicated to other WINS servers in the WINS database are called _____.

    a. inactive

    b. tombstoned

    c. cyclical

    d. archived

15. WINS is dependent upon DNS.

    a. True

    b. False

16. What is the message that is sent by the DHCP server to the client after being contacted for an IP address?

    a. DHCPOFFER

    b. DHCPACK

    c. DHCPIP

    d. DHCPCLACK

17. Which of the following commands would exclude a range of IP addresses from a scope?

    a. `dhcp server>add excluderange 192.168.10.25 192.168.10.32`

    b. `dhcp> add excluderange 192.168.10.25 192.168.10.32`

    c. `dhcp server scope> add excluderange 192.168.10.25 192.168.10.32`

    d. `server scope> add excluderange 192.168.10.25 192.168.10.32`

12

18. Which of these are reasons to use the **NETSH** command when working with WINS or DHCP? (Choose two.)

    a. The commands are much simpler than the GUI.

    b. The commands take up less bandwidth across WAN links.

    c. You can batch the commands and use them on multiple servers.

    d. DHCP can only be administered with **NETSH**.

19. DHCP uses _____ to assign IP addresses.

    a. addresses

    b. scopes

    c. zones

    d. option fields

20. DHCP and WINS are installed by default when installing Windows Server 2003.

    a. True

    b. False

DISCOVERY EXERCISES

1. Enable the DNS service on a Windows Server 2003 system. Statically place a host record for yourself into the database.

2. Install the DHCP service on a Windows Server 2003 system. Enable a scope of IP addresses and activate the DHCP service. Add another Windows 2000 Professional or Windows XP workstation on the network segment and set it for DHCP configuration. When the workstation boots up on the network, see if it receives an IP address from the scope you enabled. Try reserving that IP address in your scope and see if the workstation will renew the same address or receive a new one.

3. Install the WINS service on two different Windows Server 2003 servers. Enable one WINS server as a push/pull partner and the other as simply a push partner. Add two or three workstations on the network and see if their NetBIOS names are registered on both WINS servers.

4. Almost every business wants, or needs, to be able to send e-mail across the Internet. In order to use e-mail, you must have an e-mail server. E-mail servers use the Simple Mail Transport Protocol (SMTP) and TCP/IP. Internet e-mail servers require an IP address and two important entries into the DNS database. One type of required DNS record an e-mail needs is called an MX (mail exchanger) record. When troubleshooting e-mail problems, it is very common to verify an entry of an MX record in the DNS. Use **NSLOOKUP** to verify an MX record for your e-mail server.

5. You are the DNS administrator for your organization. You are currently responsible for a single zone. You have a primary and secondary DNS server. You are encountering problems when trying to perform zone transfers between your primary and secondary DNS servers. You ping both servers and get a response verifying that your servers are running. After troubleshooting, you want to verify that that authoritative zone data is correct. Use the Windows Server 2003 Help and Support Center to learn how to troubleshoot zone transfers using the **NSLOOKUP** command.

6. You are the LAN administrator for a large office. Your company recently purchased a new laser printer and wants it to be shared on the network. Your network is configured with a DHCP server that manages the IP addresses of all your client computers. Your new printer does not support DHCP and requires a static IP address. Use the **NETSH** command to reserve an IP address for your new printer.

12

APPENDIX

A

COMMAND DICTIONARY

<COMMAND> /?

Displays help about the specified command.

:<ROUTINE>

A batch-specific command for the *ROUTINE* tag, the place to which the GOTO command jumps. All commands after this point are executed unless another GOTO statement directs the operation to another subroutine.

@ECHO OFF

Turns command echoes off and does not display any results.

<COMMAND> >NUL

Eliminates *COMMAND* output.

><LOCATION>

At the end of a command, redirects output to *LOCATION*; *LOCATION* can be a file or port.

>><LOCATION>

At the end of a command, redirects output to *LOCATION*; appends to existing *LOCATION*; *LOCATION* can be a file or port.

AT

Schedules programs and other commands.

AT \\<COMPUTERNAME> <TIMEOFDAY> /EVERY: <DAYOFMONTH> <COMMAND>

Schedules the *COMMAND* to run at the specified time every month on the specified date (1, 2...31).

AT \\<COMPUTERNAME> <TIMEOFDAY> /EVERY: M| T| W| TH| F| S| SU <COMMAND>

Schedules the *COMMAND* to run at the specified time every day on the indicated day.

AT \\<COMPUTERNAME> <TIMEOFDAY> /INTERACTIVE <COMMAND>

Schedules the *COMMAND* to run at the specified time, allowing it to interact with the currently logged-on user.

AT \\\<COMPUTERNAME> \<TIMEOFDAY> \<COMMAND>

Schedules the *COMMAND* to occur on the networked computer at the specified time.

AT \<TIMEOFDAY> /EVERY:\<DAYOFMONTH> \<COMMAND>

Schedules the *COMMAND* to run at *TIMEOFDAY* every month on *DAYOFMONTH*; *DAYOFMONTH* is a number from 1 to 31.

AT \<TIMEOFDAY> /EVERY:M|T|W|TH|F|S|SU \<COMMAND>

Schedules the *COMMAND* to run at *TIMEOFDAY* every specified day. Days may be used in combination by listing multiple days separated by a slash (M/T/F), or a comma (M,T,F).

AT \<TIMEOFDAY> \<COMMAND>

Schedules the *COMMAND* to occur on the local machine at *TIMEOFDAY*.

ATTRIB \<DIRECTORY> \<ANY ATTRIBUTES> /S /D

Applies the specified attributes to the files within the current directory.

ATTRIB \<FILENAME>

Displays the attributes associated with the specified file.

ATTRIB \<FILENAME> +A

Changes the file's attribute to archived.

ATTRIB \<FILENAME> +H

Changes the file's attribute to hidden.

ATTRIB \<FILENAME> +R

Changes the file's attribute to read-only.

ATTRIB \<FILENAME> +S

Changes the file's attribute to system.

ATTRIB \<FILENAME> \<ANYATTRIBUTES> /S /D

Applies the specified attributes to the files in the current directory and all files in all subdirectories.

ATTRIB \<FILENAME> –A

Removes the archive attribute from the file.

ATTRIB \<FILENAME> –H

Removes the hidden attribute from the file.

ATTRIB *<FILENAME>* –R
Removes the read-only attribute from the file.

ATTRIB *<FILENAME>* –S
Removes the system attribute from the file.

BOOTCFG /DEFAULT /ID *<OS#>*
Sets the default operating system (the line number for the OS displayed using the /QUERY option) with which the system boots.

BOOTCFG /DEFAULT /ID *<OS#>* /S *<COMPUTER>* /U *<USERNAME>* /P *<PASSWORD>*
On a multi-OS system, sets the default operating system (the line number for the OS displayed using the /QUERY option) with which the remote system boots. The specified username and password are authenticated on the remote computer.

BOOTCFG /QUERY
Displays the boot and OS sections of the boot.ini file.

BOOTCFG /QUERY /S *<COMPUTER /U <USERNAME>>* /P *<PASSWORD>*
Displays the boot.ini configuration for the specified remote computer using the indicated administrative username and password.

BOOTCFG /TIMEOUT *<SECONDS>*
Sets the amount of time the system waits before automatically selecting the default OS.

BOOTCFG /TIMEOUT *<SECONDS>* /S *<COMPUTER>* /U *<USERNAME>* /P *<PASSWORD>*
On a multi-OS system, sets the amount of time the remote system waits before automatically selecting the default OS. The specified username and password are authenticated on the remote computer.

CACLS *<FILENAME>*
Displays the current permissions for the file.

CACLS *<FILENAME>* /D *<USERNAME>*
Deletes the entry for the specified user from the file.

CACLS *<FILENAME>* /G *<USERNAME>:N | R | W | C | F*
Grants the user access to the folder or file with the specified permission (None, Read, Write, Change, or Full Control).

CACLS *<FILENAME>* /G *<USERNAME>*: *N | R | W | C | F* /E

Edits the existing user access to include the specified permission.

CACLS *<FILENAME>* /G *<USERNAME>*: *N | R | W | C | F* /T

Grants the user access to the folder, its contents, and all subfolders with the specified permission.

CACLS *<FILENAME>* /P *<USERNAME>*: *N | R | W | C | F*

Replaces the existing folder or file permissions with the specified permission for the user.

CACLS *<FILENAME>* /P *<USERNAME>*: *N | R | W | C | F* /T

Same as the previous command, but applies to all subfolders.

CACLS *<FILENAME>*/R *<USERNAME>* /E

Revokes all access to the file.

CALL *<BATCHFILE>*

Executes a subsequent batch routine (subprogram), and resumes command execution once the subprogram commands have been processed.

CALL *<BATCHFILE>*: *<ROUTINE>*

Executes only the specific subroutine within the subprogram. Execution of the parent batch routine resumes after the subprogram is completed.

CALL *<BATCHFILE>* *<PARAMETER1>* *<PARAMETER2>* *<PARAMETER3>*

Executes a subroutine with the specified parameters, and resumes command execution once the specified subprogram commands have been processed.

CD ..

Changes to the parent directory of the current directory.

CD ..*<SUBDIRECTORY>*

Changes to a subdirectory of the parent directory. Also known as a sister directory to the current directory.

**CD **

Changes to the root of the current drive.

CD *<DRIVE>*:

Changes to the last-used directory located on the new drive.

CD <DRIVE>:\

Changes to the root of the new drive.

CD <DRIVE>:\<DIRECTORY>

Changes the current directory to the new drive and directory.

CHANGE LOGON /DISABLE

Disables logons for all types of network connections, including network logons and Remote Desktop logons.

CHANGE LOGON /ENABLE

Enables server logon for all sessions.

CHKDSK <DRIVELETTER>:

Scans the specified drive for physical disk problems.

CHKDSK <DRIVELETTER>: /F

Scans for and fixes physical disk problems.

CHKDSK <DRIVELETTER>: /R

Scans for physical disk errors and recovers readable data.

CHKDSK <DRIVELETTER>: /V

Scans for physical disk problems and reports file-by-file progress to the screen.

CHKDSK <DRIVELETTER>: /X

Dismounts the volume and then scans for physical disk errors.

CHKNTFS /X <DRIVELETTER>:

Excludes the specified drive from the CHKDSK process.

CHKNTFS <DRIVELETTER>:

Displays the status of whether CHKDSK runs automatically when the system boots.

CHKNTFS <DRIVELETTER>: /C

Sets the specified drive to be scanned when the system reboots.

CHKNTFS <DRIVELETTER>: /T:<SECONDS>

When the system reboots, the system displays a countdown to cancel the CHKDSK operation before it begins. /T sets the countdown timer.

CHOICE /C <*KEYLIST*>

Prompts the user to press one of the listed keys. If the user presses a key that is not on the *KEYLIST*, the entry is ignored.

CHOICE /C <*KEYLIST*> /M "<*PROMPTMSG*>"

Prompts the user to press one of the listed keys, displaying the *PROMPTMSG* before the prompt.

CHOICE /C <*KEYLIST*> /N

Prompts the user to press one of the listed keys, but does not display the *KEYLIST*.

CHOICE /C <*KEYLIST*> /T <*TIMEOUT*> /D <*DEFAULTKEY*>

Prompts the user to press one of the listed keys within the specified *TIMEOUT* period. If no entry is received, the *DEFAULTKEY* entry is specified by the system.

CIPHER /E /A <*FILENAME*>

Encrypts *FILENAME*.

CIPHER /E /S:<*DIRECTORY*>

Encrypts *DIRECTORY* and all of its contents. Any file subsequently added to this directory is automatically encrypted. Files removed from this directory are decrypted when they are saved elsewhere.

CIPHER /K

Creates a new key for the current user.

CIPHER /R:<*FILENAME NO EXTENSION*>

Restores the EFS keys for the current user from *FILENAME*.

CIPHER /U /N

Updates the current user-encrypted files to the current key.

CIPHER /X:<*FILENAME* >

Backs up the EFS keys for the current user to *FILENAME*.

CIPHER <*DIRECTORY*>*

Displays the encryption status of all files within *DIRECTORY*.

CLS

Clears the screen.

A

CMD /F:ON

Turns on directory and filename completion.

CMD /K

From the Start menu's Run line, runs the command and leaves the window open.

CMD /Q

Turns echo off.

CMD /T:BT

Changes the background and text colors: 0=black; 1=blue; 2=green; 3=aqua; 4=red; 5=purple; 6=yellow; 7=white; 8=gray; 9=light blue; a=light green; b=light aqua; c= light red; d=light purple; e=light yellow; f=bright white.

CMD <COMMAND> /C

From the Start menu's Run line, runs the command and closes the command window.

CMDKEY /ADD:<COMPUTER or DOMAIN NAME> /USER: <COMPUTER or DOMAIN NAME>\<USERNAME> /PASS:<PASSWORD>

Adds the remote resource (*COMPUTER* or *DOMAIN NAME*) to be accessed using the account (*COMPUTER* or *DOMAIN NAME\USERNAME*) with the specified password.

CMDKEY /ADD: <COMPUTER or DOMAIN NAME> /SMARTCARD

Adds the remote resource and obtains the username and password from the smartcard. A smartcard is a small physical device containing encrypted account and password information that is plugged into the system. Smartcards offer additional security against detection of an account name and password by monitoring keystrokes or watching a user enter the information.

CMDKEY /ADD:<COMPUTER or DOMAIN NAME> /USER: <COMPUTER or DOMAIN NAME>\<USERNAME>

Adds the remote resource to be accessed using the account with no password.

CMDKEY /ADD:<COMPUTER or DOMAIN NAME> /USER: <COMPUTER or DOMAIN NAME>\<USERNAME> /PASS

Adds the remote resource (*COMPUTER* or *DOMAIN NAME*) to be accessed using the account (*COMPUTER* or *DOMAIN NAME\USERNAME*) with a blank password.

CMDKEY /LIST

Lists locally stored usernames and passwords.

CMDKEY /LIST:<*COMPUTER or DOMAIN NAME*>

Searches for the specified computer or domain within the current list of stored usernames and passwords.

COMPACT /C <*FILENAME*>

Compresses the specified file.

COMPACT /C /S:<*DIRECTORY*>

Compresses *DIRECTORY* and all subdirectories within it.

COMPACT /U /F <*FILENAME*>

Forces extraction (uncompression) of the specified file and is used to fully uncompress a partially uncompressed file.

COMPACT /U /S:<*DIRECTORY*>

Extracts *DIRECTORY* and all subdirectories within it.

COMPACT /U <*FILENAME*>

Extracts the specified file.

CONVERT <*DRIVELETTER*>: /FS:NTFS

Converts the format to NTFS for *DRIVELETTER*.

CONVERT <*DRIVELETTER*>:/FS:NTFS /CVTAREA: <*FILENAME*>

Converts the *DRIVELETTER*'s format to NTFS and places the new system files at the beginning of the drive.

CONVERT <*DRIVELETTER*>:/FS:NTFS /NOSECURITY

Converts the *DRIVELETTER*'s format to NTFS and nullifies all security settings.

CONVERT <*DRIVELETTER*>: /FS:NTFS /X

Dismounts the drive prior to converting the format to NTFS.

COPY <*FILENAME1*> <*DESTINATIONPATH*>

Copies the original file, *FILENAME1*, into the destination location, *DESTINATIONPATH*.

COPY <*FILENAME1*> <*FILENAME2*>

Copies the original file, *FILENAME1*, and names it *FILENAME2*. *FILENAME1* and *FILENAME2* can be the same filename, as long as the destination directory that is included in *FILENAME2* is different from the source directory containing *FILENAME1*.

A

COPY <*FILENAME1*> <*FILENAME2*> /Y

Copies the files, and does not prompt to overwrite any pre-existing files named *FILENAME2*. Without the /Y, the system prompts you to overwrite any existing file with the *FILENAME2* name.

COPY <*FILENAME1*> <*FILENAME2*> /-Y

Copies the files, and prompts to overwrite any pre-existing files named *FILENAME2*. This is the default setup for COPY.

COPY <*FILENAME1*> <*FILENAME2*> /Z

Copies the files, and restarts a failed copy from the point of failure.

CSVDE

Imports and exports Active Directory data from a comma-separated file.

DCPROMO

Starts the Active Directory Installation Wizard.

DEFRAG <*DRIVELETTER*>: /A

Runs an analysis and determines whether the drive needs to be defragmented.

DEFRAG <*DRIVELETTER*>: /A /V

Same as above, but displays detailed status as it runs the analysis.

DEFRAG <*DRIVELETTER*>: /F

Defragments the drive only when free disk space is approaching 15 percent of total disk capacity.

DEFRAG <*DRIVELETTER*>: /V

Defragments the drive and displays detailed results.

DEL <*FILENAME*> /A:<*ATTRIBUTES*>

Deletes the specified files based on their attributes. R=read-only files, S=system files, H=hidden files, A=changed files (archive bit on), –R=not read-only files, –S=not system files, –H=not hidden, –A=unchanged files (archive bit off). For example, `del *.*  /A:S` deletes all system files in the current directory.

DEL <*FILENAME*> /F

Deletes the specified file(s), including read-only files.

DEL <*FILENAME*> /Q

Deletes the specified file(s) without confirmation.

DEL *<FILENAME>* **/S**

Deletes the specified file(s) from all subdirectories.

DIR

Lists the contents of a directory. Use /P or /MORE to display a list one screen at a time.

DIR /A

Lists a directory's contents, including system and hidden files.

DIR /AD

Lists all directories.

DIR /AH

Lists all hidden files within the directory.

DIR /AR

Lists all read-only files within the directory.

DIR /AS

Lists all system files within the directory.

DIR /OD

Lists files by date and time, from oldest to newest. Use /O-D to sort by newest file first.

DIR /OE

Lists files by file extensions alphabetically. Use /O-E to sort by reverse alphabetization.

DIR /OG

Lists contents of a directory with subdirectories shown first.

DIR /ON

Lists files alphabetically by name. Use /O-N to sort by reverse alphabetization.

DIR /OS

Lists by smallest file size first. Use /O-S to sort by largest file size first.

DIR /Q

Lists the files within the current directory, along with an additional column indicating file ownership.

DIR /S

Lists the contents of the current directory, all subdirectories, and their contents.

DIR /TA

Lists contents with the date and time the file(s) were last accessed.

DIR /TC

Lists contents with the date and time the file(s) were created.

DIR /TW

Lists contents with the date and time the file(s) were written or updated.

DIR <DRIVE>:\<DIRECTORY>

Lists the contents of the new drive and directory without navigating the prompt to the directory itself.

DIR <FILENAME>

Displays the specified file.

DIR <FILENAME> /Q

Lists the owner of the specified file.

DISKCOPY <DRIVELETTER1> <DRIVELETTER2> /V

Copies the contents of the disk in *DRIVELETTER1* to *DRIVELETTER2* and verifies successful completion.

DISKPART | ACTIVE

Mounts the specified partition.

DISKPART | ADD DISK=<DISKNUMBER>

Adds a mirror to the specified volume, where *DISKNUMBER* is the number of the second disk.

DISKPART | ASSIGN LETTER=<DRIVELETTER>

Assigns the selected volume a drive letter.

DISKPART | BREAK DISK=<DISKNUMBER>

Breaks a mirrored volume into two separate simple volumes. *DISKNUMBER* is the disk that does not belong to the selected volume.

DISKPART|BREAK DISK=<*DISKNUMBER*> /NOKEEP

Same as the previous command, but deletes the current selected simple volume and retains only one half of the mirror.

DISKPART|CLEAN

Removes all data and information from a drive.

DISKPART|CONVERT BASIC

Converts the selected dynamic disk (SELECT DISK) to a basic disk. This command only succeeds if the disk has no volumes or data on it.

DISKPART|CONVERT DYNAMIC

Converts the selected disk (SELECT DISK) to a dynamic disk. At least 1 MB of free space must be available on the selected disk.

DISKPART|CREATE PARTITION EXTENDED SIZE=<*PARTITIONSIZE*>

Creates an extended partition of *PARTITIONSIZE* with the size in megabytes.

DISKPART|CREATE PARTITION LOGICAL SIZE=<*PARTITIONSIZE*>

Creates a logical drive based on an existing extended partition.

DISKPART|CREATE PARTITION PRIMARY SIZE=<*PARTITIONSIZE*>

Creates a primary partition of *PARTITIONSIZE* with the size in megabytes.

DISKPART|CREATE VOLUME RAID SIZE=<*SPACEPERDISK*> DISK=<*DISKNUMBER1*>, <*DISKNUMBER2*>, <*DISKNUMBER3*>

Creates a RAID 5 volume whose width is *SPACEPERDISK* across the specified disks.

DISKPART|CREATE VOLUME SIMPLE SIZE=<*VOLUMESIZE*>

Creates a simple volume of *VOLUMESIZE* in megabytes.

DISKPART|CREATE VOLUME STRIPE SIZE=<*SPACEPERDISK*> DISK=<*DISKNUMBER1*>, <*DISKNUMBER2*>, <*DISKNUMBER3*>

Creates a stripe set whose width is *SPACEPERDISK* across each of the specified disks.

DISKPART|DELETE DISK

Deletes the selected disk. Applies to an entire disk (not drive), partition, or volume.

DISKPART|DELETE PARTITION

Deletes the specified partition.

A

DISKPART | DELETE VOLUME

Deletes the specified volume.

DISKPART | DETAIL DISK

Displays disk information, including type, ID, and volume information.

DISKPART | DETAIL PARTITION

Lists details on the specified partition, including volume number, drive letter, drive label, file system format, type, size, and status.

DISKPART | DETAIL VOLUME

Displays statistics for the specified volume, including number, drive letter, label, format type, volume type, and size.

DISKPART | EXTEND DISK=<DISKNUMBER> SIZE=<SIZE>

Extends a selected volume, *DISKNUMBER*, to add the *SIZE* in megabytes. Unallocated free space must exist on the disk.

DISKPART | IMPORT

Integrates another system's volume into the current server without reconfiguring the volume or losing the data.

DISKPART | INACTIVE

Dismounts the specified partition.

DISKPART | LIST DISK

Lists the physical disks installed on the server. Currently selected disk appears with an asterisk (*) to the left of the entry.

DISKPART | LIST PARTITION

Lists all partitions on the specified disk.

DISKPART | LIST VOLUME

Lists volumes on the specified disk.

DISKPART | ONLINE

Attempts to mount and bring the specified disk online.

DISKPART | REPAIR DISK=<REPLACEDDISKNUMBER>

Repairs a failed and replaced RAID disk.

DISKPART|RESCAN

Scans the systems disk configuration to reflect any changes.

DISKPART|SELECT DISK <*DISKNUMBER*>

Selects the disk upon which subsequent commands will be performed. *DISKNUMBER* is obtained from the LIST DISK command.

DISKPART|SELECT PARTITION <*PARTITIONNUMBER*>

Selects a partition for subsequent partition-related commands. *PARTITIONNUMBER* comes from the DISKPART|LIST PARTITION command.

DISKPART|SELECT VOLUME <*VOLUMENUMBER*>

Selects the *VOLUMENUMBER* that was listed in the LIST VOLUME command.

DOSKEY

Allows the system to maintain a list of previously executed commands, which are available for recall using the up and down arrow keys.

DRIVERQUERY

Displays a table containing all of the loaded drivers on the system.

DRIVERQUERY /FO *TABLE*|*LIST*|*CSV* /NH

Displays a table with the current drivers in the chosen output format (table, list, or comma delimited) with no header information.

DRIVERQUERY /S <*COMPUTERNAME*> /FO *TABLE*|*LIST*|*CSV* /NH

Displays the current drivers in either table, list, or comma-delimited format with no header information for a remote system.

DRIVERQUERY /S <*COMPUTERNAME*> /SI

Displays information about signed drivers for a remote system.

DRIVERQUERY /S <*COMPUTERNAME*> /U <*USERNAME*> /P <*PASSWORD*>

Displays a list of the installed device drivers for the specified remote computer where username and password credentials are used to access the remote system.

DRIVERQUERY /SI

Displays information about signed drivers.

DRIVERQUERY /V

Displays detailed information about system drivers.

DSADD

Adds objects such as users, computers, contacts, groups, and organizational units to Active Directory.

DSADD COMPUTER <*COMPUTERNAME*>

Adds a computer to Active Directory.

DSADD CONTACT <*CONTACTNAME*>

Adds a contact to Active Directory.

DSADD GROUP <*GROUPNAME*>

Adds a group to Active Directory.

DSADD OU <*OUNAME*>

Adds an organizational unit to Active Directory.

DSADD USER <*USERDISTINGUISHEDNAME*> -CANCHPWD *YES*|*NO*

Specifies whether the user can change his or her password. Use DSMOD to modify an existing user account.

DSADD USER <*USERDISTINGUISHEDNAME*> -DISABLED *YES*|*NO*

Setting this option to YES prevents a user from logging on to the network. Use DSMOD to modify an existing user account.

DSADD USER <*USERDISTINGUISHEDNAME*>-MAIL (*EMAILADDRESS*)

Sets the user's e-mail address. Use DSMOD to modify an existing user account.

DSADD USER <*USERDISTINGUISHEDNAME*> -MOBILE (*MOBILEPHONENUMBER*)

Sets the user's cell phone number. Use DSMOD to modify an existing user account.

DSADD USER <*USERDISTINGUISHEDNAME*> -MUSTCHPWD *YES*|*NO*

Determines whether the user must change his or her password at next logon. Use DSMOD to modify an existing user account.

DSADD USER <*USERDISTINGUISHEDNAME*> -PWD (*PASSWORD*)

Sets the user's new password. Use DSMOD to modify an existing user account.

DSGET

Shows attributes of a specified object.

DSMOD
Modifies users, computers, servers, contacts, organizational units, or groups.

DSMOVE
Renames or moves an object.

DSQUERY
Queries Active Directory for a list of objects using a specified search criteria.

DSRM
Removes objects from Active Directory.

ECHO <*MESSAGE*>
Displays the specified message on the screen.

ECHO OFF
Does not display program output on the screen.

ECHO ON
Displays program output on the screen.

EDIT
Opens the Edit program.

EDIT <*FILENAME*>
Opens *FILENAME* using the Edit program.

EDIT <*FILENAME*> /R
Opens *FILENAME* as read-only using the Edit program.

EVENTCREATE /L APPLICATION /SO <*ADMINISTRATOR* or *APPLICATION NAME*> /T ERROR|*WARNING*|*INFORMATION* /ID <*EVENT ID*> /D <*DESCRIPTION*>
Creates an event in the event viewer's application log on the specified remote computer with *ADMINISTRATOR* or *APPLICATION NAME* as the title, an event type of *ERROR*, *WARNING*, or *INFORMATION*, the specified *EVENT ID*, and the *DESCRIPTION*.

A

EVENTCREATE /S <COMPUTERNAME> /U <USERNAME> /P <PASSWORD> /L APPLICATION /SO <ADMINISTRATOR or APPLICATION NAME> /T ERROR|WARNING|INFORMATION /ID <EVENT ID> /D <DESCRIPTION>

Creates an application event for the event viewer on the specified remote computer with *ADMINISTRATOR* or *APPLICATION NAME* as the title, an event type of *ERROR*, *WARNING*, or *INFORMATION*, the specified *EVENT ID*, and the *DESCRIPTION*. *EVENT ID* can be any number, and *DESCRIPTION* should be a word or phrase that adequately describes the event.

EVENTQUERY /S <COMPUTERNAME> /U <USERNAME> /P <PASSWORD>

Displays all events in the event logs for the specified remote computer using the *USERNAME* and *PASSWORD*.

EVENTQUERY /S <COMPUTERNAME> /U <USERNAME> /P <PASSWORD> /FI "TYPE EQ ERROR| WARNING|INFORMATION"

Displays all events in the event logs for the specified remote computer where the event type is an *ERROR*, *WARNING*, or *INFORMATION*.

EVENTQUERY /S <COMPUTERNAME> /U <USERNAME> /P <PASSWORD> /FO TABLE|LIST|CSV /NH

Displays all events in the event logs for the specified remote computer in the specified output format of table, list, or comma delimited for the remote computer using the *USERNAME* and *PASSWORD*. Used primarily with redirection to a file.

EXIT

Closes the current existence of CMD.

EXPAND <CABFILE> <DESTINATIONDIR>

Extracts the contents of the .cab file into the *DESTINATIONDIR* directory. If *DESTINATIONDIR* is empty, files are extracted and placed in the destination directory.

EXPAND <CABFILE> -F:<FILENAME> <DESTINATION FILE or DIRECTORY>

Extracts the *FILENAME* from the .cab file and places it into the *DESTINATION FILE* or *DIRECTORY*.

EXPAND –D <CABFILE>

Displays a list of the .cab file contents.

EXPAND –R <DISTRIBUTION FILE> <DESTINATION FILE>

Extracts *DISTRIBUTION FILE* and renames it *DESTINATION FILE*.

FIND <FILENAME> "<STRING>"

Scans the contents of the *FILENAME* and outputs lines containing the *STRING*.

FIND <*FILENAME*> "<*STRING*>" /C

Scans the contents of the *FILENAME* and outputs the number of lines within the file that contain the *STRING*.

FIND <*FILENAME*> "<*STRING*>" /I

Scans the contents of the *FILENAME* for the specified string in either uppercase or lowercase letters, and outputs the data containing the *STRING*.

FIND <*FILENAME*> "<*STRING*>" /N

Scans the contents of the *FILENAME* and outputs line numbers and data containing the *STRING*.

FIND <*FILENAME*> "<*STRING*>" /V

Scans the contents of the *FILENAME* and outputs lines that do not contain the *STRING*.

FINDSTR /B "<*STRING*>" <*FILENAME*>

Finds and displays the entire line(s) containing the *STRING* within the *FILENAME* where the string is at the beginning of the line.

FINDSTR /C:<*STRING*> <*FILENAME*>

Finds and displays lines containing the *STRING* within the *FILENAME*. The *STRING* cannot contain any regular expressions and does not require quotation marks.

FINDSTR /E "<*STRING*>" <*FILENAME*>

Finds and displays lines containing the *STRING* within the *FILENAME* where the *STRING* is at the end of the line.

FINDSTR /I "<*STRING*>" <*FILENAME*>

Finds and displays lines containing the *STRING* within the *FILENAME* without regard to uppercase or lowercase letters.

FINDSTR /L "<*STRING*>" <*FILENAME*>

Finds and displays lines containing the *STRING* within the *FILENAME*. The *STRING* cannot contain any regular expressions.

FINDSTR /M "<*STRING*>" <*FILENAME*>

Displays *FILENAME*s containing the *STRING*.

FINDSTR /N "<*STRING*>" <*FILENAME*>

Finds and displays line numbers and lines containing the *STRING* within the *FILENAME*.

FINDSTR /P "<STRING>" <FILENAME>

Finds and displays lines containing the *STRING* within the *FILENAME* where the file(s) do not contain non-printable characters.

FINDSTR /S "<STRING>" <FILENAME>

Finds and displays lines containing the *STRING* within the *FILENAME* in the current directory and all subdirectories. Similar to the /S option for the DIR command.

FINDSTR /X "<STRING>" <FILENAME>

Finds and displays lines containing the *STRING* within the *FILENAME*. Used when the *STRING* is intended to search for an entire phrase rather than single words.

FINDSTR "$<STRING>" <FILENAME>

A regular expression that finds and displays lines containing the *STRING* within the *FILENAME* where the *STRING* is at the end of the line.

FINDSTR "\!<STRING>" <FILENAME>

Finds and displays lines containing the *STRING* within the *FILENAME* where the character represented by "!" is literal. Used to negate regular expression characters (*^$.*) when you want to search for these symbols within a regular expression. An example would be to search for the dollar amount $100, which would be `FINDSTR "/$100" *.*` .

FINDSTR "^<STRING>" <FILENAME>

A regular expression that finds and displays the entire line(s) containing the *STRING* within the *FILENAME* where the *STRING* is at the beginning of the line.

FINDSTR "<STRING>" <FILENAME>

Finds and displays the entire line(s) containing the *STRING* within the *FILENAME*.

FOR %%N IN (<FILENAME1>, <FILENAME2>) DO IF "<PARAMETERNUMBER>" =="%%N" <COMMAND>

For every file, runs the COMMAND if the *PARAMETERNUMBER* and the object are equal.

FOR %%N IN (<LIST>) DO <COMMAND>

Performs the *COMMAND* for every item on the *LIST*.

FOR %%N IN (<LIST>) DO <COMMAND> %%N

For each item on the *LIST*, the *COMMAND* is performed with a parameter of that item.

FOR %%N IN (<*LIST*>) DO IF "<*PARAMETERNUMBER*>"=="%%N" <*COMMAND*>

Compares every object on the *LIST* to the *PARAMETERNUMBER*. If the two are equal, runs the *COMMAND*.

FOR %%N IN (<*VARIABLE*>) DO <*COMMAND*>

Performs the *COMMAND* for every item in the *VARIABLE*.

FOR %%N IN (<*VARIABLE*>) DO <*COMMAND*> %%N

For each item in the *VARIABLE*, the *COMMAND* is performed with a parameter of that item.

FOR %%N IN (<*VARIABLE*>) DO IF "<*PARAMETERNUMBER*>"=="%%N" <*COMMAND*>

Compares every object in the variable to the *PARAMETERNUMBER*. If the two are equal, runs the *COMMAND*.

FORMAT <*DRIVELETTER* or *VOLUME*> /FS:NTFS /C

Formats the *DRIVELETTER* or *VOLUME* and implements compression.

FORMAT <*DRIVELETTER*>: /FS:NTFS|FAT|FAT32 /V:<*LABEL*>

Formats *DRIVELETTER* as NTFS, FAT, or FAT32 and adds a *LABEL* to the drive.

FREEDISK /S <*COMPUTERNAME*> /U <*USERNAME*> /P <*PASSWORD*> /D <*DRIVELETTER*>

Displays the available hard disk space for the specified hard drive on the specified remote computer.

FSUTIL DIRTY

Allows the disk to be marked as corrupt, even if it is not.

FSUTIL FSINFO NTFSINFO <*DRIVELETTER*>:

Displays NTFS statistics on the drive.

FSUTIL FSINFO VOLUMEINFO <*DRIVELETTER*>:

Displays volume information, including support capabilities.

FSUTIL QUOTA DISABLE <*DRIVELETTER* or *VOLUME*>:

Disables tracking and enforcement of disk quotas on *DRIVELETTER*.

FSUTIL QUOTA ENFORCE <*DRIVELETTER* or *VOLUME*>:

Restricts users from adding more disk space once the quota has been met. If quotas are not enforced, violations generate a warning to the user and also generate an event log entry.

FSUTIL QUOTA MODIFY <*DRIVELETTER or VOLUME*>: <*WARNINGSPACE*> <*MAXDISKSPACE*> <*USERNAME or GROUPNAME*>

Sets the quota limit for the volume. Users would be warned about reaching their limit and the maximum disk space limit.

FSUTIL QUOTA QUERY <*DRIVELETTER or VOLUME*>:

Displays quota status and configuration for *DRIVELETTER*.

FSUTIL QUOTA TRACK <*DRIVELETTER or VOLUME*>:

Enables and tracks disk usage on *DRIVELETTER*.

FSUTIL QUOTA VIOLATIONS <*DRIVELETTER or VOLUME*>:

Displays a report of all quota violations.

FSUTIL VOLUME DISKFREE <*DRIVELETTER*>:

Displays the amount of free disk space on the drive.

FSUTIL VOLUME DISMOUNT <*DRIVELETTER*>:

Dismounts the volume.

FTP <*SITENAME*>

Enters an FTP site.

FTP | DIR

Shows a listing of files available in the root folder.

FTP | GET <*FILENAME*>

Downloads a file from an FTP server.

FTP | PUT <*FILENAME*>

Uploads a file to the current directory open on the FTP server.

FTP | TYPE

Displays the file transfer mode in use: ASCII or Binary.

GETMAC /S <*COMPUTERNAME*>

Displays the MAC address and all associated protocols for the networked computer.

GOTO <*SUBROUTINE*>

Jumps to the specified routine header and executes commands from that point.

IF /I %<*VARIABLE1*>% <*OPERATOR*> %<*VARIABLE2*>% <*COMMAND*>

Runs the *COMMAND* if *VARIABLE1* compares to *VARIABLE2* according to the operator function. Operators can be one of the following: EQU, NEQ, LSS, LEQ, GTR, GEQ.

IF /I %<*VARIABLE1*>%==%<*VARIABLE2*>% <*COMMAND*> ELSE <*COMMAND*>

Runs the *COMMAND* if *VARIABLE1* is equal to *VARIABLE2*, and runs the second *COMMAND* if *VARIABLE1* is not equal to *VARIABLE2*.

IF /I %<*VARIABLE1*>%==%<*VARIABLE2*>% <*COMMAND*>

Runs the *COMMAND* if *VARIABLE1* is equal to *VARIABLE2*.

IF DEFINED <*VARIABLE*> <*COMMAND*>

Runs the *COMMAND* if the *VARIABLE* exists.

IF ERRORLEVEL <*NUMBER*> <*COMMAND*> ELSE <*COMMAND*>

Tests for the *ERRORLEVEL* and performs the *COMMAND*. Any other error levels perform the second *COMMAND*.

IF ERRORLEVEL <*NUMBER*> <*COMMAND*>

Tests for the specified error level number and performs the *COMMAND*.

IF EXIST <*FILENAME*> <*COMMAND1*> ELSE <*COMMAND2*>

Performs *COMMAND1* if the *FILENAME* exists; otherwise, performs *COMMAND2*.

IF EXIST <*FILENAME*> <*COMMAND*>

Performs the *COMMAND* if the *FILENAME* exists.

IF NOT /I %<*VARIABLE1*>% <*OPERATOR*>%<*VARIABLE2*>% <*COMMAND1*> ELSE <*COMMAND*>

Runs *COMMAND1* if *VARIABLE1* does not compare to *VARIABLE2* according to the operator function, otherwise, performs *COMMAND2*. Operators can be one of the following: EQU, NEQ, LSS, LEQ, GTR, GEQ.

IF NOT ERRORLEVEL <*NUMBER*> <*COMMAND*>

Tests for anything but the specified error level and performs the *COMMAND*.

IF NOT EXIST <*FILENAME*> <*COMMAND1*> ELSE <*COMMAND2*>

Performs *COMMAND1* if the *FILENAME* does not exist; performs *COMMAND2* if the *FILENAME* does exist.

IF NOT EXIST <*FILENAME*> <*COMMAND*>

Performs the *COMMAND* if the *FILENAME* does not exist.

A

INUSE <REPLACEMENTFILE> <CORRUPTFILE>
Replaces the *CORRUPTFILE* with the *REPLACEMENTFILE*.

IPCONFIG
Displays the basic IP configuration information on your interface.

IPCONFIG /ALL
Displays all IP configurations on each network interface card.

IPCONFIG /FLUSHDNS|DISPLAYDNS
Displays or flushes the contents of the DNS resolver cache.

IPCONFIG /RELEASE|RENEW <ADAPTER>
Flushes or renews IP configuration.

LABEL <DRIVELETTER>: <LABEL>
Adds a label to the *DRIVELETTER*.

LDIFDE
Creates, changes, and removes objects from the directory. Use LDIFDE to extend the Active Directory schema. Allows for bulk changes to Active Directory.

LOGOFF <SESSIONID>
Forcefully logs a session off the system based on the *SESSIONID* number.

LOGOFF <SESSIONNAME>
Forcefully logs a session off the system based on the *SESSIONNAME*.

MD ..\<DIRECTORY>
Creates the *DIRECTORY* within the parent directory. This new directory is a sister directory to the current directory.

MD \<DIRECTORY>
Creates the *DIRECTORY* as a subdirectory of the root.

MD <DIRECTORY>
Creates the subdirectory *DIRECTORY* in the current directory.

MD <DIRECTORY1>\<DIRECTORY2>\<DIRECTORY3>
Creates the specified tree of directories.

MEM

Displays the amount of used and free space in the system.

MEM /C

Displays running programs and the amount of memory they are using.

MOVE <PATH>\<DIRECTORYNAME1> <DIRECTORYNAME2>

Renames *DIRECTORYNAME1* in the specified path to *DIRECTORYNAME2* in the same location.

MOVE <PATH1>\<FILENAME1> <PATH2>

Moves the specified file(s) in *FILENAME1* to the location stated in *PATH2*. Will not move a directory tree.

NBTSTAT

Displays protocol statistics and current TCP/IP connections using NBT (NetBIOS over TCP/IP).

NET ACCOUNTS

Displays the default information that applies to all accounts.

NET ACCOUNTS /MAXPWAGE:<DAYS>

Sets the longevity of a password before it expires and must be changed.

NET ACCOUNTS /MINPWAGE:<DAYS>

Sets the minimum interval of time between password changes.

NET ACCOUNTS /MINPWLEN:<NUMBER>

Sets the minimum number of characters that can be in a logon password.

NET ACCOUNTS /UNIQUEPW:<NUMBER>

Sets the number of passwords that the system accepts. This prevents users from simply changing an old password to the same password.

NET COMPUTER \\<COMPUTERNAME> /ADD

Adds the computer to the domain database.

NET COMPUTER \\<COMPUTERNAME> /DEL

Removes the computer from the domain database.

NET CONFIG SERVER /AUTODISCONNECT:<MINUTES>

Sets the amount of idle connection time before the server terminates any given session.

NET CONFIG SERVER /HIDDEN:*YES*|*NO*

Removes the system name from server lists; it doesn't show up in My Network Places or as a listed computer within Windows Explorer.

NET CONFIG SERVER /SRVCOMMENT:"*<TEXT>*"

Creates a text message or description that displays with the computer name in My Network Places or Windows Explorer.

NET CONFIG WORKSTATION /CHARCOUNT:*<BYTES>*

Lists bytes of data stored before that data is sent to the server.

NET CONFIG WORKSTATION /CHARTIME:*<MILLISECONDS>*

Displays the amount of time data is stored before that data is sent to the server.

NET CONFIG WORKSTATION /CHARWAIT:*<SECONDS>*

Specifies the amount of time to elapse before device timeout occurs and the device is considered to be no longer connected to the network.

NET CONTINUE *<SERVICE>*

Restarts the *SERVICE* after it has been paused.

NETDOM

Allows an administrator to change and move objects within Active Directory.

NET FILE

Displays the current open files on the server.

NET FILE *<FILEID>*/CLOSE

Closes the open file based on the file identification number listed with the NET FILE command.

NET GROUP *<GROUPNAME>* /ADD /DOMAIN

Creates a domain global group called *GROUPNAME*.

NET GROUP *<GROUPNAME>* /DELETE /DOMAIN

Deletes the domain global group called *GROUPNAME*.

NET LOCALGROUP *<GROUPNAME>* /ADD

Adds the specified group.

NET LOCALGROUP *<GROUPNAME>* /ADD /DOMAIN

Creates a domain local group called *GROUPNAME*.

NET LOCALGROUP <*GROUPNAME*> /DELETE

Deletes the specified group.

NET LOCALGROUP <*GROUPNAME*> /DELETE /DOMAIN

Deletes the domain local group called *GROUPNAME*.

NET LOCALGROUP <*GROUPNAME*> <*USERNAME*> /DELETE

Removes the specified user from the specified group.

NET PAUSE <*SERVICE*>

Pauses the *SERVICE*.

NET PRINT \\<*COMPUTERNAME*> <*JOBNUMBER*> /DELETE

Deletes the print job.

NET PRINT \\<*COMPUTERNAME*> <*JOBNUMBER*> /HOLD

Pauses the print job on the printer that is attached to *COMPUTERNAME*. *JOBNUMBER* is determined by the results of running NET PRINT.

NET PRINT \\<*COMPUTERNAME*> <*JOBNUMBER*> /RELEASE

Resumes the print job.

NET PRINT \\<*COMPUTERNAME*>\\<*PRINTERNAME*>

Lists all print jobs being routed to the printer that is attached to the specified computer.

NET SESSION

Displays all current connections to the server.

NET SESSION <*COMPUTERNAME*> /DELETE

Ends the connection between the server and the specified computer.

NET SHARE

Displays all active shares on the server.

NET SHARE <*SHARENAME*> /CACHE:*MANUAL*|*AUTOMATIC*|*NO*

Allows the share to be stored as part of a user's Offline Files and Folders configuration. A cache status of "Manual" means that changes to the offline content must be manually re-synchronized with the share data. A cache status of "Automatic" means that changes to the offline content will be automatically re-synchronized with the share data. A cache status of "No" disables the Offline Files and Folders configuration for this share.

A

NET SHARE *<SHARENAME>* /DELETE

Deletes the specified share.

NET SHARE *<SHARENAME>* /REMARK:"*<DESCRIPTION>*"

Adds a description to the share. The description appears within My Network Places or Windows Explorer.

NET SHARE *<SHARENAME>* /USERS:*<NUMBEROFCONCURRENTUSERS>* | *UNLIMITED*

Configures the share for the maximum number or unlimited concurrent connections.

NET SHARE *<SHARENAME>*$=*<DRIVELETTER>*:*<DIRECTORY>*

Creates a hidden administrative share and assigns it to the specified directory.

NET SHARE *<SHARENAME>*=*<DRIVELETTER>*:*<DIRECTORY>*

Creates a share and assigns it to the specified directory.

NET START

Lists the services available.

NET START *<SERVICE>*

Starts the *SERVICE*.

NET STATISTICS *<SERVER* or *WORKSTATION>*

Displays access statistics.

NET STATISTICS SERVER

Displays session statistics, security violations, and device access information for the server since the last time the Server service was started.

NET STATISTICS WORKSTATION

Displays the connectivity, networking, and session statistics for the Workstation service since the last time it was started.

NET STOP *<SERVICE>*

Stops the *SERVICE*.

NET TIME /SETSNTP:*<SERVERIPADDRESS>*

Configures the server to synchronize its time with the IP address of an external Web time server. This can be a local server or an external Web time server.

NET TIME /SETSNTP:<*TIMESERVER*>

Synchronizes the server time using the DNS name of a time server. This can be a local server or an external Web time server.

NET TIME \\<*SERVERNAME*>

Displays the current network time of the server.

NET TIME \\<*SERVERNAME*> /SET

Configures the current system to synchronize its time with that of the server.

NET USE

Displays all mapped drives on the server.

NET USE \\<*COMPUTERNAME*>\<*SHARENAME*>

Establishes a connection to the share.

NET USE \\<*COMPUTERNAME*>\<*SHARENAME*> /USER:<*DOMAINNAME*>\ <*USERACCOUNT*>

Establishes a connection to the share using *DOMAINNAME* and *USERACCOUNT*.

NET USE <*DRIVELETTER:*> \\<*SERVERNAME*>\<*SHARENAME*>

Configures the system to assign the data located in the specified share to the specified *DRIVELETTER*.

NET USE <*DRIVELETTER:*> \\<*SERVERNAME*>\<*SHARENAME*> /PERSISTENT:YES

Configures the system to assign the data located in the specified share to the specified *DRIVELETTER*. The /PERSISTENT:YES option allows the drive mapping to be permanent.

NET USE <*DRIVELETTER:*> \\<*SERVERNAME*>\<*SHARENAME*> /DELETE

Deletes the drive mapping.

NET USE <*DRIVELETTER:*> \\<*SERVERNAME*>\<*SHARENAME*> /USER: <*USERNAME*>

Configures the system to assign the *DRIVELETTER* to the appropriate server resources using the specified user account. The system prompts the user for a password.

NET USE <*DRIVELETTER:*> \\<*SERVERNAME*>\<*SHARENAME*> /USER: <*USERNAME*> /SAVECRED

Configures the system to assign the *DRIVELETTER* to the appropriate server resources using the specified user account, and to save those credentials locally, so that (with the /PERSISTENT:YES option) the user is not required to enter a password every time the connection is established.

NET USE <*DRIVELETTER:*> \\<*SERVERNAME*>\<*SHARENAME*>\<*SUBDIRECTORY*>

Assigns the *DRIVELETTER* to the *SUBDIRECTORY*. Not available prior to Windows 2000.

NET USE <*DRIVELETTER:*> \\<*COMPUTERNAME*>\<*SHARENAME*> /USER:<*DOMAINNAME*>\<*USERACCOUNT*>

Establishes a connection to the share using *DOMAINNAME* and *USERACCOUNT* and assigns that connection to the *DRIVELETTER*.

NET USER

Lists the current user accounts stored on the server.

NET USER /DOMAIN

Displays all users within the domain.

NET USER <*USERNAME*> /ACTIVE:*NO* | *YES*

Disables the account.

NET USER <*USERNAME*> /ADD

Adds the *USERNAME*.

NET USER <*USERNAME*> /DELETE

Deletes the *USERNAME*.

NET USER <*USERNAME*> /DELETE /DOMAIN

Removes the *USERNAME* account from the domain.

NET USER <*USERNAME*> /EXPIRES: <*MM/DD/YYYY*>

Sets the account to expire on the specified date.

NET USER <*USERNAME*> /HOMEDIR:<*HOMEDIRPATH*>

Sets the home directory to the specified path.

NET USER <*USERNAME*> /PASSWORDCHG: *YES* | *NO*

Allows the user to change his or her password or prevents the user from changing his or her password.

NET USER <*USERNAME*> /PASSWORDREQ: *YES* | *NO*

Changes the account to require or not require a password.

NET USER <*USERNAME*> <*PASSWORD*>

Changes an existing user account's password.

NET USER <*USERNAME*> <*PASSWORD*> /ADD

Adds the *USERNAME* and *PASSWORD*.

NET USER <*USERNAME*> <*PASSWORD*> /ADD /DOMAIN

Adds the *USERNAME* and *PASSWORD* to the domain.

NET USER <*USERNAME*> <*PASSWORD*> /DELETE

Deletes the *USERNAME* and *PASSWORD*.

NET USER <*USERNAME*> <*PASSWORD*> /DOMAIN

Changes the password for *USERNAME* to *PASSWORD* within the domain.

NET USER <*USERNAME*> /PROFILEPATH:<*PROFILEDIR*>

Configures the stored profile location.

NET USER <*USERNAME*> /SCRIPTPATH:<*SCRIPTDIR*>

Configures the location of the logon script.

NET VIEW

Displays all computers on the network that are sharing resources.

NET VIEW /DOMAIN

Lists all domains that are available on the network.

NET VIEW /DOMAIN:<*DOMAINNAME*>

Displays all systems in the specified domain that are sharing resources. Not necessary if the current server is a domain controller or member of a domain.

NET VIEW /NETWORK:NW \\<*COMPUTERNAME*>

Displays all accessible resources on the NetWare server.

NET VIEW \\<*COMPUTERNAME*>

Displays all network shares on *COMPUTERNAME*, provided the host computer and *COMPUTERNAME* are in the same domain.

NET VIEW \\<*COMPUTERNAME*> /CACHE

Displays the cache (the ability to enable Offline Files and Folders) status for all shares on *COMPUTERNAME*.

NET VIEW \\<*COMPUTERNAME*> /DOMAIN:<*DOMAINNAME*>

Displays all network shares on *COMPUTERNAME*.

A

NETSH – A

Specifies that an alias file is used. An alias file allows you to create alias (shortcut) commands instead of using the NETSH command.

NETSH – C

Specifies the context of the command that corresponds to an installed helper DLL.

NETSH – C WINS

Enters the WINS context of the NetShell utility.

NETSH – C WINS|INIT PULL

Initiates and sends a pull trigger to another WINS server.

NETSH – C WINS|INIT PULLRANGE

Initiates and pulls a range of records from another WINS server.

NETSH – C WINS|INIT PUSH

Initiates and sends a push trigger to another WINS server.

NETSH – C WINS|INIT REPLICATE

Initiates replication of the database with replication partners.

NETSH – C WINS|INIT SCAVENGE

Initiates scavenging of the WINS database for the server.

NETSH – C WINS|SET AUTOPARTNERCONFIG

Sets the automatic replication partner configuration information for the server.

NETSH – C WINS|SET PULLPARAM

Sets the default pull parameters for the server.

NETSH – C WINS|SET PULLPARTNERCONFIG

Sets the configuration parameters for the specified pull partner.

NETSH – C WINS|SET PUSHPARAM

Sets the default push parameters for the server.

NETSH – C WINS|SET PUSHPARTNERCONFIG

Sets the configuration parameters for the specified push partner.

NETSH – F *<SCRIPTFILE>*

Specifies that all the NETSH commands in the specified script are run.

NETSH – R *<REMOTECOMPUTER>*

Specifies that the NETSH commands are run on a remote computer specified by either its name or IP address.

NETSTAT

Displays protocol statistics and current TCP/IP network connections. Only available if TCP/IP has been installed.

NSLOOKUP

Queries a DNS server.

NTDSUTIL

Performs Active Directory database maintenance.

PAGEFILECONFIG /CHANGE /I *<INITIALSIZE>* /M *<MAXSIZE>*/VO *<DRIVELETTER>*:

Changes the existing page file to the specified initial size and maximum size for the *DRIVELETTER*.

PAGEFILECONFIG /CHANGE /S *<COMPUTERNAME>* /U *<USERNAME>* /P *<PASSWORD>* /I *<INITIALSIZE>* /M *<MAXSIZE>* /VO *<DRIVELETTER>*:

Changes the existing page file on the remote computer to the *INITIALSIZE* and *MAXSIZE* for the *DRIVELETTER*.

PAGEFILECONFIG /QUERY

Displays the current page file configuration.

PAGEFILECONFIG /QUERY /FO *TABLE|LIST|CSV*

Displays the page file configuration in the specified output format (table, list, or comma delimited). This is ideal for documentation purposes when used with redirection.

PAGEFILECONFIG /QUERY /S *<COMPUTERNAME>* /U *<USERNAME>* /P *<PASSWORD>*

Displays the page file configuration on the specified remote computer using the *USERNAME* and *PASSWORD* provided.

PAGEFILECONFIG /QUERY /S <COMPUTERNAME> /U <USERNAME> /P <PASSWORD>/FO TABLE|LIST|CSV

Displays the page file configuration in the specified output format for the remote computer using the *USERNAME* and *PASSWORD*. This is ideal for documentation purposes when used with redirection.

PAGEFILECONFIG /CREATE /I <INITIALSIZE> /M <MAXSIZE> /VO <DRIVELETTER1>: /VO <DRIVELETTER2>:

Configures a page file with the *INITIALSIZE* and *MAXSIZE*. At least one volume (/VO) is required. The page file will be split across the number of /VO entries that are specified.

PAGEFILECONFIG /CREATE /S <COMPUTERNAME> /U <USERNAME> /P <PASSWORD> /I <INITIALSIZE> /M <MAXSIZE> /VO <DRIVELETTER1>: /VO <DRIVELETTER2>:

Same as the above command, but on a remote computer.

PAGEFILECONFIG /DELETE /S <COMPUTERNAME> /U <USERNAME> /P <PASSWORD> /VO <DRIVELETTER1>: /VO <DRIVELETTER2>:

Deletes the page file located on one or more disks on the remote system.

PAGEFILECONFIG DELETE /VO <DRIVELETTER1>: /VO <DRIVELETTER2>:

Deletes the page file located on one or more disks.

PATHPING /H

Sets the maximum number of hops packets will take. The default is 30.

PATHPING <IPADDRESS>

Displays the network statistics between each hop or router the ICMP packets cross.

PAUSE

Prompts the user to "Press Any Key to Continue...".

PING /i <TTL> <IPADDRESS>

Sets the time to live (TTL) on the packets.

PING <IPADDRESS> /T

Issues PING commands continuously until stopped with a Ctrl+Z keystroke.

PING<IPADDRESS>

Determine whether TCP/IP is working on the target computer *IPADDRESS* being "pinged."

POWERCFG /CHANGE <*SCHEME*> /DISK-TIMEOUT-*AC|DC* <*MINUTES*>

Shuts down the hard disks at the specified timeout for the *SCHEME* under either AC or DC power.

POWERCFG /CHANGE <*SCHEME*> /HIBERNATE-TIMEOUT-*AC|DC* <*MINUTES*>

Hibernates the system at the specified timeout for the *SCHEME* under either AC or DC power.

POWERCFG /CHANGE <*SCHEME*> /MONITOR-TIMEOUT-*AC|DC* <*MINUTES*>

Shuts down the monitor at the specified timeout for the *SCHEME* under either AC or DC power.

POWERCFG /CHANGE <*SCHEME*> /PROCESSOR-THROTTLE-*AC|DC NONE|CONSTANT|DEGRADE|ADAPTIVE*

Alters the processor performance based on the specified throttle type.

POWERCFG /CREATE <*SCHEME*>

Creates a blank power configuration scheme and assigns it the *SCHEME* name.

POWERCFG /EXPORT <*SCHEME*> /F <*FILENAME*>

Exports the *SCHEME* to the *FILENAME*.

POWERCFG /IMPORT <*SCHEME*> /F <*FILENAME*>

Imports the *SCHEME* from the *FILENAME*.

POWERCFG /LIST

Displays a list of the current power schemes.

POWERCFG /QUERY <*SCHEME*>

Displays the power configuration associated with the *SCHEME*.

POWERCFG /SETACTIVE <*SCHEME*>

Assigns the *SCHEME* as the current scheme. The system will henceforth associate the current status with that particular scheme.

PRNJOBS –L –S <*COMPUTERNAME*> –U <*USERNAME*> –W <*PASSWORD*>

Lists all print jobs on the printer attached to *COMPUTERNAME* using the *USERNAME* account and *PASSWORD*.

PRNQCTL –X –S <*COMPUTERNAME*> –U <*USERNAME*> –W <*PASSWORD*> –P <*PRINTERNAME*>

Deletes all print jobs from the printer queue for the printer attached to *COMPUTERNAME*, using the *USERNAME* account and *PASSWORD*.

A

PROMPT

Displays the current prompt configuration.

PROMPT $D

Displays the date as the prompt.

PROMPT $G

Displays > as the prompt.

PROMPT PG

Displays the C:\> prompt.

PROMPT $T

Displays the time as the prompt.

QUERY SESSION

Displays all current sessions on the server. These include console sessions where the user is logged on locally and Remote Desktop sessions.

RD <DIRECTORY>

Deletes the *DIRECTORY*. Does not delete the *DIRECTORY* if it has files in it. When using a full directory path (e.g., C:\Profiles and Settings\ Administrator), the last directory in the path is deleted, not the entire tree.

RD <DIRECTORY> /S

Deletes the *DIRECTORY*, including all files and subdirectories. Prompts for confirmation.

RD <DIRECTORY> /S /Q

Deletes the *DIRECTORY*, including all files and subdirectories. Does not prompt for confirmation.

RECOVER <DRIVELETTER>:\<PATH>\<FILENAME>

Attempts to recover a file that has been corrupted by a physical disk problem (or other corruption).

REG COPY <SOURCEKEY> <DESTINATIONKEY> /S /F

Copies the contents of the *SOURCEKEY* into a new *DESTINATIONKEY* within the registry.

REG EXPORT <KEYORHIVENAME> <FILENAME>

Exports the contents of the specified hive or key into the *FILENAME*. Used to export hives and keys to other servers.

REG IMPORT <FILENAME>

Imports the contents of the *FILENAME* into the registry.

REG QUERY \\\<COMPUTER>\\<KEYORHIVENAME>

Displays the entries and first-level subkeys for the listed key or hive.

REG QUERY \\\<COMPUTERNAME>\\<KEYNAME>

Displays the remote computer's registry entries for *KEYNAME* and first-level subkeys for the specified key or hive.

REG QUERY \\\<COMPUTERNAME>\\<KEYNAME> /S

Displays the remote computer's registry entries for *KEYNAME* and subkeys for the specified key or hive, including the entire subtree structure.

REG QUERY \\\<COMPUTERNAME>\\<KEYNAME> /V <ENTRY>

Displays the remote computer's specified subkey entry data that is located in the specified key.

REG QUERY <KEYNAME> /V <ENTRY>

Displays the specified entry data that is located in the specified key.

REG QUERY <KEYORHIVENAME>

Displays the entries and first-level subkeys for the specified key or hive.

REG QUERY <KEYORHIVENAME> /S

Displays the entries and subkeys for the listed key or hive, including the entire subtree structure.

REG RESTORE <FILENAME>

Performs the same action as REG IMPORT but must be performed on the same system that the REG SAVE file was created on.

REG SAVE <KEYORHIVENAME> <FILENAME>

Performs the same action as REG EXPORT, only with a file format that is not transferable to a different system.

REM <STATEMENT>

Documentation that does no processing. REM statements are informative for the programmer, but are ignored by the batch.

RENAME <FILENAME1> <FILENAME2>

Renames *FILENAME1* to *FILENAME2*.

RESET SESSION <SESSIONID>

Forcefully closes all applications and logs off a session.

A

ROUTE ADD <DESTINATION> MASK <SUBNETMASK>

Adds a specific subnet mask other than the default 255.255.255.255 to the destination.

RUNAS /NOPROFILE /USER:<USERNAME> <PROGRAM>

Runs the *PROGRAM* on behalf of the user without loading that user's profile. The password will be prompted as the program is run.

RUNAS /PROFILE /USER:<USERNAME> <PROGRAM>

Runs the *PROGRAM* on behalf of the user and loads that user's profile. The password will be prompted as the program is run.

RUNAS /SAVECRED /USER:<USERNAME> <PROGRAM>

Runs the *PROGRAM* on behalf of the user, prompts for a password, and saves the *USERNAME* and password locally. These credentials must be saved prior to automating other RUNAS commands.

RUNAS /SMARTCARD <PROGRAM>

Runs the *PROGRAM* using the username and password stored on the smartcard.

SC \\<COMPUTERNAME> ENUMDEPEND <KEYNAME>

Displays the services that depend on the specified key.

SC \\<COMPUTERNAME> GETKEYNAME <DISPLAYNAME>

Returns the formal service keyname for the specified display name.

SC \\<COMPUTERNAME> QUERY

Displays a list of all the services on the specified remote computer.

SC \\<COMPUTERNAME> QUERY <KEYNAME>

Displays the services associated with the *KEYNAME*.

SC CONFIG <SERVICENAME> START=BOOT|SYSTEM|AUTO|DEMAND|DISABLED

Configures the specified service to start on boot, when the system kernel is loaded, automatically without logon, manually, or not at all.

SC CONTINUE <KEYNAME>

Restores the service after it has been paused.

SC CREATE <KEYNAME> BINPATH= <EXEFILE> TYPE= SHARE START= AUTO

Instructs the system to start the program (*EXEFILE*) as a service without requiring an active logon.

SC ENUMDEPEND <*KEYNAME*>

Displays the services that depend on the *KEYNAME*.

SC GETKEYNAME <*DISPLAYNAME*>

Returns the formal service name for the key *DISPLAYNAME*.

SC PAUSE <*KEYNAME*>

Pauses the service.

SC QUERY

Displays a list of all of the services on the local machine.

SC QUERY <*KEYNAME*>

Displays the entries associated with the *KEYNAME*.

SC START <*KEYNAME*>

Starts the service.

SC STOP <*KEYNAME*>

Stops the service.

SET

Displays all current environmental variables.

SET <*VARNAME*>

Displays the contents of the *VARNAME* variable.

SET <*VARNAME*>=%<*VAR1*>% %<*VAR2*>%

Sets *VARNAME* with the values of the predefined variables *VAR1* and *VAR2*.

SET <*VARNAME*>=<*VALUE*>

Creates a new variable called *VARNAME* and sets the value at *VALUE*.

SET PATH

Displays the current path.

SET PATH=<*PATHDATA*>

Sets the path to equal *PATHDATA*.

SETX /S <COMPUTER> /U <USERNAME> /P <PASSWORD> <VARIABLENAME> <VARIABLEVALUE>

Creates the variable *VARIABLENAME* on the remote computer and assigns it the value of *VARIABLEVALUE*. *USERNAME* and *PASSWORD* are authenticated on the remote computer.

SHIFT

Deletes the contents of the current %1 parameter, and reassigns the %2 parameter as %1.

SHUTDOWN /I

Executes the Remote Shutdown dialog box on the local computer. From within the GUI, you can specify one or more computers to shut down or restart, along with reason codes for the reboot.

SYSTEMINFO

Displays system information.

SYSTEMINFO /FO *TABLE | LIST | CSV* /NH

Displays system information and outputs it in the specified format (table, list, or comma delimited) with no header information.

SYSTEMINFO /S <COMPUTERNAME> /U <USERNAME> /P <PASSWORD>

Displays system information for the specified remote computer.

SYSTEMINFO /S <COMPUTERNAME> /U <USERNAME> /P <PASSWORD> /FO *TABLE | LIST | CSV* /NH

Displays system information for the remote computer and outputs the specified format (table, list, or comma delimited).

TAKEOWN /F <FILENAME>

Takes ownership of the *FILENAME*.

TAKEOWN /S <COMPUTERNAME> /F <FILENAME>

Takes ownership of the *FILENAME* located on the network computer *COMPUTERNAME*.

TAKEOWN /S <COMPUTERNAME> /U <USERNAME> /P <PASSWORD> /F <FILENAME>

Takes ownership of the file using the *USERNAME* and *PASSWORD*.

TASKKILL /FI "SERVICES *EQ | NE* <KEYNAME>"

Stops all tasks associated with the listed service name.

TASKKILL /FI "STATUS *EQ | NE RUNNING | NOT RESPONDING*"

Stops any process that matches the criteria (equal/not equal) of running or not responding.

TASKKILL /FI "WINDOWTITLE *EQ|NE* <*WINDOWNAME*>"

Stops all processes associated with the specified application window (*WINDOWNAME*).

TASKKILL /IM <*PROCESSNAME*>

Stops the specified process.

TASKKILL /S <*COMPUTER*> /U <*USERNAME*> /P <*PASSWORD*> /FI "STATUS *EQ|NE RUNNING|NOT RESPONDING*"

Stops a process that matches the criteria (equal/not equal) of running or not responding.

TASKKILL /S <*COMPUTER*> /U <*USERNAME*> /P <*PASSWORD*> /IM <*PROCESSNAME*>

Stops the specified process on the remote computer.

TASKKILL /S <*COMPUTERNAME*> /U <*USERNAME*> /P <*PASSWORD*> /FI "SERVICES *EQ|NE* <*KEYNAME*>"

Stops all tasks on the remote computer associated with the specified service.

TASKKILL /S <*COMPUTERNAME*> /U <*USERNAME*> /P <*PASSWORD*> /FI "WINDOWTITLE *EQ|NE* <*WINDOWNAME*>"

Stops all processes associated with the specified application window on the remote computer.

TASKLIST

Displays all of the current processes on the system.

TASKLIST /FI "SERVICES *EQ|NE* <*KEYNAME*>"

Displays a list of processes that are associated with a service where SERVICES are either equal to or not equal to the *KEYNAME*.

TASKLIST /FI "STATUS *EQ|NE RUNNING|NOT RESPONDING|UNKNOWN*"

Displays a list of all processes matching the criteria (equal or not equal) of running, not responding, or unknown.

TASKLIST /FI "WINDOWTITLE *EQ|NE* <*WINDOWNAME*>"

Displays a list of processes that are associated with a particular application's window where the window title is either equal to or not equal to the *WINDOWNAME*.

TASKLIST /FO *TABLE|LIST|CSV* /NH

Displays all processes in the specified format (table, list, or comma delimited). Used primarily with redirection to a file.

TASKLIST /S <*COMPUTER*> /U <*USERNAME*> /P <*PASSWORD*>

Displays all processes currently running on the remote system.

TASKLIST /S <*COMPUTERNAME*> /U <*USERNAME*> /P <*PASSWORD*>

Displays all processes currently running on the remote computer. /U and /P are used to authenticate against the remote computer to ensure that the user is a member of the remote computer's Administrators group.

TASKLIST /S <*COMPUTERNAME*> /U <*USERNAME*> /P <*PASSWORD*>/FO *TABLE*|*LIST*|*CSV* /NH

Displays all the processes in the specified output format (table, list, or comma delimited) for the remote computer using the *USERNAME* and *PASSWORD*. Used primarily with redirection to a file.

TRACERT <*IPADDRESS*>

Displays the name and IP address of every router or gateway that a packet travels across as it moves from a local computer to a remote host.

TREE

Displays the directory structure of a drive.

TREE /F

Displays the directory and file structure of a drive.

TSDISCON <*SESSIONID*>

Forcefully disconnects a session: the session is orphaned.

TYPE <*FILENAME*>

Displays the contents of the specified file on the screen.

TYPE <*FILENAME*> |MORE

Displays the file on the screen, one screen at a time. Pressing the spacebar displays the next screen.

TYPE <*FILENAME1*> >> <*FILENAME2*>|<*LOCATION*>

Redirects the contents of *FILENAME1* to another file (*FILENAME2*) or specified location such as a printer port.

XCOPY <*FILENAME1*> <*FILENAME2*>

Copies the original file, *FILENAME1*, to destination *FILENAME2*.

XCOPY <FILENAME1> <FILENAME2> /F

Copies files and displays source and destination filenames.

XCOPY <FILENAMES> <PATH OR DRIVELETTER:>

Copies multiple files (wildcards assumed) to the destination directory or drive. Does not include system or hidden files. Will prompt to overwrite read-only files.

XCOPY <FILENAMES> <PATH OR DRIVELETTER:> /A

Copies multiple files whose archive attribute is set to the destination directory or drive. Does not reset the archive bit. Use this command when performing a routine data backup.

XCOPY <FILENAMES> <PATH OR DRIVELETTER:> /C

Copies multiple files and does not abort if an error occurs.

XCOPY <FILENAMES> <PATH OR DRIVELETTER:> /D

Copies multiple files whose date and time stamp are more recent than identically named files residing in the destination directory or drive. If one of the files contained in *FILENAMES* does not exist, that file will also be copied to the destination. Use this command when updating data that resides in an alternate location, or when performing an irregular or occasional data backup.

XCOPY <FILENAMES> <PATH OR DRIVELETTER:> /D:MM-DD-YYYY

Copies multiple files whose date and time stamp are on or after the specified date (MM-DD-YYYY) to the destination directory or drive.

XCOPY <FILENAMES> <PATH OR DRIVELETTER:> /EXCLUDE: <FILENAME1>

Copies all files to the destination directory except the specified file.

XCOPY <FILENAMES> <PATH OR DRIVELETTER:> /H

Copies multiple files to the destination directory or drive and includes hidden and system files. Often used when copying system directories or when performing a backup.

XCOPY <FILENAMES> <PATH OR DRIVELETTER:> /K

Copies multiple files and their attributes to the destination directory or drive. Use this command when performing network backups.

XCOPY <FILENAMES> <PATH OR DRIVELETTER:> /M

Copies multiple files whose archive attribute is set to the destination directory or drive. Resets the archive bit. You can also use the /M option when performing a routine data backup.

XCOPY <FILENAMES> <PATH OR DRIVELETTER:> /O

Copies multiple files, along with their ownership and security access settings, to the destination directory or drive. Use this command when performing network backups.

A

XCOPY *<FILENAMES> <PATH OR DRIVELETTER:>* /R

Copies multiple files to the destination directory or drive and overwrites read-only files. Often used when copying system directories or performing a backup.

XCOPY *<FILENAMES> <PATH OR DRIVELETTER:>* /U

Copies multiple files that already exist in the destination to the destination directory or drive.

XCOPY *<FILENAMES> <PATH OR DRIVELETTER:>* /X

Copies multiple files, along with their audit settings, to the destination directory or drive. Use the /X option in conjunction with others for routine backups.

XCOPY *<FILENAMES> <PATH OR DRIVELETTER:>* /-Y

Copies multiple files to the destination directory or drive. Prompts to overwrite existing files.

XCOPY *<FILENAMES> <PATH OR DRIVELETTER:>* /Y

Copies multiple files to the destination directory or drive. Does not prompt to overwrite existing files.

XCOPY *<FILENAMES> <PATH OR DRIVELETTER:>* /Z

Allows checkpoint restart to occur on a failed XCOPY process.

XCOPY *<PATH OR DRIVELETTER:> <PATH OR DRIVELETTER:>* /E

Used in conjunction with /S or /T to include empty directories.

XCOPY *<PATH OR DRIVELETTER:> <PATH OR DRIVELETTER:>* /S

Copies an entire directory tree to the destination directory or drive. Data inclusive. Does not include empty directories.

XCOPY *<PATH1> <PATH2>* /T

Copies an entire directory tree to the destination directory without data. Does not copy empty directories.

B

ADVANCED NETWORKING COMMANDS

TERMINAL SERVICES COMMANDS

CHANGE LOGON   Displays and changes the status and ability for the terminal server to accept connections.

CHANGE PORT   Lists and changes COM port mappings for DOS backward compatibility.

CHANGE USER   Changes user .ini file mappings for terminal server consoles.

MSTSC   Runs the terminal server client.

QUERY PROCESS   Displays process information about a specific terminal server process.

QUERY SESSION   Displays all current terminal server sessions.

QUERY TERMSERVER   Displays all terminal servers on the network.

QUERY USER   Displays information about terminal server users who are currently connected.

TSKILL   Ends a terminal server process.

TSPROF   Copies a terminal server's user configuration and changes the profile path.

TSSHUTDN   Shuts down a terminal server.

INTERNET INFORMATION SERVER COMMANDS

IISBACK   Backs up the IIS database.

IISCNFG   Exports and imports the IIS database.

IISFTP   Creates, lists, and deletes FTP sites.

IISFTPDR   Creates, lists, and displays FTP virtual directories.

IISVDIR   Creates and deletes virtual directories.

IISWEB   Creates, deletes, and lists Web sites.

CERTIFICATE SERVICES COMMANDS

CERTREQ	Requests certificates from a CA (certificate authority).
CERTUTIL	Configures certificate services.

CLUSTERING COMMANDS

CLUSSVC	Starts and stops the cluster service in debug mode.
NLB	Starts, stops, and configures network load balancing and clustering.
NLBMGR	Manages load-balanced or clustered servers.

NEW COMMANDS FOR WINDOWS SERVER 2003

ADPREP	Prepares Windows 2000 servers for upgrade to Windows Server 2003.
BOOTCFG	Configures boot.ini settings.
CHOICE	Prompts the user to make a choice in a batch program.
CLIP	Redirects output to the clipboard.
CMDKEY	Creates, lists, and deletes stored usernames and passwords or credentials.
DEFRAG	Defragments the hard disk drive.
DISKPART	Manages disks, partitions, or volumes.
DRIVERQUERY	Displays a list of drivers and driver properties.
DSADD	Adds a computer, contact, group, organizational unit, or user to a directory.
DSGET	Displays attributes of a computer, contact, group, or organizational unit in Active Directory.
DSMOD	Modifies an existing user, computer, contact, group, or organizational unit in Active Directory.
DSMOVE	Moves any object from its current location in the directory to a new location in Active Directory.
DSQUERY	Queries Active Directory for specific directory objects.
DSRM	Deletes an Active Directory object.

B

EVENTCREATE	Creates an event-viewer event.
EVENTTRIGGERS	Displays and configures event triggers—performance-type counters that trigger an event-viewer event when they reach a certain threshold.
FORFILES	Selects files in a folder or tree for batch processing.
FSUTIL	Manages the file system on a disk.
GETMAC	Displays the MAC address for the current system.
GETTYPE	Defines the %errorlevel% parameter for a command or batch program.
GPRESULT	Displays resulting Group Policy settings for a user or computer.
IISBACK	Backs up the IIS database.
IISCNFG	Imports and exports the IIS database.
IISFTP	Creates, deletes, and lists FTP sites.
IISFTPDR	Creates and deletes virtual directories of FTP sites.
IISVDIR	Creates and deletes virtual directories.
IISWEB	Creates, deletes, and lists Web sites.
INUSE	Replaces locked operating system files.
LOGMAN	Manages and schedules performance counter and event trace log collections on local and remote systems.
NLB	Starts and stops the network load balancing and clustering services.
NLBMGR	Configures and manages network load balancing clusters and all cluster hosts from a single computer.
OPENFILES	Queries, displays, or disconnects open files.
PAGEFILECONFIG	Displays and configures the page file.
PRNCNFG	Displays and configures printer information.
PRNDRVR	Adds, deletes, and manages printer drivers.
PRNMNGR	Adds, deletes, and manages printers.
PRNPORT	Creates, deletes, and displays TCP/IP printer ports.
PRNQCTL	Controls and administers a printer queue.

RELOG	Extracts data from performance monitor logs into separate files.
RSS	Enables remote storage.
SC	Displays and modifies services.
SCHTASKS	Schedules commands and programs. Similar to AT.
SETX	Sets environment variables.
SHUTDOWN	Shuts down or restarts a local or remote computer.
SYSTEMINFO	Displays system information.
TAKEOWN	Allows an administrator to take ownership of a file or folder.
TASKKILL	Terminates a task or process.
TASKLIST	Displays a list of processes running on the system.
TIMEOUT	Pauses the command processor for the specified number of seconds. Similar to the PAUSE command, without requiring user intervention.
TRACERPT	The event-viewer equivalent of RELOG.
TYPEPERF	Displays all performance monitor information on the screen or redirects it to a text file.
WAITFOR	Synchronizes networked computers. Does not reset time.
WHERE	Locates files that match a given parameter. Batch-exclusive.
WHOAMI	Displays logon information for the current user.

Glossary

access control entry (ACE) — An entry in a DACL that specifies a permission for a particular group or user. There are typically many ACEs in every DACL.

access control list — A list of users that indicates various permissions that each user has.

Active Directory — The directory service for Microsoft Windows Server 2003.

Active Directory integrated zone — A type of DNS zone that stores its zone information inside Active Directory.

administrative share — A hidden share that contains a dollar symbol ($) after its name. The share itself does not appear when using Windows Explorer or **NET VIEW.**

advanced computer and power interface (ACPI) — A power standard that allows the OS to fully control the power status (on or off) of hardware components on the system.

Alerter service — Enables administrative alerts over the network.

APM (advanced power management) — A power standard that allows the BIOS to shut off or suspend power to certain components.

archive bit — The bit that, when turned on, indicates that a file has been modified.

ASCII — American Standard Code for Information Interchange. A file format in which every numeral or character has an assigned ASCII code number.

attributes — Specialized properties of a file, including read-only, archive, system, and hidden.

authentication — The process of determining whether someone or something is, in fact, who or what it is declared to be.

automation — The process of executing a series of tasks using a script, batch file, or other executable program without user intervention.

backup — A copy of data that is stored for purposes of file, system, and disaster recovery. Also, the process of copying data for emergency retrieval.

backup job — A list of files and folders that is referenced during a backup procedure.

backup pool — A backup that consumes more than one tape.

basic disk — A disk type that can contain primary or extended partitions.

batch — A type of automation script that uses commands that are written in a plain text file with a .bat extension.

battery backup — An external battery power source.

Binary — A mathematical system that uses either a 1 or a 0 to designate whether a bit is on or off. Also used to describe the sending of applications or executable files in a file transfer process.

bind operation — An association between two or more programming objects or value items for some scope of time and place. In the realm of LDAP, a bind operation makes an association between a query and the object you are requesting.

bitmap — A simple picture file.

boot — The process in which a computer turns on and loads the operating system.

boot drive — The disk and drive that contain the operating system.

browse master — A central computer that is responsible for maintaining the authoritative list of computers and shares on the network.

Browser service — Maintains a list of computers on the network.

business continuity — The idea or concept of being able to continue business when disaster strikes, specifically when the office building has been destroyed or is otherwise uninhabitable.

byte — Eight bits. The basic unit of data.

carriage return — The literal end-of-line marker that generates a new line; it is created using the Ctrl+Enter key combination.

checkpoint restart — A process that enables a failed download to restart at the failed location rather than starting over.

child node — A node in the DNS structure beneath a parent node; a subdomain.

Clipbook service — Enables copy and paste functions with network data.

command line — A text-based interface for running commands.

command prompt — The environment, interface, and location for running commands.

compression — The reduction in file size resulting from the removal of redundant space in the file.

computer administration — The process of administering and maintaining local computer hardware, software, and services.

conditional forwarder — A new feature of the Microsoft DNS service incorporated into Windows Server 2003. This features allows a DNS server to forward DNS queries according to specified domain names.

conditional processing — A type of process in which certain commands are executed based on specifically defined conditions.

console — A locally logged-on session that includes login and desktop settings, a Start menu, icons, and a user profile.

context — A grouping of commands for a specific network component.

copy backup — A backup type that copies selected files and does not reset the archive bit.

CPU throttling — A procedure that allows the CPU to change its performance based on power needs.

daily backup — A backup type that copies selected files and folders that have been created or modified that day.

DHCP Client service — Enables a client machine to automatically receive TCP/IP configuration information from the nearest DHCP server.

differential backup — A backup type that copies selected files and folders that have been created or modified since the last incremental or normal backup. Does not reset the archive bit.

directory — A container of data that can contain other directories (including subdirectories) or files.

Directory Access Protocol (DAP) — A protocol for querying and updating a directory database. Used in X.500 implementations. It was replaced by LDAP.

directory and filename completion — A feature that allows a system to display directory names and filenames based on one or two characters of entered text.

directory information tree (DIT) — Hierarchy on which Active Directory is based.

directory service — A network service used to store information. Directory services typically store information about network resources, security, and network configuration.

directory tree — A hierarchical view of the directory structure on a hard drive.

Discretionary Access Control List (DACL) — A list of access control entries that define who can do what to an object.

disk — A physical medium for storing data.

disk fault tolerance — The ability of a server to sustain a drive failure without having the entire server fail.

disk quota — A feature that allows restrictions to be placed on the amount of disk space used by one or more user accounts.

disk thrash — The constant use of the hard disk resulting from a fragmented drive.

distinguished name — The unique name of an object in Active Directory.

distribution files — Files containing compressed data that are used to install an application.

domain — A logical security boundary covering a group of networked computers, user accounts, and other network resources.

domain administration — The process of administering and maintaining the security of objects belonging to a domain.

domain controller (DC) — A Windows NT, 2000, or Server 2003 server that contains the directory service database.

DNS — Domain naming system.

domain tree — A relationship between multiple branches and a single root. Trees are commonly used to describe the relationship between child domains and their parent domain.

DOS — Disk operating system. The first operating system used on PCs.

drive — A volume, logical drive, or partition that has a drive letter.

drive compression — A feature that allows files and folders to consume less space on a drive.

driver — A software program that allows the OS or application to communicate and interface with a specific hardware component.

duplexing — Identical to mirroring, only with a disk controller for each disk, providing controller fault tolerance in addition to disk fault tolerance.

dynamic disk — A disk type that can contain simple, extended, spanned, striped, mirrored, or RAID 5 volumes.

Dynamic Host Configuration Protocol (DHCP) — A protocol that is part of the TCP/IP protocol suite and dynamically assigns IP addresses to hosts on a network segment. Typically runs on a Windows Server 2003 system.

dynamic link library (DLL) — A collection of small programs, any of which can be called when needed by a larger program that is running on the computer. The small program that lets the larger program communicate with a specific device such as a printer or scanner is often packaged as a DLL program.

echo — A command line feature that displays non-critical messages on the screen.

Encrypting File System (EFS) — The service that provides encryption within Windows Server 2003.

encryption — The process of enabling a user to exclusively view file and folder data. Encryption works by making the data unreadable without the user's specific credentials. Permissions do not modify the data. Instead, they grant and restrict file and folder access based on users' accounts.

environment variable — A variable that resides on a computer system and contains data relevant to the system, such as date, time, or username.

exclusion range — A range of IP addresses that are excluded from a scope. They are typically used for Web servers and other computers that need to have an IP address that is set statically.

exit codes — Hidden command output that indicates the success, failure, or status of the command.

extended partition — A type of partition that cannot contain an OS. There can only be one extended partition on a disk. There is no practical limit on the number of logical drives that can be created from an extended partition.

extended volume — A volume that occupies multiple locations on a single disk.

FAT (File Allocation Table) — A type of disk format that has little security, and has limitations on disk size, partition size, and filename conventions.

FAT32 — A type of disk format that has little security, but does not have the same limitations on disk size, partition size, and filename conventions that FAT does.

file compression — A feature that shrinks a file size.

file extension — The last three characters of a filename following a period. Directories do not have extensions, and not all files have extensions. The file extension often indicates what application created the file. Examples of extensions are .exe (an executable file), .bat (a batch file), .doc (a Microsoft Word document), .xls (a Microsoft Excel spreadsheet), .gif (a bitmapped color graphics file), and .jpg (a compressed graphics file).

File replication service — Allows coordination between domain controllers.

File Transfer Protocol (FTP) — A TCP/IP protocol that allows you to send and receive files over networks.

filter — An option that enables the suppression of certain pieces of data.

flag — An attribute. Used as a verb to refer to the on or yes state of an attribute. For example, "The file is flagged as read-only."

focus — The current location of the cursor. Within Windows, the focus may be indicated by a dotted rectangle around the item of focus.

forest — One or more domains sharing a common schema, configuration, and Global Catalog. Domains in a forest are linked with a two-way transitive trust.

format — The process of preparing a disk or drive to receive data.

forward lookup zone — Resolves a hostname to an IP address.

fragmentation — The splitting of a single file across multiple sections of a drive.

full backup — A normal backup of all files on a server.

functions keys — The F-numbered keys that provide shortcut access to frequently used commands.

gigabyte — 1,000 megabytes.

Global Catalog — A subset of Active Directory used by clients and applications to query and locate objects in a forest. The Global Catalog is maintained on one or more domain controllers in the forest.

Global Catalog server — Windows Server 2003 domain controller maintaining the Global Catalog.

graphical user interface (GUI) — An interface that uses graphics and color to enhance a computer's ease of use and the input/output of commands and data.

hibernation — A process in which current settings are stored on the hard disk, and the system is powered off. When the system is powered on again, the current settings are restored.

hidden file — A file whose hidden attribute makes it not viewable by standard methods.

hive — The primary or first-level section (key) in the registry. There are five hives in the registry: HKLM, HKCC, HKU, HKCR, and HKCU.

home directory — A directory that is generated by the system and contains exclusive permissions for the user account.

hosts — Computers or interfaces that exist on a network. Also called node.

incremental backup — A backup type that copies selected files and folders that have been created or modified since the last incremental or normal backup. Resets the archive bit.

Internet Group Management Protocol (IGMP) — An Internet protocol that provides a way for a computer to report its multi-cast group membership to adjacent routers.

InterNIC — An organization licensed to the Internet Corporation for Assigned Names and Numbers, it registers public domain names.

Kerberos version 5 — The default authentication mechanism used by Windows Server 2003 to validate a user's credentials.

key — An entry within a hive that contains subentries.

key distribution model — A security model that operates by giving out keys or tickets to authenticate objects.

keylogger — A type of Trojan horse virus program that records all key entries into a log.

kilobyte (K) — 1,024 bytes.

Lightweight Directory Access Protocol (LDAP) — The main protocol used to access Active Directory, it is based on X.500's DAP.

linear — A method of processing in which the program executes commands line by line.

LMHOST file — A text file located in the %systemroot%\ system32\drivers\etc folder that contains static records of IP address to NetBIOS names to IP address resolution. Replaced by WINS. Similar to a HOSTS file.

log file — A simple text file that contains the output results of commands.

logic — The ability to compare or judge two items based on given conditions and to execute commands based on the status of those conditions.

logic processing — A type of command or process that indicates some amount of conditional processing.

logical drive — A drive that can be created on an extended partition. Not bootable.

logon script — A batch file that executes when the user logs in to a system or domain.

loop — A reiterative process that continues until the specified reiterations have occurred. Within batch, loops reiterate until the end of the file or list has been reached.

loopback — An address set up on a local network interface card that allows you to test the TCP/IP setup. Typically this value is 127.0.0.1, but you can use any IP address in the 127 address range.

MAC address — A unique identifying address on the NIC.

macro — A group of commands or procedures that is assigned a name and executed as a whole.

megabyte (M) — 1,024 kilobytes.

Messenger service — Enables a client machine to receive alerts and console messages.

metacharacters — Specialized characters that are used to find patterns of characters specific to regular expressions.

mirrored volume — A volume that is replicated with an identical volume on another disk.

mirroring — A fault-tolerant disk storage method in which the contents of a disk or drive are constantly replicated to another disk or drive.

mixed domain — A domain that contains non-Windows Server 2003 domain controllers.

monitoring — Checking a system for problems in normal operations.

multi-master replication model — A model for distributing Active Directory data between all domain controllers. Other methods for distributing data include the distributed method where only parts of the data are replicated, or the single-master replication model as used in Microsoft Windows NT.

name server — The server component in the client-server architecture of a DNS system.

native domain — A domain that exclusively contains Windows 2000 or Server 2003 domain controllers.

NetBEUI — The protocol that transports NetBIOS.

Netlogon service — Handles system logon and authentication.

network administration — The process of maintaining and administering connectivity between computers on a network. This type of maintenance can involve cables, hardware, and computer administration components such as network card drivers and protocols.

Network Basic Input Output System (NetBIOS) — The API that was developed by IBM to allow computers to communicate over a LAN.

network interface card (NIC) — A piece of hardware that provides a means for Windows Server 2003 and other OSs to package data and place it on a network.

network share — A folder that has been configured for network access.

nodes — Computers or interfaces that exist on a network. Also called hosts.

normal backup — A backup type that copies selected files and resets the archive bit.

NTFS (New Technology File System) — A type of disk format that provides additional security and efficiency over FAT and FAT32.

NTFS permissions — Security-level permission associated with all files and folders on an NTFS-formatted drive.

Open Systems Interconnection (OSI) — A standards body that defines network communications protocols and the mechanisms for transporting those messages.

operating system (OS) — A software interface that runs the computer and aids the user in executing programs and utilizing hardware.

operator — Math-based comparison symbols that can be used to compare numbers and characters.

optimization — The process of fine-tuning a system's performance to its optimal capacity.

option — Text that modifies a command to perform the command in a specific way.

organizational unit (OU) — An Active Directory container object used to store such items as users, computers, and groups within Active Directory.

orphaned session — A task or session that continues even when the parent process has stopped.

output redirection — The process of directing the output from a given command that would normally appear on the screen elsewhere. Redirection of this sort is usually used for logging but can be used to test data communications.

owner — The creator of an object, or someone who has seized ownership of an account to be able to change the permissions.

packets — Small pieces of files and e-mail messages that travel over networks and are reassembled into their original form upon reaching their destination.

page file — A file that is used by the OS as supplemental RAM.

pane — An enclosed section of a window.

parameter — The batch equivalent of a command option.

partition — A portion or all of a basic disk; can either be primary or extended.

peer-to-peer network — A network in which all of the computers share files with each other. In this environment, accounts for each user must exist on every "peer" computer in the network.

permissions — Specific access privilege that is attached to data and associated with users. Permissions grant and deny specific levels of access to the data.

Plug and Play service — Enables the system to automatically detect and install hardware.

power scheme — A power configuration that is based on a specific system state.

primary partition — A type of partition that is bootable, can have a drive letter assigned, and is formattable. A single disk can have up to three primary partitions and one extended partition or a total of four primary partitions on a disk.

print job — A document that has been transmitted to the printer for printing.

print queue — A memory or disk location that contains all print jobs waiting to be printed.

process — One or more tasks that are performed on behalf of an application.

profile — A directory containing a user's Start menu and desktop icons, My Documents, and other user-specific items, including portions of the registry.

prompt — The location on the screen where the computer accepts typed input from the user. A blinking cursor indicates a prompt.

properties — Details of a file, including attributes; creation, access, and modify dates; permissions; and ownership information.

protocol — A standard or set of rules that allows communication between computers. A method of communication shared by a source and destination. Typically protocols are developed in layers or "stacks" with elements operating at each layer.

protocol suite — Multiple applications and services operating within a protocol stack.

Raid 1 — A technology that creates a synchronized copy of a volume or disk on another disk, enabling the system to sustain a single disk failure without loss of data or performance. Also called mirroring or duplexing.

Raid 5 — A technology that distributes data across three or more disks and maintains parity information, allowing the system to sustain a single disk failure without loss of data. Also called striping with parity.

Recovery Agent — A designated user account that allows a user to decrypt files encrypted by a different user.

registry — A system database that contains system and application settings.

registry key — Any entry that exists within a hive that contains subentries or subkeys.

registry value — A registry entry that contains specific information.

regular expression — A string that allows the use of wildcards to locate specific pieces of data.

remark — A statement that is documentary in nature and is ignored within a batch routine. Represented within batch as REM.

Remote Assistance — A remote control application that allows someone to connect to an active user console and take control of the system.

Remote Desktop — A remote administration application that allows a user to connect to a server and log on as if he or she were physically at the server.

remote storage — Backup data storage that is remote to the server.

resolver — The "client" component in the client-server architecture of a DNS system. Clients send DNS query requests to name servers.

reverse lookup zone — Resolves an IP address to a hostname.

roaming profile — A profile that is portable between multiple computers. Requires a common network storage location that can be accessed by all computers.

root node — The topmost node in the DNS hierarchy, it is represented by a period (.) or "".

round-robin rotation — A method of load distribution used by DNS servers.

router — A host that determines the best way for packets to reach their destinations.

schema — The set of object definitions indicating what can be stored in Active Directory.

scope — The full consecutive range of possible IP addresses for a network. Typically a subnet or logical network segment.

script — A specific file that is used to perform multiple tasks and logic. Scripts are generally platform-specific, language-specific, and simpler in nature than a full-blown programming language. Unlike standard programs, scripts do not have to be compiled, but they usually require an agent or service to run them. One exception is batch scripts, whose processing agent is embedded within the command environment.

security identifier (SID) — A unique code that is assigned to each resource object within a domain.

Server service — Enables a computer, workstation, or server to share resources over a network.

service — An automated background program that performs actions based on specific events.

session — A connection between two or more hosts over a network.

share caching — A server feature that enables different levels of Offline File and Folder storage for network clients.

share permissions — Network-only permission that is associated with network shares.

shortcut — A link to a program or file that is represented by an icon.

simple volume — A volume that is not extended, spanned, striped, mirrored, or RAID 5.

site — One or more reliably connected IP subnets. Sites form a replication boundary and help make up the physical structure of Active Directory.

sniffer — An application that examines packets by recording information that passes through a router.

spanned volume — A volume that occupies multiple locations on more than one disk.

Spooler service — Coordinates and feeds print jobs to a printer.

string — A group of characters (symbols, letters, and numbers) used in searching.

striping with parity — A fault-tolerant disk storage method where data is spread across three or more disks, along with parity. This provides fault tolerance.

subkey — A key that exists as part of another key.

subnet mask — A 32-bit binary number that identifies the network and host portion of an IP address.

subprogram — A batch program that is executed from within another batch program.

subroutine — A section of a batch, program, or script that is separate from the main processing and is used for processing conditional tasks.

swap file — A page file.

system file — A file that is used by the operating system for functionality and maintenance. Usually flagged as a system file.

system state — A backup term specifically referring to system-specific files, including the registry and Active Directory database.

tape rotation — A method of recycling and reusing backup tapes for archive and cost-saving purposes.

text file — A document file that contains letters and numbers that can be edited. Text files typically cannot be formatted or include graphic elements.

Transmission Control Protocol/Internet Protocol (TCP/IP) — A set of protocols that allows hosts to communicate with each other. It is used for communications over the Internet.

trust — A logical connection between domains allowing one domain to authenticate users from another domain. Trust relationships allow users to securely share resources between domains.

Universal Naming Convention (UNC) format — A standardized format for identifying the location of data on remote computers. The format is \\servername\sharename.

UPS (uninterruptible power supply) — Another term for a battery backup.

user account — A system account that consists of a username, password, and various properties and allows a user to log in to a computer and gain access to data.

user group — A collection of user accounts that is organized by similar access and permissions privileges. Permissions are assigned to the user group instead of to individual group members.

variable — A memory location that represents data that can change over time.

Visual Basic script language — A scripting language supported by Windows Server 2003 that incorporates a subset of the Visual Basic programming language.

volume — A drive or partition.

volume number — A number that is assigned to each volume by the system for internal reference.

wide area network (WAN) — A network that is connected by fiber (optic), ISDN, DSL, dial-up, T1, 56K, broadband cable, or other medium that is intended to span large distances.

wildcard — A symbol that is used to represent one or more numeric, symbolic, or alphabetical characters in any combination.

wildcard parameter — A type of variable that does not exist outside the bounds of the command that uses it. Wildcard parameters begin as wildcards, but can be temporarily assigned a value within the **FOR** command.

Windows Scripting Host (WSH) — The Windows Server 2003 service that enables scripts to be executed.

workstation — A computer that is not a server. Sometimes workstations do not have an operating system installed and rely on a server for the operating system.

Workstation service — Allows a system to access data on a remote server.

X.500 — A standard way to develop an electronic directory of people in an organization so that it can be part of a global directory available to anyone in the world with Internet access. Such a directory is sometimes called a global White Pages directory.

X.509 version 3 — A security certificate that contains information about the user as well as the user's public key.

zone — A storage database for a single DNS domain name.

Index

Microsoft® Windows® Server 2003
Enterprise Edition 180-Day Evaluation

The software included in this kit is intended for evaluation and deployment planning purposes only. If you plan to install the software on your primary machine, it is recommended that you back up your existing data prior to installation.

System requirements

To use Microsoft Windows Server 2003 Enterprise Edition, you need:

- Computer with 550 MHz or higher processor clock speed recommended; 133 MHz minimum required; Intel Pentium/Celeron family, or AMD K6/Athlon/Duron family, or compatible processor (Windows Server 2003 Enterprise Edition supports up to eight CPUs on one server)
- 256 MB of RAM or higher recommended; 128 MB minimum required (maximum 32 GB of RAM)
- 1.25 to 2 GB of available hard-disk space*
- CD-ROM or DVD-ROM drive
- Super VGA (800 × 600) or higher-resolution monitor recommended; VGA or hardware that supports console redirection required
- Keyboard and Microsoft Mouse or compatible pointing device, or hardware that supports console redirection

Additional items or services required to use certain Windows Server 2003 Enterprise Edition features:

- For Internet access:
  - Some Internet functionality may require Internet access, a Microsoft Passport account, and payment of a separate fee to a service provider; local and/or long-distance telephone toll charges may apply
  - High-speed modem or broadband Internet connection
- For networking:
  - Network adapter appropriate for the type of local-area, wide-area, wireless, or home network to which you wish to connect, and access to an appropriate network infrastructure; access to third-party networks may require additional charges

Note: To ensure that your applications and hardware are Windows Server 2003–ready, be sure to visit **www.microsoft.com/windowsserver2003**.

* Actual requirements will vary based on your system configuration and the applications and features you choose to install. Additional available hard-disk space may be required if you are installing over a network. For more information, please see **www.microsoft.com/windowsserver2003**.

Uninstall instructions

This time-limited release of Microsoft Windows Server 2003 Enterprise Edition will expire 180 days after installation. If you decide to discontinue the use of this software, you will need to reinstall your original operating system. You may need to reformat your drive.